D0990960

BOWLING GREEN STATE UNIVERSITY
DISCARDED
LIBRARY

Realism in EEO

Realism in EEO

HAROLD P. HAYES

JOHN WILEY & SONS New York • Chichester • Brisbane • Toronto

Library of Congress Cataloging in Publication Data:

Hayes, Harold P 1920–
Realism in EEO.

Includes index.
1. Discrimination in employment—United States.
2. Minorities—Employment—United States. 3. Women—Employment—United States. 4. Affirmative action programs—United States. I. Title.

HD4903.5.U58H39 331.1'33 79-25295
ISBN 0-471-05796-7

Printed in the United States of America

10 9 8 7 6 5 4 3 2 1

Preface

During my lifetime I have had the opportunity of working with many wise and wonderful people. Among the wisest was the friend who taught me the "take away" test. At the end of a presentation to a panel of executives or a speech at the Kiwanis luncheon or a career discussion with an employee, what are the take away items? What nuggets do you want the audience to retain? What things do you want them to do differently? These are the take aways—the end results of the communication process.

This book has a variety of expected take aways because it is directed to several different audiences:

*The practitioner of EEO, the day-to-day doer—the professional—can expect to find a logic pattern with which to integrate the many tasks inherent in EEO work. He or she can also find a number of specific techniques useful in support of the logic pattern. In essence, there is a "theory of the case" in the EEO arena that, if followed, simplifies the decision-making process and leads to creative contributions much beyond the routine of responding to administrative regulations.

*The managers—those who have the jobs to fill—can find their "theory of the case," their logic pattern for participation in the EEO system. The more all participants understand about a system with complex interfaces, the more the authority of the situation rather than personal opinions governs the decision-making process.

*The policy makers—the top people in an enterprise who set the EEO climate and direction—can find new insights into short- and long-range strategies.

*The regulators—the public officials who plan and operate the EEO thrust nationally and locally—can find some ways to redirect and sharpen their efforts in meeting the responsibilities assigned to them by law.

*Potential litigants—prospective plaintiffs and defendants in lawsuits—can find ways of reducing litigation by properly planned preventive steps.

*Citizens at large—the basic source of EEO legislation, regulation, and acceptance—can find their "theory of the case" for the manner in which they participate in the social/cultural evolution that is occurring.

I, too, have a personal take away. If the stakeholders in the EEO arena will meet on common ground and plan and work together, genuine long-range EEO progress can be made. That is the real purpose of the Civil Rights Act and subsequent presidential orders. If this book results in more effective redirection and application of energies and resources, more focus on relevant education and training for minorities and women, reduced litigation, reduced frustration and haggling, and increased attention to the very long time frame needed to produce significant results, I will have my take away in the satisfaction of a modest contribution to the great, important national effort in the EEO arena.

I express my thanks and indebtedness to a number of people and institutions for their help:

*Corporate management and my colleagues at General Electric for the learning and growing climate they provided.

*The Bureau of National Affairs for generous permission to quote and excerpt from their publications.

*The Institute of Labor Relations at Cornell University.

*The Aerospace Industries Association of America, Inc.

*The California State Department of Education and the school districts that shared their affirmative action plans.

*Those employers who shared privately their thoughts about EEO progress and problems.

HAROLD P. HAYES

Atascadero, California
January 1980

Contents

Realism in EEO

CHAPTER ONE

An Overview

The setting for this vignette is Vandenberg Air Force Base, sometimes referred to as the Cape Canaveral of the West. Vandenberg occupies sprawling acreage in the central coast of California and is landlord to most of the big names in the aerospace industry. As federal contractors, these companies have to prepare affirmative action plans in compliance with Executive Order No. 11246 and its subsequent revisions. From time to time, on relatively short notice, some contractors are selected for on-site reviews of their plans and performance.

This is the story of one such contractor, who perhaps overstates the situation when he describes the compliance reviewer showing up with his golf clubs and a handful of forms, remarking "fill these out, I'll be back later." Overstated or not, the description is illustrative of the adversary relationship about which so many employers have voiced complaints. The contractor claimed that the reviewer had little interest in the 51-page affirmative action plan for that year. Instead, the focus was on one thing—what share of your upcoming hires will be targeted for minorities and women? Faced with the suspension and possible loss of a pending multimillion dollar contract, the contractor was willing to negotiate on this particular goal. The negotiations can best be described as a "seat of the pants" effort, because neither reviewer nor contractor had adequate labor market data on which to base a decision.

Vandenberg is situated in a rural area on the northern boundary of Santa Barbara County, some 70 miles from the major population center of Santa Barbara City/Goleta. Yet the reviewer insisted that the labor market data for the county be used as the basis for determining whether or not the contractor had any shortfalls in the representation of women and minorities in his work force. Moreover, both reviewer and contractor were basing judgments on the broad census categories of managers, professionals, crafts, and so forth, without any further breakdown into job families such as engineers, missile launch mechanics, machinists, and welders. In effect, elementary school teachers in the City of Santa Barbara, a long automobile ride away, were counted as part of the contractor's labor market.

In comparison with the gross demographics for the county, the contractor was clearly underrepresented in a number of employment categories. This shortfall, by the regulations, required corrective goals. The contractor, in essence, said, "I'll agree to a 25% share of placements for women and minorities in all categories." The reviewer, in essence, replied, "I want 25% for women and 25% for minorities or your contract will be held up." Faced with the potential loss or at least a major delay in a multimillion dollar package, the contractor capitulated and agreed to the combined 50% share of placements for women and minorities. Performance against that goal is almost an impossibility.

Although the location is isolated, the vignette is not. A spokeswoman for another company described much the same type of experience. Describing the compliance review process as one of "jumping through hoops," she talked about a newly designed affirmative action plan submitted in June of the year which was required to be resubmitted under a previous, older format. She did this, but a few months later was subject to another pre-award-of-contract review. She prepared her plan under the "old format" but was required to redo it in the newer "June version." She, too, was pressured into some unattainable goals, and described the agony of explaining missed goals. In order to hire 600 people in a year, she had to make about 2,400 offers. To accomplish the latter, she had to screen 10,000 applications. When the goals were not met, she had to explain the action taken literally on each of the 10,000 applications.

A large manufacturer in the Midwest reported receipt of a telephone call announcing that a compliance review would be held. The reviewing agency pointed out that "we will have to look at your applicant flow." The response to the loud groan of the company that "we have 50,000 applicants a year" was that "we'll just have to deal with that in some way."

A young black M.B.A. responsible for an affirmative action plan covering more than 10,000 employees takes pride in his knowledge of the EEO process, because he worked previously for a monitoring agency. Speaking with the knowledge of "both sides of the fence," he pointed out that the employer must always yield on something during the negotiation process. "If you don't, they'll keep you busy the year around with nit-picking paper work. It's a lot easier just to roll over." His favorite story is one in which he won a minor victory, although he had to pay for it later by the opening up of other areas of investigation. The demand was that he post the official statement of company EEO policy on *all* bulletin boards. He was able to win the argument that the compliance requirement was limited to *official* company bulletin boards, excluding the many on which union announcements, garage sales, employee association outings, et al., are posted as a way of factory life.

The voices of complaint are growing louder and more penetrating. Some are beginning to question the legitimacy of the entire goals and timetables process as not actually called for under Executive Order No. 11246. In December, 1978, Firestone Synthetic Rubber and Latex of Orange, Texas, was granted a hearing on the single issue of whether the Constitution prohibits the Federal Government from imposing goals on its contractors in the absence of a finding of discrimination.* Attacking from another direction, on January 24, 1979, Sears, the nation's largest retailer filed suit against 10 U.S. government agencies, alleging that conflicting and sometimes unenforced government rules, regulations, policies, and laws were the cause of racial, sexual, and age discrimination in retail employment. Among other things asked for in the suit, Sears wanted a ruling that a number of actions of the federal Equal Employment Opportunity Commission were either illegal or violated the firm's constitutional rights.

The EEO arena is indeed a turbulent one.

THE LEARNING PROCESS

Government and employers alike were ill prepared to cope with all of the ramifications spawned by the passage of the Civil Rights Act in 1964 and the subsequent Executive Order No. 11246. At best, the translation of law into agency regulations and the ultimate response of those affected is often a long and arduous process. In the EEO arena, this has been painfully true. New ground was being plowed. There was no history of relevant court decisions on which to build a

*B.N.A. Fair Employment Practices, January 4, 1979.

rationale for the host of regulations that poured forth. Nor was there an organized discipline of facts and knowledge available from the academic research world or other sources. In a 1978 feasibility study to support a proposal for an Institute of Human Resource Management for Equal Employment Opportunity to be established at Cornell University, the conclusion was reached that:

> Surprisingly, however, the research effort directed to finding definitive answers to the myriad questions facing employers, regulators, and everyone, is modest and diffuse. As of this writing, there is no neutral research source devoted to research and education in the management of human resource systems to implement equal employment opportunity policies.
>
> Interviews with corporate and government officials covered the following topics: internal and external availability determination; monitoring of affirmative action; orientation programs for new protected-class and incumbent employees; affirmative action modeling; reverse discrimination problems; the relationship between the legal and personnel departments; relationships between firms and their compliance agency (or agencies); and any special problems not covered in the above categories. Their responses, almost unanimously, point to numerous conceptual, technical, and administrative problems. A few examples are illustrative: How should EEO/AA performance be measured? What is par? At what rate should industry be required to effect social change? How many women/minorities are available in various labor markets? What is statistical parity? Must the compliance process continue on an adversary basis? What are the costs and benefits of EEO policies and programs? And many others.
>
> The study leads to the general conclusion that there is a gap in the research-training resources available to deal with these problems.

This study finding, 14 years after the passing of the Civil Rights Act of 1964, well describes the state of the knowledge discipline so essential to real progress for women, minorities, and other protected classes. In the absence of an organized academic discipline of knowledge, the concepts and processes which will ultimately circumscribe the EEO arena are being established on a trial and error basis through litigation in the courts, or in precedent-setting consent decrees and conciliation agreements. This is a slow, agonizing process as court decisions in particular keep rolling in. From the statistical point of view alone, the Equal Employment Advisory Council (basically an association of employers) found it worthwhile to commission the publication of a book (1977) entitled, "Current Trends in the Use (and Misuse) of Statistics in Employment Discrimination Litigation." In an appendix entitled Table of Authorities, the book lists 158 court cases as references. Bit by bit the legal jigsaw puzzle is being pieced together, but the overall picture is far from complete. To some extent, the seniority issue has been clarified and, in the Hazelwood School District Case (Chapter X), light has been shed on the use of share of opportunities as an appropriate measure of legal compliance. But the decision rules by which internal and external labor markets can be defined still remain to be determined.

From another view, as regulatory staffs were assembled, a dichotomy of interests, motivation, and background developed between government and the world of business and industry. Either through lack of knowledge or a conscious decision, some regulatory personnel have not recognized a number of the realities in the work of the private sector. Certainly, the EEO Commission staff clung too stubbornly too long to the use of the Civilian Labor Force as a measure of women and minority representation that could reasonably be expected in most job categories. It is probably fair to say that regulatory staff assumed an advocacy role which later resulted in the view by employers that compliance monitoring is done in the mode of adversary relationships. With perhaps some exceptions, employers view themselves as running a business, not as agents of social change. There is at the least a natural dichotomy of interests between the EEO monitor and the employer. That dichotomy has been considerably exacerbated by the advocacy posture of monitoring agencies. The neutral ground on which to meet for a seeking of the real facts, the identification of the problems and their solutions, has not yet been found.

Generally, much of the learning that has taken place has been legal and procedural. Monitoring agencies and employers now have a decidedly better understanding of the legal limits and pitfalls. They have also learned much about computerized systems, how to acquire data, how to massage it, and how to handle it in negotiations. In the main, the EEO arena is characterized as negotiations against a legal backdrop. Perhaps that is the way it should be or at least has to be. On the other hand, one could view the arena as standing on a tripod with the law as one leg, data-based negotiations as another, and fundamental principles of human resources dynamics as the third. The latter leg seems not to have developed as well as the other two—leaving the arena in a shaky if not more seriously unstable condition. As learning continues, growth in the human resources leg needs to be accelerated and communicated.

THE NEW LOOK

Late in 1978, as part of President Carter's plan to reorganize the federal civil rights bureaucracy, Executive Order No. 12086 consolidated federal contract compliance authority for equal employment opportunity and affirmative action in the Labor Department. Under the Order, the EEO compliance monitoring of government contractors and subcontractors became the responsibility of the Labor Department's Office of Federal Contract Compliance Programs. Commonly known as the OFCCP, this office now has the enforcement authority previously shared with 11 other compliance agencies.

At about the same time, the EEO Commission was given the authority to direct and coordinate the equal employment opportunity enforcement activities of all federal civil rights agencies. The EEOC was thus empowered to:*

- Establish uniform standards, guidelines, and policies defining the nature of employment discrimination.
- Establish uniform standards and procedures for investigations and compliance reviews.
- Designate the agency to be responsible for conducting investigations or compliance reviews of particular employers or classes of employers.
- Establish uniform record-keeping and reporting requirements concerning employment practices.

Additionally, all federal departments and agencies must now have any proposed EEO policies and procedures screened by the Commission prior to public announcement.

Thus, in a more tightly knit chain of command, the federal efforts will be spearheaded by the EEO Commission. That thrust will continue to be threefold:

- The handling of individual complaint cases, where a once-reached backlog of more than 100,000 cases is being whittled down by more streamlined procedures.
- Affirmative action plans, most of which are now consolidated under OFCCP.
- Systemic charges similar to the one on which the Commission and the General Electric Company reached a conciliation agreement in

*B.N.A., June 8, 1978.

1978 involving the expenditure of $32 million by the company but with no finding nor admission of guilt.

The task at hand is a massive one. For example, the Director of OFCCP was quoted* as planning for 1,800 employees throughout 52 regional offices to attend to compliance for 15,000 contractors employing 31 million people. Earlier in the year (June 22, 1978), the same publication quoted Donald Elisburg, assistant secretary of labor for employment standards to the effect that the OFCCP would add offices in 60 cities and would conduct 17,000 compliance reviews in the upcoming year. Regardless of which numbers are correct, it all adds up to an almost incredible level of activity in attempting to regulate the placement dynamics of the national work force.

AN INDUSTRY VIEW

How well the new look in federal administration will address the "noise signals" from employers remains to be seen. One industry's view of the compliance problems was well articulated in October, 1977, by the Aerospace Industries Association of America, Inc. In a letter to OFCCP, the Association expressed the opinions quoted below:

AEROSPACE INDUSTRIES ASSOCIATION OF AMERICA, INC.

1725 De Sales Street, N.W., Washington, D.C. 20036, Tel. 347-2315

October 21, 1977

Mr. Robert Hobson
Associate Director
Office of Federal Contract Compliance Programs
Department of Labor
200 Constitution Avenue, N.W., Room C-3325
Washington, D.C. 20210

Dear Mr. Hobson:

Pursuant to a discussion with you, Mr. James Cisco and members of AIA's Equal Employment Opportunity and Affirmative Action Plans Subcommittee, we wish to comment on the OFCCP Task Force

*B.N.A., October 26, 1978.

Study on the Revitalization of the Federal Contract Compliance Program submitted to Secretary Marshall on September 16, 1977.

The subcommittee appreciated the frank discussion that prevailed during our all-day meeting earlier this month. It was especially gratifying to learn that DoL is sensitive to the frustrations and dilemmas of aerospace industry contractors in carrying out affirmative action programs effectively. These concerns do not reflect foot-dragging or lack of commitment to the policy of ending employment discrimination wherever it exists, rather they are the product of day-to-day experience with anomalies and conflicts within the present system. Among these concerns are the following principal problems:

1. The frequent existence of an adversary relationship between a compliance officer and a contractor fostered by a "guilty until proven innocent" attitude and aggravated by inconsistencies in the definition and administration of EEO standards.

2. The requirement that excessive effort be expended on "form" over "substance," as evidenced by the voluminous amount of paper work generated.

3. The lack of credibility of the basic data upon which elaborate and detailed AAP's must be based.

4. A "gun to your head" climate in which pre-award compliance reviews are carried out resulting in unrealistic and often unattainable "promissory notes."

5. The frequent need for a contractor to engage in repeated defenses of the same issue due to lack of standards between the various government agencies responsible for equal employment opportunity.

6. The prevalence of a contractor's "no win" situation when there is a conflict between provisions of a labor agreement and an affirmative action requirement.

7. The tendency of compliance agencies to hold contractors responsible for coping with a demonstrated lack of supply, a situation over which they have very limited control, leads contractors to engage in "stealing" the same employees back and forth from each other.

The foregoing concerns have given rise to the following comments reflecting the general consensus of the subcommittee regarding specific findings and recommendations of the study:

1. Until such time as it can be demonstrated that the efforts of OFCCP and EEOC can be merged into an equitable and effectively administered entity, the two agencies should remain separate, although philosophically it is difficult to justify the existence of two large governmental bodies having the same basic objectives.

2. While there is concern over separating the "affirmative action" obligations of a contract with the government from other contractual obligations, experience has demonstrated that multiple agency enforcement has led to conflict, inconsistencies and duplication of effort. Therefore, practicality dictates that all affirmative action compliance effort be removed from the various contracting agencies and centralized under OFCCP. While the subcommittee supports such a consolidation, it is their prayer that OFCCP not concern itself only with affirmative action to the exclusion of other contractual priorities. Conversely, the contracting agency should not divorce itself completely from compliance requirements. Arbitrary separation of the award-making and compliance monitoring functions can only lead to deadlocks between the OFCCP and the respective procurement agency.

3. To use the number of debarments as a criterion for measuring the effectiveness of OFCCP is counterproductive. Likewise, to count the number of systemic discrimination findings or the dollar value of sanctions as a measuring device of effectiveness is out of step with the essential "affirmative" approach of the Executive Order. Success should be a simple matter of "how many more were employed" rather than "how many employers were punished."

4. Since "availability" is the most critical statistic in any affirmative action program, it is essential that a high degree of credibility accompany it; therefore, the subcommittee completely endorses the Task Force recommendation for more reliable data. There is a question of whether or not the DoL is the logical agency to develop this information. Would it not be more realistic for the Census Bureau to assume this responsibility?

5. The subcommittee recognizes that increasing availability is a must if the EEO goals of this country are to be met. It disagrees, however, with the administrative imposition of training on contractors under the guise of testing good faith effort to meet goals and timetables. However, there are instances where a contractor may be uniquely qualified to train. Where this condition exists, OFCCP and the contractor would best be served by permitting the contractor to substitute training for goals and timetables.

6. Current narrow job groupings for determining utilization result in endless detail; therefore, broader job categories in affirmative action plans are necessary.

7. Ultimate affirmative action goals are obviously unrealistic due to the nonpredictability of job opportunities in the aerospace industry and the fact that work force parity is not a constant; therefore, a five-year maximum on goals is appropriate.

8. While the subcommittee has no serious quarrel with the proposition that the OFCCP should be concerned with the detection of systemic discrimination, we disagree with the suggestion that it is chronically subtle or difficult to perceive. The recommendation of extension of the time limits for completion of compliance reviews in order to focus on systemic discrimination, smacks of "fishing expeditions" which can only add to the current level of frustration already being experienced by contractors in the whole EEO arena. Systemic violation by every aerospace company should not be regarded as a foregone conclusion by OFCCP.

9. The subcommittee opposes the proposal that OFCCP depart from the fundamental prospective affirmative action concept of the Executive Order by demanding individual relief in the form of back pay or benefits for particular members of so-called affected classes. The mission of the Secretary of Labor under Executive Order 11246 is one of monitoring the policies of government contractors to determine whether the equal employment opportunity clause is being honored, and of assisting contractors by defining uniform, understandable guidelines of acceptable job practices. We do not believe that OFCCP is authorized or empowered—nor should it be empowered in the future—to compel payment of monetary damages, back pay or other financial redress to individual employees. Retroactive remedial measures benefiting individuals—as distinguished from classwide general measures to ensure nondiscrimination—rests with EEOC and the courts under Title VII of the Civil Rights Act of 1964.

10. Contract passover should not be permissible pending an appeal from a nonresponsibility decision of the compliance agency to the administrative law judge under the Task Force recommendation. Unless such a limitation on passovers is added, contractors will be subjected to loss of contracts before final agency action has occurred and a due process review becomes available.

11. The subcommittee cannot endorse the proposal that formal administrative hearings must be subjected to deadlines of sixty to ninety days. In practice, such acceleration would constitute a denial of due process to the parties, whose ability to resort to adequate discovery and preparation would be compromised, if not precluded.

We are confident that changes resulting from the Task Force study will provide positive guidance and assistance to contractors in carrying out their affirmative action responsibilities.

Very truly yours,

Daniel J. Nauer

Daniel J. Nauer
Executive Secretary
Industrial Relations Committee

The "new look" should please the aerospace industry in at least one aspect—the consolidation of monitoring activities within the OFCCP. A number of the other problems will not be solved by an administrative reorganization per se but must be addressed in terms of fundamental philosophy, operational concepts, and actual field practices. The latter may be the most difficult of all—maintaining consistency of behavior and judgments among OFCCP personnel in more than 50 field offices as they conduct many thousands of compliance reviews (perhaps 17,000) during any single year.

SOME OTHER VIEWS

The Cornell study referred to earlier found employers generally saying the same things expressed by the Aerospace Industries Association:

> Employers are troubled and irritated with many aspects of the compliance process. In summary form they note these types of difficulties: rules and regulations that are fuzzy and imprecise leading to no-win decisions; lack of uniformity and consistency in the rules and in their interpretation by sometimes competing compliance agencies; standards and rules that change too frequently; conflicts between and among local and federal agencies; and perhaps the single greatest complaint or difficulty is the lack of trust and cooperation from compliance officials. Put differently, it is the adversarial relationship between the compliance officials and themselves that they find troubling. . . .

Several very specific problems were noted in the following comments:

- Why can't the feds get together and use the same forms—we supply employee data to two different agencies on two incompatible forms?
- How can we implement affirmative action when we are drastically shrinking in size?
- The IRS is disallowing some training expenses claiming that training is an individual's perk—isn't it counterproductive for EEO if the IRS taxes our training?
- There is a real conflict between Title IX Education Amendments of 1972 and OFCCP regulations.
- How do we handle the problem of a move from the city to

suburbia where the percentage of minorities dropped from 30 percent to 4 percent, or the geographical moves of larger scope such as a company moving from the Northeast to the South? . . .

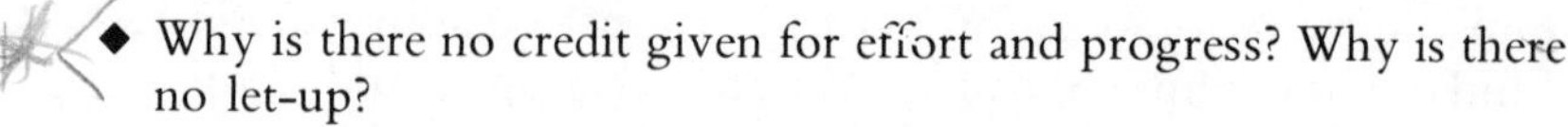

- Why is there no credit given for effort and progress? Why is there no let-up?

In conjunction with a lecture at the University of Kansas in January, 1979, then Attorney General Griffin Bell called for the curtailment and perhaps the abolishment of the so-called rule-making powers of the independent regulatory commissions. Bell pointed out that the rule-making power has developed over the past five years as a means of avoiding lengthy adversary proceedings at which all sides are heard. "Rule making is a total substitute," said Bell, "for all other forms of government. . . . Its abuse can stymie and frustrate the government of whole states and the operations of entire industries." Bell, although not speaking specifically of the EEOC, but more generally about all federal regulatory commissions, pointed out that the paper work and compliance burden on smaller American businesses is simply impossible, that the net result is a wholesale disobedience which then breeds disrespect for the law generally.

The views of the EEO Commission and other monitoring agencies are more difficult to express succinctly. At the top levels, the views are statesmanlike, as they understandably must be. The EEO regulatory agencies are subjected to considerable pressures from the many constituencies and individuals who are stakeholders in the arena. For example, Commissioner Eleanor Holmes Norton was not too long ago criticized for failing to devote enough attention to the employment discrimination problems of Spanish-speaking people. Of course, there can be little other response than a pledge that the problems will be attended to.

As another example, the General Electric Conciliation Agreement was passed by only a 2 to 1 vote of a then short-handed Commission. Commissioner Daniel Leach was quoted as saying that he had evaluated the case differently and did not consider it adequate. He did not elaborate further. The 13 unions that represent G.E. workers refused to sign the agreement. In the agreement, there is a statement that it is not to be precedent setting. Thus from a $32 million settlement there comes little specific view of what the next one will be like. The general view is that there will be more such systemic charges forthcoming. On the other hand, the Commission must surely get some reinforcement for its forceful stands when it notes a court judgment which describes top to bottom discriminatory practices at a particular company where coworkers boisterously speculated about the virginity of a female employee and circulated a crude drawing depicting her at a nudist colony. The supervisor's response to her complaints was simply that she must expect such things in a man's world. In the same forceful vein is a preliminary court approval of a consent decree whereby 50% of the additions to the San Francisco police force must be minorities and an additional 20% women for the next 10 years (there is some alleviation by permitting double counting of minority women). Perhaps the clearest indication of the view of the Commission lies in its reaction to the Bakke Case. The thrust is that if employers follow certain Commission-issued guidelines, they can be immunized against reverse discrimination charges that result from their affirmative action plans. Employers who see some reasonable risk that they have violated the Civil Rights Act and could be found guilty of discrimination are encouraged to take appropriate remedial action without having to face Commission findings of liability for reverse discrimination. This thrust proved to be exceptionally visionary as the Weber case (Chapter IX) progressed to the ultimate Supreme Court decision on June 27, 1979. Elated by the Court's findings, the Commission will undoubtedly continue to encourage very strong affirmative action plans by private employers.

NARROWING THE DIFFERENCES

It is difficult to tell whether the dichotomy between monitoring agencies and employers is widening, closing, or not changing much at all. Yet until differences in views are narrowed and areas of common understanding can be agreed upon, the EEO arena will continue in what can be described as a chaotic condition. With some risk of overstatement, there are two polarized views. The regulatory agency says, "we know you are guilty and we'll catch up with you sooner or later." The employer says, "we are doing the best we can; we're being held for ransom for things beyond our control." Constituency groups and individuals can also be found at both poles. Yet there must be some common ground between the two extremes where mutual understanding can be reached and from which genuine long range EEO progress can be launched.

There appear to be two basic thrusts in the arena. The first is the searching out and elimination of discriminatory personnel practices. The second is the changing of the profiles of work forces such that race/sex/ethnic distributions are more equitable in the future than they now are. To assure that the latter not merely takes place but is accelerated, goals and timetables come into being as a way of life in the world of employment. These, in turn, generate and trigger other arguments and events related to what is par, how can labor markets be defined, what is fair share, systemic charges, various lawsuits, and disrupting emotional reactions. The conclusion reached in frustration and a sense of helplessness is that "it's all just a numbers game."

Paradoxically, the numbers can lead the way to more common understanding and more effective operations and results in the EEO arena. When approached from an analytical view, the "numbers" can be used to identify the critical parameters and, in some instances, certain almost indisputable mathematical relationships. In others, they at least suggest what may be some generally acceptable logic patterns. The analytical patterns and logic may be the common ground on which all of the stakeholders in the arena can accept some of the inevitable realities and proceed from there in a more orderly and productive fashion.

The chapters which follow are a search for that common ground.

CHAPTER TWO

A Human Resources Model

Independent of race/sex/ethnic considerations, there are numerous realities in the world of work. Most people during their working lives inevitably come to grips with some of these. Some jobs provide for upward mobility; some end in stagnation; others disappear as the character of the United States economy changes over time. Unless the individual orchestrates a career plan with exceptional insights and determination, the good life that is hoped for may not be found in its entirety, and some less than desirable trade-offs may have to be made. This is true not only for individuals but for enterprises as well. Unless a business likewise orchestrates its future with wisdom and insight, the actual profitability and growth may fall far short of expectations.

Planning for the future, by an individual or a business, is no easy task. There is a temptation to forecast the future in the shape of a hockey stick curve as shown in Figure 1.

However success may be defined, whether profits or personal income or life satisfaction, the theme of the curve is "ever onward and upward." Often when the future is faced analytically and objectively, there is little basis for the hockey stick enthusiasm. There are generally some realities that define the limits of what is achievable. Unless these are identified and dealt with in the planning process, the future will contain undesirable surprises and frustrations. Setting aside the element of luck, the best results come from planning, not wishing; from in-depth understanding, not from guesswork; from facing realities rather than turning away from them.

All of these thoughts are particularly applicable to the EEO arena. If there were no race/sex/ethnic considerations, the employer would still have to deal with human resources in the planning and implementation process. He or she would still have to address such

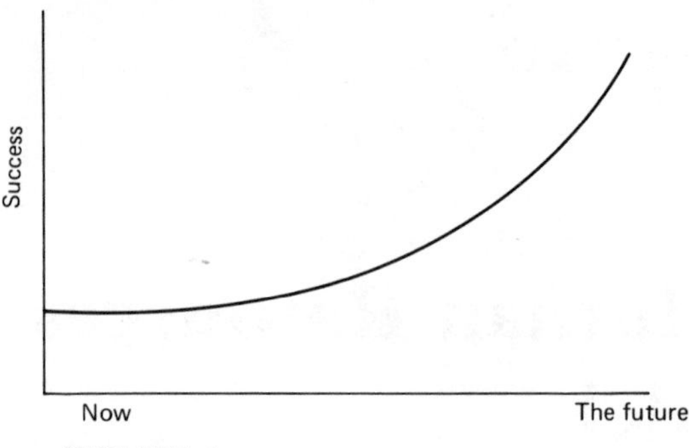

FIGURE 1.

things as job qualifications, hiring from the external market, promoting within the organization, growth or reduction of the work force, turnover—all of these factors which are so necessary to the attainment of business objectives. The basic impact of EEO requirements is simply that personnel activities be done in a way that is nondiscriminatory for minorities, women, and other protected classes. The additional impact, of course, is retribution for any past discriminatory actions and some future-oriented remedies. In the main, EEO requirements do not change the natural personnel dynamics which occur as a result of business activity. They address the question of what the minority and women's participation in those activities should rightfully be.

Rationally, the first step in realistic EEO planning is to examine the natural personnel dynamics that occur independent of race/sex/ethnic considerations. Assuming that redistribution of minorities and women in the national work force is a principal EEO objective, the attainment of the objective depends on the opportunities for change which the American economy produces. Similarly, redistribution within a specific employer's work force is a function of the personnel dynamics which occur therein.

There are methodologies available for studying personnel dynamics. Regretably, they have not been adequately applied to the EEO arena. If they were, the "transfer of technology" could greatly enhance EEO progress in the long run. If employers and monitoring agencies could meet on some common ground of analytical understanding, issues could be resolved more quickly and the sense of working together to solve a common problem greatly expanded. Until such understanding is reached, there will be a considerable number of surprises along the way that can significantly dampen EEO momentum for change. Unfortunately, such surprises result in expedient solutions which set precedent for more expediencies. The end result is an empirical feeling the way along, rather than a well planned, well executed thrust.

Even when applied on a minimal, illustrative basis, the techniques applicable to human resources planning in general contribute greatly to the in-depth understanding of EEO dynamics. The dynamics—the hires, promotions, losses, and end results—are a critical element. Presumably, the objective of EEO is to change the status of minorities and women in the work force from what it now is to something better. A process of getting from here to there requires a definition of there, a time frame, and some action steps. Unless the practical dynamics of the work force as a whole are well understood, and the planned EEO dynamics fall within achievable limits, EEO projections for the future may well be unattainable hockey stick curves.

Somewhere in the files of most businesses there are records which can be used to describe the flow of people into and within the work force. What the records themselves cannot do is to explain why the particular flow occurred and what flow patterns can be expected to occur in the future. For example, the records might show that during the past year 50 people were promoted from machinist to group leader. What factors created these 50 opportunities? Is it reasonable to assume that this same number of promotions will occur next year and each year thereafter? Similarly, suppose the employer recognizes a general need to start an apprentice training program. How many trainees should there be—20, 50, 100?

One approach that has been successfully used to answer such questions is to build a mathematical model that describes the work force dynamics. That model can then be used to explain historical dynamics and, more importantly, to explore a range of scenarios applicable to the future. First mention of applying mathematics to the flow of people sometimes produces negative reactions, such as "stay in the real world" or "that's good for textbooks but it's too abstract to be practical." Yet models in other areas of activity are widely accepted and, in fact, have considerable impact on each of us individually. For example, the econometric models that address such things as gross national product, unemployment rates, trade balance, and inflation rates are a major factor in national policy. Such models are far more complicated than human resources ones, yet their answers are often accepted to an accuracy of one decimal place.

Factory flow models are another good example. With the advent of computers, it has become practical to simulate the production flow through a factory before any concrete is poured or equipment purchased. The ability to do this offers enormous advantages, because the whole system can be optimized before irretrievable investments are made. For example, the flow model or simulation can help decide whether one or several machines are required at a particular work station. If the model shows that a long queue forms when only one machine is in service, machines can be added until the queue disappears and flow through the factory can occur at the desired rate.

In the human resources area, it is possible to build models ranging from the very simple to the very complex. In general, it is not necessary that the models be complex. In fact, it is better if they are not because the more readily they are understood, the more confidently and universally they will be used. All it takes is a few variables, some simple equations which relate those variables, and some data and assumptions as input to the equations. For a modest amount of effort, there can be large payoffs in practical applications.

AN ILLUSTRATIVE MODEL

Background

Human resources models can be kept simple, if they are directed to specific ad hoc questions. In many instances, they do not require the use of a large computer but can be exercised with the aid of a hand calculator.

The model described in the following discussion is one used by the General Electric Company as an aid in determining the number of college recruits that should be hired into a company training program each year. It was designed as an ad hoc model to address a specific question, but it serves a number of other purposes equally well. The numbers used in the illustration are hypothetical to protect General Electric proprietary information.

G.E., like most large corporations, recruits actively on college campuses. The new graduates from the colleges and universities each year are one of the major sources for renewal (and sometimes expansion) of the professional work force. As a high technology company, G.E. has traditionally been among the most active in recruiting engineering graduates. G.E. also tends toward a grow your own human resources strategy. As a result of these two factors, the

Company places heavy emphasis on the recruiting process and early-years development programs. For example, a Manufacturing Management Training Program has been operated continuously since 1953. The input is mostly recent engineering graduates; the output is a flow of future leaders of the manufacturing work within the company.

In theory, training programs are a great concept. They make the recruitment of top talent somewhat easier; they offer a focus for specific development activities; and they provide a steady flow of well qualified people for the future needs of the business. It's that part about the steady flow that makes reality different from theory. In lean business years, the input to training programs tends to shrink; in other years, it may expand considerably. The result is not the smooth input/output flow that theory envisions, but a much more erratic pattern. However, when the real dynamics are fully understood, smoothing out can be accomplished in a rational way.

Management's Questions

In 1971, top management became keenly interested in two questions:

1. How do we know how many college recruits we should have each year—500, 5000, or what?
2. What should be the annual input to the Manufacturing Management Program?

These were good questions and worth answering for three reasons:

1. Top management wanted an answer.
2. Personal professionalism called for a better rationale in recruiting.
3. Strategic planning was a new philosophical business thrust in the Company, with implications for college recruiting and human resources planning.

There were two possible approches to the problem. One was to seek out masses of data and search for some kind of correlation by regression analysis or other mathematical techniques. The other was to analyze the problem in the abstract and subsequently cross check the logic with real data. Within a very short time, it became apparent that a mathematical model could be built to describe the work force dynamics and the questions could be answered as a derivative of the model.

The Model

With some exceptions, General Electric's college graduates are a part of a total professional population classified as exempt in terms of the National Fair Labor Standards Act. As one might expect, this population exists in hierarchical layers of pay and responsibility. G.E. uses the Hay position level system, which describes a pyramid of people with large numbers at the bottom and lesser numbers at the top. This is depicted graphically in Figure 2. The number of people at each position level is shown to scale by the horizontal bars. The result is the classic textbook picture of the personnel pyramid in industry. Whether or not this shape is the ideal one for business needs is an interesting question. For purposes of discussion, let's assume the shape is to remain the same. What are the factors that cause flow to occur, into and within the pyramid? The two obvious ones are replacing losses and satisfying growth if any occurs. But there is a third factor—the manner in which external hires are distributed by position level is a major determinant of promotion flow. These variables can be related by some simple equations. When the arithmetic is done, the flow dynamics of the work force are the output of the model.

The techniques for constructing the model are discussed in Chapter Seven because of their direct relationship to EEO upward mobility. Meanwhile, let's assume the model has been built and exercised for the following assumptions:

- 5% external loss rate at each level.
- 0% growth rate at each level.
- At PL 12 and up, 10% of all vacancies at each level are from external sources; similarly 20% for PL 8 through 11; similarly 90% at PL 7.
- College recruits enter at PL 7.

The output of the model is shown in Figure 3. Promotion flow is diagrammed for each position level. External hires are shown only for PL 7 because that is the area of interest, the focus of the model. External hires at higher levels are known but merely omitted from the diagram for purposes of simplification.

Position level	Number of people
23	1
22	0
21	1
20	11
19	15
18	19
17	77
16	124
15	184
14	284
13	461
12	500
11	666
10	755
9	940
8	1,014
7	894

FIGURE 2.

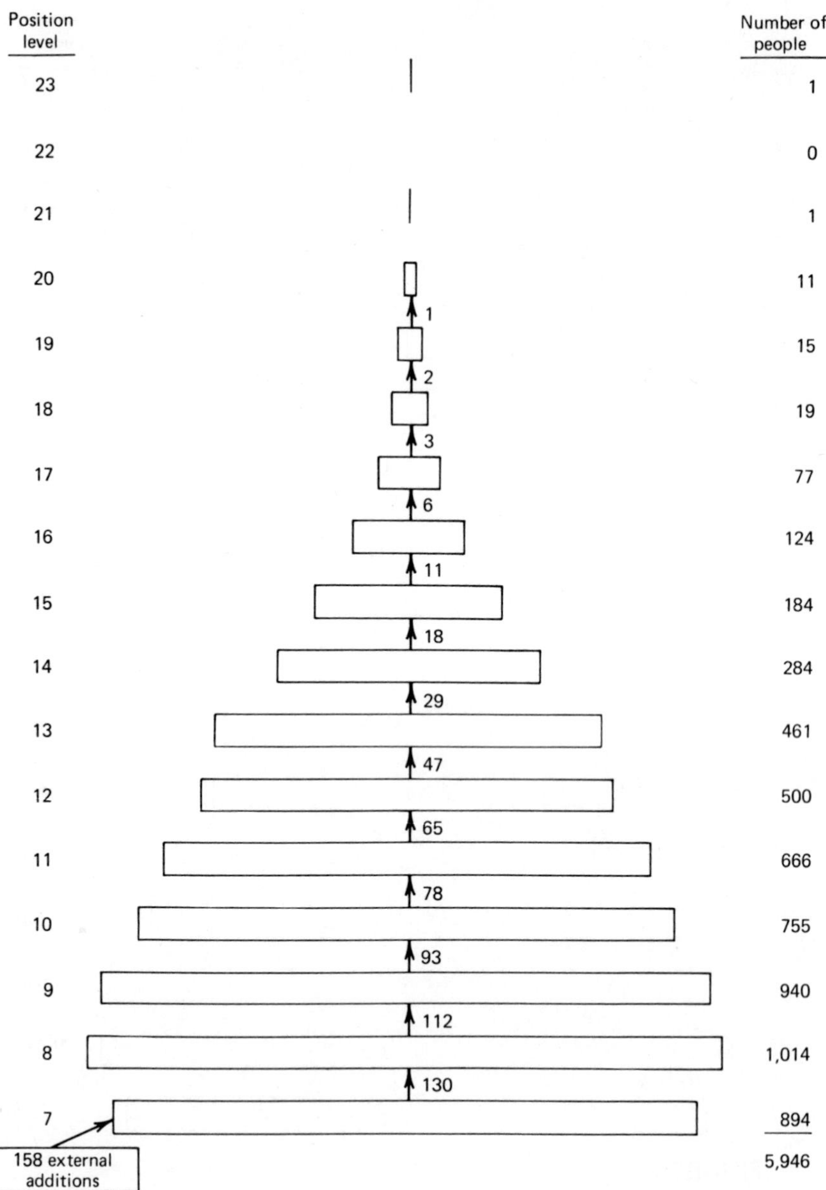
Position level
Number of people
23
1
22
0
21
1
20
11
1
19
15
2
18
19
3
17
77
6
16
124
11
15
184
18
14
284
29
13
461
47
12
500
65
11
666
78
10
755
93
9
940
112
8
1,014
130
7
894
5,946
158 external additions

FIGURE 3.

Obviously, the model should be exercised under different sets of assumptions related to possible ranges of growth rates, loss rates, and external hires distributions. But for the sake of illustration, let's assume the assumptions are close to the anticipated real world behavior.

At this point, we know the number of entry-level external additions, and we have a picture of upward mobility opportunities within the exempt population. So far, we have not introduced any qualitative elements such as engineers, physicists, nondegreed. People are simply people at this point. But we are ready to try to answer the questions which led to the construction of the model.

The Answers

The same methodology can be used to answer both questions because the concepts are the same. The question concerning all college recruits relates to the total population; the question regarding Manufacturing Management Program trainees relates specifically to that portion of the total population engaged in manufacturing work. That simply calls for a similar model dealing only with the manufacturing function.

Because Figure 3 is based upon a no-growth assumption, each year in the future will look the same as the one displayed. There will be 158 external additions at PL 7. The question is: how many of these should be top-notch college recruits?

Now the model forces one to come to grips with a fundamental question: What is the purpose of college recruiting? The answer "to get new blood into the organization" is not sufficient because the question of *how much* new blood still remains. At this point, management needs to agree on three parameters:

1. What is the target level for the college recruits input?
2. What per cent of promotions into the target level should be filled by college recruits?
3. How rapid should the upward mobility be?

Let's assume the answers to these questions are

1. The target level is PL 12.
2. The share of promotions is 50%.
3. The upward mobility rate is one level every two years.

Promotion opportunities at PL 12 during the 11th year hence	65
Opportunities to be filled by college recruits (50% of 65)	33
College recruits input now allowing 5% annual loss rate	54

FIGURE 4.

These specifications now clearly delineate the problem. What must be this year's input in order to fill 50% of the promotions into PL 12 during the 11th year from now? The answer is shown in Figure 4.

The allowance for annual losses from this year's college recruits can be determined from Figure 5. At a 5% annual loss rate, only about 60% of the initial input will remain after a 10-year period.

For perspective, the total external hires input at all levels was 281. Of these, 158 or slightly more than half came in at entry level, PL 7. Of these 158, roughly one-third should be high upward mobility college recruits. Management has a rational system which assures a smooth upward flow of top-notch entry-level talent upward but has retained a high degree of flexibility in its hiring patterns, including experienced people at levels above entry.

Some Additional Checks

The application of the model should not stop with Figure 4. Possibly PL 12 is not the most appropriate target level. Similarly, a share of promotions other than 50% may be desirable. Assuming that upward mobility continues to occur at one level every two years, Figure 6 shows the effect of changing the other specifications.

A calculation also needs to be made to determine that the opportunities in the upward flow movement from entry level can sustain the desired college recruits flow. This is done by constructing a table (Figure 7) that relates time, position level, and upward flow of college recruits.

One can conclude from Figure 7 that there are no numerical impediments in the upward flow channel.

Effects of Varying Loss Rates From Populations

N	1%	2%	3%	4%	5%	6%	7%	8%	9%	10%
1	.9900	.9800	.9700	.9600	.9500	.9400	.9300	.9200	.9100	.9000
2	.9801	.9604	.9409	.9216	.9025	.8836	.8649	.8464	.8281	.8100
3	.9703	.9412	.9127	.8847	.8574	.8306	.8044	.7787	.7536	.7290
4	.9606	.9224	.8853	.8493	.8145	.7807	.7481	.7164	.6857	.6561
5	.9510	.9039	.8587	.8154	.7738	.7339	.6957	.6591	.6240	.5905
6	.9415	.8858	.8330	.7828	.7351	.6899	.6470	.6064	.5679	.5314
7	.9321	.8681	.8080	.7514	.6983	.6485	.6017	.5578	.5168	.4783
8	.9227	.8508	.7837	.7214	.6634	.6096	.5596	.5132	.4703	.4305
9	.9135	.8337	.7602	.6925	.6302	.5730	.5204	.4722	.4279	.3874
10	.9044	.8171	.7374	.6648	.5987	.5386	.4840	.4344	.3894	.3487
11	.8953	.8007	.7153	.6382	.5688	.5063	.4501	.3996	.3544	.3138
12	.8864	.7847	.6938	.6127	.5404	.4759	.4186	.3677	.3225	.2824
13	.8775	.7690	.6730	.5882	.5133	.4474	.3893	.3383	.2935	.2542
14	.8687	.7536	.6528	.5647	.4877	.4205	.3620	.3112	.2670	.2288
15	.8601	.7386	.6333	.5421	.4633	.3953	.3367	.2863	.2430	.2059
16	.8515	.7238	.6143	.5204	.4401	.3716	.3131	.2634	.2211	.1853
17	.8429	.7093	.5958	.4996	.4181	.3493	.2912	.2423	.2012	.1668
18	.8345	.6951	.5780	.4796	.3972	.3283	.2708	.2229	.1831	.1501
19	.8262	.6812	.5606	.4604	.3774	.3086	.2519	.2051	.1666	.1351
20	.8179	.6676	.5438	.4420	.3585	.2901	.2342	.1887	.1516	.1216

Example: If I start with 100 people and lose 5% of the balance at the end of each year, at the end of 10 years I have 60 (59.87) people left.

FIGURE 5.

College Recruits Input Now to Satisfy Future Share of Opportunities

Target Level	Per Cent Share 10	20	30	40	50	60	70	80	90	100
14	6	12	18	24	30	35	41	47	53	59
13	9	17	26	34	44	52	61	71	78	87
12	11	22	32	43	(54)	65	76	86	97	108

Note: Circled (54) is answer for previous illustrative example.

FIGURE 6.

Comment

We need to remind ourselves again that the total work force model was exercised under a single set of assumptions to simplify the illustration. The really great value of a model, particularly if computerized, is its ability to generate answers for a wide range of assumptions. It leads to more consideràtion of what if questions and minimizes the risk that a single set of assumptions might be used to arrive at a single point answer. In short, it permits the testing of the sensitivity of the flow dynamics to changes in the value of the input variables. Planning and decision making can then be based upon a matrix of options, rather than on a single set of data or one or more subjective opinions.

Year	Arrival Level	No. of. Oppor-tunities	No. Filled by College Recruits	%
Now	7	158	54	34
+2	8	130	49	38
+4	9	112	44	39
+6	10	93	40	43
+8	11	78	36	46
+10	12	65	32	49
				(Approx 50)

FIGURE 7.

When the model has been sufficiently exercised, management has sufficient data to exercise some judgments and arrive at an operational decision. Although other targets could be set, the 50% share of promotions at PL 12 has considerable merit as a specification.

1. The college recruits share of all entry level (PL 7) additions is only 34%. This means that having enough training assignments available should pose no serious problems.
2. PL 12 is the bottom layer of the top 25% of the total professional work force. This is a reasonable definition of middle management and there is a substantial pool of people to draw on for top management positions.
3. There is still opportunity for continued upward movement of the college recruits into PL 13—a sort of safety factor in the design. The input of 54 to fill half of the promotion opportunities into PL 12 will satisfy only 62% of the promotion need at PL 13.
4. The promotion share for college recruits as they move progressively up the position level ladder is small enough to avoid animosity and bitterness by fellow workers who might otherwise resent being shunted aside by the "crown princes."

THE QUALITATIVE ASPECTS

Human resources planning obviously consists of much more than numbers. The model helps to outline the problem before the more qualitative planning begins. The target level concept provides a focus for the qualitative analysis. Such questions arise as:

- What are the types of jobs at PL 12?
- What are the characteristics of the present incumbents?
- Do we want to change the characteristics of the future incumbents?
- What college recruits input characteristics do we want now to meet the PL 12 needs?
- What types of training and development experiences do we want to provide for this upwardly mobile population?
- What schools are the best potential sources of recruits?
- What kind of tracking system do we want to monitor the plan and to provide information regarding possible changes?
- What development experiences could serve this special population to prepare it for responsibilities beyond PL 12?

One begins to get a message that the model forces an in-depth analysis of the work force, both quantitatively and qualitatively. Therein lies the opportunity to generate some genuine human resources planning—a process sometimes more talked about than actually done.

AN UNFORESEEN BENEFIT

The model achieved its objectives. How it was validated and has been used by the General Electric Company is proprietary information and, in any event, is not relevant to this book. What is important is that the company had a technique for understanding the upward mobility dynamics of its work force and a much improved rationale for college recruiting.

As the modeling project moved from a development to an operational status, significant applications to EEO began to emerge. It is probably fair to say that until 1971 and for sometime thereafter, the national EEO effort was one of getting minorities into the civilian labor force without too much attention to their upward mobility. Women were already in the work force in large numbers and tended to be a secondary matter of concern nationally. The required reporting process in the EEO arena was simply an adaptation of the basic United States census reporting categories. Those were (and still are):

1. Officials and managers
2. Professionals
3. Technicians
4. Sales
5. Office and clerical
6. Crafts
7. Operatives
8. Laborers
9. Service workers

The question of upward mobility for professionals and managers within an exempt work force was almost totally masked by the reporting system. Moreover, the goal-setting process of that era caused additional problems. In general, the process was to set some end of year percentage representation goal for minorities and women. For example, if the start of year representation of minorities in the officials and managers category was 3.5%, the end of year goal might be set at 4.5%. Some improvement in this percentage was expected annually. At General Electric and other companies that are large users of engineers, the college recruiting effort was becoming difficult because the minority and women supply lines for engineers were running woefully thin, but the minority goals were nevertheless taken very seriously. The situation clearly called for a scenario to see where the fierce competition for minority engineering graduates would lead everyone in the long run.

The college recruiting model proved to be an excellent vehicle for addressing the problem. In hindsight, it's easy to see that a minority engineering graduate supply of less than 5% simply left many of the companies in the industrial sector empty-handed. It was a year-to-year struggle and the time frame of the problem was not very well identified. The longer range goal was generally "parity." This meant that representation of minorities in the work force should equal their percentage in the civilian labor force. For the high technology companies, this could well be demonstrated as impossible. General Electric has openly published the fact that 65% of its middle management and higher incumbents have technical degrees, primarily in engineering. When the data from a study of minority engineering degree holders were put into the model, the results were awesome and shocking.

1. In terms of extremely modest minority representation at middle management levels, the time frame for planning had to be 20 years or more.
2. Minorities could not possibly have any significant representation at the middle management levels of technology industries in *any* time frame unless the number with engineering degrees was increased tenfold.

From these findings came a national effort known as PIMEG, the program to increase minorities among engineering graduates. This program is described in detail in Chapter Three. PIMEG is a classic example of what can be accomplished in the EEO arena when government, industry, education, and a profession combine efforts in a major thrust.

EEO IMPLICATIONS

The college recruitment model used as an illustration is only one of many that can be built. However, it does help to put in perspective some of the more important things models can be used to do in the EEO arena.

- Identify the important variables in the EEO goal-setting process.
- Identify the relative leverage of each of the variables under different sets of circumstances.
- Focus attention on the need for a reliable data base from which to draw the necessary modeling assumptions.
- Focus attention on the assumptions from which results follow rather than on subjective opinions about single point answers.
- Provide a rationale for evaluating the attainability of specific goals and timetables.
- Provide a rationale for evaluating the current level of EEO attainment (by exercising a model backward rather than forward).
- Provide a rationale for evaluating the realism of the expectation levels of the various stakeholders in the EEO arena.
- Help to identify opportunities for business and industry joint efforts with government to generate long range programs such as PIMEG.
- Provide a basis for integrating operating component EEO activities into an effective total corporate thrust.
- Eliminate some of the myths which tend to surround the demographics and movement dynamics of a work force.

It is important to note that models are only one of a number of analytical techniques that can be brought to bear in the EEO arena. Each major EEO case seems to have its own peculiarities, flowing largely from the different products and services offered by the firms. To cope with the analytical challenges, one needs a broad array of techniques woven into a custom-designed logic pattern for each case. In the main, these techniques must address the dynamics of the total work force before the realities of EEO progress can be seen in proper perspective. Often there is a wide gap between levels of expectation and achievable realities. A sound analytical approach can help to identify these gaps. Once the character of the gap is clearly in focus, the way is at least partially paved for equitable resolution of issues. Equally important, insights are generated for long range planning and programs to bring about genuine EEO progress.

CHAPTER THREE

PIMEG

There are several reasons for discussing the national Program for Increasing Minority Engineering Graduates, more commonly known as PIMEG.

- The program, which had its origins in the Human Resources model described in Chapter Two, was a major vote of confidence in the usefulness of dynamic demographic models.
- The very long time frame required for genuine EEO progress at the professional level and the necessity for planning on a long range basis were recognized.
- The program illustrates the need to take a root causes approach in addressing the question of minority upward mobility.
- The enthusiastic support of the major technology companies in the United States highlights the existence of a generally untapped national spirit to address EEO issues in a constructive, fruitful manner.
- The task of increasing minority representation at higher levels in the professional ranks of the industrial sector is being faced, not only with realism, but also with dogged, constructive efforts to meet the challenge.
- The complexities of determining what goals should be established and their elusiveness when expressed as percentages are illustrated.
- The PIMEG experiences have spin-off value in stimulating thinking and action on the creation of other programs which are important to minority and women's upward mobility.

THE BEGINNING

One advantage gained by using models in human resources planning is that the magnitude of a problem and the time frame required for its solution can be identified in a very short time. Often only a few days or weeks are needed to paint a broad-brush picture that can draw the needed attention to the problem.

In the case of PIMEG this was certainly true. In early 1971, thinking about future progress in minority upward mobility, General Electric asked itself such questions as: "How many minority should we recruit each year from the college campuses in order to achieve 10% minority representation at the first rung of the middle management/professional layer in the 20th year from now?" When the answer was divided into technical and nontechnical people with degrees and into specific minority categories, the need for black engineers, for example, was found to be in the range of 200 to 300 per year. At that time, the number of black graduates from the schools of engineering was about 400 per year. Even on a 20-year time frame, General Electric, which usually recruits about 2% of all engineering graduates annually, would have to hire 50% or more of the black engineering graduates each year.

This finding was an attention getter. In searching the literature of the period, one can find other references to the need for increasing black engineering graduates. But for the first time, within the General Electric Company at least, the need had been quantified in terms that top management could clearly understand. The rhetoric had been translated into numbers and related to the long-range interests and needs of the company. Only a few months later, in May of 1971, the finding was conveyed to all corporate officers by Hershner Cross, senior vice-president of the company, at a corporate-wide division managers' meeting.

However, conveying a message can only call attention to a problem—it doesn't provide a solution. Under the direction of Dr. Lindon Saline, head of Professional Development, intensive efforts were launched to find a solution to what was accepted as a serious problem, or in the General Electric jargon of the day, "a challenging opportunity."

THE FIRST PROPOSED SOLUTION

In May of 1972, Dr. Saline was ready to report in depth to top management. By then J. Stanford Smith, who later was to become top man at the International Paper Company, had taken the place of Hershner Cross as senior vice-president. Much of the credit for launching PIMEG and its subsequent success can be attributed to his enthusiastic participation and dedicated commitment. He was chairman of the meeting at which Dr. Saline, using the theme "To Make a Difference," pointed out several items of major significance and led the way to a proposed solution. As excerpted from the General Electric Company's publication, "A Report on the First Two Years of the Program to Increase Minority Engineering Graduates," the conclusion was:

a) The demographic manpower model of company employees showed that General Electric is a 'degreed culture' and in fact a highly 'engineering-degreed culture'. The majority of the higher technical positions and 60% of the top 20% positions are occupied by persons who hold four-year technical degrees. Only about 1% of the top 20% of the jobs were filled by minority persons at that time.

b) The dimensions of the shortage of minority engineers is so massive, that the traditional patterns and pace of attracting, educating, recruiting, developing, and promoting of minority engineers could not achieve parity* even by the turn of the next century. Therefore, a broad scale massive change, on the order of 10 to 15 fold, would be needed 'to make a difference' towards achieving parity within the next 10 to 15 years.

c) The depth of the shortage in the educational pipeline stretches back through the colleges down to the high schools and junior high schools because minority persons tended or were counseled to shy away from math, science, and other school work essential to college students in engineering.

d) Some of the alternate solutions considered at that time were:

- Massive scholarship aid utilizing existing colleges.
- Long term loan program.
- Engineering scholarship program for members of families of minority employees in the company.
- Operate (and pay costs of) the engineering school at an existing black college.
- Buy an existing black college.
- Establish a General Electric Institute (similar to General Motors Institute).

*Parity is defined and discussed later in this chapter.

> The strategy selected for further pursuit was to establish a Minority Co-Op Program with existing schools. This would entail some additional 2,000 co-op jobs for 4,000 students in order to yield about 600 minority hires per year for GE. The national objective of supplying 6,000 minority engineering graduates would require 30,000 *new* co-op jobs for 60,000 four-year minority engineering students! The "Minority Co-Op program" would be of such magnitude as to involve many other employers, the colleges of engineering, the Office of Education of HEW and other government agencies, minority organizations, professional societies and associations, foundations, and various other segments of society.

The selection of the Co-Op strategy was based on some preliminary studies which had pinpointed finances as the major obstacle to a successful program. In many quarters, the mistaken view was held that "there is plenty of scholarship money around—minorities are just not interested in engineering." This was clearly not the case. Even with scholarships available, the problem of subsistence funds alone was a staggering one. The Co-Op approach, an earn-while-you-learn opportunity, seemed the best way to solve the financial problem.

TESTING THE CO-OP CONCEPT

In July of 1972, 44 Deans of Engineering were called together in a conference given by General Electric to discuss "strategic Considerations in Engineering Education." Foremost among the topics discussed was that of increasing the number of minority engineering graduates. In a stirring address, J. Stanford Smith called for a 10-fold increase as he posed the problem, outlined its dimensions, and appealed for bold, innovative, all-out action. Although aimed specifically at engineers, Smith's remarks could apply to many occupations where minorities were woefully under-represented—only the numbers used in the examples would change:

> Of 43,000 engineers graduated in 1971, only 407 were black and a handful were other minorities and women. One per cent. It takes about 15 to 25 years for people to rise to top leadership positions in industry. So if industry is getting 1% minority engineers in 1972, that means in 1990, that's about the proportion that will emerge from the

competition to the top leadership positions in industry. Not 5%, or 10%, or 17%, but *1*%.

Gentlemen, that is a formula for tragedy. Long before the year 1990, a lot of minority people are going to feel that they have been had. Already there are angry charges of discrimination with regard to upward mobility in industry, whereas the real problem, clearly visible today, is that there just aren't enough minority men and women who have taken the college training to qualify for professional and engineering work. . . . There has been much talk of job restructuring. A certain amount of that can be done, and openings made for minority technicians without the full range of engineering education. But these jobs will not be a major source of professional and managerial leadership in the future, any more than they are today.

From time to time, one hears hints that we in industry might drop our standards, hire unqualified people, perhaps even call them "engineers". Then if they fail in the competition for leadership, that's their fault, not ours. What a sorry game!

First of all, it can't be done for competitive reasons. Our competitors here and abroad have first-rate engineers, and we can't compete with second-raters. The waste and inefficiency would knock us out of business. The United States is having trouble enough in international competition, without adding the problem of unqualified engineers.

And furthermore, the blacks and other minorities would quickly see through the sham and resent it. . . . Perhaps it has crept into your mind that we might be able to get away with excuses. We in industry could prove that we are hiring our fair share of the available population of minority engineers, and pass the buck along to the engineering schools. You, in turn, could point to your programs to attract black enrollments, and demonstrate that the problem lies with the blacks; they just don't sign up for engineering. And the blacks would place the blame on a white society that they would believe discriminates against blacks in professional work. Then the situation would stand exactly where it is today, except by that time the blacks might dominate the civil service ranks of local, state, and federal government, while the whites would hold the centers of technology, and that form of segregation could have disastrous results for all concerned.

During the many informal discussions that took place at this five-day conference, a strong signal could be heard that the Co-Op route was not the best one to follow. Further study confirmed the strength of and the reason for that signal. Many of the schools of engineering and the operating businesses which provide employment could simply not gear up for a program of the needed magnitude. For that reason, the conclusion was reached that the program had to be bigger than just Co-Op. What was needed "to make a difference" was a plurality of approaches, efforts, and organizational involvement.

In hindsight, the conclusion was extremely fortuitous, for a large scale Co-Op program could not have withstood the business recession of 1974. The effort would probably have died as employers struggling for survival could no longer make Co-Op jobs available.

THE REVISED APPROACH

The shunting aside of the Co-Op approach to a lesser role by no means dampened the enthusiasm and commitment for the objective. It merely stimulated the search for more viable alternatives. One of these was to find a national sponsor who could rally all of the necessary participants under a single, non self-serving banner. Among all of the many possibilities, the National Academy of Engineering proved to be the best, and in September of 1973, it accepted the national coordination and leadership role for the effort to increase minority engineering graduates.

One year later, at a conference held in Croton, New York, Dr. Robert C. Seamans, Jr., then president of the National Academy of Engineering, announced:

> . . . the NAE's master plan for its nationwide campaign to bring about a 10-fold increase in the number of minority engineering graduates within the next decade. The planning drafted by the NAE Committee on Minorities in Engineering sets forth methods for coordinating all present and future programs aimed at encouraging young Americans of Black, Indian, Puerto Rican, and Mexican/Chicano heritage to take up engineering careers. It also proposes several initiatives by the NAE, including the design of a 'National Engineering Financial Assistance Fund' and management of a program to provide more minority students with summer jobs in the engineering field.
>
> Under the plan, the NAE through its Committee on Minorities in Engineering would serve as the national focal point for development of programs at the junior high school, high school, and college levels. The programs would identify potential engineering students from minority groups, help motivate and qualify them for matriculation in an engineering school, and assist them educationally and financially to successfully complete an engineering curriculum. There would be comprehensive supporting programs to increase the effectiveness of

high school math and science teachers (including more bilingual teachers), more information on college placement and financial assistance, and greater emphasis on recruiting qualifiable engineering candidates from high school and college. The master plan establishes linkages on the decision-making level with the organizations and institutions which influence the career choice and education of minority students and their eventual employment.

Dr. Seamans' remarks show clearly how much broader and deeper the revised approach is in comparison to the original Co-Op concept. As additional studies revealed, the financial problem was only one of several root causes for the shortage of minority engineering graduates. In the case of PIMEG, it was necessary to reach down to the junior high school level to clear impediments to the program. (One has to wonder what root causes searches might uncover in other occupational fields.)

Under the revised approach, the General Electric Company and other major employers of engineers still have an important role to play. However, they are appropriately out of the educational mainstream, which is more properly the function of educators. Under the aegis of the National Academy of Engineering and through its Committee on Minorities in Engineering, stakeholders in the PIMEG process are positioned to do those things which they can do best.

NATIONAL ADVISORY COMMITTEE ON MINORITIES IN ENGINEERING (NACME)

One of the roles played by the major employers of engineers is participation in NACME, an informal body of high level executives that provides advice and counsel to the president of the National Academy of Engineering and to the Committee on Minorities in Engineering. Having committees which give free advice is nothing new, but NACME is exceptional in the quality of its membership. When the top corporate leaders of General Electric, Du Pont, Exxon, International Paper, and many others assemble, they really achieve a great deal more than provide advice and counsel. They reflect a high level commitment to make PIMEG a success and very directly make things happen in their own enterprises. Nor do they take the associated publicity and then send substitutes to the meetings. They personally participate and contribute much.

Membership in NACME is not limited to industrial corporations. By the end of 1978, the roster read:

Industrial Corporations	36
Industrial Associations	1
Minority Groups	6
Technical/Education Societies	3
Universities	4
Government Advisors	7
Total	57

In addition to NACME members at the advice and counsel level, there is widespread participation in PIMEG by other individuals and organizations—engineers, scientists, businessmen and their staffs, professors and administrators in colleges and universities, teachers and administrators in public and private schools, and members of civil rights groups. As described by Dr. Thomas Martin, chairman of the Committee on Minorities in Engineering, the PIMEG effort "is not being masterminded from some Washington-based cockpit. It is the collective result of many local actions, local initiatives, and local people."

For the PIMEG effort, a great national spirit has been found and activated. How much untapped national spirit exists for occupations other than engineering is an unanswered question. But one could speculate that there is indeed very much, if only the right "turn ons" could be found.

A BLUEPRINT FOR ACTION

In the fall of 1973, the Sloan Foundation organized "The Planning Commission for Expanding Minority Opportunities in Engineering" (informally known as the Sloan Task Force). Led by Dr. Louis Padulo of Stanford University, the Task Force focused particularly on costs and funding required. However, it did not stop there and in effect drew up a blueprint that has guided the NAE Committee on Minorities in Engineering through the early years of PIMEG efforts. In a summary booklet entitled, "Minorities in Engineering—A Blueprint for Action," the Task Force put forth 20 far-reaching recommendations covering numerous facets of the efforts needed at the college level. These are quoted here to illustrate that upward mobility for minorities involves far more than monitoring or enforcing numerical objectives. Although the need for financial support for PIMEG is a recurring theme, the recommendations reach out in many directions ranging from role models at the professional level to the stimulation of interest in engineering in the elementary schools.

The Recommendations

1. The Task Force recommends that U.S. schools of engineering increase the percentages of Black American, Chicano, Puerto Rican, and American Indian students enrolled as freshmen, with the national goal of achieving approximate population parity in the freshman class of 1982, and in all classes by 1987.
2. The Task Force recommends the establishment of a single national organization to raise and distribute essential new funds for financial aid to minority engineering college students.
3. The Task Force recommends that financial-aid programs for engineering students be planned to cover five years of undergraduate study.
4. The Task Force recommends that corporations, foundations, and other organizations wishing to support engineering education for minorities give part of their scholarship contributions through the new fund-raising organizations called for in Recommendation 2. Organizations still desiring to make contributions directly to certain educational institutions or individual students should continue to do so but should commit some additional resources to the national scholarship effort.
5. The Task Force recommends that foundation support be provided to defray administration and operating costs of the new fund-raising organization for the first five years of its operation. Such support would offset overhead and high start-up costs and assure donors that a maximum share of money contributed would be utilized for direct assistance to students.
6. The Task Force recommends that the National Academy of Engineering (NAE) assume a leadership role in coordinating the efforts of the many organizations working to increase minorities in engineering and in stimulating development of new programs that may be needed nationally. Without surrendering their independent prerogatives, these interested organizations should participate in the coordination effort and cooperate fully with each other, discussing their current activities and future plans and carry out a cohesive national effort.

7. The Task Force recommends that some existing or specially created organization undertake to match and place qualified minority applicants with engineering schools seeking minority students.
8. The Task Force recommends that the six traditionally Black universities with engineering programs be supported at optimum levels to insure that these programs achieve maximum minority enrollment during the next five years. An increase of 100% in their present enrollment is a realistic goal to be achieved at this time.
9. The Task Force recommends that programs be developed with a selected number of colleges which have heavy concentrations of Chicanos, Puerto Ricans, and American Indians to provide pathways into engineering for these minorities as the Black colleges have traditionally provided for Black youth.
10. The Task Force urges support for efforts by engineering colleges to improve the articulation between engineering education and other institutions of higher education (two-year colleges and four-year institutions without engineering programs) in order to smooth the transition into engineering and to retain more transfer students in engineering.
11. The Task Force recommends that all schools of engineering provide remedial and tutorial programs, improved orientation and counseling, flexible curricula and, wherever possible, cooperative engineering programs with engineering employers. These should not be looked upon as merely "affirmative action" programs for minorities but should be recognized as essential for large numbers of students, whatever their racial or ethnic background.
12. The Task Force recommends that U.S. engineering schools develop programs to increase the output of Ph.D.'s from minority groups so that minorities will be adequately represented among faculty and administration leaders and will also serve as role models for engineering students.
13. The Task Force recommends that programs be implemented to capitalize upon educational opportunities in the armed forces in order to channel more minority military personnel and veterans into engineering.
14. The Task Force recommends that federal Special Services programs, now supported by the U.S. Office of Education (USOE) for providing tutorial and support assistance for disadvantaged college students, be maintained; and that engineering institutions and organizations explore with the USOE the feasibility of setting up jointly supported and operated pilot programs for engineering students.
15. The Task Force recommends that a small number of honorific scholarships of, say $1,000 each, be awarded to the top finalists and semi-finalists in competitions run by the National Achievement

Scholarship Program and the Upper Division Scholarship Competition for minority students—such awards to be used in an engineering educational institution. To provide greater access to higher education for other minority groups, the National Achievement Scholarship Program should be encouraged to expand its programs to include Chicanos, Puerto Ricans, and American Indians, as well as Blacks.

At the Pre-College Level

16. The Task Force urges that programs be initiated to train greater numbers of elementary and high school teachers in bilingual and bicultural education. Particularly needed are minority science and mathematics teachers who can teach within their students' cultural experience and who can serve as role models for minority children.

17. The Task Force recommends the continuation of summer training programs for high school students and particularly urges that new programs be developed to attract minority students to engineering.

18. The Task Force recommends strengthening present school-year programs and developing new efforts to interest minority high school and elementary school students in engineering, and to motivate them toward securing necessary high school preparation for college.

19. The Task Force recommends establishing programs to educate minority parents, science and mathematics teachers, and high school counselors concerning the opportunities in engineering, utilizing a field staff to reach minority community organizations, teachers, and counselors, and providing promotional material directed at the four underrepresented minority families and social structures.

20. The Task Force recommends expansion of the U.S. Office of Education's project, Talent Search, to identify and assist potential engineering students from the seventh grade on. In addition, the Task Force recommends the dedication of several pilot Upward Bound programs and experimental minority high school curricula to pre-engineering and science, perhaps in cooperation with engineering employers, as well as engineering colleges, to see if early career orientation will increase the desire of minority youth to acquire the skills necessary for success in college.

THE COMMITTEE ON MINORITIES IN ENGINEERING (CME)

On July 1, 1974, the CME was transferred from the NAE to the newly formed Assembly of Engineering in the reorganized National Research Council. The organizational structure is shown in Figure 1.

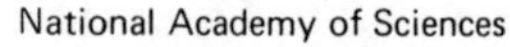

Corporate Entity

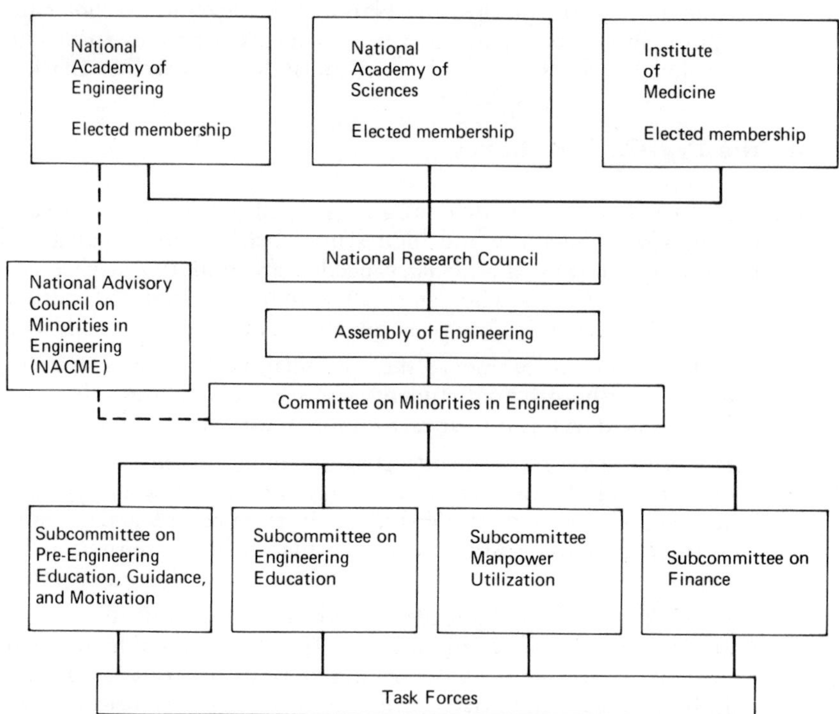

FIGURE 1.

The connection with the National Academy of Engineering still exists, although it is obscured somewhat by organizational detail. In actuality, the chairman of CME is appointed by the chairman of the Assembly of Engineering, who is also the president of the National Academy of Engineering.

It is important to recognize that the CME consists of two distinct groups of people—volunteers and employees of the National Research Council, Assembly of Engineering. The latter essentially provides logistics and staff services for the volunteers and for the National Advisory Committee on Minorities in Engineering (NACME).

Aside from organization charts and committees, what is CME's approach to the problem of increasing the number of minority engineering graduates? In a well thought-out, well articulated statement, the Committee had this to say:*

Engineering Career Trajectory

It is clear that an engineering career trajectory has three distinct phases: The pre-college phase, the college phase and the post graduate, or career development, phase. For minorities to have truly equal opportunities for leadership positions, they must achieve parity in all three phases of the engineering career path. One or more strategies aimed at overcoming the barriers to minorities along this trajectory have been developed for each—for pre-college, for retention through the college phase, for career development. And additional strategies are required to raise the necessary funds to support these strategies.

Obstacles in the Pre-College Phase

The two largest obstacles to minority entrance into college engineering programs—that is, the largest pre-college obstacles—are:

1. Lack of knowledge on the part of minority students about engineering, and
2. Lack of sufficiently strong preparation in mathematics and science for those students especially who attend predominantly minority schools.

These two main obstacles result from combinations of other considerations and factors which can be categorized briefly as follows:

1. The 8th or 9th grade is the critical point in students' careers when they make choices about the mathematics and science courses they will or will not take. And these decisions then determine their subsequent admissibility into an engineering school.
2. Because of a lack of role models and a general lack of information about engineering, minority students generally lack motivation toward engineering. It is well established that this motivation is the most important single factor in determining whether or not a student enrolls in engineering and whether or not he or she succeeds once enrolled.

*The Committee on Minorities in Engineering, "Scope and Activities," National Research Council.

3. A long standing lack of demand for upper division courses of high quality in mathematics and science in predominantly minority schools has created a lack of teachers who are qualified or interested in teaching substantial courses.
4. The high school and junior high school courses, particularly in mathematics, must be interesting and of a quality appropriate to pre-engineering. They must be well taught and attractive to students.
5. The atmosphere in many predominantly minority schools is not strongly academic in many important aspects and does not encourage the kind of academic excellence a potential engineering student must exhibit.
6. High school teachers and counselors in the minority schools are usually unfamiliar with engineering, its opportunities and requirements.

Pre-College Strategies

The apparently successful pre-college strategies attack these obstacles and factors through the following processes:

1. Identifying intellectually able minority students early in their education, not later than their junior year, and preferably as early as the 8th or 9th grade; the tools and techniques for accurate early identification are not fully understood.
2. Motivating them toward engineering careers through a wide variety of programs and activities.
3. Providing them with proper academic guidance and counselling so that they complete the requisite academic courses in high school.
4. Improving the capabilities of the high school faculty who are teaching the mathematics and science courses and who, in turn, will improve the quality of the courses;
5. Removing the financial barriers affecting both entry into an engineering college and continuation through to graduation; and
6. Informing parents, teachers, counselors and school administrators about opportunities for minorities in engineering.

Most of the strategies that seem to have been successful have occurred at the local level, each specialized to the particular requirements of the local situation. Most have been joint efforts among NACME members, engineering colleges, local school systems and ethnic organizations.

There are examples where other factors have been the catalyst and many other cases where there have been other co-contributors. The apparent successes* of PRIME, MESA, TAME, FAME, GCAP, CIC$^+$, MITE, JETS and others prove these points. In addition, ME^3 and the National Fund play critical supporting roles in many of these strategies, but the local action programs have been the key.

The task of increasing the number of minorities qualified for entry into an engineering college is complicated by the fact that we do not yet have common agreement, or possibly common understanding, of the precise definition of "success" in these programs.

The foregoing programs and strategies, while aimed at opening engineering careers to minorities, have the additional effect of opening up many *other* career opportunities as well. This is an important by-product, but it is only a by-product—the focus of the Committee is centered upon *engineering* careers as pathways to vertical equal opportunity in the corporate world.

Science and Engineering High Schools

To substantially increase the pool of qualified minorities, bolder and more comprehensive strategies are required. One such strategy requires the establishment of comprehensive high schools of excellence which meet the academic needs of students oriented toward engineering and science. Hopefully, these schools will offer programs similar to those available at the Bronx High School of Science, the High School of the Engineering Profession in Houston, and St. Augustine High School in New Orleans. The development of such secondary school programs must be encouraged in other appropriate metropolitan areas. The resources needed to make this happen already exist in federal, state and local agencies and can be channeled into such a development. Agency and program guidelines may require change or modification.

Disaggregating "Minorities"

The word "minorities" assembles an extraordinary diversity of peoples in very different situations under a single rubric. It is obvious that the problems of Blacks in Chicago are different from those in Detroit or Atlanta and all are different from those in the rural South.

*The 1977 Annual Report of the Committee on Minorities provides a more comprehensive list of organizations and their acronyms.

They differ from those of the Cubans in Miami, which also differ from the Puerto Ricans in New York and the Mexicans in Las Cruces. All differ from those faced by the American Indian on the reservation, whose problems also differ from those of his counterparts in upper New York State. And so it goes. There is no one approach. Each problem needs to be understood in its own particular context, and strategies must be developed that recognize this uniqueness. This need is best illustrated by the brief reference to the American Indians in the next section.

Our program has chosen to limit its scope of concern to the four minority groups—Black, Mexican American, Puerto Rican, and American Indian—that are clearly underrepresented in the engineering profession.

American Indians

American Indians comprise a unique minority group (0.4% of the population) that suffers from all of the obstacles previously enumerated for other minorities in traversing engineering career trajectories. These can be attacked by the six strategies listed earlier. However, the special circumstances of North America are such that the mechanics of implementing these strategies, as developed elsewhere (GCAP, PRIME, etc.), and which are primarily adapted to minority needs in large metropolitan areas, are not applicable to American Indians in their reservation environments.

There are nearly 52 million acres in trust for the American Indians—about 15 million are semi-arid. Indians own a substantial fraction of all U.S. energy reserves of coal, oil, gas and uranium and they are determined to develop these resources and their lands and forests. Such development is necessary to meet the present and future needs of the U.S., particularly in energy. But, Indians lack the trained manpower capable of dealing with this matter. Until they acquire the necessary skills, the U.S. will be unable to deal effectively with its energy needs across the present interface between Indian reservations and the balance of American society. Special programs are required that have not yet been developed.

Need for Government Support of Pre-College Strategies

All of the programs and activities described so far have been supported almost entirely by private sources, by the NACME companies and by the Sloan Foundation primarily. This is an unstable situation that cannot be maintained indefinitely—the total problem simply exceeds the ability of the private sector to pay for its solution. There must be a renewed vitality and a more effective use of government funds in support of education which advances the national goal of vertical equal opportunity. A resolute commitment by the executive branch of the federal government is urgently needed.

The provision of government assistance must be handled with great care. It would be a mistake for the various government agencies to assume that the traditional paths, programs and assumptions of government support are sufficient to cause more minority students to follow engineering career trajectories. If conventional approaches are followed, huge sums of money will be spent, but no progress is likely to be achieved.

Government support should be channeled into specific local action programs through local organizations of proven success as well as to national organizations with proven track records. Plans will need to be developed to address this problem.

The College Phase

For the college phase of the engineering career trajectory, retention of the minority student becomes the key strategy, specifically, achieving a retention rate that is the same as for majority students. One fact that emerged from our January 1978 Committee report was that the two most important factors influencing retention were associated with the pre-college experience:

1. The student's high school mathematical background and skills.
2. The motivation of the student toward engineering.

All other "academic factors" such as class standing, SAT scores and the like were of minor importance in comparison. Similar conclusions were documented at the MIT Workshop on Retention. The Workshop Report is now being prepared.

That first factor, motivation toward engineering, is an exceedingly complex factor. It involves a host of other factors such as:

1. On the job engineering experience—which, in addition to providing motivation, also provides real life examples of the barriers to upward mobility for those who lack the proper academic preparation.

2. Personal background.
3. Home environment.
4. Quality and breadth of high school mathematics and science instruction and the relevance of the courses to the student's world.

The strategies aimed at retention must consider all of these issues, and action programs addressing each are required. Further, because of the intensely personal character of each of these factors, a high level of individualized personal involvement with each student is necessary.

Other factors also bear on the issue of retention. Engineering colleges with minority programs must plan to provide a variety of programs of social support for their students. Minority students are often less sure of themselves than their majority counterparts—they are less at home in the highly competitive engineering college environment.

They need help, advice and counseling on a close, individual and personal basis. These requirements impose a serious additional financial burden upon the colleges. Here again is an area where additional financial resources must be provided.

Finally, the excessive rigidity of the typical engineering curriculum increases the difficulty of dealing with bright, talented youths who are intellectually capable but who may have critical disadvantages that interfere with their progress. Faculty imagination must confront this issue.

In particular, more consideration must be given to attracting more mature students into engineering programs. This includes those people who may have several years of experience as engineering technicians. The motivation and retention rate of such students tend to be above average and their financial needs tend to be greater than younger students.

The Career Development Phase

The number of minorities in the career development phase of the engineering career trajectory is small, and will remain small in the near future. Thus, this phase has not received much time or attention. This cannot remain so. The potential career development obstacles to minority graduates must be identified and corrective programs initiated before large numbers of minorities enter this phase. In view of the promises made and the expectations aroused in the pre-college and college phases, failure to develop programs aimed at the career development obstacles would be an ethical and social disaster. It would also make it impossible to achieve the Committee goal of parity with the population for minorities in engineering careers.

At this point, one can observe how carefully and thoroughly each step has been taken.

- Appropriate in-depth problem definition and program planning studies were made by the Sloan Foundation Task Force.
- A sound organizational structure is in place in the form of the Committee on Minorities in Engineering.
- High level endorsement and support are assured through NACME and the National Academy of Engineering.
- Strategies have been carefully thought out and agreed upon.
- A volunteer army of participants continues to be built—addressing many of the challenges at the grass roots level.
- In short, PIMEG has been institutionalized to make certain that efforts continue throughout the very long time frame necessary to achieve its goals.

GOALS AND RESULTS

In the 1974 Sloan Task Force Report, recommendation number one read:

> The Task Force recommends that U.S. schools of engineering increase the percentages of Black American, Chicano, Puerto Rican, and American Indian students enrolled as freshmen, with the national goal of achieving approximate population parity in the freshman class of 1982, and in all classes by 1987.

It is important to note that Orientals were not included in PIMEG, because they had already achieved relevant population parity.

Four years later, there was still considerable discussion over a precise definition of parity. Initially, the four under-represented minorities were estimated to make up 18% of the college age population in the year 1980. Thus 18% was articulated as the numerical goal. Subsequently, arguments were raised that:

- The proportion of minority members in the relevant age population will continue to increase beyond the year 1980—Blacks alone to 18% by the year 1984.

- The percentage of minority students entering postsecondary education is considerably less than that for nonminorities. In the fall of 1976, 14.5% of all full-time students at all institutions of higher education were Black-nonHispanic, Hispanic, and American Indian/ Alaskan native. At four-year institutions, the percentage was 12.4, and in engineering schools (predominantly male) only 10.7% of the total enrollment was male minority.
- The engineering school retention rates, although not precisely established, appear to be considerably lower for minorities than for others. Perhaps two separate minority goals are needed—one for entering students and one for graduates.

In the PIMEG December 1978 report on financial aid needs for minorities, the recommendation was to stay with the 18% goal for both entering students and graduates on the assumption that minority retention would be improved by the 1980s, and to stay consistent with the original task force report for measurement purposes.

Regardless of the specific numbers, the PIMEG experience illustrates the difficulties in arriving at an acceptable, agreed upon definition of parity. The analogy to employers in formulating their affirmative action plans almost speaks for itself. Some of the numbers change with time, some data always seem to be lacking, and the EEO objectives are not as easy to state as they first might appear to be.

How well has PIMEG succeeded in its early years? The clearest indication is shown in Figure 2.

In absolute terms, the minority participation in the freshman class was 4,146 students more in 1977 than in 1973. However, when minority participation is expressed as a per cent of the total, the improvement was only 2.2 percentage points. The great surge in total first-year enrollment makes the percentage goal task a much more difficult one. However, if engineering enrollments follow their traditional up and down pattern, the future minority percentage participation rates will probably appear in a more favorable light.

The Financial Aid Needs Study Committee did a thorough, professional job culminating in its December 1978 report. The data from Figure 2 illustrate the elusiveness of the target. Recognizing the many possible things that can happen, the committee constructed a number of scenarios to describe what might. The estimated range of possible times in which the 18% minority first-year engineering enrollment might be met was somewhere between 1982 and 1985. Even if the goal is not met until 1985, a slippage of three years from the original target, PIMEG will have been a remarkable accomplishment. If

Year	First-Year Engineering Enrollment		
	Total	Minority	%
1973	51,920	2,987	5.8
1974	63,440	4,018	6.3
1975	75,343	5,344	7.1
1976	82,250	6,309	7.7
1977	88,780	7,133	8.0

FIGURE 2.

minority retention rates can be improved, 18% parity in the graduating classes could be reached in the year 1990, just about 20 years from the articulation of the short supply problem by General Electric in early 1971.

Only time will tell whether or not the PIMEG projections contain some of the hockey-stick optimism discussed in Chapter Two. It appears that they do. By the end of 1978, the Committee on Minorities in Engineering, recognizing this possibility, had begun to call for stepped up efforts on all fronts, following the theme "Building the Multiplier Effect." One thing appears certain. If PIMEG falls short of objectives or misses on its timetable, it will not be from lack of trying nor from failing to use the best known state of the art in its efforts.

A ONE PER CENT SOLUTION

If PIMEG succeeds in meeting its graduates-based goal at some time in the last decade of this century, 18% of the output from the nation's engineering schools will be from the four targeted groups—Blacks, Mexican Americans, Puerto Ricans, and American Indians. The flow stream of the future will be open and contributing its appropriate share of minorities to the main body of engineers in the civilian labor force. Yet, only the first two steps of the journey will have been taken—parity in entering students and parity in graduating students. The final step, the real objective, will be upward mobility for these minorities in the technology-based industries and parity throughout the technical-professional work force at all levels at some time well into the 21st century.

But as massive as the undertaking has proven to be, PIMEG is directed only at engineering degree-based employment—at less than 2% of the jobs in the total civilian labor force. Moreover, PIMEG concentrates on only four minority groups in a professional field which consists predominantly of men. It does not address the question of women in engineering and could well be described as a one per cent solution, albeit in a very important sector of the world of work.

Participation in PIMEG is not an exemption from the compliance arena, nor should it be. Rather it is an overlay on the more short-range, on-going compliance activity. But it does emphasize the necessity for finding and facing up to EEO realities in the other 99% of the arena. In many instances, more pressure from regulating agencies for increased goals and shortened time-tables cannot be nearly as productive as might be hoped. In fact, it can be counter-productive if it masks the realities of low availability of minorities and women and other inherent limitations on what can actually be achieved in any given time frame. Nor does exhortation to do more generally lead to results, unless it is supported by thorough study, problem identification, and solution formulation.

In PIMEG, many stakeholders in EEO found common ground on which to build for the future. Where is the common ground for the other 99% of the civilian labor force?

CHAPTER FOUR

Women and Minority Representation

One indicator commonly used to evaluate an employer's EEO performance is the percentage representation of minorities or women in a particular work force category. For example, suppose an employer reports that at the close of last year, minorities held 8% of the jobs in the crafts category. When this 8% is compared to some external reference number such as the percent of minorities in the community or the percent of minorities in crafts in the local labor market, a judgment of the employer's EEO performance is made. If several years of data have been accumulated, a trend line can be drawn to show the improvement or lack of it in the minority representation over a period of time. This trend line is used in two ways—to evaluate the past and to predict the future. For example, the employer whose crafts category is now 8% minority may have had only 4% minorities in crafts five years ago. If this trend continues for another five years, minorities might be expected to hold 12% of the crafts jobs.

What does all of this really tell us? The judgment lies mainly in the eye of the beholder. The employer's press release might proclaim that minority representation doubled in five years and the outlook for continued progress is very bright. A monitoring agency might take a dimmer view—that compared to the 14% minority in crafts that other employers in the area have achieved, the present 8% is too low and the projection for the future needs to be sharply increased. The minority community might argue that compared to a 40% minority representation in the local labor market, the employer's results are woefully inadequate.

In reality, the use of minority representation in work force categories either as a specific statistic or as a trend indicator can be very misleading. Annual snapshots of representation do not get at the real dynamics of the EEO process. The basic issue is how well did the employer do with the available opportunities. Over the five-year time period in this example, minorities shared to a high or low degree in the job placements made in the crafts category. The reporting process based on annual representation gives no indication about what that share was. Even if that share were known, there would still be plenty of room for argument and judgment, but the basis of evaluation would be shifted closer to the real heart of the matter.

The future's forecast is a particularly troublesome part of the example. Can the minority community, or the monitoring agency, or the employer rationally assume that the historical rate of change will continue? It is a risky assumption to make, amounting to little more than guesswork. One of the most serious mistakes one can make in the EEO arena is to project the future by simply extending past performance on a straight-line basis. The dynamics are considerably more complex than simple linear relationships. Until these dynamics are explored in detail, judgments of past performance and predictions of the future are on shaky ground.

Let's begin the exploration of the dynamics by working from a specific numerical example—a model that demonstrates some of the relationships among the variables in the EEO process.

A SHARE OF HIRES MODEL

The simplest form of model deals with a gross population, such as the total work force of an employer. In this type of model, we have a total population, and we are not concerned about the distribution within the population. The distribution can be addressed later on with an upward mobility model such as the one described in Chapter Seven.

The dynamics are illustrated in Figure 1.

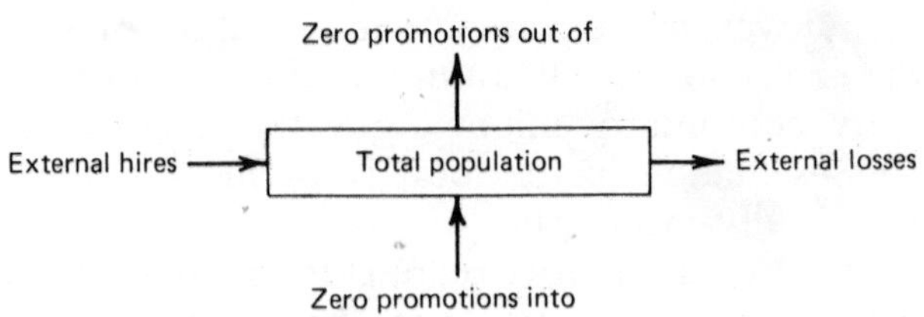

FIGURE 1.

If there is no growth in the total population, the dynamics are simply that external losses are replaced by external hires.

Suppose we have the following data:

Total population	= 1000
Minority population	= 40
Total population loss rate	= 10%/year
Minority population loss rate	= 10%/year
Annual growth rate is zero	

Each year there will be 100 external hires to replace the losses. These hires are opportunities in which minorities should share. In subsequent chapters we will discuss ways of determining how large the minority share should be. Meanwhile, let's arbitrarily assume a value of 10%. Of the 100 people hired each year, 10 will be minority.

The action which takes place during the first year is:

◆ Total Losses = .10 × 1000 = 100

◆ Minority Losses = .10 × 40 = 4

◆ Because growth rate is zero, we hire a total number of people equal to total losses.

$$\text{Hires} = \text{Losses} = 100$$

◆ Minority share of total hires is 10%.

$$\text{Minority Hires} = .10 \times 100 = 10$$

◆ The end of year number of minorities in the total population is the start of year number plus the difference between minority hires and minority losses.

$$\text{Minority, End of Year} = 40 + (10 - 4) = 46$$

◆ The per cent representation of minorities in the total population has changed from

$$\text{Start of Year} = \frac{40}{1000} = 4\%$$

to

$$\text{End of Year} = \frac{46}{1000} = 4.6\%$$

Minority Dynamics: 10% Share, 10% Loss Rates

Year	Start Total	Lose	Hire	Net Gain	End Total	% Rep.
1	40	4	10	6	46	4.6
2	46	5	10	5	51	5.1
3	51	5	10	5	56	5.6
4	56	6	10	4	60	6.0
5	60	6	10	4	64	6.4
6	64	6	10	4	68	6.8
7	68	7	10	3	71	7.1
8	71	7	10	3	74	7.4
9	74	7	10	3	77	7.7
10	77	8	10	2	79	7.9

FIGURE 2.

This process can be repeated for any desired number of years. The exercise can be done in tabular form, using conventional arithmetic rounding. Because of the zero growth assumption, the annual number of hires remains constant at 100 per year. Because the minority share of hires is 10%, the annual number of minority hires remains constant at 10. The results for a ten-year period are shown in Figure 2.

Note that in the early years, the minority representation increases by 0.5 percentage points a year. Later on, this rate drops to 0.2 points a year. In this particular example, the curve which describes minority representation from year to year is not linear but something considerably less. If the model is extended for an additional 10 years, making 20 years in total, the minority representation reaches 9.2%. The results are shown graphically in Figure 3.

What is Figure 3 telling us? Let's hold off drawing any conclusions until we add another curve. Suppose the loss rates were not 10% but were only 5% per year. What would happen? The number of opportunities in which minorities could share would be reduced from 100 down to 50 per year. If the minority share of hires remains at 10%, the resulting dynamics would be those shown in Figure 4. If the model is extended for another ten years, the minority representation would be only 7.7% at the end of the 20th year.

Let's now depict the results from Figures 2 and 4 on the same chart, Figure 5.

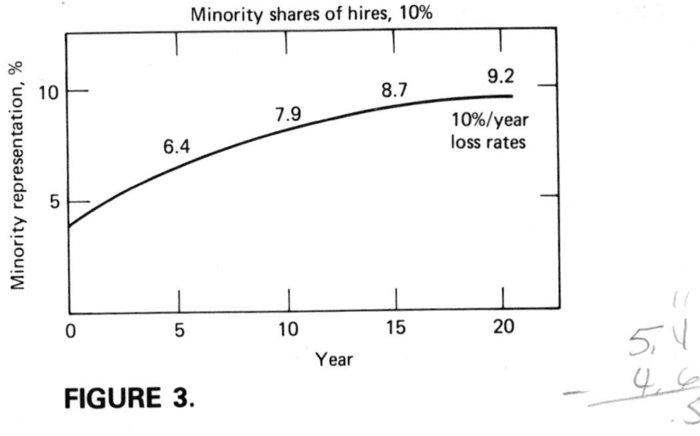

FIGURE 3.

Minority Dynamics: 10% Share, 5% Loss Rates

Year	Start Total	Lose	Hire	Net Gain	End Total	% Rep.
1	40	2	5	3	43	4.3
2	43	2	5	3	46	4.6
3	46	2	5	3	49	4.9
4	49	2	5	3	52	5.2
5	52	3	5	2	54	5.4
6	54	3	5	2	56	5.6
7	56	3	5	2	58	5.8
8	58	3	5	2	60	6.0
9	60	3	5	2	62	6.2
10	62	3	5	2	64	6.4

FIGURE 4.

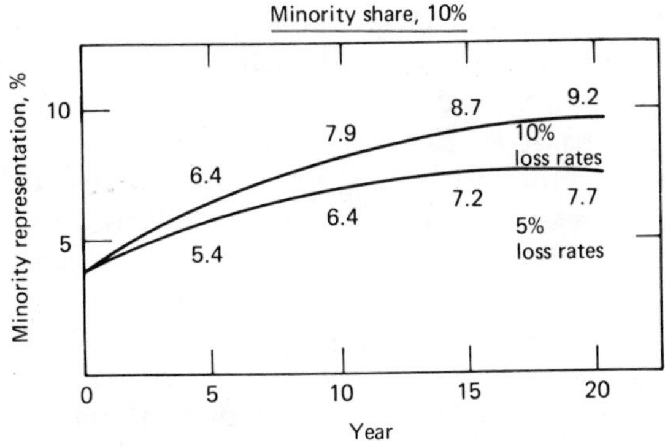

FIGURE 5.

What do the curves in Figure 5 tell us? There are several messages. For the given data and assumptions:

1. The rate of increase in representation achieved in the first few years cannot be sustained in later years. As progress is made, each additional step of progress becomes more difficult.
2. Loss rates are a major determinant of the end results. The accuracy of future representation forecasts depends upon how well the loss rates can be predicted.
3. An employer who sets goals based on representation forecasts runs considerable risk of missing the goals if loss rates prove to be lower than expected. The only alternative, if goals *must* be met, is to adjust the share of hires upward. On the other hand, if loss rates are higher than expected, the employer can adjust the share downward and meet the goals with less relative effort.
4. Surprisingly, doubling the opportunities (which is what occurs as loss rates move from 5% to 10%) comes nowhere near producing a doubling of representation even over a 20-year time frame.

Let's do more exploration with this model. Suppose an employer is committed to representation goals corresponding to the 10% loss rate curve in Figure 5, but loss rates turn out to be only 5% per year. How much would the share have to be changed to obtain the desired results? This calculation can be done in tabular form as displayed in Figure 6.

Similarly, Figure 7 shows the reverse situation. The goals have been set on the basis of the 5% loss curve, but actual losses prove to be 10% per year.

What are the results displayed in Figures 6 and 7 telling us about evaluating EEO performance? Suppose two similar employers operating in the same community and the same labor market started at 4% minority representation and reached 7.9% in ten years. Until we have the share of hires data, we are in no position to evaluate their absolute or comparative EEO performance.

Let's now conclude the exploration of this particular model. What we need is some way of generalizing the results. It isn't possible to do so from the single set of data we have used so far. On the other hand, we can't go on hand-building models indefinitely on a trial-and-error basis. Fortunately, there is a general mathematical equation which describes total work force, no-growth models of the kind we have built. When that equation is exercised under different sets of assumptions, many what if questions can be answered fairly quickly.

Minority Dynamics: Variable Share					
Year	Start Total	Lose	End Yr. Need	Must Add	% Share
1	40	2	46	8	16
2	46	2	51	7	14
3	51	3	56	8	16
4	56	3	60	7	14
5	60	3	64	7	14
6	64	3	68	7	14
7	68	3	71	6	12
8	71	4	74	7	14
9	74	4	77	7	14
10	77	4	79	6	12

FIGURE 6.

Minority Dynamics: Variable Share					
Year	Start Total	Lose	End Yr. Need	Must Add	% Share
1	40	4	43	7	7
2	43	4	46	7	7
3	46	5	49	8	8
4	49	5	52	8	8
5	52	5	54	7	7
6	54	5	56	7	7
7	56	6	58	8	8
8	58	6	60	8	8
9	60	6	62	8	8
10	62	6	64	8	8

FIGURE 7.

Before we discuss the general algebraic equation, it is worth noting that we can follow any one of three modelling approaches.

1. Continue hand-calculated exercises as we have done in the foregoing.
2. Develop a computer program to do the arithmetic.
3. Work from a general equation, either manually or by computer.

The option chosen is a matter of individual preference and resources available. It also depends upon the audience for whom the work is being done. In general, algebraic equations tend to look too complicated and to generate some fears that things are being manipulated. Printed computer outputs are generally believable. Hand-done exercises are the simplest to explain.

A GENERAL SOLUTION

The general algebraic equation for a gross population model with zero growth rate is

$$R_{m_n} = R_{m_o}\,(1 - L_m)^n + XL_t\,(\alpha)$$

where $\alpha = 1 + (1 - L_m) + (1 - L_m)^2 + \cdots (1 - L_m)^{n-1}$

R_{m_n} = Minority representation in total at the end of the nth year of interest, per cent.

R_{m_o} = Minority representation in the total at the start of the first year, per cent.

L_m = The annual minority loss rate, decimal fraction.

L_t = The annual total loss rate, decimal fraction.

X = The minority share of hires, per cent.

n = The number of the year.

Although the equation looks formidable, it's not too difficult to apply with the aid of a hand calculator, and it does open the way to some useful EEO generalizations.

First of all, let's make sure the equation yields the same results as the hand-built model for the 10% minority share, 5% loss rate assumptions (Figure 4). Let's use the year 10 as the checkpoint. For the hand-built model, the minority representation at the end of the 10th year was 6.4%. What does the equation yield as an answer?

$R_{m_o} = 4\%$
$L_m = .05$
$L_t = .05$
$X = 10$
$n = 10$

$$(1 - L_m)^n = (1 - .05)^{10} = .5987$$

$$\begin{aligned} \alpha = \ & 1.000 \\ & 0.950 \\ & 0.903 \\ & 0.857 \\ & 0.815 \\ & 0.774 \\ & 0.735 \\ & 0.698 \\ & 0.663 \\ & \underline{0.630} \\ & 8.025 \end{aligned}$$

$$\begin{aligned} R_{m_{10}} &= R_{m_o} (1 - L_m)^{10} + XL_t (\alpha) \\ &= 4.0 (.5987) + 10 (.05) (8.025) \\ &= 2.39 + 4.01 \\ &= 6.4\% \end{aligned}$$

The equation and the hand-built model yield the same result. For those who choose to work with the general equation, the tables in Appendix A are a very useful aid in doing the necessary arithmetic.

In addition to simplifying the modelling tasks, the equation is helpful in visualizing what is happening. The first term describes the annual reduction in the initial minority population because of losses. The other term shows that the effect of minority share of opportunities on the future representation is less than might be anticipated, because some of the minority additions each year are lost in the subsequent years. Note also that except for the term n which represents number of years, all other parameters are expressed as percentages or decimal fractions. As long as representation is expressed as a percentage, the results are independent of actual numerical scale, except for differences in rounding.

To illustrate the use of the equation for generalizing, let's examine the effect of doubling the loss rates, assuming they are the same for the total and minority workers. In the hand-built model, we were surprised that when loss rates increased from 5% to 10% and minority share of hires was 10%, the representation in the 10th year increased only from 6.4% to 7.9% (Figure 5). Why was this change so small considering the fact that opportunities doubled?

If we look at the general algebraic equation, we see that the future representation has two components. Let's calculate these separately for two cases, using the same data as for the hand-built model.

Case 1

$X = 10\%$

$R_{m_0} = 4.0$

$L_t = .10$

$L_m = .10$

$n = 10$ (using the 10th year as a basis of comparison)

$R_{m_0}\ (1 - L_m)^{10} = 1.40$

$\alpha = 6.5$

$XL_t\alpha = 6.5$

$R_{m_{10}} = 1.4 + 6.5 = 7.9$

Case 2

$X = 10\%$

$R_{m_0} = 4\%$

$L_t = .05$

$L_m = .05$

$n = 10$

$R_{m_0}\ (1 - L_m)^{10} = 2.4$

$\alpha = 8.0$

$XL_t\alpha = 4.0$

$R_{m_{10}} = 2.4 + 4.0 = 6.4$

When the total loss rate is doubled, it is true that hiring opportunities

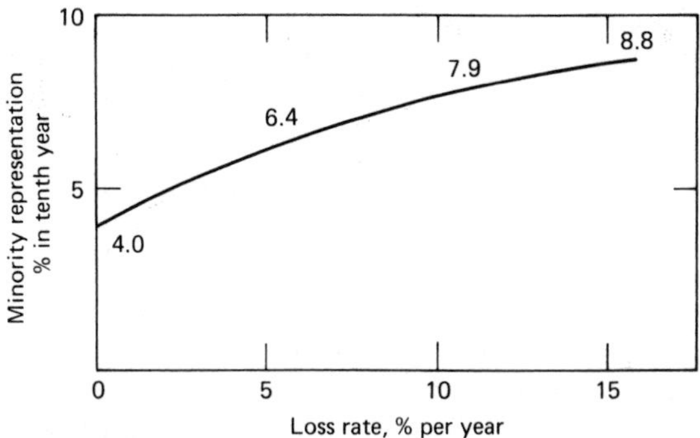

FIGURE 8.

also double. But the minority loss rate also increases and that effect is felt very heavily in both components which add together to yield the total minority representation. Note that the initial population shrinks more rapidly at the higher loss rate and the α term is also reduced. The end result is inevitably disappointing vis-a-vis intuitive expectations.

If we do some additional calculations for loss rates other than 5% and 10%, we can construct the curve shown in Figure 8,* which clearly shows the effect of increasing loss rates on ultimate representation. Note how far below linear this curve is.

In the no-growth mode for a total work force, the only factor that generates opportunities is the overall loss rate (L_t). Even when the loss rate increases substantially (assuming $L_t = L_m$), the opportunities generated fall far short of intuitive expectations. For the employer or monitoring agency attempting to forecast future representation, the relatively small yield from a sizable increase in loss rate is a critical and sobering factor.

AFFIRMATIVE RETENTION

In the examples we have used so far we have assumed that minority loss rate is equal to that for the total population. This is not necessarily the case. If minority loss rate is higher than that for nonminorities,

*Initial minority representation, $R_{m_0} = 4\%$
Minority share of hires = 10%
Minority loss rate = Total loss rate

future representation will be disappointingly low. Conversely, if an employer could hold minority losses to a relatively low rate, substantially higher future representation could be achieved for the same minority share of hires. The employer whose EEO performance is being measured in terms of minority representation would do well to institute affirmative retention programs. Although affirmative action is usually associated with the input process—the seeking out and hiring of minorities—it really should include the exit process also.

How sensitive is future representation to differential loss rates? The general algebraic equation can provide some useful insights. Suppose we continue with the example for which the initial minority representation is 4%, the total loss rate is 10%, and the minority share of hires is 10%. When the minority loss rate is equal to that for the total population, representation increases from 4% to 7.9% over a 10-year period. But if minority loss rate were only 5%, the representation at the end of the 10th year would be 10.4%. On the other hand, if the minority loss rate jumped up to 15% for some reason or other, while the total loss rate stayed at 10%, the representation at the end of the 10th year would be only 6.1%.

Strictly speaking, minority loss rate has some impact on the total loss rate, but mathematically it is relatively small in this instance. For illustrative purposes, this impact can be neglected—the general scale of results is not appreciably affected.

In some work categories where minority supply is relatively small and recruiting competition among employers is intense, it is quite possible that a particular employer will have to face the problem of differential loss rates unfavorable to improvement of minority representation. There are only two main alternatives available—affirmative retention efforts or intensifying recruiting efforts to increase minority share. In this particular example where the plan assumes a 10% minority share to reach a 10th year representation goal of 7.9%, the share would have to be ratcheted upward by an additional one-third to offset the differential loss rate of 15% for minority versus 10% for total. Such ratcheting may or may not be possible. If the original 10% estimate of share contained strong affirmative action elements, further attempts to go higher could leave the employer struggling with a very difficult if not impossible task.

SHARE OF HIRES

In the examples so far, we have been assuming a 10% share of hires for minority. Rationally, the share of hires should be derived by thorough analysis of the external market as described in Chapter Six. However, regardless of its numerical value, its resulting impact on changing future representation relates mathematically to the initial minority representation. Mathematically, the ratio $\frac{X}{R_{m_0}}$ must be fairly large to produce significant changes in future representation. For example, when share is 10%, loss rates are 5%, and initial representation is 4%, the ratio $\frac{X}{R_{m_0}}$ is equal to 2.5. But the end result is only 6.4% minority representation after a 10-year period.

In predicting future results to be achieved as a result of hiring share, it is important to think in terms of this ratio rather than some absolute value for share. One more generalization of the algebraic equation can be helpful in this regard. If both sides of the equation are divided by R_{m_0}, the result is:

$$\frac{R_{m_n}}{R_{m_0}} = (1 - L_m)^n + \frac{XL_t\alpha}{R_{m_0}}$$

The term $\frac{R_{m_n}}{R_{m_0}}$ is a measure of the progress in representation that can be achieved in a given time period. For example, a value of two for this term over a 10-year time period means that representation will double in that amount of time.

The equation is now expressed in its most useful form. By using the tables in Appendix A, one can very quickly make estimates of the impact of changing share. Similarly, for any desired future results, the share necessary to achieve them can be calculated with just a few minutes of effort.

For illustration, we have been using a 10-year time period. Most consent decrees or conciliation agreements involve only a five-year time period. At this point, let's switch to a five-year time basis to illustrate how large a share is required to produce substantial changes in representation in such a relatively short time period.

Suppose that an employer wants to double minority representation in a work force category within a five-year time period. The initial representation is 4% and loss rates are 10% per year for total and for minority. The desired value for the term $\frac{R_{m_5}}{R_{m_0}}$ is two. From the tables in Appendix A, $(1 - L_m)^5$ is 0.59 and α is 4.10. In order to achieve the desired result, the term $\frac{X}{R_{m_0}}$ must be 3.4. The absolute value of share must be 3.4 times the initial representation, or 13.6%.

If the loss rates were only 5% per year, the required ratio would be 5.4 corresponding to an absolute share of 21.6%.

Why would an employer want to double minority representation in five years? One circumstance could be that a careful analysis of external labor market data shows that other similar employers in the area have achieved 8% minority representation, but this particular employer is at the 4% level. The 8% achieved by other employers is a measure of the availability of minorities in the labor market. If the employer in this particular example could improve minority representation from 4% to 8%, the external labor market bench mark would be equalled and the chances of a prima facie case of discrimination greatly reduced.

Here we see one of the principal dilemmas in the EEO arena. To achieve substantial improvement in minority representation, share of hires must be relatively high. But the minority representation in the external labor market may be considerably below the required share. To make up this difference, the employer has to exceed the reasonable supply by a sizable amount. When that happens, the goal becomes more of a wish than a reality.

In this particular numerical example, the employer would have to exceed the minority representation in the labor market by a factor of 1.7 in the case of 10% loss rates, or 2.7, if the loss rates are only 5%. The alternative, of course, is to settle for something less than a doubling of representation in five years and run the risk of being viewed as a discriminatory employer. When EEO performance is measured in terms of representation, the employer is literally between a rock and a hard place.

ONE APPROACH TO GOAL SETTING

One of the major insights to be gained from gross representation models at zero growth is the difference between intuitive expectation levels, and what is mathematically possible. An equally important lesson is the importance of setting EEO goals on the basis of share of opportunities rather than some forecasted representation. A realistic process for setting goals should begin with a determination of labor market and from that a reasonable share of opportunities. The representation which results over a period of time should be the dependent *not* the independent variable.

Let's do a detailed example to illustrate how share of hires can be used as a basis for goal setting. Suppose an employer has the following end-of-year data available for a total work force.

Total population = 1000
Minority population = 60
Minority representation = 6%

The objective of the goal-setting process is to estimate what share of hires might reasonably be expected for minorities and what that share will lead to in terms of representation after five years.

The first step is a thorough analysis of the external labor market. What is a reasonable estimate of percentage availability of minorities? In Chapter Six we will discuss some ways of doing this. Meanwhile, let's assume that the answer is 12%.

The next step is to study historical data to establish some approximate loss rates for the total population and for minority. Let's assume that this study results in an estimate of 10% per year for the total and also the minority population.

As a third step, let's assume that the business forecast is for no growth in the work force.

As an additional step we need to establish some possible ranges in values of the variables. The future is best predicted in terms of ranges rather than single point values. However, in this example we will not establish a range for growth in the work force. That is an additional complexity to be addressed in Chapter Five.

When all of these steps have been taken, we can construct the data table shown in Figure 9.

What can we expect the minority representation to be at the end of five years? The answer can be presented in a table which shows a most likely value and a range of possible results. From this point on,

		Possible Range
Total Population	= 1000	
Minority Population	= 60	
Minority Representation	= 6%	
Total Loss Rate	= 10%/year	5–15%
Minority Loss Rate	= 10%/year	5–15%
Population Growth Rate	= Zero	
External Labor Market	= 12%	
Estimated Share of Hires	= 12%	8–16%

FIGURE 9.

Minority Representation, Percent End of Fifth Year			
Share of Hires, %	Loss Rate, %/year 5	10	15
8	6.5	6.8	7.1
12	7.4	8.5*	9.3
16	8.3	10.1	11.6

*Most likely value

FIGURE 10.

the derivation of the table is merely a matter of arithmetic. The results are shown in Figure 10, assuming there are no differential loss rates for total versus minority.

An employer who has a results display as in Figure 10, has a reasonably clear picture of the outcomes of various courses of action or various degrees of success in EEO efforts. To a certain extent, all of the possible outcomes depicted are disappointing against those intuitively estimated or hoped for. But at least the employer has a rational basis for decision making and has eliminated some of the elements of surprise, which tend to occur so frequently in EEO results forecasting.

SUMMARY

In summary, several significant conclusions can be drawn from total work force, zero growth models.

1. There is a generalized equation which relates six variables.

- Initial minority or women representation.
- Share of opportunities filled by minorities or women.
- Annual total population loss rate.
- Annual minority or women's loss rate.
- Minority or women's representation in some future year.
- Number of years in the future.

This equation can be used to predict future minority and women's representation.

2. Intuitive estimates of the rate at which minority or women's representation can be increased may often be considerably in error. There are mathematical inevitabilities that significantly limit the rate of progress.

3. If employer goals are to be set, they should be based on share of opportunities, not on forecasted minority representation. Mathematically, the independent variable should be share. Representation is a dependent variable.

4. Increases in minority representation occur more rapidly in the early than in the later years unless share of opportunities is increased each year. The results are analogous to walking up a hill that is increasing in steepness.

5. Because of the need to increase share of opportunities each year if the previous year's rate of progress is to be sustained, the real EEO leverage lies in finding ways to increase that share. That can be done arbitrarily at the risk of facing unrealistic goals or by programs directed at increasing the supply of minorities and women.

6. Annual snapshots of minority and women's percentage representation in a work force are not a valid basis for evaluating an employer's EEO performance. They do not get at the real EEO dynamics nor at the basic issue of how well an employer did with the opportunities that were available.

CHAPTER FIVE

The Growth Factor

In Chapter Four we worked with total work force models using a zero growth rate. When growth rate is considered as a variable, the models become more complex but are still manageable. It's important to note that growth rate can be positive or negative. In periods of high business activity, new jobs are created and opportunities for increasing minority and women's representation are increased. In periods of low business activity, there can be elimination of some jobs by attrition and the reduction of others by forced layoffs. When the growth rate is negative, seniority can sometimes be a significant factor if it produces higher loss rates for minorities and women than for others. As has been pointed out, such differential loss rates can be a serious impediment to increasing minority and women's representation in a work force.

A GROWTH MODEL

Let's apply a grow factor to the 5% loss rate model previously discussed. The basic data are:

Total population	1000
Minority population	40
Minority representation	4%
Total population loss rate	5%/yr
Minority population loss rate	5%/yr
Minority share of hires	10%
Growth rate of total work force	5%/yr

What will be the effect of growth and the opportunities resulting therefrom on the end of 10th year minority representation?

Now the model gets a little more complex, because the number of hires increases each year. The action that takes place during the first year is:

- Total losses = .05 × 1000 = 50
- We need to grow the total population by 5% or 50 people.
- The total hires must be 100.
- The end of year population will be 1,050 people.
- Minority losses = .05 × 40 = 2
- Minority hires = .10 × 100 = 10
- Minority net gain = 10 − 2 = 8
- Minority end of year population = 48
- Minority end of year representation = 4.6%

The balance of the model can be done in tabular form, one for the total population (Figure 1) and one for minorities (Figure 2).

How do these results compare with those for the corresponding no-growth model in Chapter Four? For a 5% loss rate, the no-growth model yielded a 6.4% minority representation at the end of the tenth year. For a 10% loss rate, the 10th year result was 7.9%,

Total Population Dynamics

Year	Start Total	Lose	Needed Growth	Total Hires	End Total
1	1000	50	50	100	1050
2	1050	53	53	106	1103
3	1103	55	55	110	1158
4	1158	58	58	116	1216
5	1216	61	60	121	1276
6	1276	64	64	128	1340
7	1340	67	67	134	1407
8	1407	70	70	140	1477
9	1477	74	74	148	1551
10	1551	78	78	156	1629

FIGURE 1.

Minority Dynamics

Year	Start Total	Lose	Hire	Net Gain	End Total	% Rep
1	40	2	10	8	48	4.6
2	48	2	11	9	57	5.2
3	57	3	11	8	65	5.6
4	65	3	12	9	74	6.1
5	74	4	12	8	82	6.4
6	82	4	13	9	91	6.8
7	91	5	13	8	99	7.0
8	99	5	14	9	108	7.3
9	108	5	15	10	118	7.6
10	118	6	16	10	128	7.9

FIGURE 2.

exactly the same as the 7.9% obtained from a combined 5% loss rate and 5% growth rate. As far as percentage representation is concerned, the 5% growth rate appears to have behaved mathematically as if it were simply an incremental additional 5% loss rate. If this is generically always the case, we have learned something very important. Remember that we have already discovered that increased loss rates (Figure 8, Chapter Four) do not produce anywhere near the improvement in representation that one might intuitively expect. If the same is true for growth rates, we have reinforcement of the concept that actual achievements will inevitably fall appreciably short of intuitive expectations. One might have hoped that growth is a high leverage parameter as far as minority representation improvement is concerned. Generally, growth rates will be considerably smaller than loss rates. Unless they provide high leverage, they may not be a major contributor to accelerated changes in minority and women percentage representation.

Let's do another spot check. Although a growth rate of 10% per year combined with a loss rate of 5% per year would be a most extreme and unusual combination, we can at least check the result in that circumstance with that in Figure 8, Chapter Four, for a 15% loss rate in a no-growth mode. There the result was 8.8%. If we get about that same result from this exercise, we are one step closer to a generalization. Figures 3 and 4 show the results of those calculations.

Total Population Dynamics

Year	Start Total	Lose	Needed Growth	Total Hires	End Total
1	1000	50	100	150	1100
2	1100	55	110	165	1210
3	1210	61	121	182	1331
4	1331	67	133	200	1464
5	1464	73	147	220	1611
6	1611	81	161	242	1772
7	1772	89	177	266	1949
8	1949	97	195	292	2144
9	2144	107	214	321	2358
10	2358	118	236	354	2594

FIGURE 3.

The results for the end of 10th year minority representation are surprisingly close. Numerically, of course, the number of minorities in the work force has increased dramatically. But as far as percentage representation is concerned, the denominator in the equation has also increased substantially, resulting in a much lower percentage than might have been expected.

Minority Dynamics

Year	Start Total	Lose	Hire	Net Gain	End Total	% Rep
1	40	2	15	13	53	4.8
2	53	3	17	14	67	5.5
3	67	3	18	15	82	6.2
4	82	4	20	16	98	6.7
5	98	5	22	17	115	7.1
6	115	6	24	18	133	7.5
7	133	7	27	20	153	7.9
8	153	8	29	21	174	8.1
9	174	9	32	23	197	8.4
10	197	10	35	25	222	8.6

FIGURE 4.

A GENERALIZED EQUATION, POSITIVE GROWTH

There is a general algebraic equation, which describes the total work force, growth model. As would be expected, it is more complex than in the no-growth case because it requires provision for the growth variable. The general equation is

$$R_{m_n} = \frac{R_{m_0}\,(1 - L_m)^n}{(1 + i)^n} + X(Lt + i)B$$

where i is the annual growth rate in decimal fraction

$$\text{and } B = \frac{1}{1 + i} + \frac{1 - L_m}{(1 + i)^2} + \frac{(1 - L_m)^2}{(1 + i)^3} + \cdots \frac{(1 - L_m)^{n-1}}{(1 + i)^n}$$

Let's spot check this general equation against Figures 1 and 2 using the end of fifth year representation as the basis for comparison. The hand-built model yielded a minority result of 6.4%. The solution to the equation is

$$\frac{Rm_o\,(1 - L_m)^5}{(1 + i)^5} = \frac{4.0\,(1 - .05)^5}{(1 + .05)^5} = 2.43$$

$$Lt + i = .05 + .05 = .10$$

$$X = 10$$

$$B = \frac{1}{1.05} + \frac{.95}{(1.05)^2} + \frac{.90}{(1.05)^3} + \frac{.86}{(1.05)^4} + \frac{.81}{(1.05)^5} = 3.93$$

$$R_{m_5} = 2.43 + 10\,(.10)\,(3.93)$$

$$= 6.4\%$$

The equation checks out all right against the hand-built model. Although the equation is somewhat cumbersome to use, we now have an analytical tool that can be used to examine the sensitivity of the model to changes in the variables.

As was the case in the no-growth mode, the minority representation at the end of any year is made up of two components. The first term is the residual from the initial population after losses have occurred. The second term describes the effect of minority participation in the available opportunities. Note that the growth term i generates opportunities in the same way as the total loss rate Lt because the two terms are added together in the equation. But it also appears in the denominator and tends to reduce the resulting percentage minority representation. The net effect is that growth produces

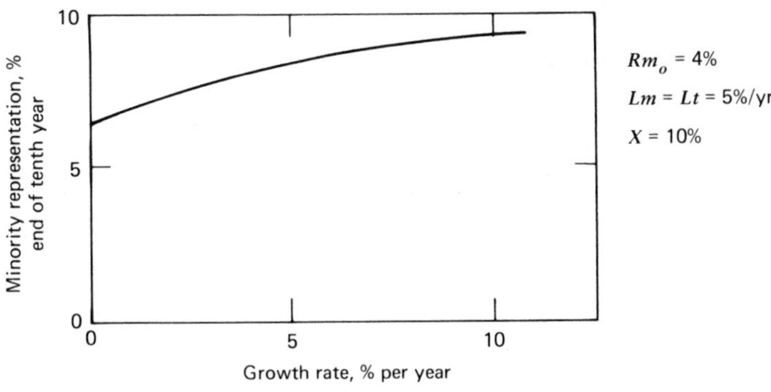

FIGURE 5.

about the same resulting percentage representation as if it were simply treated as an increase in loss rate for a no-growth model.

To illustrate graphically the effect of increasing growth rate, we can use the three results we have already calculated for the example of a 4% initial minority representation, a 5% loss rate, and a 10% share.

% Growth Rate	% 10th Year Representation
0	6.4
5	7.9
10	8.6

Figure 5 displays these results graphically. The curve is very shallow, showing that for the given values of the other variables increased growth rates have a much lesser impact than might be expected.

NEGATIVE GROWTH

Most employers always keep a watchful eye on the size of the work force. Even when business is moving along at a brisk pace, the so-called head count is a major factor in budgetary controls. When the number of people on the payroll is carefully monitored, growth in the size of the work force will not correlate directly with growth in business activity. For example, the annual sales may increase by 20%, but the size of the work force may remain the same or show only a modest increase of a few percentage points. This is all a part of the concept of productivity—higher annual output per individual worker.

When business activity slows down, the already strong interest in head count control further intensifies. Usually, there will be some specific target such as a 10% cut in work force size or a stated number to be removed such as 50 or 100 people. Depending upon how deeply the planned reduction bites into the size of the work force, it can be achieved in one of two ways. Even in a recession environment there are often natural losses from the work force such as resignations and retirements. One way of achieving a reduction in work force is not to replace losses, a process sometimes referred to as a reduction through attrition. However, if natural losses are not sufficient for the achievement of the head count target, forced layoffs are the only alternative available.

In terms of impact on minority and women's representation, negative growth rates in the total work force need to be analyzed for three sets of circumstances. For purposes of illustration, we can use the same basic data for each of the three cases. Let's assume the following data:

Total population	1000
Minority population	40
Minority representation	4%
Total population natural loss rate	10%/yr
Minority population natural loss rate	10%/yr
Minority share of hires	10%

Case 1

Management desires to reduce the work force from 1,000 at the start of the year to 950 at the end of the year. Natural losses at a 10% rate would number 100 people. But since the desired reduction is only 50 people, there will still be some hiring done during the year even though the growth rate of the total work force is negative. What will happen to minority representation? During the year, four minority will be lost and five will be hired. At the end of the year, there will be 41 minority workers in a work force of 950 people or a 4.3% representation. Even though the total work force was reduced, there were still some opportunities in which minority groups shared, and thus there was an increase in minority representation.

Case 2

Management desires to reduce the work force from 1000 at the start of the year to 900 by the year's end. Natural losses would be 100 people and the target would be exactly met by attrition. There would be no opportunities for hires. During the year, four minority would be lost, resulting in 36 minority workers out of 900 at year's end or a representation of 4%.

Case 3

Management desires to reduce the work force from 1,000 at the start of the year to 800 by the year's end. Natural loss rates would result in 36 minority workers out of 900 total people as in Case 2, but an additional 100 people must be removed from the payroll. How should that be done?

If there is a seniority system, the order of layoff will be predetermined on a last-in, first-out basis. It is possible that the entire remaining 36 minority workers could be forced off the payroll as a result of unfavorable seniority.

If there is no seniority system, it seems reasonable to prorate the necessary layoffs in terms of minority representation in the total work force. Of the necessary 100 layoffs, four would be minority. By the end of the year, there would be 32 minority persons out of 800 total or a representation of 4%.

From an overall view of the three cases, we can conclude that in general negative loss rates impede improvement in minority representation but do not cause a reduction below the initial value. The one exception is when minority loss rates are disproprotionately high which might happen with forced layoffs where a seniority system prevails.

VARIABLE GROWTH RATES

In the examples earlier in the chapter, we assumed that growth rate remains constant each year. In the ups and downs of the business world, that is seldom the case. However, longer range business plans are often made on a five-year time frame and annual forecasts of the size of the work force are a part of the plan. When data of this kind is available, it can be used as the basis for a five-year EEO model.

Suppose we have the following information:

Total population	1000
Minority population	40
Total population loss rate	10%/yr
Minority population loss rate	10%/yr
Minority share of hires	10%
Annual work force growth rate:	

Year	Rate, %
1	5
2	−10
3	5
4	10
5	10

Total Population Dynamics					
Year	Start Total	Lose	Needed Growth	Total Hires	End Total
1	1000	100	50	150	1050
2	1050	105	0	0	945
3	945	95	47	142	992
4	992	99	99	198	1091
5	1091	109	109	218	1200

FIGURE 6.

This information might describe a business that is phasing out a production contract in year 1, is in the design stages of a new project in year 2, and moves into full production during years 3, 4 and 5. The results of a hand-built model are shown in Figures 6 and 7.

Over the five-year period, the total work force increased by 20%. There were a total of 708 hires of which 71 were minority workers. Yet at the end of five years, minority representation is only 7%. For the no-growth mode, the representation at the end of the fifth year would be 6.4%. In net effect, the 20% growth contributed less than one percentage point to minority representation over and above what would have been produced in the no-growth mode.

Suppose instead of doing the year-by-year model, we had simply used the general algebraic equation with a 4% per year growth factor. How close would that result come to the one from the hand-built model? The answer from the general equation is 7.1%,

Minority Dynamics						
Year	Start Total	Lose	Hire	Net Gain	End Year	% Rep
1	40	4	15	11	51	4.9
2	51	5	0	−5	46	4.9
3	46	5	14	9	55	5.5
4	55	6	20	14	69	6.3
5	69	7	22	15	84	7.0

FIGURE 7.

very close to the 7.0% obtained by the other method. As a general rule, when detailed data is available from a business plan, it is best to spend the time necessary to address that specific data. The closer one works to real data, the more believable the results. When one is attempting to identify the gap between intuitive expectations and actual realities, credibility is a very important factor. However, for more general approximations, a trend line growth rate used in the general algebraic equation yields reasonably good results.

SOME BROADER IMPLICATIONS

In all of the models we have studied, there has been an inflow and outflow of people. Where do they come from and where do they go? This is an important question, because the activities of one employer generally must interrelate with those of other employers. For example, referring back to Figures 3 and 4, during the first year the employer adds 15 minority workers out of a total of 150 hires—this is the 10% minority share of hires assumed for the model. But out of 50 losses only two are from a minority—this is a 4% exit share. If all of the people who are lost find work in the local community, other employers must have been hiring at only a 4% minority share for this particular group of people. The dynamics that enable the employer in the model to increase minority representation over a period of time act as a downward drag on minority representation for other employers. Similarly, if the employer in the model acquired all 150 hires including 15 minority employees from other employers in the community, there would be a very distorted balance of trade. The other employers would be contributing minority workers on a 10% share basis but getting them in return at only 4% share.

This example is a simplified one, but it is not unreal. The employer in the model could be a particular campus within a total university network. There are faculty transfers between campuses and some faculties may grow in size while others decline. If the total university faculty size stays constant, and there are no external losses due to retirements or resignations, the total university minority representation will stay constant. But the dynamics described in this example would cause one campus to improve minority representation at the expense of one or more of the others.

Should we take a micro or macro view of progress in the EEO arena? From the point of view of the single campus, the 50 people who were removed from payroll were losses that generated hiring opportunities in which minorities could share. The same is true for the 100 opportunities generated by growth. But from the point of view of the total university, these were not opportunities for changing minority representation but simply transfers within a system.

If one extends the macro view to a national basis, all university faculty members constitute a work force population. The only real opportunities for changing women and minority representation in this macro view come from the growth factor and from "real" losses out of the total faculty work force. These opportunities result in new additions from new supply sources. Aside from redistribution by rank, which is a separate upward mobility issue, all other movements are merely transfers within the national faculty population.

Micro measurements can be extremely misleading, as a simple example can illustrate. Suppose there are two universities. University A has 1000 faculty of whom 40 are minority. University B has 1000 faculty of whom 100 are minority. On a combined basis, the minority representation is 7%. University A grows by 100 faculty per year and achieves a 10% minority share in the opportunities generated by the growth. On the other hand, University B is shrinking in size also at a rate of 100 faculty per year and becomes the supply source for University A. These are the only dynamics that take place. The results for a five-year period are shown in Figure 8.

The EEO performance of both universities looks good. Despite a reduction in work force, University B has managed to maintain a 10% minority representation. Meanwhile, University A has steadily improved minority representation by achieving a 10% share of growth opportunities. But on a combined basis, the minority representation is still 140 out of 2,000, or 7%.

	University A			University B		
End Year	Total Faculty	Minority	% Min	Total Faculty	Minority	% Min
0	1000	40	4.0	1000	100	10
1	1100	50	4.5	900	90	10
2	1200	60	5.0	800	80	10
3	1300	70	5.4	700	70	10
4	1400	80	5.7	600	60	10
5	1500	90	6.0	500	50	10

FIGURE 8.

In many work force categories on a national scale, loss rates and the growth factor will be small and opportunities for changes in minority and women's representation will be limited. As the models demonstrate, share of hires is the high leverage variable. As a nation we must get to the issue of increasing minorities and women in the supply lines. Unless we can do something effective there, we will lose the leverage associated with share of opportunities.

SUMMARY

When growth rate is considered as a variable, the following observations can be made:

1. There is a generalized model which can be used to analyze the effects of the growth factor on minority and women's representation. Given specific values for the variables, certain results are mathematical inevitabilities.

2. Intuitive estimates of the influence of growth on changes in minority representation can be grossly in error. Growth is a relatively low leverage variable when EEO progress is measured in percentage representation of minorities.

3. When growth is negative, opportunities are reduced and the improvement of minority and women's representation is seriously impeded. If negative growth results in forced layoffs, seniority may produce differential loss rates unfavorable to minorities and women resulting in an actual reduction of their representation in the work force.

4. The time frame needed to produce appreciable changes in minority and women's representation is not significantly reduced by the growth factor.

5. The high leverage factor for the growth mode as well as for the no-growth mode is minority and women share of hires.

6. It is important to evaluate EEO progress in terms of both the micro and macro view. In some instances, EEO progress as measured by percentage representation of minorities and women may be made by one employer at the expense of another. Or several employers may have what appear to be favorable results, yet on a combined basis, there has been no improvement at all in minority and women's representation. Unless a more national macro view is taken, results can be misleading and the real issue of attacking the EEO problem at the supply source may be neglected.

7. Thus far, we have limited the discussion to total work force populations. They imply a homogeneity to the extent that a single share of hires can be applied to the total population. In reality, most work forces need to be segmented both vertically and horizontally for thorough analysis. However, the total work force model principles can be applied to specific job categories. Ultimately, these separate analyses can be connected together in a flow pattern to analyze upward mobility.

8. Thus far, we have simply arbitrarily assumed some values for shares of hires in order to do some illustrations. In practical applications, it is necessary to do very thorough external market analysis.

CHAPTER SIX

The External Labor Market

We have seen to date that minority and women's share of external hires into a work force is an extremely important variable in EEO dynamics. How might one go about determining what those shares could reasonably be expected to be? How low can share be before it suggests discrimination in the personnel processes? How high can it realistically be?

There are obviously no precise answers, as the volume of EEO litigations and conciliations clearly shows. However, there are some analytical approaches that can help narrow the range of possible answers and substantially reduce the amount of intuitive guesswork which might otherwise exist.

CONCEPT OF A LABOR MARKET

The concept of a labor market is based on the view of labor as a commodity that is bought and sold. An individual seeking work is essentially offering labor for sale. An employer who has jobs to fill needs to buy labor. When there is an appropriate match up, a job offer and acceptance occur—a labor market transaction has taken place. Independent of race, sex, or ethnic considerations, an employer needs to know the geographic area within which certain types of labor transactions might reasonably be expected to occur.

This information is important not only for knowing where to seek out new employees, but also for determining appropriate wage rates. For example, there has recently been considerable political furor over the so-called prevailing wage rate practices of some cities and counties. Ordinances require that city or county employees' pay be comparable to that for similar jobs in other public agencies and in private enterprise as well. Sometimes the basis for comparison will include counties several hundred miles away. Opponents of the prevailing wage rate practices argue that such comparisons are irrational, that there is a local "labor market" which is the logical basis for determining wages for county employees. Regardless of who wins the political argument, the example helps to illustrate the point that a labor market description will contain at least a specification of the kind of work and the geographic domain. For example, it might be said that the labor market for plumbers in the City of Pismo Beach, California, is the County of San Luis Obispo of which the city is a part. The statement simply means that an employer in Pismo Beach seeking to fill a plumber's job could reasonably expect to satisfy that need from somewhere within the county. The determination of reasonable could be based upon historical data or some other factors such as commuting distance, pay scales, and availability of public transportation.

Labor markets for the professions such as medicine, law, architecture, and engineering could possibly be international, national, statewide, or very local depending upon the particular set of circumstances. Those who remember the boom days in the aerospace industry in the 1960s would readily agree that the labor market for engineers was a national one. Since then, there has been a growing reluctance to make major geographic moves from coast to coast, and now perhaps the market is much less national than in the past.

In contrast to the professions, a local restaurant owner's labor market for short-order cooks would tend to be very limited geographically. The geography could be as limited as a corridor due east of the restaurant, only two miles wide by five miles long, if it contained the principal means of public transportation.

From a practical point of view, there are one or more geographic areas that contain the people most likely to accept offers and go to work for an employer filling positions at a particular location. The number of people with the relevant job skills in the geographic area(s) constitute the employer's labor market.

LABOR MARKETS AND EEO

The identification of labor markets is of particular importance in the EEO arena because therein lies a basis for estimating the share of hires that can reasonably be expected to go to minorities and women. Unfortunately, there are so many variables and unknowns in sizing labor markets that the process is far from an exact science. Labor markets often differ from skill to skill. Likewise, they are far from static; they change with supply and demand, wage rate differentials, life styles, and many other factors which influence the offer and acceptance transaction. The geographic boundaries are often somewhat elusive; so are the appropriate skills match ups and the true availability of people. There may be many with the appropriate skills within the geographic boundaries who for all sorts of reasons will reject job offers.

The vagaries associated with a precise definition of a labor market are further compounded when equal employment opportunity is introduced into the picture. Perhaps a labor market has traditionally been the northwestern sector of the city. If that sector is nonminority and minority are concentrated in the southeastern sector, should the labor market be redefined for EEO purposes? One point that came to light when Watts, California, was burned in a racial outburst was the lack of public transportation available to residents. Watts was essentially excluded from labor markets by this single factor.

In addition to concern for the geographic factor, EEO has produced intensive study of job descriptions and specifications—the skills aspect of the labor market definition. Many improvements have been made and more are sure to follow. On the other hand, the assumed willingness of people to move into nontraditional work is a matter of serious debate in sizing the race/sex/ethnic distribution of a labor market. What percent of women now doing light assembly work are interested in moving to heavy foundry work? What percent of males entering the marketplace are interested in clerical and secretarial work? The male voices we now hear when we talk with telephone operators are an indicator that movement into nontraditional work is indeed taking place. Things are happening, but they are difficult to assess with any degree of precision. A simple one-on-one case can always be resolved—even if the decision is by a judge in court. But EEO cannot be managed on a micro basis. On a larger scale, monitoring agencies and employers will have to settle for a considerable number of approximations in sizing external labor markets.

A SYSTEMIC APPROACH

Shortly after becoming Chairwoman of the Equal Employment Opportunity Commission in 1977, Eleanor Holmes Norton issued the following statement: "Each field office also will have a special unit to handle cases involving patterns and practices of discrimination." Norton said then that the Commission had not had a systematic approach to addressing "systemic" discrimination. Targeting companies for investigation under Section 707 of Title VII has been like "pinning the tail on the donkey." In addition Norton said:

> The primary vehicle for attacking systemic discrimination will be the use of Commissioners' charges. Where relevant statistics demonstrate an employer has fallen significantly below comparable employers, there exists a prima facie case of discrimination. By the use of statistics, the Commission will be able to identify those employers and industries which are appropriate targets for a challenge to systemic discrimination. Individuals and civil rights organizations also will be able to petition the Commissioners to conduct investigations of patterns of discrimination.*

The Commission cannot, of course, abrogate its micro responsibilities, but it has clearly declared an additional thrust based on macro, systemwide, large-scale activities. In pursuing this course, the Commission has taken on a responsibility for thorough labor market analysis. Otherwise, systemic charges will still be like pinning the tail on the donkey. However, the further one moves away from a micro basis in labor market analysis, the spongier the results become. What looms on the horizon is a sizing negotiated between the employer and the Commission. This is a very practical way to get at the problem—provided that both parties avoid extreme emotional positions and mutually seek to use available data in a rational, objective way. If this task is properly done, it will lead to the identification of critical supply areas. Once identified and agreed upon, critical problems of supply can be alleviated by training programs—local and possibly national in scope.

However, the external labor market analysis should not be used solely as the basis for suspecting an employer of systemic discrimination. We will talk more about that in subsequent chapters. External labor market analysis is only one of many factors at work in the dynamics of EEO. It is merely one step in a lengthy analytical process.

**Fair Employment Practices*, #325, August 4, 1977. Bureau of National Affairs, Washington, D.C. 20037.

LABOR MARKET DATA

U.S. Census data are abundant and, despite the fact that it is nearly ten years old, it can be extremely useful. In many respects, it is a major cornerstone on which to base external market analyses. However, it is by no means the only data available. Other excellent data are available for selected segments of the nation's work force. The Engineers' Joint Council has done an outstanding job of data collection for engineers. The U.S. Department of Labor has good data on registered apprentice programs. Occasionally, there are some other excellent pieces of data such as the degreed work force details in the Manpower Report of the President. Sometimes, a friendly librarian can be of great help for ad hoc tidbits of information—such as finding in a relatively obscure study the percent of nurses who have college degrees. Wherever one may find the data, the important thing is that it be reputable and be used objectively.

Because the 1970 U.S. Census data are so commonly used in the EEO arena, some brief discussion of how it was collected and organized is useful in developing confidence or lack thereof in its applicability to a specific situation.

CENSUS DATA COLLECTION PROCEDURES

The following description of U.S. Census data collection procedures was extracted from the Bureau of Census Publication PC(2)-7A.

> The 1970 census was conducted primarily through self-enumeration. In 1960, self-enumeration was first introduced on a nationwide scale as a substitute for the traditional census direct interview.
>
> A census questionnaire was delivered by postal carriers to every household several days before Census Day, April 1, 1970. This questionnaire contained certain explanatory information and was accompanied by an instruction sheet; in areas with comparatively large proportions of Spanish speaking persons, a Spanish version of the instruction sheet was also enclosed. Facsimiles of the questionnaires and instructions to respondents are included in the Volume I reports.
>
> In the larger metropolitan areas and some adjacent counties, altogether containing about three-fifths of the population of the United States, the householder was requested to fill out and mail back the form on Census Day. Approximately 87 percent of the householders returned

their forms by mail. The mailed-back forms were reviewed by the census enumerator (or, in some localities, a census clerk), and if the form was determined to be incomplete or inconsistent, a followup was made. The bulk of these followups were made by telephone, the rest by personal visit. For the households which did not mail back their forms, a followup was also made, in almost all cases by personal visit and in the remainder by telephone.

For the remaining two-fifths of the population, the householder was requested to fill out the form and give it to the enumerator when he called; approximately 80 percent did so. Incomplete and unfilled forms were completed by interview during the enumerator's visit.

Three types of questionnaires were used throughout the country; 80 percent of the households answered a form containing a limited number of population and housing questions, and the remainder, split into 15-percent and 5-percent samples, answered forms which contained these questions as well as a number of additional questions. Some of the additional questions were the same on the 15-percent and 5-percent versions; others were different. A random procedure was used to determine which of the three forms any particular household answered.

In the metropolitan and adjacent areas, the designated type was sent to each household. In the remaining areas, the questionnaire with a limited number of questions was distributed to all households, and the enumerators asked the additional questions in those households designated for the 15-percent and 5-percent samples.

The following questions were used to collect industry and occupation information in the 1970 Census of Population.

33–35. Current or most recent job activity

Describe clearly this person's chief job activity or business last week, if any. If he had more than one job, describe the one at which he worked the most hours.

If this person had no job or business last week, give information for last job or business since 1960.

---

33. Industry

a. For whom did he work? *If now on active duty in the Armed Forces, print "AF" and skip to question 36.*

(Name of company, business, organization, or other employer)

b. What kind of business or industry was this?
Describe activity at location where employed.

(For example: Junior high school, retail supermarket, dairy farm, TV and radio service, auto assembly plant, road construction)

c. Is this mainly— *(Fill one circle)*

○ Manufacturing
○ Wholesale trade
○ Retail trade
○ Other *(agriculture, construction, service, government, etc.)*

34. Occupation

a. What kind of work was he doing?

(For example: TV repairman, sewing machine operator, spray painter, civil engineer, farm operator, farm hand, junior high English teacher)

b. What were his most important activities or duties?

(For example: Types, keeps account books, files, sells cars, operates printing press, cleans buildings, finishes concrete)

c. What was his job title?

---

35. Was this person— *(Fill one circle)*

Employee of private company, business, or individual, for wages, salary, or commissions ...... ○

Federal government employee .... ○
State government employee .... ○
Local government employee *(city, county, etc.)* ..... ○

Self-employed in own business, professional practice, or farm—
Own business not incorporated .... ○
Own business incorporated .... ○
Working without pay in family business or farm .... ○

DATA REDUCTION

The reduction of this enormous mass of data to something useful in labor market analysis is an incredible task. But the Bureau of Census has detailed decision rules which guide the data reduction process. The publication *Classified Index of Industries and Occupations* explains in detail how about 25,000 job titles are finally collapsed into 417 occupational categories, classified into 12 major groups. For example, Transport Equipment Operatives is one of the groups. It contains the occupational category Parking Attendants. All of the jobs listed below fall into that category.

711 Parking attendants
Attendant, n.s.—Parking lot 749
Auto hiker—639–649, 749, 757
Auto parker—(749)
Car chaser—639–649, 749, 757
Car hiker—639–649, 749, 757
Car hop—639–649, 749, 757
Car hopper—639–649, 749, 757
Car hostler—639–649, 749, 757
Car jockey—639–649, 749, 757
Car parker
Car shagger—639–649, 749, 757
Hiker—639–649, 749, 757
Lot boy—Parking lot 749
Parking attendant—(749)
Parking-lot attendant—(749)
Parking-lot laborer—(749)
Ramp jockey—(749)
Shag boy—639–649, 749, 757
Truck spotter

When the task of collapsing this data has been completed, the results are displayed in a wide array of tables. For example Table 171, Detailed Occupation of Employed Persons by Residence, Race, and Sex: 1970, in Appendix A. This table and similar ones provide one basis for EEO external labor market analysis. Table 171 is known as sixth count data. It contains the most detailed job titles generally available. Sixth count data can be purchased in the form of magnetic computer tapes for those who wish to have computer capability in sizing external labor markets. It is expensive but extremely useful for large projects.

The term "standard metropolitan statistical area" is so commonly used that a quote from the Bureau of Census publication PC(2)-7A about SMSAs is appropriate.

> *Standard Metropolitan Statistical Areas*—except in the New England States, a standard metropolitan statistical area is a county or group of contiguous counties which contains at least one city of 50,000 inhabitants or more, or 'twin cities' with a combined population of at least 50,000. In addition to the county, or counties, containing such a city or

cities, contiguous counties are included in an SMSA if, according to certain criteria, they are socially and economically integrated with the central city or cities. In the New England States, SMSA's consist of town and cities instead of counties. Each SMSA must include at least one central city, and the complete title of an SMSA identifies the central city or cities.

The population living in SMSA's is designated as the metropolitan population. The population living outside SMSA's constitutes the nonmetropolitan population. The metropolitan population may be subdivided into those living in the central city or cities and those living in the balance of the SMSA.

EXTERNAL LABOR MARKET FOR WOMEN IN CRAFTS

As was mentioned, external labor markets can be international, national, state, SMSA, or even more localized. For most jobs, the SMSA is a rational starting point. Let's see what Table 171 for the Baltimore SMSA (Appendix B) tells us about women in the external labor market for crafts.

At the micro level, it may be only a matter of reading an appropriate line from the table. For example, if an employer has a plumbing shop in Baltimore, Maryland, and needs to recruit experienced plumbers, the SMSA is the rational geographic area in which to begin the search. In Table 171 for Baltimore, there are 4,649 males and 52 female plumbers and pipe fitters. The women's representation in the labor market is 1.1%. If one suspects that Baltimore might be an aberration in that regard, a check of Census Table 232 for the total USA can be made. There the figures are 377,769 men and 4,100 women plumbers and pipe fitters yielding a percentage of 1.1% for women. Aside from the possibility of some just-graduating women apprentices or some unemployed women plumbers, the external labor market contains somewhere around 1% women. Whether the expected women's share of plumber hires should be 2% or 3% rather than 1% may be open to discussion. But based on the SMSA data, it most likely should not be 5%, and clearly not 10% or higher.

When EEO is being monitored and managed at a more macro level, there is some inclination to take an approach that says "crafts are crafts" and base the expected women's share of hires on the total category. For example, Table 171 for the Baltimore SMSA shows 112,163 males and 5419 females in the crafts category. On this basis,

Job	Male	Female	% Female
1. Foremen, n.e.c.*	15,538	1,214	7.2
2. Mechanics and repairmen	23,180	504	2.1
3. Tailors	793	375	32.1
4. Crafts and kindred† allocated	7,097	340	4.6
5. Bookbinders	243	340	58.3
6. Decorators and window dressers	417	338	44.8
7. Bakers	963	299	23.7
8. Compositors and typesetters	1,875	263	12.3

*n.e.c. means not elswhere classified.
†Those returns from the Population Census which do not have an occupation entry are allocated among the major groups during the computer processing.

FIGURE 1.

women constitute 4.6% of the crafts category. That figure can be very misleading as a deeper look into the data will illustrate.

A useful technique is to rank-order the jobs where women exist in the largest numbers. The results of this exercise are displayed in Figure 1.

One could continue further rank-ordering, but this is far enough to make a significant observation. Masked by the total crafts numbers is a division of the category into traditional and nontraditional jobs for women. This can be seen in Jobs 3, 5, 6 and 7. These four jobs together account for 25% of all the women in the crafts category.

If one is determining the percent of women in crafts for a manufacturing enterprise, Jobs 1, 3, 5, 6, 7 and 8 should be subtracted from the total. Strictly speaking, Job 1 is supervision; the others are not relevant to a manufacturing enterprise. The results are shown in Figure 2.

This exercise could be further refined by searching out additional job titles that are representative of the profile of the employer's work force. But the approach is at least illustrated by this abbreviated example. Within the crafts category, one can get a range of expected women's share of hires ranging from 1.1% for a plumbing firm to 2.7% for a manufacturer to 23.7% for a bakery.

In general, the rank-ordering approach and the deletion of irrele-

	Male	Female	% Female
Total	112,163	5,419	4.6
Less Job 1	15,538	1,214	7.2
Sub Total	96,625	4,205	4.2
Less Sum of Jobs 3,5,6,7,8	4,291	1,615	27.3
Sub Total	92,334	2,590	2.7

FIGURE 2.

vant jobs is a good compromise between the short cut of attempting to use the total category and the enormous detail involved in trying to address each individual job listing.

Regardless of how the data is analyzed, when the traditional women's craft jobs are set aside, the resulting percentage of women in crafts is very low. As employers attempt to increase their representation of women in crafts, not much progress is possible by competing for shares of a shortage. The data literally cry out for massive training thrusts for women in nontraditional crafts work. To what extent such a thrust is culturally and financially possible is as yet an unanswered question. But without such an effort, it is obvious that shares of hires amounting to a few percentage points will not contribute much to increased women's representation in the nontraditional crafts subgrouping.

WOMEN IN PROFESSIONAL JOBS

Patterns similar to those for crafts emerge when other categories are analyzed in depth. The category "professional, technical, and kindred workers" provides a good example. For the Baltimore SMSA, Table 171 shows:

	Male	Female	% Female
Total	79,196	49,395	38.4

First of all, technicians are a separate EEO-1 category from professionals. Three technician groupings should be subtracted: health

Job	Male	Female	% Female
1. Teachers, except college & university	7,559	19,212	71.8
2. Registered nurses, dietitians & therapists	688	9,318	93.1
3. Professional, technical & kindred workers allocated	3,437	2,773	44.7
4. Social & recreation workers	1,495	2,430	61.9
5. Writers, artists & entertainers	5,782	2,256	28.1
6. Accountants	5,754	2,100	26.7
7. Personnel & labor relations workers	2,675	1,405	34.4
8. Teachers, college & university	2,731	1,112	28.9
9. Librarians, archivists	277	1,016	78.6

FIGURE 3.

technologists and technicians; engineering and science technicians; other technicians. The result is:

	Male	Female	% Female
Total (less technicians)	67,722	45,898	40.4

Now let's rank-order the jobs which contain the largest numbers of women as shown in Figure 3.

In the main, Jobs 1, 2, 4, 5, 8 and 9 do not constitute labor markets for industrial enterprises. Job 3 is an allocation; the jobs themselves are an unknown quantity. When Jobs 1, 2, 3, 4, 5, 8 and 9 are subtracted from the total (less technicians) the result is:

	Male	Female	% Female
Total (less technicians)	67,722	45,898	40.4
Less Jobs 1,2,3,4,5,8,9	21,969	38,117	63.4
Remainder	45,753	7,781	14.5

From the point of view of an industrial employer, 85% of the women in the "professionals" labor market are concentrated in seven job categories that generally do not provide experience relevant to industrial work. Even on this broad brush basis, the expected women's share of hiring opportunities would be much closer to 15% than to 40%. Yet, at times, monitoring agencies operating on the prima facie evidence concept are tempted to use figures as high as 40% women's representation as the basis for evaluating an employer's EEO performance.

The issue of whether or not to include teachers in the external labor market for industrial enterprises is of particular interest. A high percentage are tenured and are not genuinely available for other employment. On the other hand, teachers have willingly and successfully made the transition from academia to industry. The question is not whether employers have the right to arbitrarily reject teachers who apply for nonteaching work. They clearly do not. What we are seeking, however, is some estimate of the share of hiring opportunities that could reasonably be expected to be filled by women. Would teachers be attracted to noneducational employers in sufficient numbers to influence the percentage share? Employed, tenured teachers? Probably not. Unemployed teachers? Possibly yes, depending upon the circumstances.

For an employer with a technology-oriented professional work force, the expected women's share of hires could be considerably less than the 14.5% derived in the first broad brush pass. For example, Table 171 for Baltimore shows that women constitute 1.8% of the engineers category. Even if engineers are viewed as a national market, that percentage does not change significantly (it is 1.6% nationally). If an employer's work force is made up of half engineers and half "others," the expected share could be estimated on a weighted basis. It would be (0.5)(1.8) + (0.5)(14.5) or 8.2%—a long way from the 40.4% in the professionals category.

WOMEN IN OPERATIVES JOBS

Although the rank-ordering exercise gets repetitive, one more example can add some additional perspective. If we rank-order jobs held by women in the operatives (except transport) category, we get the results shown in Figure 4 for Baltimore.

Within these seven job listings, we have accounted for 82% of all women operatives. For a "light" manufacturing employer, perhaps all of these listings are relevant and a part of the labor market. For a "heavy" manufacturer, perhaps Jobs 1, 3 and 7 are not relevant. When they are subtracted from the total, the results are:

	Male	Female	% Female
Total	60,322	36,840	37.9
Less Sum of Jobs 1,3,7	3,446	13,859	80.0
Remainder	56,876	22,981	28.8

Once again, a very broad brush pass at the data shows a traditional/nontraditional job distribution for women. For an extreme example, note in Table 171 that welders and flame cutters are only 8.3% women; meat wrappers in retail trade are 96.5% women.

For purposes of estimating a reasonable expected women's share of hiring opportunities, it is necessary to go much deeper than a simple broad brush first pass. The end point is to come as close as possible to finding counterpart jobs in the external market for those in the employer's work force. Even within the operatives category, the detailed effort is worthwhile despite the fact that many of the jobs are unskilled, entry level ones. However, before the detail work is done, the broad brush rank-ordering approach is extremely useful in

Job	Male	Female	% Female
1. Sewers & stitchers	564	7,316	92.8
2. Miscellaneous & not specified	18,829	7,186	27.6
3. Packers & wrappers, except meat & produce	2,233	4,797	68.2
4. Assemblers	4,359	3,550	44.9
5. Operatives, allocated	4,715	3,359	41.6
6. Checkers, examiners, etc.	3,252	2,401	42.5
7. Clothing ironers & pressers	649	1,746	72.9
	34,601	30,355	46.7

FIGURE 4.

crossing the emotional bridge from the total civilian labor force to something much more rational (even though considerably smaller) as an EEO bench mark.

BEYOND TABLE 171

In the discussion so far, we have used data for employed persons in the civilian labor force as the basis for illustrations. On the whole, this is a valid approach for purposes of estimating a reasonable expected minority and women's share of hiring opportunities. However, there are some exceptions that require consideration of other sources of employees.

- When there are no serious aberrations in the race/sex/ethnic distribution of the unemployed, the addition of another 6% to 10% unemployed people to Table 171 will not appreciably change the results of the illustrations. But we do know of one major aberration—the high unemployment rate for minority young people. This could significantly affect an estimate of expected minority share of hires into unskilled entry level jobs. For example, an SMSA Table 171 might show 25% male minority in the *employed* laborers category. When *unemployed* unskilled male minorities are taken into consideration, the real external market for laborers might turn out to be 35% minority.
- Those discharged from the military service seeking work in the civilian labor force will be predominantly men. In such categories as technicians and crafts and in some operatives jobs, the real labor market may have a higher percentage of men than Table 171 would suggest. This is especially true from the shares point of view because there is no question about availability—the candidates are on the spot, ready to be hired.
- New entrants into the work force may have a race, sex, or ethnic distribution substantially different from those employed. For example, the percentage of minorities among recent engineering graduates is well above the percent minority among employed engineers. In the extreme case of an employer who recruits recent engineering graduates and no other persons, the employed engineers in the SMSA are not at all a measure of the external labor market. The real measure for share is the percentage of minority engineering graduates from the schools that would normally constitute the supply source independent of race, sex, or ethnic considerations.

BENCH MARK JOBS AND WEIGHTING

The rank-ordering approach to estimating the minority and women's reasonable share of hiring opportunities enables one to focus very quickly on the jobs that have the most impact on the end result. In the crafts example displayed in Figures 1 and 2, eight key jobs were identified, and they accounted for more than two-thirds of all the women in crafts. When some of these were judged as not relevant to a manufacturing employer, the result was a 2.7% quick estimate of expected women's share of hires. We could continue the rank-ordering until all jobs in the crafts category had been examined and accepted or rejected as relevant to a manufacturing employer. In terms of negotiations between a monitoring agency and an employer, another 50 or so jobs would have to be discussed and evaluated for relevancy. Considerable time could be spent arguing the relevancy of jobs that have no significant impact on the end result. For example, Figure 5 shows a continuation of the rank-ordering process for eight more jobs.

Jobs 10, 13 and 14 could be judged not relevant to a manufacturing employer. When these are subtracted from the subtotal in Figure 2, the results are as shown in Figure 6.

In this exercise, eight more jobs were reviewed, three were judged irrelevant, but the end result was no different from the 2.7% determined in the first broad brush pass.

Job	Male	Female	% Female
9. Inspectors, n.e.c.	1,593	169	9.6
10. Pressmen & plate printers	2,231	156	6.5
11. Electricians	5,632	131	2.3
12. Machinists	4,354	118	2.6
13. Carpenters	8,923	109	1.2
14. Shoe repairmen	268	106	28.3
15. Painters, construction & maintenance	3,843	94	2.4
16. Crafts & kindred, n.e.c.	1,147	75	6.1
	27,991	958	3.3

FIGURE 5.

	Male	Female	% Female
Sub Total (Figure 2)	92,334	2,590	2.7
Less Jobs 10,13,14	11,422	371	3.1
Sub Total	80,912	2,219	2.7

FIGURE 6.

An alternative to the rank-ordering approach is to use selected bench mark jobs that approximate the kinds of skills required in an employer's work force. For example, after reviewing hundreds of in-house job titles, the employer might conclude that the skills associated with plumbers and pipefitters, electricians, machinists, and mechanics and repairmen are representative of those required in the crafts category in the factory work force. Women's share of hiring opportunities would be expected to correspond to their representation in those four bench mark jobs in the external labor market.

There are three ways to use the data. One approach is simply to add up the numbers for the four jobs and determine the percent of women in the total. The other is to use a weighting process in which the external distribution is matched against the internal on a composite basis. The third is to stay completely on a micro basis, in which case four expected shares instead of a single composite would be determined.

The Aggregate Approach

In this approach, the data from Table 171 are displayed as in Figure 7.

For the crafts category, the expected women's share of hires would be about 2%.

The Weighted Approach

In this approach, the employer must first determine how the work force is distributed vis-a-vis the four bench mark jobs. This is done

Job	Male	Female	% Female
Plumbers & pipe fitters	4,649	52	1.1
Electricians	5,632	131	2.3
Machinists	4,354	118	2.6
Mechanics & repairmen	23,180	504	2.1
	37,815	805	2.1

FIGURE 7.

independent of race, sex or ethnic distributions. For example, the work force skills distribution might consist of:

20% equivalent to plumbers & pipefitters
10% equivalent to electricians
30% equivalent to machinists
40% equivalent to mechanics & repairmen

This distribution is then weighted against the percent of women in the external bench mark jobs as shown in Figure 8.

For the crafts category, the expected women's share of hires would be about 2%.

The Micro Approach

In this approach, there is neither aggregation nor weighting. Instead of expressing the expected women's share in terms of a single figure

Job	% Internal Dist.	% Women External	Weighted Factor
Plumbers & pipefitters	20	1.1	.22
Electricians	10	2.3	.23
Machinists	30	2.6	.78
Mechanics & repairmen	40	2.1	.84
			2.07

FIGURE 8.

for the crafts category, there would be four figures—one for each subcategory. For example, external hires into the machinists category would be monitored as an entity and the expected women's share of machinists equivalent hires would be 2.6%.

What is the best approach to use? There is no one best way to analyze external labor markets, because so much depends upon the type and size of the work force. The important thing is for both monitoring agency and employer to approach the task with a high degree of integrity and objectivity. The purpose is to arrive at a reasonable expected minority or women's share of hiring opportunities. Whatever it takes to achieve that purpose has to be done. Guesswork or emotionally based estimates of share can too easily lead to what in reality may be unfounded charges of discrimination at one end of the spectrum or reverse discrimination on the other end. In short, both the monitoring agency and the employer have a responsibility to seek out reputable data and to process it thoroughly in pursuit of reasonable, well founded results.

SUMMARY

1. The determination of reasonable expected minority and women's share of external hiring opportunities into a work category is an important factor in the EEO process. The well established concepts of external labor markets can be applied, with some extensions, to this task of determining share.

2. U.S. Census data for 1970, although old and sometimes lacking in detail, is the most universally available basis for analyzing and sizing external labor markets. More current supplementary data for some occupations can be found by some diligent library research work.

3. The EEO Commission's systemic thrust cannot be managed at a micro level. It calls for a macro approach, which has the weakness of masking the real facts with generalizations that can be too broad. However, there are some analytical approaches that help to minimize the shortcomings of the macro approach.

4. Rank-ordering of the jobs that have the highest numbers of women incumbents in a labor market is one very useful approach. It leads very quickly to an estimate of a reasonable expected minority and women's share of hires into a work category. Of equal importance, it helps to unmask those situations where a composite women's representation percentage is hiding the fact that relatively few women hold nontraditional jobs.

5. A bench mark job approach is useful in determining reasonable expected minority and women's share of hires. It is particularly helpful when the EEO issue is systemic and decision rules must be applied uniformly in several components of a total company. If the bench mark jobs are well chosen, the share results will usually be close to those obtained by a more detailed study of all jobs in a labor market.

6. Perhaps the most important element of all is a commitment to objectivity by both the monitoring agency and the employer—a willingness to seek out good data and use it wisely.

CHAPTER SEVEN

Upward Mobility

By the mid-1970s it became apparent that upward mobility for minorities had been added to representation in the total work force as a major issue for the future. The very term upward mobility suggests that a total work force can be segmented into some kind of hierarchy and that movement upward from one layer to the next is an important consideration. To some extent, the EEO-1 reporting categories constitute a hierarchy. For example, the EEO-6 Crafts category on the whole represents a higher level of skills and pay than the EEO-7 Operatives category. Similarly, EEO-3 Technicians in the main constitutes a higher skills and pay level than EEO-5 Office and Clerical.

Three very important variables now appear which cause upward mobility models to become considerably more complex than simple gross representation models.

1. The work force must be segmented into some kind of hierarchical layers.
2. Internal markets must now be defined, because they provide source populations for upward mobility.
3. The share of total additions into a layer that comes from external/internal markets must be considered. Generally, management tries to reserve the right to fill a position from either external or internal sources. There may be few or many constraints on this right, but, in any case, it must be provided for in a model.

A BASIC MODEL

Let's build our first upward mobility model independent of race/sex/ethnic considerations. Subsequently, we can factor minority external

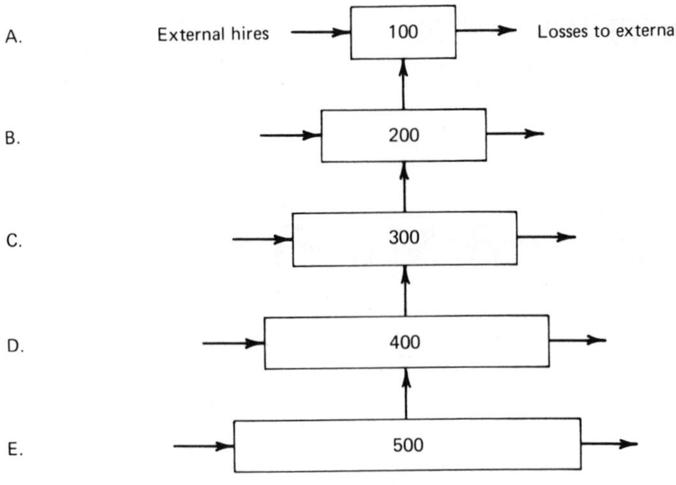

FIGURE 1.

additions, promotions, and the resulting representation into the model.

Assume that a work force of 1500 total is segmented into five hierarchical layers or work zones. This is shown graphically in Figure 1. The number inside each box is the total number of people in that particular work zone.

The horizontal arrow on the left side of each box represents external hires. The horizontal arrow on the right side of each box represents losses—quits, retirements, discharges, layoffs, and so forth. The vertical arrows represent upward movement (promotions) from one layer to the next. Work Zone E represents entry level into the total work force.

For this first model, a basic assumption is that promotions occur one level at a time.

Let's suppose this model simulates the hourly work force in a factory. Work Zone A might be highly skilled crafts; Work Zone E might be beginning assemblers. Let's also assume zero growth rate to simplify the construction of the model. We need some additional assumptions:

- Loss rates for each work zone.
- Some decision rule which allocates share of total additions to a work zone between external and internal sourcing.

Work Zone	% Annual Growth Rate	% Annual Loss Rate	% of Total Additions That Are External
A	0	5	0
B	0	10	0
C	0	15	0
D	0	20	0
E	0	25	100

All promotions occur in the progression E-D-C-B-A.

FIGURE 2.

For the first basic model, assume that external additions to the work force occur only at entry level E. Subsequently, we can study the effect of external hiring at levels above entry.

Figure 2 summarizes the data and assumptions for the model.

In an upward mobility model we have to start at the top of the hierarchy and work our way down to the entry level.

At Work Zone A, the loss rate is five percent. This means that five of the original population will be lost. Since growth rate is zero, five jobs will have to be filled to replace the losses. Since there is no external hiring at this level, five jobs will be filled by promotion. Figure 3 shows this schematically.

At Work Zone B, external losses are 20 people. However, the five people who were promoted into Work Zone A also have to be replaced. Because there is no external hiring at this level, there must be 25 promotions from C to B. Figure 4 shows this schematically.

Similarly at Work Zone C, there will be 45 losses. But there were also 25 promotions upward out of C, so there must be 70 promotions from D to C. Figure 5 shows these results schematically and also those for Work Zones D and E.

Note that in the zero growth mode, total external hires must equal

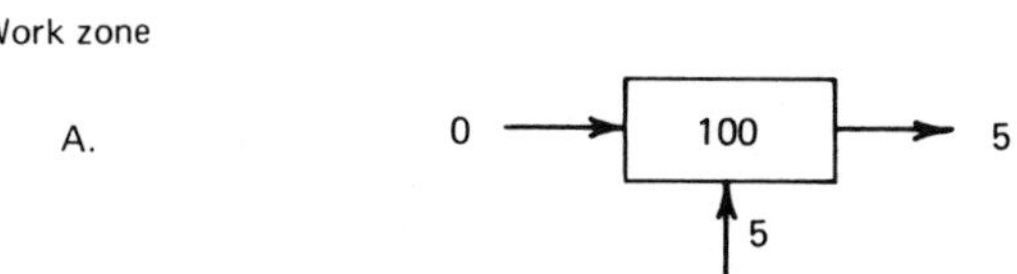

FIGURE 3.

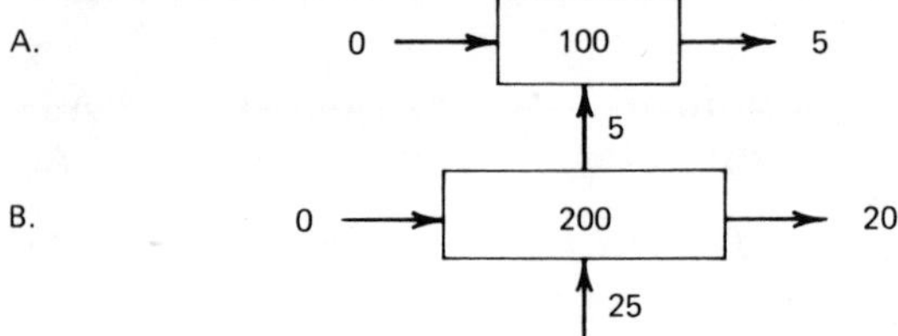

FIGURE 4.

total external losses. There were 275 hires and 275 losses, so our arithmetic checks out properly.

Note also the effect of promotions on the external hires needed at entry level. An additional 150 hires must be made beyond those needed to replace entry level external losses. This is an item of significance for minority concentrations at entry level.

In a situation such as the one described in this model, no hires above entry level, there is a very useful mathematical relationship. The number of total additions that must be made to a work zone depends upon what happens at that work zone and all those above it.

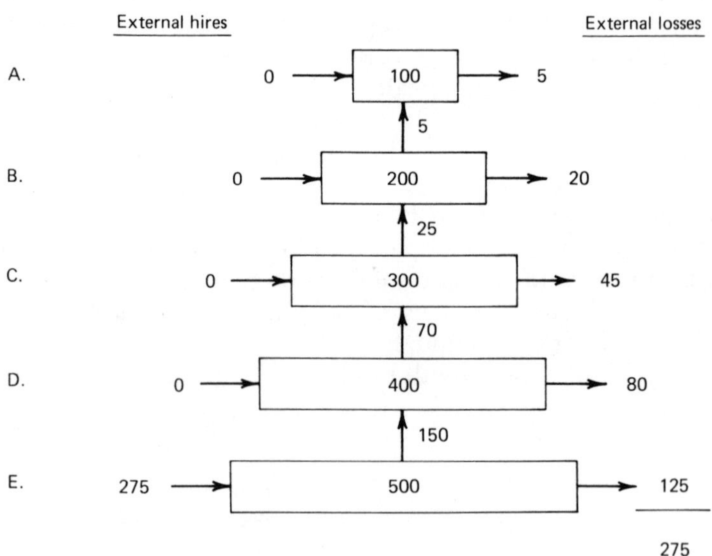

FIGURE 5.

$$V_N = \Sigma_N^A Lt_N N_N$$

where V_N = vacancies at any work zone, N
Lt_N = loss rate at any work zone, N
N = number of people in work zone, N

For example, the vacancies at Work Zone C for the year would be

$$\begin{aligned} V_C &= Lt_A N_A + Lt_B N_B + Lt_C N_C \\ &= .05(100) + .10(200) + .15(300) \\ &= 70 \end{aligned}$$

Note this is the value derived in the hand-built model.

The equation also tells us that the shape of the distribution pyramid is very significant. Upward mobility would be more rapid, if the population were distributed equally among the five work zones. If the pyramid had a rectangular shape (300 people in each work zone), the vacancies at Work Zone C would be

$$\begin{aligned} V_C &= Lt_A N_A + Lt_B N_B + Lt_C N_C \\ &= .05(300) + .10(300) + .15(300) \\ &= 90 \end{aligned}$$

The number of promotions into Work Zone C would increase, but, more importantly, the chances of the people in Work Zone D for promotions would also increase. The random chance for being promoted is the ratio of the promotions out of the work zone to the population in the work zone.

In the case of the pyramid shape, chances of promotion out of Work Zone D $= \frac{70}{400} = .175$. The corresponding ratio for the rectangular shape is $\frac{90}{300} = .300$. Figure 6 shows a comparison of promotion chances within a pyramid shape to those within a rectangular shape.

For the data and assumptions of this model, the random chance of being promoted out of Work Zone C for the pyramid configuration is only 1 in 12. For the rectangular configuration it is 1 in 6.

This random chance concept is a useful measure of the upward mobility opportunities available within a particular work force. In both cases displayed in Figure 6, upward mobility could at best be

Chances of Promotion Out of Work Zone

Work Zone	Pyramid Shape	Rectangular Shape
A	0	0
B	.025	.050
C	.083	.150
D	.175	.300
E	.300	.500

FIGURE 6.

described as sluggish. One can also see why qualifications of one individual vis-a-vis another becomes such an important issue. When the supply pool is large and the opportunities are few, management may have to use a very fine sieve to separate one individual from another in the selection process.

A MORE COMMON MODEL

In building the basic model, we assumed there was no external hiring above entry level. A more realistic model should allow for external hiring at all levels. Let's make some assumptions as shown in Figure 7. Figure 7 summarizes the basic data and assumptions for the model.

Work Zone	Population	% Annual Growth Rate	% Annual Loss Rate	% of Total Additions That Are External
A	100	0	5	20
B	200	0	10	20
C	300	0	15	20
D	400	0	20	40
E	500	0	25	100

All promotions occur in the progression E-D-C-B-A.

FIGURE 7.

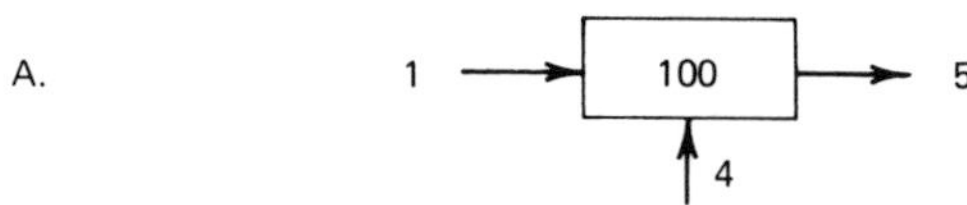

FIGURE 8.

This model is the same as the initial one except external hires are distributed over all five work zones.

At Work Zone A, the loss rate is 5%. Five people will be lost. Since growth rate is zero, five jobs will have to be filled to replace the losses, 20% (or one job) will be filled from external sources. Four jobs will be filled by promotions. Figure 8 shows this schematically.

At Work Zone B, external losses are 20 people (10% of 200). However, the four people who were promoted into Work Zone A have to be replaced. So there are 24 total additions into Work Zone B. Five of these will be hired from the external market (20% of 24; result rounded). The other 19 will be promotions out of Work Zone C. Figure 9 shows this schematically.

At Work Zone C, external losses are 45 people (15% of 300). Also, the 19 people promoted out of C into B must be replaced. So there are 64 total additions. Thirteen of these will be hired from the external market (20% of 64; result rounded). The other 51 will be promotions out of Work Zone D. Figure 10 shows these results schematically and also completes the arithmetic for Work Zones D and E.

As before, in the zero growth mode, total hires must equal total losses. There were 275 hires and 275 losses so our arithmetic checks out properly.

We can now compare the two cases. Model 1 assumed no external hiring above entry level. Model 2 allowed for external hires per the stated assumption. All other factors were the same. The results are shown in Figure 11.

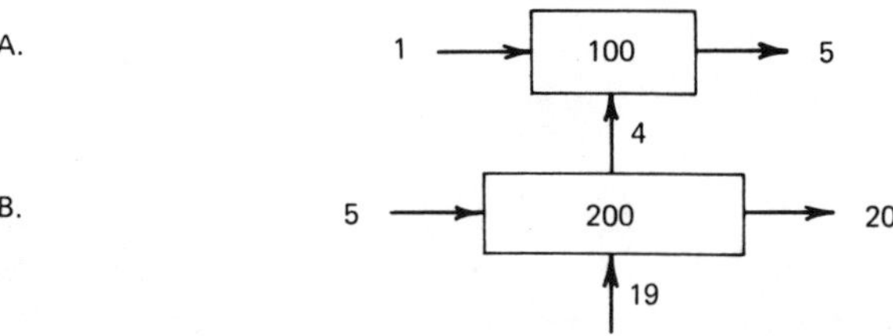

FIGURE 9.

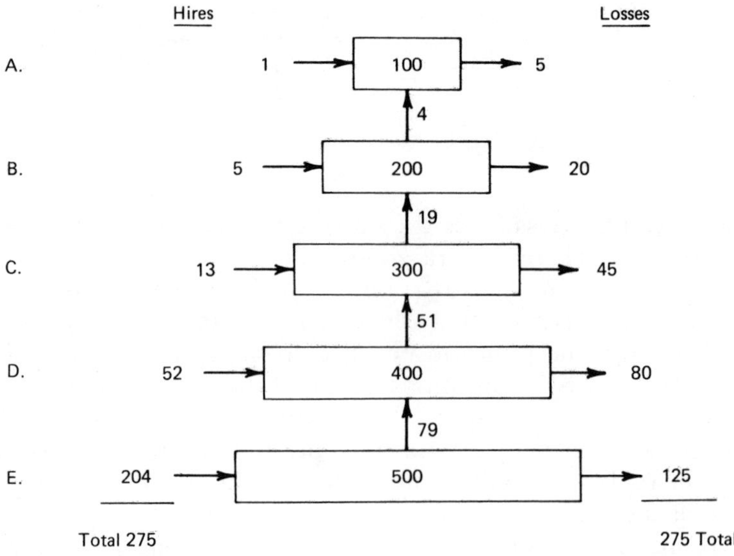

FIGURE 10.

The total external hires remain the same in each case. But when external hiring occurs at above entry level, the available promotions and the total additions decrease. For the overall work force, total promotions are reduced by 39% (from 250 to 153) and total additions by 18% (from 525 to 428). The pattern of external hiring is clearly a significant factor in the upward mobility rates within a work force.

Work Zone	Total Population	External Hires into Work Zone Case 1	External Hires into Work Zone Case 2	Promotions into Work Zone Case 1	Promotions into Work Zone Case 2	Total Additions to Work Zone Case 1	Total Additions to Work Zone Case 2
A	100	0	1	5	4	5	5
B	200	0	5	25	19	25	24
C	300	0	13	70	51	70	64
D	400	0	52	150	79	150	131
E	500	275	204	0	0	275	204
Total	1500	275	275	250	153	525	428

FIGURE 11.

The impact of experienced external hires at higher levels is felt all the way down to entry level.

MINORITY UPWARD MOBILITY

For the zero growth assumption, the results of this model, which provides for hiring above entry level, are simply repeated every year. The model can now be extended to include the dynamics for the minority population.

To do so, it's necessary to make some assumptions for minorities. In Chapter Six we examined some mechanisms for sizing external labor markets. In Chapter Eight we will examine some additional mechanisms for sizing internal markets. For purposes of this model, assume the minority share of promotions into a work zone is equal to the minority representation in the next lower work zone (seniority might not permit this). Similarly, assume the minority share of external hires into a work zone is equal to the percentage of minorities in the relevant external labor market. Also assume that minority loss rates are the same as those for the total population within each work zone. The data are displayed in Figure 12.

This is the kind of distribution pattern that makes upward mobility for minorities a major issue in the EEO arena. Minorities constitute 24% of the total work force, but they are 50% of Work Zone E and only 5% of Work Zone A. More than two-thirds of all minorities in the work force are in the entry level work zone. It is common practice to call this a concentration of minorities at the lowest level. Upward mobility by means of internal promotions is a

Work Zone	Total Number	Minority Number	Minority Rep.,%	Ext. Mkt. Minority,%	Minority Loss Rate,%
A	100	5	5	12	5
B	200	16	8	18	10
C	300	30	10	20	15
D	400	60	15	25	20
E	500	250	50	30	25
Total	1500	361	24		

FIGURE 12.

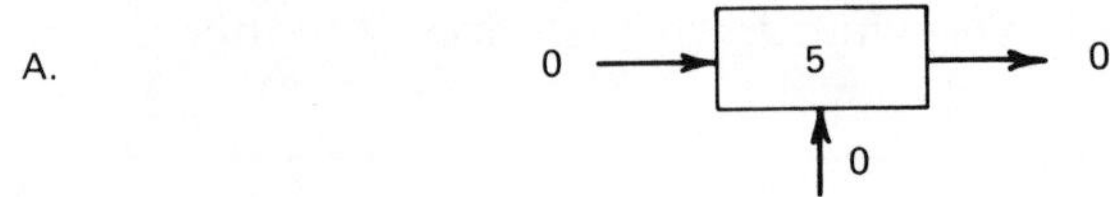

FIGURE 13.

potential mechanism for relieving the concentration and redistributing minorities throughout the work force.

The minority movement dynamics can be established in much the same way as for the total population. At Work Zone A, we will lose zero minority workers (5% of 5; result rounded). From Figure 10, we know that there were four promotions and one external hire into Work Zone A. The minority share of the one external hire is the 12% external market share. By conventional rounding, this reduces to zero. The minority share of the four promotions is the 8% minority representation in the next lower work zone. This (result rounded) is zero minority promotion into Work Zone A. These results are shown schematically in Figure 13.

At Work Zone B, the minority losses are two (10% of 16); the external hires are one (18% of 5); the internal promotions are two (10% of 19). These results and those for the rest of the work zones are shown in Figure 14.

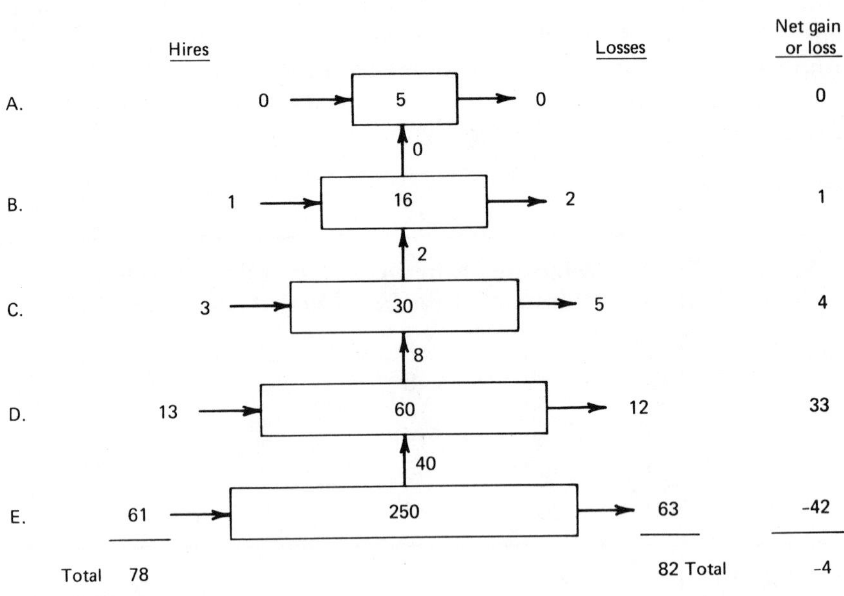

FIGURE 14.

Work Zone	Total Number	Minority Number Start Yr 1	Minority Number End Yr 1	Minority Representation, % Start Yr 1	Minority Representation, % End Yr 1	Minority Representation, % Ext. Mkt.
A	100	5	5	5.0	5.0	12.0
B	200	16	17	8.0	8.5	18.0
C	300	30	34	10.0	11.3	20.0
D	400	60	93	15.0	23.3	25.0
E	500	250	208	50.0	41.6	30.0
Total	1500	361	357	24.0	23.8	

FIGURE 15.

We can now construct a minority distribution table for the end of Year 1. This is shown in Figure 15.

A redistribution of minority has occurred during the year—more at Work Zones E and D, less at Work Zones C, B, and A. The model can be continued over some period, say five years, making sure to take into account the annual changes in the percentage of minorities in the internal market. The results are shown in Figure 16.

Over the five-year period, a substantial redistribution of minority has taken place—except at Work Zone A. Because the number of opportunities available decreased as one progressed up the work force pyramid, five years is simply not enough time for minority penetration into Work Zone A. In order to shorten the time frame for

Work Zone	Total Number	Minority Number Start Yr 1	Minority Number End Yr 5	Minority Representation, % Start Yr 1	Minority Representation, % End Yr 5	Minority Representation, % Ext. Mkt.
A	100	5	5	5.0	5.0	12.0
B	200	16	24	8.0	12.0	18.0
C	300	30	62	10.0	20.7	20.0
D	400	60	116	15.0	29.0	25.0
E	500	250	157	50.0	31.4	30.0
Total	1500	361	364	24.0	24.3	

FIGURE 16.

increasing minority representation at Work Zone A, one would have to bypass the usual upward flow system by increasing the placements directly into Work Zone A. This could be done perhaps by more aggressive external recruiting, but that would produce a shortage for some other companies. The better alternative would be special education and training aimed at direct placement into Work Zone A. One useful outcome of the model is to pinpoint that need. There are also some further observations that can be made.

- The model assumes a minority share of entry level hires to be 30% even though the representation is at 50%. If a 50% share had been used, additional redistribution would have occurred at Work Zones B, C, D, but the concentration at E would have remained at 50%.
- The model assumes that minority share of promotions is equal to the minority representation in the next lower work zone. That may not be a valid assumption if seniority is unfavorable to minorities or if minority interests and qualifications are not on a par with those for non-minorities. The sizing of the internal market is a very critical factor.
- The model demonstrates that with the given data, substantial redistribution of minorities can occur within a five-year period. When it can occur but doesn't, a model can pinpoint the need for in-depth exploration of the reasons why.
- For Work Zones C and D, the minority representation at the end of the fifth year exceeds that in the external market. This is an interesting finding because it has been argued in some EEO cases that the external market is the appropriate bench mark to aim for in minority representation. The model suggests that further exploration of that concept would be worthwhile.

EXTERNAL LABOR MARKET AS A BENCH MARK

Let's explore the logic of using minority representation in the relevant external labor market as a bench mark by asking the question: If the minority representation in each work zone were equal to its relevant external labor market, what would be the minority representation for the total work force?

This question can be answered by the weighting process shown in Figure 17.

In this particular case, the bench mark would be a reasonable one. The total work force population which began at 24% would be

Work Zone	Total Number	Minority Ext. Mkt.,%	No. Minority to Equal Ext. Mkt.
A	100	12	12
B	200	18	36
C	300	20	60
D	400	25	100
E	500	30	150
Total	1500	23.9%	358

FIGURE 17.

reduced very slightly to 23.9%. But suppose the circumstances pictured in Figure 18 existed.

If the same weighting process were applied to the data in Figure 18, the results would be as shown in Figure 19. The weighting process yields a 20% overall minority representation versus an initial 26.1%. If this bench mark approach were used in a strict application, the minority population would be reduced by 91 people. These minorities would have to find work somewhere else or be unemployed even though the company had perfectly matched the relevant external labor market.

This is an imposing dilemma. Under some sets of circumstances, a redistribution of minority workers based on equalling their percentage in the relevant external labor market for each work zone cannot be achieved without decreasing the overall minority representation.

Work Zone	Total Number	Minority Number	Minority Rep.,%	Minority Ext. Mkt.,%
A	100	3	3	5
B	200	16	8	10
C	300	42	14	15
D	400	80	20	20
E	500	250	50	30
Total	1500	391	26.1	

FIGURE 18.

Work Zone	Total Number	Minority Ext. Mkt.	No. Minority to Equal Ext. Mkt.
A	100	5	5
B	200	10	20
C	300	15	45
D	400	20	80
E	500	30	150
Total	1500	20.0%	300

FIGURE 19.

On the other hand, holding the minority representation in the total work force constant would most likely be done by excessive hiring of minorities at entry level. But if that is done, there is a concentration of minorities at the bottom of the work force. This calls for increased efforts at redistribution through upward mobility. Unknowingly, a company that has been overly attractive to minorities at entry level may have taken on a larger redistribution task than its less successful entry level peers.

One has to conclude that the percentage of minorities in the external labor market by itself is not a valid measure of the appropriate minority distribution in the work force. This can be seen from the extreme case of the first model we built in this chapter, the one for which there was no external hiring above entry level. The distribution of minorities in the work force above entry level is solely the result of promotions. The real measure is whether the minority share of promotion opportunities over time was equal to, greater than, or less than the real minority internal market. As the models show share and minority loss rates determine the distribution that results from available opportunities. An underlying assumption appears to be that a company should not be expected to do any better in distribution than the average of the relevant portion of the SMSA. The assumption would quickly lose validity, if, over a period of time, the company had a high number of opportunities, while the relevant SMSA did not. The external bench mark would be too low. The company could have been highly discriminating, but it would look good by comparison. The converse, of course, could also happen.

One would have to conclude that the measure of the distribution of minorities in a work force is some combination of internal and external market data, because a significant variable is the extent to which positions are filled from external or internal sources.

MINORITY CONCENTRATIONS AT ENTRY LEVEL

Upward mobility models must usually be custom built for specific situations. Much of the time the generalized equations are unmanageable except on a computerized basis. Even then, they are less useful than a specific algorithm. However, there is one generalized equation that is very useful in addressing concentrations of minorities, particularly at entry level.

One very obvious and often used piece of data is that minorities tend to be concentrated at the bottom end of the employment hierarchy. Reduction of such concentration can come about only through some form of upward mobility, unless one is willing to accept a reduction of minority entry level hires share as an alternative. A model that addresses minority concentration at the entry level work zone can provide a basis for planning upward mobility programs and an understanding of the time frame within which they might produce significant results. The dynamics are illustrated in Figure 20.

In the zero growth mode, opportunities for external hires and internal promotions are generated by losses that have to be replaced. When the replacements are made by promotions, the effect is to increase the entry level hires beyond those necessary simply to replace entry level losses. The promotions provide a domino "suction" effect on the entry level layer. All of these actions are interrelated and *for entry level* can be described by the equation for the first year:

$$Rm_1 = Rm_o\,(1 - Lm) + XLt + \frac{\mathrm{P}}{\mathrm{Nt}}\,(X - KRm_o)$$

where Rm_1 = minority representation, percent, end of first year
Rm_o = initial minority representation, percent
Lm = minority loss rate, percent per year (decimal fraction)
X = minority share of external additions, percent
Lt = total loss rate, percent per year (decimal fraction)
P = number of promotions out of entry level
Nt = entry level total population, number
K = a coefficient that establishes minority share of promotions as a function of minority representation.

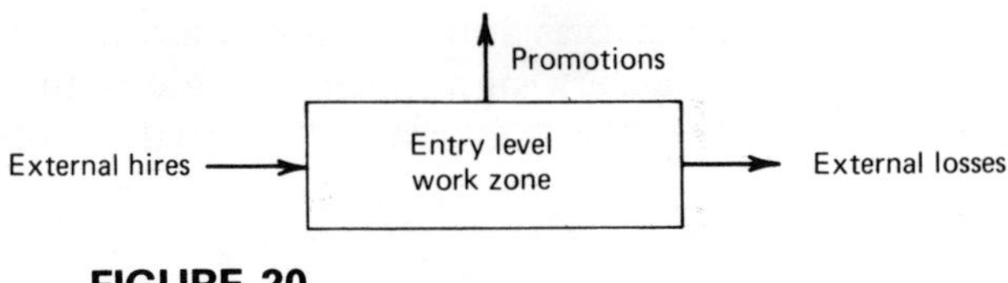

FIGURE 20.

There are limits to the value of K that can be used:

- The number of minority promoted is limited to their population remaining after losses have occurred. If Rm_o is less than $\frac{P}{Nt}$, the limiting value of K is $\frac{1 - Lm}{P/Nt}$.
- The number of minority promoted cannot exceed the number of promotions available. If Rm_o is greater than $\frac{P}{Nt}$, the limiting value of K is $\frac{1}{Rm_o}$.

Note that the first two terms in the equation describe a gross representation model as discussed in Chapter Four. The third term, $\frac{P}{Nt}(X - KRm_o)$, describes the effect of promotions on minority representation. P would be a maximum if there were no hiring above entry level. P would be zero if there were no promotions upward from one layer to another. In the latter case, the third term would equal zero and we would simply have a gross representation model.

This equation explains how concentrations come into being and what it takes to relieve them. If the minority share of promotions is less than the minority representation, a concentration develops. Let's put some assumed values into the equation.

$$\begin{aligned} Rm_o &= 25\% \\ Lm &= 25\% \text{ (.25 decimal fraction)} \\ Lt &= 25\% \text{ (.25 decimal fraction)} \\ P &= 250 \\ Nt &= 500 \\ K &= 0.5 \\ X &= 25\% \end{aligned}$$

$$Rm_1 = 25(1 - .25) + 25(.25) + \frac{250}{500}[(25 - .5(25))]$$

$$Rm_1 = 31.25\%$$

The end of first year minority representation at entry level has increased to 31.25% even though the hiring share was only 25%. For subsequent years

$$Rm_2 = 34.4\%$$
$$Rm_3 = 35.9\%$$
$$Rm_4 = 36.7\%$$
$$Rm_5 = 37.1\%$$

The concentration will reach steady state when the minority representation is 37.5%. When the minority promotion share out of entry level was only half of the minority representation ($K = 0.5$) an input share of 25% produced a 37.5% concentration.

By inspection of the equation, one can see that a K value of 1.0 would have held the minority representation at 25%. A K value greater than 1.0 would have decreased the minority representation. For example, if K were 1.5 (its maximum possible value for this example), the minority representation would be reduced to a steady state value of 18.75%.

Assuming loss rates remain unchanged, there are three factors which affect concentrations:

- $\frac{P}{Nt}$, which is a measure of the opportunities produced by the promotion flow system.
- X, which is the share of external hires.
- K, which is a measure of promotion share.

If one sets out to avoid a concentration or to relieve one, these three factors must be considered as a package. For a fixed value of $\frac{P}{Nt}$, the mathematical fact is that once a concentration has developed, there are only two ways of reducing it—controlling minority share of hires or increasing the value of K to greater than one. In many instances, controlling the minority share of hires means reducing it. This is hardly a viable alternative in the face of high minority unemployment rates. If share of hires cannot be used as the mechanism for reducing a concentration, the only alternative is an "affirmative action" multiplier (K greater than one). This says, in effect, that "the process which built the concentration must be reversed in order to relieve it. K values less than one built it; K values greater than one are needed to relieve it."

The maximum effect that can be achieved by a K value greater than one is to promote each year all of the minority in the entry level work zone after losses have taken place. Although that is hardly likely, it does represent a mathematical limit. Under these circumstances, the end of year minority representation will be:

$$Rm = X\left(Lt + \frac{P}{Nt}\right)$$

If Lt and $\frac{P}{Nt}$ are fixed, the entry level representation depends directly upon the share of external hires. This result suggests the incompatibility of two major EEO goals:

1. To bring minority into the work force by aggressive entry level recruiting.
2. To distribute minority throughout the work force in proportion to their representation in the SMSA or some equivalent bench mark.

For example, a community which constitutes a labor market has a minority representation equal to 20%. But minority unemployment is high. A particular company recruits aggressively at the unskilled entry level and achieves a 40% minority share of hires. By careful job placement and training, the company is able to achieve a K value of one. Suppose:

$$\begin{aligned} Rm_0 &= 20\% \\ Lt &= 20\% \\ Lm &= 20\% \\ \frac{P}{Nt} &= 0.5 \\ X &= 40\% \end{aligned}$$

$$\text{Limiting value of } K = \frac{1 - Lm}{\frac{P}{Nt}}$$

The minority representation will increase to 40%. (In the limit it would be 28%, if the maximum possible value of K could be achieved.) But the parity distribution goal would be the 20% minority in the community which serves as the labor market. Given these circumstances it is a mathematical impossibility to achieve both goals.

Therein lies one fallacy in focusing on numbers. In a truly open personnel system, there will be natural shares of hires and promotions based upon objective job placements. Concentrations may still occur even with ideal objectivity. But if they do occur, they are a mathematical inevitability rather than evidence of on-going discrimination.

ANOTHER EXAMPLE OF CONCENTRATIONS

In the examples used to describe an entry level concentration, the assumed value of $\frac{P}{Nt}$ was 0.5. That number is representative of a work force with relatively high upward mobility opportunities. In some types of manufacturing plants, a much lower value for $\frac{P}{Nt}$ occurs. A good example is a plant that has been highly automated except for assembly work at the unskilled entry level. Above entry level, a relatively small number of skilled and semiskilled workers maintain the automated machines and the general physical plant. The configuration of the work force is illustrated in Figure 21.

If we make the following assumptions, we can derive a value for $\frac{P}{Nt}$

- ◆ Loss rates 10% per year for Work Zones A through D.
- ◆ Loss rate 25% per year for Work Zone E.
- ◆ No external hiring above entry level.
- ◆ Zero growth rate.

(◆ Limiting value of K is $\frac{1}{Rm_o}$.)

Figure 22 shows the dynamics of movement for one year.

Internal promotions generate 20 external hires at entry level beyond those needed to replace entry level external losses. The value of P is 20 and $\frac{P}{Nt} = \frac{20}{800} = .025$. Suppose minority constitute 60% of Work Zone E and 60% of external hires. If all available promotions went to minority, the limiting value of K would be $\frac{1}{Rm_o}$, or 1.67.

$$Rm_1 = Rm_o\,(1 - Lm) + XLt + \frac{P}{Nt}\,[X - KRm_o]$$

$$Rm_1 = 60(.75) + 60(.25) + .025[60 - 1.67(60)]$$

$$Rm_1 = 60 - 1 = 59\%$$

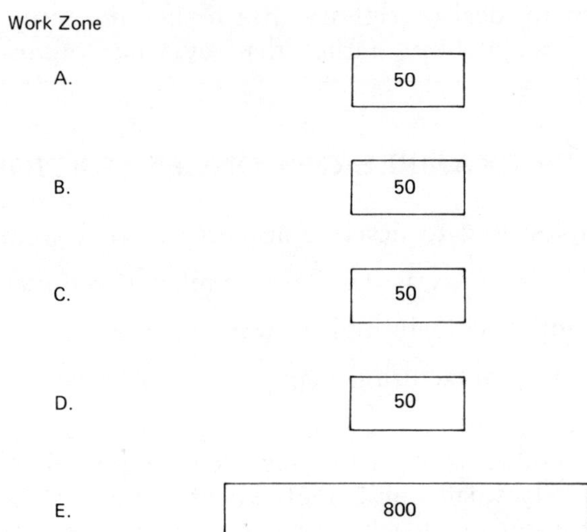

FIGURE 21.

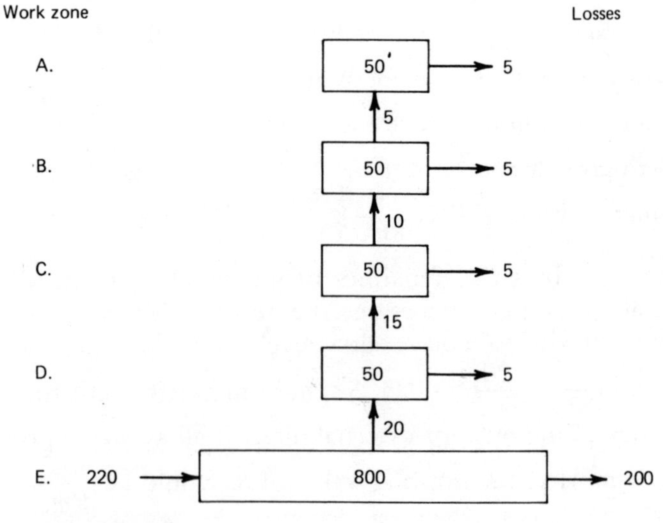

FIGURE 22.

If the model is extended for additional years, the minority representation will not go below 56%. Here is a case (not uncommon with women assemblers in particular) where the entry level concentration cannot be significantly reduced even if all promotions go to minority. The *only* way to relieve the concentration is to reduce share of external hires at entry level. But if job applications were 60% minority and the selection process was random, we would expect 60% of the hires (plus or minus some statistical tolerances) to be minority. That is a real dilemma.

The 60% minority concentration does not in itself indicate discrimination. However, if 60% is the steady state condition for a K value of one, representation in excess of that value could be an indication of discrimination. A steady state representation of 65% corresponds to a K value of 0.15. Thus, with the given data, 65% representation might be a clue to discrimination because it could come about only if K were 0.15. The reasons for such a small value of K would need to be examined very carefully because therein lies the key to whether the system is discriminatory.

GROWTH IN UPWARD MOBILITY MODELS

The model displayed in Figures 10, 15, and 16 was based upon zero growth of the total population over a five-year period. If a growth rate of 10% per year were used, the first year dynamics would be as shown in Figure 23. A 10% annual growth rate is an unusually large one, but the somewhat extreme case helps to high-light the effect of growth as a factor.

The broken lines symbolically represent the growth of the total population at each layer. A comparison of Figures 10 and 23 reveals the following:

- Total external additions have increased by 150, from 275 to 425. The increase is simply 10% of the 1500 total population.
- Promotions and external hires into each layer have increased substantially. For example, at Work Zone E external hires have increased by 50% and promotions by 62%. Growth provides high upward mobility leverage.

When the model is exercised for five years, and minority movements are determined using the same assumptions as for the zero growth model, the minority results are those shown in Figure 24.

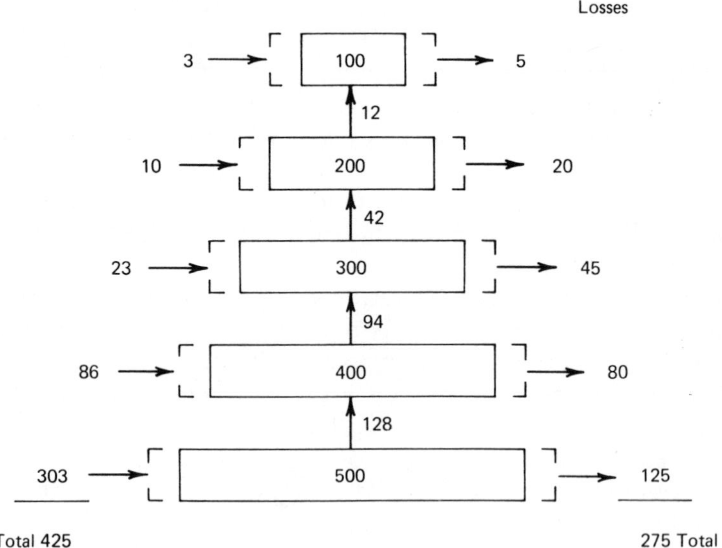

FIGURE 23.

Note that expressed as a percentage, the overall minority representation has increased only slightly. This is consistent with the gross population model findings in Chapter Five. Growth is not a major factor in improving overall minority representation.

A comparison of Figures 16 and 24 for the end of fifth year minority results shows little percentage difference for Work Zones E

	Total Number		Minority Number		Minority Representation,%		
Work Zone	Start Yr 1	End Yr 5	Start Yr 1	End Yr 5	Start Yr 1	End Yr 5	Ext. Mkt.
A	100	161	5	12	5.0	7.5	12.0
B	200	322	16	51	8.0	15.8	18.0
C	300	483	30	122	10.0	25.3	20.0
D	400	644	60	188	15.0	29.2	25.0
E	500	804	250	244	50.0	30.3	30.0
Total	1500	2414	361	617	24.0	25.6	

FIGURE 24.

and D. Growth has resulted in improved minority representation in Work Zones C, B, and A, but not as much as one might have intuitively hoped for. A 10% per year growth rate for a five-year period produced only 2.5 percentage improvement at Work Zone A over that in the zero growth model. Similarly, there was only a 3.3 percentage points incremental improvement at Work Zone B and 4.6 at Work Zone C. Growth has produced an increase of 256 minorities in the work force (a 71% increase), but this is not reflected very much in the percentage representations. The denominator in the percentage calculation increases sufficiently to offset the actual numerical improvement in minorities in the work force.

GROWTH IN ENTRY LEVEL CONCENTRATION MODELS

Similarly, one could include the growth factor in concentration models without significantly altering the conclusions drawn from the zero growth models. The general equation with growth accounted for is

$$Rm_1 = \frac{Rm_o\,(1 - Lm) + X(Lt + i) + \dfrac{P}{Nt}(X - KRm_o)}{1 + i}$$

The data for the upward mobility model with hiring above entry level can be used as an example. (See Figures 7 and 12.)

$$Rm_o = 50\%$$

$$Lm = 25\%$$

$$Lt = 25\%$$

$$X = 30\%$$

$$K = 1.0\%$$

$$\frac{P}{Nt} = 0.158 \text{ for no growth}$$

$$\frac{P}{Nt} = 0.256 \text{ for 10\% annual growth}$$

The results are shown in Figure 25 for Work Zone E.

The results differ slightly from those in the hand-built model because of rounding.

	Zero Growth	10% Growth
Rm_1	41.8	39.0
Rm_2	37.0	34.1
Rm_3	34.1	31.8
Rm_4	32.4	30.8
Rm_5	31.4	30.4

FIGURE 25.

SEGMENTING THE WORK FORCE

We have already seen that when upward mobility has to be addressed, the work force must be segmented into layers. The decision rules by which the segmentation is done are of critical importance. The basic concept is to develop segments or layers that establish a hierarchy of work related skills. One approach which is often used in local affirmative action plans is to rank every job by pay rate. Here, the underlying assumption is that pay rate is a measure of the level of skills required to do the work. This approach is clouded by the existence of overlapping pay rates for different kinds of work. For example, a journeyman plumber might be paid more than a college graduate starting out in an accounting job. But the upward mobility trails for the two people are substantially different. The plumber might move upward into the role of foreman of an installation crew. The accountant might move up to vice president of finance. Clearly there need to be other parameters.

The EEO-1 categories are a good starting point. They have their roots in U.S. Census decision rules, and they can readily be related to census data in determining external labor markets. They also provide segmentation into white collar and blue collar groupings, and hierarchies within those two groupings.

But EEO-1 categories tend to be too general to get to specific upward mobility paths or trails. The use of some kind of job families is necessary to really pinpoint upward mobility patterns and opportunities. How many job families should there be? The answer is the usual trade-off between a macro and micro approach. We start with the EEO-1 categories and do further segmentation by job families until we reach the point of practicality in tracking the system and making it work.

In the General Electric Company's conciliation agreement stemming from its Track I EEO Commission charge, the decision was to establish 10 work zones. General Electric is a massive company, engaged in 16 of the 21 major industries defined by the Standard Industrial Code. It operates in several hundred locations in the United States. Since the Track I charge was systemic, the response was systemic. The result was 10 work zones based upon the nine EEO-1 categories and broadly defined job families. The GE Work Zones can be diagrammed into upward mobility trails as shown in Figure 26.

The EEO-1 segmentation basis is:

Work Zone	**EEO-1 Category**
I, II	1, 2, 4
III, IV	3
V, VI	4, 5
VII, VIII	6
IX, X	7, 8, 9

The arrows show the general upward mobility flow patterns. For example, a person might take a job in Work Zone X as an assembler; after acquiring experience move to Work Zone IX as a quality control inspector; and subsequently move to Work Zone II as an assembly foreman. In the main, there are two white collar paths and one blue collar path upward to the managerial/professional work zones. There could have been a much larger number of paths simply by subdividing the work zones into additional job families. In this particular agreement, the broad scale macro approach won out over the micro.

SUMMARY

1. Consideration of upward mobility requires four factors beyond those used in gross representation models.

- The work force must be segmented into a hierarchy of layers or work zones.
- Internal markets must be determined because they provide source populations for upward mobility.
- The division of total additions to a work zone between external hires and internal promotions must be considered.

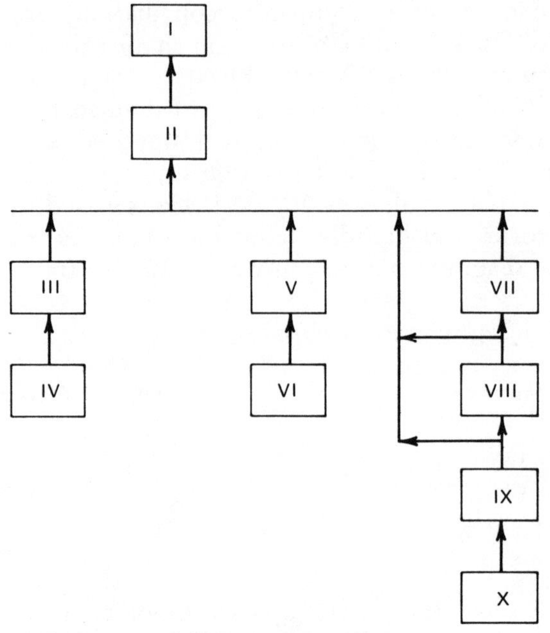

WORK ZONES

I Managers & Professionals, PL 7–9
II First Level Managers & Professionals, PL 1–6
III Skilled Technicians
IV Other Technicians
V Clerical & Administrative
VI Other Clerical
VII Apprenticed & Equivalent Crafts
VIII Other Crafts
IX Semi-Skilled Operatives
X Entry Level Operatives

FIGURE 26.

- Seniority, to the extent it affects minority share of promotions, must be considered.

2. The configuration of the work force hierarchy provides a visual clue to upward mobility opportunities. If one is in a particular upward mobility chain, the more people there are above him or her, the greater the potential prospects for a promotion.

3. Redistribution of minorities throughout the work force by means of internal promotions will generally require a long time frame.

4. Concentrations of minority workers at entry level are caused when their external hires input is relatively high and their promotions out of entry level relatively low. Once a concentration has developed, it may not be possible to relieve it by means of internal promotions. If share of external hires remains relatively high, the concentration may continue to exist even if minorities are allocated a share of promotions significantly higher than their representation in the work zone. There is a general algebraic equation which is useful in analyzing concentrations and determining what might be done about them.

5. Redistribution of minorities based on equalling the percent of the minority population in the external market corresponding to each work zone may result in a reduction of minorities in the work force. This will tend to occur when there is a concentration of minority applicants at entry level in excess of their representation in the relevant external labor market. On the other hand, maintaining a disproportionately high minority input at entry level and simultaneously attempting to relieve a concentration there will force higher than external market targets at each of the other layers.

6. A goal of increasing the entry level share of hires for minorities may be mathematically incompatible with a goal of having minority distributed throughout the work force in proportion to their overall representation in the community or the labor market.

7. The real end point of upward mobility is a personnel system that provides for upward flow of people in a nondiscriminatory way. That is a valhalla that is not just a hope but a necessity. In a truly nondiscriminatory system, there will be a natural flow which will establish values for such variables as shares of hires and promotions. When these are established, the resulting representations are mathematical inevitabilities. Even then, the results may be viewed as unsatisfactory. Such a view could be caused simply by hoping for too much achievement in too short a time frame. In that case, the issue is one of accepting the mathematical inevitabilities associated with upward mobility. On the other hand, such a view based upon understanding and acceptance of the mathematics could be very legitimate. It would suggest, however, that cultural changes and education and training are major issues which need to be addressed.

Until the truly non-discriminatory personnel system valhalla is reached, "numbers" will continue to be a major EEO consideration. Hopefully, the mathematics will be a useful tool in keeping those numbers in reasonable perspective

CHAPTER EIGHT

The Internal Labor Market

Share of promotions out of one job level into another is a critical factor in upward mobility. How can one go about determining what that share should be? The natural assumption tends to be that promotion share should be equal to the percentage representation in the job level from which promotions are occurring. For example, if women constitute 50% of the entry job level population, they would be expected to receive 50% of the annual promotions to the next higher job level. Often they receive considerably less than this "fair share." Is that because of discriminatory personnel practices, or could there be other factors which produce a lower share than would be intuitively expected? Three such possible factors will be explored in this chapter.

1. Not all jobs prepare a person for higher level jobs. This is particularly true for unskilled entry level jobs. Some are simply a dead end, contributing no learning experiences useful for upward mobility. If women are concentrated in the dead end jobs and men are not, women will receive a lesser share of promotions than their representation in the total entry level population.
2. Seniority can be a major deterrent to upward mobility for women. In a strict seniority system, women's share of promotions could be considerably less than what otherwise might be expected.
3. Not everyone is interested in being promoted. In reality, only a portion of the total population in a job level may be interested in promotions to a higher level. The supply for promotions may not be the total population in the job level, but only some fraction thereof. If women's interest in promotions is less than that of men's, their share can turn out to be less than their representation in the job level.

These factors are difficult to address because they require so much detail work, some of which may be inconclusive anyway. But share of promotions is such a critical factor in upward mobility that monitoring agencies and employers have considerable obligation to make the detail effort.

For proper analysis of internal markets, vertical segmentation such as that discussed in Chapter Seven must be done. But that is not sufficient. There must also be horizontal segmentation—a detailed but extremely useful procedure.

INTERNAL LABOR MARKET SEGMENTATION

The blue collar work force in a production plant provides a good vehicle for a discussion of internal labor markets. The skills differentiation among crafts, operatives, laborers, and service workers is generally understood and accepted. Not too many would argue that job skills for a waitress in the plant cafeteria are different from those for a steam fitter in plant maintenance. Although not all differences are that obvious, at least some broad brush categories or job families can be arrived at without too many differences of opinion. The delineation of the job families is very important to internal market analysis, because they are the key to upward mobility trails. Without further special training, it is not likely that a waitress will become a plumber nor a grounds keeper a tool and die maker. It can be postulated that not all jobs, independent of race/sex/ethnic of the incumbents, lead to better jobs. So the task of understanding and sizing internal markets begins with a segmentation into job families that bear some relationship to each other in terms of upward mobility.

VERTICAL SEGMENTATION

Assume that a factory blue collar work force consists of 20 job rates—ranging from unskilled entry level at Job Rate 1 (JR1) to highly skilled tool and die makers at Job Rate 20 (JR20). It is natural to assume that the job rate reflects skill level. In some cases this assumption can be challenged. For example, a job which is a truly dirty, undesirable one may have a rate higher than the appropriate skill level should command simply because no one would take the job at lower pay. Or, where different unions exist in the same plant, one may have been more successful in negotiating job rates than another. Also, it has been argued (successfully in some cases) that job rates for women are sometimes artificially depressed when the supply is high and the woman's only alternative is unemployment. However, as a starting point, let's set aside these potential challenges because they can be factored into the segmentation later on. Let's assume that job rate is a measure of the required skills level. We can then proceed with a segmentation.

Our first choice is the usual micro/macro one. We can treat each JR as a work zone, making a total of 20, or we can collapse the 20 into some smaller number. A fairly natural grouping that fits many blue collar work forces reasonably well is that of four work zones.

Work Zone

- **A.** Crafts, apprenticed and equivalent
- **B.** Other crafts
- **C.** Semi-skilled
- **D.** Other blue collar workers

This grouping would be characteristic of a hierarchy such as:

- **A.** Tool and die maker
- **B.** Machinist
- **C.** Precision machine operator
- **D.** Assembler

How do we determine the boundaries of the work zones? Generally, one can find some levels in the job hierarchy where there are appreciable changes in the skills required compared with lower job levels. For example, Work Zone A contains the apprenticed crafts—tool and die makers, plumbers, electricians, and others. The lower boundary of Work Zone A is the job rate below which there are no significant numbers of apprenticed crafts workers. Similarly, there is a change in skills requirements between Work Zones B and C. Workers in B are machinists who do their own set up work; workers in C simply operate automatic machines such as spot welders or small punch presses. The job rate at which this change occurs is the lower boundary for Work Zone B. Similarly, there is a break point between the semi-skilled in Work Zone C and the unskilled in Work Zone D.

Work Zone	Job Rates
A	JR16–20
B	JR11–15
C	JR 6–10
D	JR 1–5

FIGURE 1.

When the task of defining work zone boundaries is completed, a table such as Figure 1 can be constructed.

In this example, the job rate ranges uniformly span five JR numbers. This need not always be the case but will depend upon the specific job structure for any particular plant. It is important to note that the work zone boundaries have been established on a skills demarcation basis using apprenticed and machining jobs as bench marks. What about all the other jobs in the factory besides these particular ones? Here is where the assumption that job rates reflect skills requirements is so important. All of the other jobs are placed in work zones according to their job rates. For example, an inspector at JR7 would fall into Work Zone C; a chauffeur at JR17 would fall into Work Zone A. As mentioned earlier, one can challenge the job rate/skills requirement assumption, but in the main it is a reasonable one. The alternative would be to analyze all of the blue collar jobs in the factory on a skills basis. However, that was already presumably done in establishing the pay structure to begin with. If one is willing to accept the imprecision associated with the job rate/skills assumption, it is possible to arrive at least at some approximate internal market sizes.

The use of four work zones on a collapsed basis rather than 20 work zones each of which is a JR number can also be challenged. In using this particular methodology, one must bear in mind that promotions can occur *within* a work zone and *between* work zones. If the objective is to find possible impediments to upward mobility for women, the four work zone basis is very useful. One could assume that there are few impediments within a work zone—the real problem is clearing the change of skills hurdles at the work zone boundaries. Also, the vertical segmentation is only the first step in a lengthy process. For purposes of analyzing internal markets, the vertical segmentation does not provide enough detail. The next step has to be a horizontal segmentation within each work zone.

HORIZONTAL SEGMENTATION

Although the vertical segmentation boundaries were based on apprenticed and machining jobs, each work zone will actually contain a variety of jobs. The numerical distribution of these various jobs is critical to upward mobility, because that is what determines the type of opportunities that will be available to both men and women. For a manufacturing enterprise, jobs can generally be categorized as shown in Figure 2.

Each job within a work zone can be placed in one of the eight categories. When the vertical and horizontal segmentation has been completed, there are four work zones each of which has eight subcategories—a total of 32 job cells or job families. The value of using only four work zones is clear at this point. If each job rate had been selected as a work zone, there would have been 160 job families—a difficult data task to cope with. With the help of a computer, the task could be manageable, but it implies a precision that is not very realistic for internal market analysis.

The results of all of these efforts can be displayed in the matrix of Figure 3, using numbers that approximate the real world.

Distributions such as those shown in Figure 3 depend mainly on the type of products, the degree of mechanization, and the use of purchased versus made components. This particular distribution is typical of what might occur in a mass production, light assembly manufacturing plant for a product that requires a wide variety of manufacturing processes. It is important to note that this matrix has been developed independent of race/sex/ethnic data. It is a profile of

Category	Examples
1. Machining	Drilling, milling, boring
2. Fabrication	Welding, sheet metal
3. Process	Painting, anodizing
4. Assembly	Putting parts into the whole
5. Inspection	Checking against specifications
6. Material Handling	Moving material
7. Material Expediting	Clearing bottlenecks in flow
8. Maintenance	Electrical, plumbing repair

FIGURE 2.

Segmentation Data

Work Zone	Total	Mach	Fab	Proc	Assy	Insp	Mat Hnd	Mat Exp	Maint
A	200	100	40	10	10	—	—	—	40
B	200	100	50	20	10	10	—	—	10
C	400	100	50	50	50	50	50	50	—
D	800	50	50	50	400	100	100	50	—
Total	1600	350	190	130	470	160	150	100	50

FIGURE 3.

the work force skills and numbers necessary to produce the product in the desired quantity and quality.

A quick glance at the data is revealing. Of the 1600 total jobs, 470 are in assembly. But nearly all of the assembly jobs are in the entry level work zone. Unless assemblers have or can acquire the skills necessary to move to other job families, their prospects for upward mobility are very low.

In tabular form, the implications of the segmentation do not stand out as clearly as they do in bar charts. Figure 4 displays the distribution of jobs in each work zone, drawn to scale. Half of the jobs in Work Zone A are in machining; half of the jobs in Work Zone D are in assembly. If upward mobility were purely vertical within a job category, eight models for upward mobility could be built. The results would be substantially different for each of the eight categories—good for machining, fabrication, and maintenance, but not so good for the others.

For the first time we can begin to see that lateral moves are a key to upward mobility, independent of race, sex or ethnic background. Somehow one has to develop at the lower levels by experience or training the skills necessary to capitalize on higher level opportunities

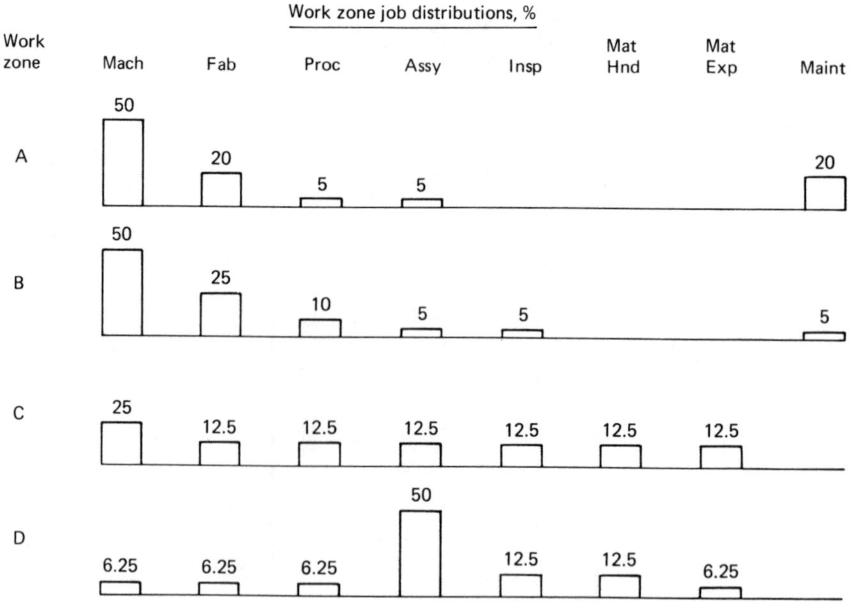

FIGURE 4.

as they become available. Lateral moves are one way of doing so. In hindsight, this should not really be any surprise. Lateral movements have been a basic factor in many training programs at higher levels. They are a reasonably well validated training technique. It would appear, however, that there has not been much application of the concept at lower levels of the blue collar work force. There lies an interesting possibility for EEO progress.

WOMEN IN THE INTERNAL MARKET

When the segmentation has been completed independent of race/sex/ethnic data, women in the internal market can be objectively considered. They can be placed in the individual job families as displayed in Figure 5.

The column headed Total shows the results of vertical segmentation. Women constitute 29.6% of the work force, but they occupy only 2% of Work Zone A and 50% of Work Zone D. This is the same pattern that has been seen in earlier chapters. There is a concentration of women at entry level, and upward mobility almost automatically becomes an important issue. Without looking at the horizontal segmentation, one might assume that women's share of promotions out of Work Zone D should equal their representation of 50%. But the horizontal segmentation sheds considerably more light on what that share actually might be. The column headed Assembly is the key one. Women occupy 80% of the assembly jobs—a category that offers relatively low upward mobility possibilities.

The distribution by job category for women in Work Zone D is shown in Figure 6.

As women at entry level figuratively look up at jobs in Work Zone C, they see the distribution displayed in Figure 7.

If some simplifying assumptions are made, the data in Figures 6 and 7 can be used to estimate what the women's share of promotions out of the entry level work zone might be.

1. Job openings in Work Zone C occur in proportion to their percentage distribution by job grouping.
2. Movements into Work Zone C are strictly vertical. There is no cross over from one job grouping to another.
3. All job openings in Work Zone C are filled by internal promotions.
4. Seniority is not a determining factor.

Work Zone		Total	Mach	Fab	Proc	Assy	Insp	Mat Hnd	Mat Exp	Maint
A	Total	200	100	40	10	10	—	—	—	40
	Women	4	2	—	2	—	—	—	—	—
B	Total	200	100	50	20	10	10	—	—	10
	Women	10	2	—	—	4	4	—	—	—
C	Total	400	100	50	50	50	50	50	50	—
	Women	60	20	—	—	25	15	—	—	—
D	Total	800	50	50	50	400	100	100	50	—
	Women	400	5	5	5	320	50	5	10	—
Total	Total	1600	350	190	130	470	160	150	100	50
	Women	474	29	5	7	349	69	5	10	—

FIGURE 5.

Women in Work Zone D	
Job Category	**Percent Women**
Machining	10.0
Fabrication	10.0
Process	10.0
Assembly	80.0
Inspection	50.0
Material Handling	5.0
Material Expediting	20.0
Maintenance	0

FIGURE 6.

Given these assumptions, a weighting process can be applied to approximate the women internal market as shown in Figure 8.

Although women's representation in Work Zone D is 50%, it's possible that they constitute only 24.4% (call it 25%) of the internal market. In that case, their promotion share would be only half of their actual representation in the work zone (mathematically, a *K* factor of 0.5).

This illustration of sizing the internal market is clearly only an approximation. Whether or not the actual women's share of promo-

Jobs in Work Zone C	
Job Category	**Percent of All Jobs in Work Zone C**
Machining	25.0
Fabrication	12.5
Process	12.5
Assembly	12.5
Inspection	12.5
Material Handling	12.5
Material Expediting	12.5
Maintenance	0

FIGURE 7.

Job Category	% Jobs in Work Zone C	% Women in Jobs in Work Zone D	Weighting Factor
Machining	25.0	10.0	2.50
Fabrication	12.5	10.0	1.25
Process	12.5	10.0	1.25
Assembly	12.5	80.0	10.00
Inspection	12.5	50.0	6.25
Material Handling	12.5	5.0	.63
Material Expediting	12.5	20.0	2.50
Maintenance	0	0	0
			24.4%

FIGURE 8.

tions in a truly open personnel system would be higher or lower than the calculated value of 25% is open to discussion. The illustration does suggest, however, that the real value of *K* could be substantially less than one. This conclusion stems directly from the data—the women are in jobs which do not have higher level counterparts.

IMPLICATIONS FOR UPWARD MOBILITY

If this internal market analysis yields anywhere near the real value for women's promotion share, the results are indeed discouraging. It has already been established (Chapter Seven) that a promotion share less than the percentage representation will cause the concentration to increase unless women's share of hires is reduced. A numerical example is worth repeating here, because it leads to an upward mobility concept not yet discussed.

As usual, it is necessary to make some assumptions for the numerical example. Assume for Work Zone D:

- Zero growth.
- 100 promotions annually.
- 20% total loss rate, annual.
- 20% women loss rate, annual.

- 25% women share of promotions.
- 50% women share of hires.

The movements dynamics are:

◆ Total external losses	20% of 800 = 160
◆ Total promotions out of D	100
◆ Needed external hires	160 + 100 = 260
◆ Women external hires	50% of 260 = 130
◆ Women promotions	25% of 100 = 25
◆ Women external losses	20% of 400 = 80
◆ Net change in women in D	130 − (25 + 80) = 25
◆ New representation of women in D	425 ÷ 800 = 53.1%

This same answer could also have been obtained by using the general algebraic equation from Chapter Seven.

$$Rm_1 = Rm_o(1 - Lm) + XLt + \frac{P}{Nt}(X - KRm_o)$$

When the data are placed into this equation, the result is also 53.1%. But the equation has an added usefulness, because it can predict the ultimate steady state conditions. For example, how long will the representation of women in Work Zone D continue to increase? Is there some value at which the increase will level off? Yes—that value is the steady state condition.

The technique for arriving at the steady state condition is a straightforward one. During some year in the future, there will be some value for the representation equal to that for the prior year. This can be expressed mathematically as:

$$Rm_n = Rm_{n-1} = Rm_{n-1}(1 - Lm) + XLt + \frac{P}{Nt}(X - KRm_{n-1})$$

For the data in the preceding example when the value for K is 0.5, the steady state representation is 62%. As long as women continue to be so heavily concentrated in assembly work, their representation will increase until it reaches a steady state value of 62%.

What if management could do a better job of distributing women by job category in Work Zone D and achieve a *K* factor of 1.0? If the share of entry hires remained at 50%, the steady state representation would be 50%. Finally, suppose management could somehow achieve a *K* factor of 1.5. In that case, the steady state representation would be 42%.

More will be said later on about this steady state concept, because it leads to an interesting conclusion—under certain circumstances, the percentage representation of women in the higher work zones must inevitably be less than that at the lower levels. That is disappointing but is nevertheless a mathematical reality.

SENIORITY IN THE INTERNAL MARKET

The effect of seniority on the internal market, and thus its effect on redistribution of women in the work force, can be seen in good perspective by using a greatly simplified numerical example. Let's begin by making the following assumptions:

- Zero growth rate.
- 1000 men at entry level, each of whom has one year of service.
- Zero women at entry level initially.
- 20% per year loss rate for men.
- 20% per year loss rate for women.
- No promotions of men or women are made during their first year of service.
- No losses of men or women occur during their first year of service.
- Women share of annual external hires is 20%.
- All promotions, losses, and hires occur on the first day of each year.
- 200 promotions annually are made out of the entry level, all of which are on a strict seniority basis.

All of the men who remain with the company will have to be promoted before any women can be promoted. There will be some losses of men at entry level, and it will take less than five years to remove the backlog of senior men. Figure 9 summarizes what will happen to the men's population over a period of time and, similarly, Figure 10 for women.

Men's Population by Years of Service

End Year	1	2	3	4	5
0	1000	—	—	—	—
1	320	600	—	—	—
2	320	256	280	—	—
3	320	256	205	24	—
4	320	256	205	19	—
5	320	256	205	19	—

FIGURE 9.

By the end of the fourth year, steady state conditions have been reached. The men's seniority backlog has been removed. Women constitute 20% of the external hires, 20% of the total population, and they are receiving 20% of the promotions. The effect of the seniority system strictly applied was to produce a *K* value of one. Mathematically, a *K* value of one produces a steady state condition where the women's representation equals the share of external hires.

In this example, the initial representation of women was zero. Let's change the initial representation to 800 men with two years service and 200 women with one year service. The results are displayed in Figures 11 and 12. The same steady state condition is reached at the end of the same time period, four years. The only difference is that the women's representation temporarily increased above 20% in the transient state years.

Women's Population by Years of Service

End Year	1	2	3	4	5
0	0	—	—	—	—
1	80	—	—	—	—
2	80	64	—	—	—
3	80	64	51	—	—
4	80	64	51	5	—
5	80	64	51	5	—

FIGURE 10.

Men's Population by Years of Service					
End Year	**1**	**2**	**3**	**4**	**5**
0	—	800	—	—	—
1	320	—	440	—	—
2	320	256	—	152	—
3	320	256	205	—	—
4	320	256	205	19	—
5	320	256	205	19	—

FIGURE 11.

While the entry level work zone is passing through a transient condition into steady state, seniority is impeding the flow of women into the next higher work zone. It introduces a time delay in upward mobility because backlogs of senior men have to be cleared before redistribution of women can occur. In the long run, this is the major significance of seniority. It can be a major contributor to extending the time needed for any substantial redistribution of women in the work force.

Seniority is a paradox. In the long-run steady state condition, seniority does not produce concentrations of women at lower levels in the work force. Other factors do that. If seniority temporarily contributes to a concentration of women, it adjusts to relieve what it created (Figures 11 and 12). It tends to assure representative shares of promotions for women because, in the long run, it tends to produce a *K* value of one. But seniority can have a significant effect on the time frame within which redistribution of women can possibly occur. For

Women's Population by Years of Service					
End Year	**1**	**2**	**3**	**4**	**5**
0	200	—	—	—	—
1	80	160	—	—	—
2	80	64	128	—	—
3	80	64	51	24	—
4	80	64	51	5	—
5	80	64	51	5	—

FIGURE 12.

a work force in which there is no hiring above entry level, backlogs of senior men in the hierarchy of work zones must be removed in sequence. This can prolong the time frame substantially over that which would otherwise be required to reach steady state conditions.

Perhaps the most useful view is that seniority distributions unfavorable to women generally are not caused by the seniority system itself. They are caused by other factors in the personnel system. But once a seniority distribution unfavorable to women has developed, seniority can be a significant deterrent to upward mobility. This is a temporary condition (sometimes a long one) that is ultimately self-adjusting to a steady state condition providing for representative shares of promotion opportunities for women, that is, K values of one.

One exception to this occurs when two unions exist in the same plant, and seniority is not transferable from one to the other. An individual with 20 years of service in the plant in Union X, who transfers to Union Y could possibly hold zero years of seniority in the new union. Dual seniority systems of that nature clearly can be generators of seniority distributions unfavorable to women.

INDIVIDUAL INTERESTS IN THE INTERNAL MARKET

Individual interests in seeking and accepting promotion to a higher level job have to be addressed on a micro rather than macro basis. Generalizations are not very useful in determining the effect of individual interests on promotion share. One might generalize that men seek macho jobs such as fabrication and women seek clean jobs such as light assembly. Even if such a generalization were valid, it would be difficult to quantify in a specific situation without additional data. For example, the display in Figure 8 shows that 80% of the assembly jobs are held by women and 90% of the fabrication jobs are held by men. The generalization, if valid, would establish that some men-women distribution different from 50–50 might be expected. But it could not lead to a conclusion that the 80-20 or 10-90 shares truly reflect differential interests of that magnitude between men and women.

Given the data in Figure 8, interest becomes a very important factor for three reasons:

1. If the initial placements into the work zone do not reflect differential interests of men and women, there is possible evidence of dis-

criminatory practices. Even if the placements are nondiscriminatory, they nevertheless have a disparate effect on subsequent upward mobility for women.

2. The present concentration of women in assembly could be relieved by lateral transfers into other kinds of work. Women would then be better positioned for upward mobility in subsequent years.
3. Whatever the distribution in the work zone might be, differential men-women interests have an impact on promotion share.

It is important to note that before an actual placement or promotion can occur, there must be sufficient interest in a specific job to trigger acceptance of an offer. The decision to accept or reject may be the result of a weighted judgment based on a large number of factors; or it may be as simple as "I don't want to do that kind of work." The list of factors which might influence the accept-reject decision can be a very long one. Since men and women place different values on these factors, the result can be differential interests in accepting or rejecting.

Some of the questions which influence the resulting decision are

- ◆ Can I really do the job well?
- ◆ Is the pay increase worth the change?
- ◆ How well will I fit in with other employees in the group?
- ◆ Is the job a stepping stone to better things or is it dead end?
- ◆ Does the job involve unfavorable environment such as odors, heat, dust?
- ◆ Does the job requires a change from first shift to graveyard?
- ◆ Will I really like the work?
- ◆ Will I like my new boss?
- ◆ Will the job tire me too much physically?
- ◆ If I wait, can I get a better job?
- ◆ Would they really offer that job to a woman?

In assessing the internal market, it is probably best to assume that there are no differential interests unless there is actual proof. This assumption forces a testing of the personnel system. To know whether women will consistently choose assembly over fabrication jobs, offers have to be made to women in both categories. When enough data has been collected, the existence or absence of differential interests can be established. More important, the progressive employer can try to determine the causes for differential interests where they do exist and initiate programs to remedy those causes.

Mathematically, one has to be a little careful in translating differential interests into their effect on promotion share. Not all of the men and women in the work zone may be interested in promotions. For example, assume an entry level work zone consists of 100 assembly jobs. There are 50 men and 50 women. The assembly experience qualifies the incumbents for 25 inspection jobs which become available during the year in the next higher work zone. The job posting-bidding system identifies 30 men and 20 women who are interested in the higher level jobs. On this basis, men appear to be more interested than women. The *K* factor for men would be 1.2 and for women it would be 0.8. If seniority and qualifications are equal, random selection would result in 15 offers to men and 10 to women. If all these 25 offers were accepted, these values for the *K* factors would be correct.

But it is possible to have acceptance ratios different from expressed interest ratios. Suppose that all 10 women accepted their offers, but five men rejected theirs. After this first round, there would be five unfilled jobs and 15 men and 10 women available to choose from. Three offers would be made to men and an additional two to women. If these five offers were accepted, the scorecard would read:

Women ....12 acceptances for 12 offers.
Men ....13 acceptances for 18 offers.

The net effect is that promotion shares would be 48% for women and 52% for men. This is a much better picture for women than the 40% share which would have been assumed on the basis of the distribution of initial job bids. Expressed mathematically, the *K* factor for women would be $\frac{48}{50}$ or 96%. For practical purposes in this set of circumstances, one might as well assume equal interests for men and women.

There is one additional caution in attempting to quantify differential interests between men and women. Many job posting-bidding systems provide for multiple expressions of interest. For example, one system sometimes permits each employee to register interest in a number of different jobs, even though none are available at that particular time. As a job becomes vacant and needs to be filled, personnel uses the file of expressed interests for that job as the source of candidates. One person's name may be in a number of different job interest files. Simply adding up the total number of men and women's expressions of interest for a family of jobs can be misleading. One has to know whether one woman was interested in 10 different jobs, or 10 different women were interested in one job. This may seem rather obvious, but it is sometimes overlooked.

LOWER REPRESENTATION AT HIGHER LEVELS

The effect of promotions out of the entry level on the next higher work zone depends upon how much external hiring occurs above entry level. Let's build a zero growth model to explore what can happen. The basic data are displayed in Figure 13.

The dynamics corresponding to Figure 13 are shown in Figure 14, for the total population.

In the ideal case, women's share of promotions out of any work zone would equal their representation in that work zone; mathematically, the K factor would be one all the way up the line.

Similarly, assume that women's share of external hires is equal to their percentage in the relevant external market, except at entry level where it is 50%. Annually, 23 women will be promoted into Work Zone C, while their representation in Work Zone D remains constant at 50%.

What happens at Work Zone C? If the external market representation for women does not change over time, the percentage of women in Work Zone C will finally reach some steady state value. This value can be calculated by using a simple flow balance given in Figure 15.

Zero Growth Mode

Work Zone	Total	Women	Loss Rate %/Yr Total	Loss Rate %/Yr Women	% Ext Hires	% Women Ext Mkt
A	200	4	5	5	50	5
B	200	10	10	10	40	10
C	400	60	15	15	40	20
D	800	400	20	20	100	40

FIGURE 13.

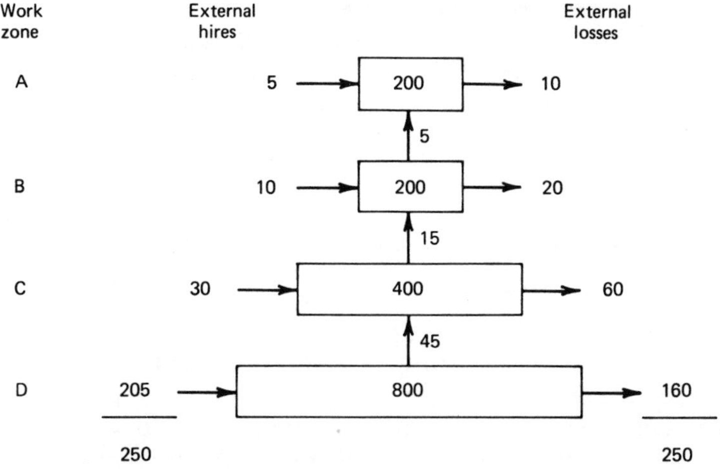

FIGURE 14.

N is the number of women in Work Zone C when steady state is reached. Twenty-three women will flow into the work zone by promotions from below. Six women will move in as external hires. At a loss rate of 15% per year, .15*N* women will be lost; and women will receive *N*/400 of the 15 promotions out of the work zone.

$$\text{Flow in} = \text{Flow out}$$

$$23 + 6 = .0375N + .15N$$

$$N = 155$$

$$\%\ \text{Rep} = \frac{N}{400} = 38.8$$

Similarly, the steady state representations are 27% for Work Zone B and 14% for Work Zone A. (Results depend upon how rounding of fractions is done.)

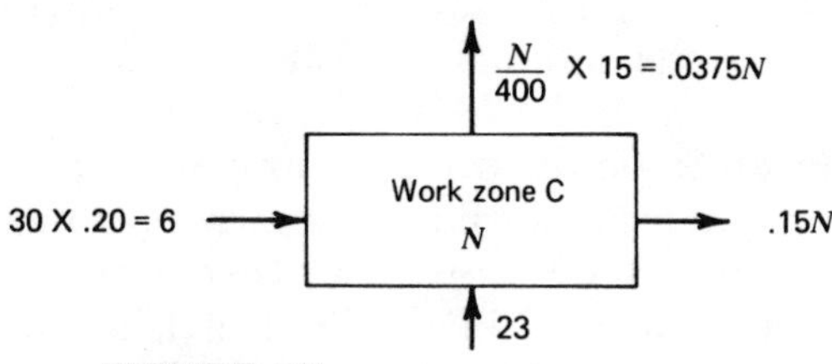

FIGURE 15.

Work Zone	% Women Steady State
A	12
B	23
C	32
D	40

FIGURE 16.

Given the particular set of data, and assuming the women's percentage in the external market remains constant, the representation of women will decrease as the measurement is taken at increasingly higher levels. Would the results have been any different if the women's share of entry level hires were equal to their external labor market (40%) share? Numerically, yes—but conceptually, no. The steady state values would be as shown in Figure 16.

In the numerical examples, the percentage of women in the external market was assumed to remain constant. In reality, it would probably increase. At least one would expect it to do so as a result of EEO efforts. The amount of increase depends partly upon how well all of the companies within the labor market have utilized their internal markets. In fact, the utilization of the internal markets by employers can be a major determinant in the size of their external markets. This is a principle which to date has probably not received adequate EEO attention. For example, in an SMSA (Standard Metropolitan Statistical Area) the number of women in the semi-skilled labor market is simply the total of all those so employed. If employers are successful in utilizing internal markets, that number and therefore the percentage of women in the relevant external labor market will increase. However, even then the conclusion drawn here is a valid one. As employers reach out for advanced placement people in the external market, they now find a shortage of many types of skills that cannot be acquired simply by the on-the-job experience which characterizes the internal market. For example, knowledge and skills associated with the MBA degree or advanced degrees in engineering and other occupations or apprentice programs require special education and training. Until women's (and minority workers') participation in such development experiences is approximately equal to their representation in the civilian labor force, advanced placements from the external market will be disproportionately low

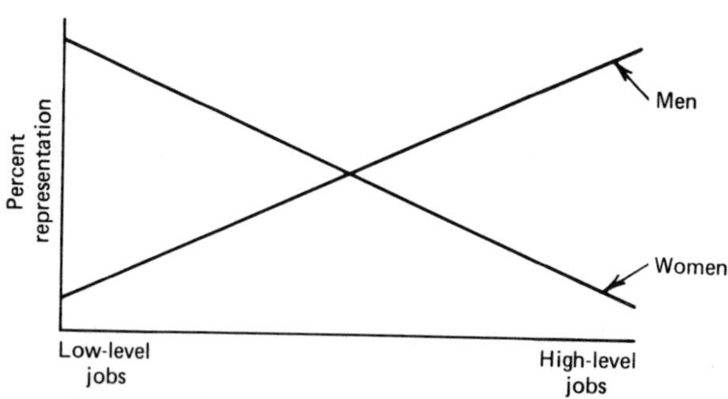

FIGURE 17.

and result in the types of distributions illustrated by Figure 16. Such results can be seen in perspective in the well known "X" shown in Figure 17.

Under many common sets of circumstances each employer is almost inevitably faced with this dilemma until all employers are fully utilizing their internal markets for women, and women (minority groups also) are participating fully in the off-the-job development experiences required to compete successfully in the work world.

SUMMARY

1. Internal market analysis requires a segmentation of the labor force both vertically and horizontally into job families on a hierarchical basis. This segmentation identifies the natural upward mobility trails that exist independent of race, sex or ethnic considerations. That identification is fundamental to planning for redistribution of minorities and women and for approximating the changes that can occur under varying sets of circumstances.

2. Four major factors determine the share of minority and women promotions:

- **a.** Personnel practices.
- **b.** Individual qualifications vis-a-vis job requirements.
- **c.** Seniority.
- **d.** Individual interests.

3. The minority and women shares of external hires and internal promotions determine the extent to which redistribution is possible.

Even when the internal market is utilized to the maximum to produce upward mobility for minorities and women, it is almost certain that their representation will be progressively lower at higher levels in the hierarchy until such time as their representation in the external market is greatly increased through special off-the-job development programs.

4. Lateral movements of minority workers and women from one job to another within a work zone may be a prerequisite to increased upward mobility. Not all jobs lead to a higher level—some are simply dead ends. Minority groups and women in dead end jobs are not really a part of the internal market. They must be repositioned in jobs that lead to better jobs before upward mobility and redistribution can occur.

5. Initial placements at entry level are a critical factor in upward mobility. The process of bringing minorities and women into the work force at entry level must be managed very carefully. If they are placed disproportionately in dead end jobs, upward mobility can be stymied before it has a chance to get started.

6. Redistribution of minority workers and women must be analyzed in both the transient and steady state conditions. Unless the potential steady state condition is at least approximated, transient results can be misleading.

7. Seniority can be a major deterrent to redistribution during the transient condition, because backlogs of seniority must be removed before upward mobility can occur. But in the long run, seniority works on behalf of redistribution, because in itself it produces a share of promotions equal to minority and women representation in the work zone.

8. Not everyone is interested in upward mobility. There may be differential interests for men and women, for minorities and nonminorities. However, one should probably assume that there are no differential interests unless there is proof to the contrary.

CHAPTER NINE

Numerical Objectives

There is probably no issue more packed with emotional and potential legal activity than that of numerical objectives, goals, or quotas. In most personal relationships, it is desirable to set up win-win situations. However, when it comes to filling a job, many times there is one winner and a number of losers. The profile of the civilian labor force throughout the United States suggests that as far as the better jobs are concerned, minority groups and women have not fared well. They not only may have been losers a disproportionately high amount of the time, but also perhaps in some instances they may not even have been entered into the competition. Simply stated, minorities and women are not distributed throughout the vertical and horizontal segments of the labor force in proportion to their overall representation. From that point of view, the profile of the labor force is distorted. This results in three basic EEO issues.

1. How much of the distortion is the result of discrimination?
2. Where and to what extent does discrimination continue to exist?
3. When discrimination has contributed or is contributing to the distortion, what remedial steps should be taken?

In some specific instances, these questions have been answered by judges in courtrooms as a result of litigation. In many other instances, the questions are not really answered but are finessed under the general banners of consent decrees, conciliation agreements, and affirmative action programs. Most of these contain some provision for goals or numerical objectives that are expected to produce changes in the representation and/or distribution of minorities and women in a work force. In essence, it is conceded that there is a distortion of some kind in the profile of the work force, and that corrective action is necessary. There is generally no concession, however, that discriminatory practices produced the distortion.

For example, in California an education code requires all school districts to develop affirmative action plans. The question of whether a particular school district has been discriminatory in the past is finessed. Similarly, in 1978 General Electric signed a conciliation agreement involving an outlay of $32 million over a five-year period and a very complex numerical objectives process. But there was no official finding by the EEO commission nor admission by the company of any discrimination.

Whether by court decree, consensus, compromise, or general lack of resistance, numerical objectives for minority groups and women have become a way of life for most employers. How numerical objectives should be established and what their long-term effects may be is one of the least understood elements in the total EEO process. In the early years of EEO monitoring, an in-depth understanding was not particularly needed, because the main thrust was to get minorities into the work force without particular emphasis on the types of jobs. However, the picture has now changed for two reasons.

- There is the added thrust of redistributing minority workers and women in the work force. This involves all of the complexities associated with segmenting the work force and utilizing internal as well as external markets.
- As each step of progress is made, the next step becomes more difficult. The rate of success in the early years cannot be achieved in future years unless affirmative action is intensified. However, there are practical limits resulting from availability within the internal and external labor markets.

If the courts are not to be glutted with EEO discrimination law suits, the numerical objectives process must be much better done in the future than it has in the past.

REVERSE DISCRIMINATION

The question of reverse discrimination has been addressed by the U.S. Supreme Court in two landmark cases. The following article from the *Los Angeles Times* (September 15, 1978) briefly summarizes the issues in the Bakke and the Weber cases.*

*Reprinted by permission from The Associated Press.

Reverse-Bias Issue Returns to High Court
Affirmative Action Program Challenged in Louisiana Case

WASHINGTON (*AP*)—The momentous legal question left unanswered by the U.S. Supreme Court's "Bakke decision"—whether employers illegally discriminate against whites when they give special preferences to minorities—returned to the nation's highest court Thursday.

The question presented itself in two appeals stemming from the job-discrimination lawsuit of Louisiana worker Brian F. Weber, a suit that poses a major threat to government efforts to improve employment opportunities for minorities.

Attorneys for Kaiser Aluminum & Chemical Co., Weber's employer, and the United Steelworkers Union asked the justices to overturn a lower court's ruling that federal law bars Kaiser from voluntarily setting up so-called affirmative action programs.

The Supreme Court, which begins its new term Oct. 2, is not expected to announce whether it will grant full review to the twin appeals until Weber's attorneys file written responses. They have 30 days in which to do so.

In a much-publicized decision last June, a deeply divided court ruled that the state-run medical school at the University of California at Davis illegally discriminated against Allan Bakke, who is white, when it denied him admission.

Bakke had charged that less-qualified applicants had been admitted ahead of him under the school's special program aimed at increasing its number of minority students.

Though the justices ordered the school to admit Bakke, they did not destroy the affirmative-action concept. They ruled that race may be considered as one of many factors in school admission decisions in order to assemble a diverse student population.

Because the decision was grounded in a federal law dealing with discrimination in education, it provided few clear signals on the court's view of similar, on-the-job affirmative action programs that affect millions of Americans.

Weber, a white employee of Kaiser's Gramercy, La., plant, sued the company in 1974 after being refused participation in a craft training program Kaiser had established at its 15 plants nationwide.

The program, approved in a company-union agreement, trained one black for each white for craft jobs with the goal of raising black representation in the higher-paying jobs.

> If trainees had been selected solely on a seniority basis, no blacks would have been included in the program at Gramercy.
>
> Weber's lawsuit charged that the selection of black workers with less seniority than he made him a victim of racial discrimination—in violation of the Civil Rights Act of 1964.
>
> A federal trial court and the 5th U.S. Circuit Court of Appeals ruled in Weber's favor.

Note the difference in issues between the Bakke and the Kaiser Aluminum cases. In Bakke, the issue was that a less qualified person was given priority over a more qualified. In Kaiser, the issue was seniority. Both, however, involved an admission or entry share for minorities.

Subsequent to the article in the *Los Angeles Times,* the United States Supreme Court agreed to hear the Weber versus Kaiser Aluminum and Chemical Corporation case. *Time Magazine* reported the case in its Christmas Day issue (December 25, 1978).*

Law

Bigger Than Bakke?

"Reverse discrimination" returns to the court

> The headline-grabbing Bakke decision last summer left open more questions about reverse discrimination than it answered. The Supreme Court outlawed explicit racial quotas for admission to universities receiving federal funds, while ruling that race could still be a factor in selecting applicants. But the court did not say how far employers could go with affirmative-action programs designed to give minorities a break, programs that often use quotas and also affect millions of workers.
>
> Last week the court decided to face that issue. It agreed to review the case of Brian Weber, 32, a white employee at the Gramercy, La., plant of Kaiser Aluminum & Chemical Corp. who had been rejected by a craft training program that reserved half its places for minorities. Weber sued Kaiser and his union, the United Steelworkers, and won: two federal courts ruled that under Title VII of the 1964 Civil Rights Act Kaiser cannot use racial quotas without proof that it discriminated in the past.

*Reprinted by permission from TIME, The Weekly Newsmagazine; Copyright Time Inc. 1978.

The lower courts reasoned that employers could use affirmative action only to remedy past wrongs. But making an employer show past discrimination puts the firm between a rock and a hard place. If an employer gives preference to nonwhite workers without admitting past errors, it opens itself up to suits from passed over white workers like Weber. But if the employer admits past discrimination, it invites suits for substantial back pay from nonwhites. Allowing the decision to stand, argued the Justice Department in its petition, "can be expected to chill voluntary affirmative-action programs throughout the country." The Equal Employment Opportunity Commission also disagrees with the Weber decision. The same day the high court decided to review the case, the EEOC announced final guidelines designed to encourage voluntary affirmative action.

Kaiser and the Steelworkers agreed to their affirmative-action program voluntarily, notes Yale Law School Professor Bruce Ackerman, but "with the Government looking over their shoulders." Fewer than 2% of the 273 skilled craft workers at the Kaiser plant where Weber works were black, while the surrounding area's work force was 39% black. Discrimination had been shown at two other Kaiser plants in Louisiana, and the company risked losing federal contracts. But Kaiser still insisted in the lower courts that there had been no past discrimination. Why? Because the company did not want to lay itself open to suits by black workers. "People are being made to feel that Kaiser would set up this kind of program even though it had not discriminated in the past," says EEOC Chief Eleanor Holmes Norton. "That's nonsense."

The EEOC and the Justice Department want the Weber case sent back so lower courts can reconsider evidence of Kaiser's past discrimination. But Weber, now a $20,000-a-year lab technician at the Kaiser plant, says he is optimistic about winning in the high court. If he does, he may become an even more important symbol than Allan Bakke. Unlike Bakke, who used to duck publicity, Weber says he doesn't mind "the notoriety." A loquacious Cajun and father of three who is fond of fishing, he likes to be photographed in his hard hat. In fact, Weber plans to go to Washington to hear his case argued in the Supreme Court's marble temple this winter. Says he: "I wouldn't miss it." ■

On June 27, 1979, the U.S. Supreme Court dismissed Weber's reverse discrimination suit by a vote of five to two, holding that private employers and unions may voluntarily adopt affirmative action plans that give special preference to blacks. The justices based their decision on the intent of the 1964 Civil Rights Act rather than on the 14th Amendment of the Constitution. The latter applies only to the conduct of government agencies, not to private employers.

Although the Court's decision is a major step in clarifying the legality of affirmative action plans, it probably does not put totally to rest the issue of reverse discrimination in the private employment arena. First of all, the Court did not say whether its decision is applicable to women or to minorities other than blacks. Secondly, Justice William J. Brennan, Jr. who wrote the majority opinion, listed three specific factors that made the Kaiser-USW program legal:

- It was designed to eliminate conspicuous racial imbalance in traditionally segregated job categories.
- It was only a temporary agreement, to end when the percentage of blacks in the skilled crafts category at the Kaiser Gramercy plant equaled their percentage in the general work force in the community.
- It did not require the firing of any white employees and did not create an absolute bar to the advancement of white workers.

The concept of the temporary character of the Kaiser training program is particularly interesting. At the Gramercy plant before 1974, blacks represented 1.83% of the skilled crafts category and 39% in the general Gramercy area work force (five blacks out of 273 total). Closing a gap of that magnitude will take a very long time.

Whether the issue of reverse discrimination has truly been settled, there is no question that affirmative action plans involving numerical goals have and will continue to be a major consideration in the EEO arena. It is a fertile field on which all stakeholders in the arena can join forces to attack the basic long-range problems associated with bettering the lot of women and minorities in the work world.

FIVE BASES FOR NUMERICAL OBJECTIVES

Fundamentally, numerical objectives can be set in five ways:

1. Share of hires.
2. Share of promotions.
3. Share of combined hires and promotions.
4. Representation at some point in the future.
5. Numerical count at some point in the future.

In chapter Four the argument was made that share is a more rational basis than some forecast percentage representation or numerical count at some future point. The mathematical a is compelling, and there is U.S. Supreme Court argum shares basis (see Chapter Ten). Yet, surprisingly, man action numerical goals are still set on the basis of prec representation.

For example (Chapter Twelve), the California State Department of Education Guidelines for Affirmative Action Programs (1975) call for the correction of "any identifiable deficiencies in representation from racial and ethnic minority groups at all employment levels" within all school districts. When translated into an affirmative action plan by a particular school district, the guidelines result ultimately in a forecasted number of women and minority workers at some future point. For example, one particular district states that the goal is "to have between 25 and 36 (minority) in teaching jobs and between 37 and 49 in nonteaching jobs by the year 1982–83."

This is a risky way to set goals, assuming they are intended to be meaningful and there is determination to meet them. Unless goals or numerical objectives are set on a shares basis, there can be considerable risk of missing the goals by a wide margin. In the example of the school district, suppose the anticipated opportunities for changing minority and women's representation do not materialize. Share becomes the dependent variable and may have to artificially exceed rational external labor market sourcing if the goal is to be met. For governmental bodies, not included in the Weber decision, excessive shares may pose serious reverse discrimination problems.

Numerical objectives based on share of combined hires and promotions have some advantages but also contain pitfalls. We will look at that in more detail later on when we examine and discuss the General Electric numerical objectives process.

THE EEOC SYSTEMIC THRUST

EEO efforts and results are measured by a number of agencies when they appear in the form of affirmative action plans. Overlaid on this relatively micro approach is the systemic thrust by the EEO Commission. The Commission has made it clear, even in the post-Bakke period, that it will continue to press aggressively for the "rightful place" of minorities and women in the labor force profiles of the larger, multi-division, multi-location corporations. Where patterns and practices that appear discriminatory occur more or less repeatedly throughout the corporation's holdings, a system-wide remedy will be sought. Instead of picking at the corporation location by location, the Commission will confront the corporate entity and hold it responsible for its component parts.

The systemic approach has solid logic to support it, flowing out of the Italian economist Vilfredo Pareto's treatment of maldistributions. Pareto found that very often a small number of the participants in an activity produce a dominant share of the results. American business and industry understand this concept very well. The Pareto concept (sometimes called the A-B-C principle) has been used successfully in a number of areas in marketing, inventory control, and simply personal time budgeting. "A" items typically represent 20% of the effort but account for 80% of the results. The EEOC, in its systemic thrust, is looking for the "A" items. How well this concept will work remains to be seen. In any event, it will require additional resources or at least a reallocation from individual case load work into system design, implementation, and monitoring. It also raises the level of complexity of the numerical objectives process by several orders as we will see when we subsequently discuss what was done in the G.E. systemic charge settlement.

Large corporations are used to thinking, planning, and doing in terms of systems. They are also very much accustomed to setting and meeting numerical objectives in matters of sales and profits. But success doesn't come by guesswork. It comes from extremely careful planning based upon the best available data, by carefully establishing plans for the business and a structure for implementing the plans. Tradeoffs are carefully evaluated. When an annual business plan finally emerges, its implementation depends upon system and subsystem designs with effective monitoring and feedback loops.

Businesses that are based on "wish lists" rather than hard data don't last very long. Perhaps this is the link pin to setting numerical objectives for equal employment opportunity. Government and industry need to agree at the outset that "wish lists" are ruled out—the best principles of system design are ruled in.

It could be argued that in the long run the systemic approach will not be as fruitful as approaching EEO progress on an SMSA by SMSA basis (Chapter Thirteen). But it is now a major thrust of the Commission, and large corporations will have to deal with it.

THE GENERAL ELECTRIC NUMERICAL OBJECTIVES PROCESS

The General Electric conciliation agreement resulting from the 1973 Commissioner's Track I charge contains an interesting approach to setting numerical objectives. Caution needs to be observed in extending the formulas and the process to other systemic situations, because this was indeed a custom-tailored settlement related specifically to the great size, diversity, and complexity of General Electric. But this particular numerical objectives approach is a good example of how a reasonable search for common ground can result in generally satisfying the interests of the many stakeholders in a specific EEO arena.* How useful this particular process may prove to be, in whole or part, to other major employers remains to be seen. But it does merit in-depth discussion to illustrate that even massive, seemingly unsolvable complexities can be reduced to a manageable system, if EEO dynamics are approached in an analytical fashion, reducing intuitive judgments to a minimum.

The numerical objectives portion of the G.E. decree has these basic elements:

- The work force at each company division location with 100 or more employees is divided into ten work zones by carefully prescribed decision rules. (143 locations are listed in Appendix D of the agreement.)
- External labor markets for male minorities and women for six of the work zones were determined by decision rules not spelled out in the decree. (These results are displayed in Appendix D of the agreement.)
- Internal labor markets are determined by carefully prescribed decision rules. When these are applied, the result is a percentage of minorities or women which is then used in a numerical objectives formula. The question of whether minority and women's share of promotions should be greater than, equal to, or less than their representation in the supplying work zone is reduced to several macro formulas. Ideally, as was discussed in Chapter Eight, one might set out to study the effect of qualifications, seniority, and interest on minority and women's expected share of hires and promotions. A number of such studies were in fact made, enough to form the basis for confidence in the realism and fairness of the formulas when applied system-wide.
- Several different formulas appear in the agreement. The applicable formula defines a share of total opportunities (the sum of hires and promotions) for entry into a particular work zone. In this numerical objectives process, movements within a work zone or into a lower work zone do not count as opportunities. The share of opportunities concept is a cornerstone of the agreement. No future representation targets are defined nor is there a projection of the results that the numerical objectives might produce in the future. The approach is

*See Appendix C.

Numerical Objectives Formulas

N.O. = $E + .2I$	N.O. = $1.9E$
N.O. = $2E$	N.O. = $2.3E$
N.O. = $1.5E$	N.O. = $0.5E$
N.O. = $1.2E$	N.O. = $0.5I$

FIGURE 1.

strictly limited to shares of opportunities on an annual basis over the five-year life of the agreement.

Numerical objectives are established for male minorities and women for eight of the 10 work zones at each G.E. division with more than 100 employees. These local objectives are aggregated on a weighted basis to the total company level for purposes of measurement and tracking.

The formulas used are listed in Figure 1. The symbol E is used to represent the percent of male minorities or women in the external labor market; similarly, the symbol I represents the percent of male minorities or women in the internal labor market. When calculations are made, the result is the numerical objective (N.O.) expressed as a percentage share.

In most instances, several formulas may be applicable, but the one yielding the highest result is used.

As an aside, it is apparent that the use of a family of formulas is a practical mechanism for recognizing the imprecision associated with sizing external labor markets in general and internal labor markets in a company as diverse as General Electric.

- There are decision rules that specify whether a numerical objective is necessary. Although the numerical objectives are based upon a share of opportunities, the need for one is based upon a comparison of male minority or women's representation with either the external or internal market, depending upon the circumstances. The decision rules describe how this comparison is to be made and interpreted.

THE BASIC FORMULA

The formula N.O. = $E + .2I$ is one of the main themes in the numerical objectives process. As an example of how the formula works, let's assume that for a particular work zone, it has been determined that for women E equals 10% and I equals 20%. This particular formula yields a result of 14% for the numerical objective. If there were 50 hires and 50 promotions into the work zone, the 14% share would be applied to a total of 100 opportunities. The result would be 14 women additions to the work zone. However, there is no specification about how many will come from promotions, and how many will come as external hires.

Why use this particular formula? Is there a logic pattern behind it or was it simply plucked from the sky? Let's take a closer look.

There is an algebraic solution to the problem of designing a formula that applies to total opportunities rather than formulas which apply separately to external hires and promotions.

Let V = total jobs to be filled
S = decimal share of jobs filled by internal hires
$1 - S$ = decminal share of jobs filled by external promotions
E = external women's market, percent
I = internal women's market, percent
$N.O.$ = numerical objective applied to V.

For equivalency between the two approaches, we can set the result obtained from one to equal that obtained from the other. The outcome is the equation that should logically be used to set numerical objectives on the basis of total opportunities.

Total Women Additions Combined Basis	=	Women External Hires	+	Women Internal Promotions

$$N.O. \times V = (1 - S) \times E \times V + S \times I \times V$$

This equation reduces to:

$$N.O. = (1 - S) \times E + S \times I$$

If we knew ahead of time the exact value of S for a coming year and used that value in the equation, as far as total additions to a work zone are concerned, it wouldn't make any difference whether we used a composite or a separate hires and promotions approach.

For example, if 100 total opportunities were divided equally between external hires and internal promotions into a work zone, the value for the variable S would be 0.5. Note that this value is independent of race, sex or ethnic considerations. It merely reflects the way in which the employer satisfies job-filling needs. Suppose the value for E is 10% and for I is 20%. Women should get 10% of 50 hires and 20% of 50 promotions, for a total of 15 additions to the work zone. On the composite basis, the equation would read:

$$N.O. = 0.5E + 0.5I$$

The share of total opportunities would be 15%, resulting in a total of 15 women.

Usually, the split of total opportunities between external hires and internal promotions (mathematically, the value for S) is difficult to predict. Although the equation is theoretically correct, it is not really very practical in application unless the split or the S value can be accurately forecast. What are the alternatives? In this case, General Electric wanted to stay with a numerical objectives process based on total opportunities for two reasons. First of all, there is only one total measurement instead of two separate ones for hires and promotions. That simplifies the monitoring and reporting activities. Secondly, management has the freedom to determine where it can best meet both business and conciliation agreement objectives.

In attempting to use the theoretically correct equation, one alternative is to estimate the split or the S value at the start of a year, set numerical objectives on that basis, and then at the end of the year evaluate what actually happened. This is an almost unmanageable process. Another alternative is to depart from the purely theoretical and establish an equation satisfactory to both the EEOC and the employer, but an equation which stays close to the theoretically correct concept.

The latter approach is the one that emerged in the General Electric settlement. The theoretical equation can be rewritten as:

$$N.O. = aE + bI$$

where a and b are merely numerical coefficients. Theoretically, b is equal to S and a is equal to $1 - S$. In reality, since S is too difficult to approximate each year, the coefficients a and b are given some fixed values on a negotiated basis. What should those values reasonably be? It seems rational that the value for a should not be less than 1.0. Otherwise, an employer who has no minority or women workers in the internal supply source ($I = 0$) could hire them externally at a share smaller than their actual representation in the labor market. For b in the General Electric settlement, the value was set at 0.2. The reasons for this particular decision will become clearer in subsequent discussion. As a result of shifting from the theoretical to a more practical working basis, the goal setting formula becomes:

$$N.O. = E + 0.2I$$

This is one of the primary formulas in the General Electric settlement.

ADDITIONAL FORMULAS

It is simply too much to expect that the numerical objectives for an EEO system of the magnitude of that within General Electric can be reduced to a single formula. Others were developed as in-depth studies illuminated problems or needs that could not be attended to by $E + .2I$. Interestingly enough, only one of these ($N.O. = 0.5I$) contains an internal market term. All of the others are keyed directly to the external market ($1.2E$, $1.5E$, $2.0E$, etc.). They can be viewed as:

- External markets with affirmative action multipliers.
- External markets defined by standardized decision rules but corrected by coefficients rather than by changes in the decision rules.
- Some combination of the above.

All of the formulas attempt to help the company stay on a path bounded by aggressive affirmative action on one side and realistic doable achievements on the other.

Several formulas may be applicable to a particular work zone. The one that yields the highest value in any particular case determines the numerical objective. For example, when $E = 10\%$ and $I = 50\%$, the formula $0.5I$ would take precedence over $E + .2I$, because it yields a higher value for the numerical objective as shown below:

$$N.O. = E + .2I = 20\%$$

$$N.O. = 0.5I = 25\%$$

Regardless of which formula is applicable, it is important to remind ourselves again that the numerical objective is a percentage share of the sum of external hiring and internal promotions into a particular work zone. The manager who is filling a job has the flexibility of sourcing male minorities or women from any combination of external and internal sources. This feature of numerical objectives process makes it difficult to understand the implications of the formulas without an in-depth examination of what they produce under different sets of circumstances.

Let's take a detailed look at three formulas:

$$N.O. = 0.5I$$
$$N.O. = E + .2I$$
$$N.O. = 1.5E$$

For the sake of consistency in discussion, the numerical objective for women in Work Zone IX will be used. The value of E is assumed to be 15%. The value for I will be changed to show the applicability and results for each formula.

WHEN NUMERICAL OBJECTIVE = 0.5*I*

The 0.5I formula assures that the numerical objective applied to total opportunities will never be less than half of the percentage representation of women in the internal labor market. For simplification, let's assume that the internal labor market consists of all of the people in the next lower work zone. This will not always be the case, because the decision rules for defining internal labor markets sometimes result in something less than the total population in the supplying work zone. What we have, for purposes of illustration, is Work Zone IX, which consists of semi-skilled workers such as precision machine operators, being supplied by an internal market which consists of unskilled entry jobs and an external market of semi-skilled workers.

The 0.5I formula does not mean that women's share of promotions into Work Zone IX will only be half of their representation in Work Zone X. The actual share depends, first of all, on how total additions to Work Zone IX are divided between external hires and internal promotions. Secondly, it depends upon how the job-filling manager exercises the flexibility to source women externally or internally as long as the combined objective is met.

Let's look at a specific numerical example as displayed in Figure 2.

There are 100 total additions to Work Zone IX of which 50 are external hires and 50 are promotions. Women constitute 15% of the external market (E = 15%) and 60% of the internal market (I = 60%). The numerical objective is equal to 0.5I or 30%. When this share is applied to the total additions, the result is an expected 30 women additions to Work Zone IX. How many of these will come

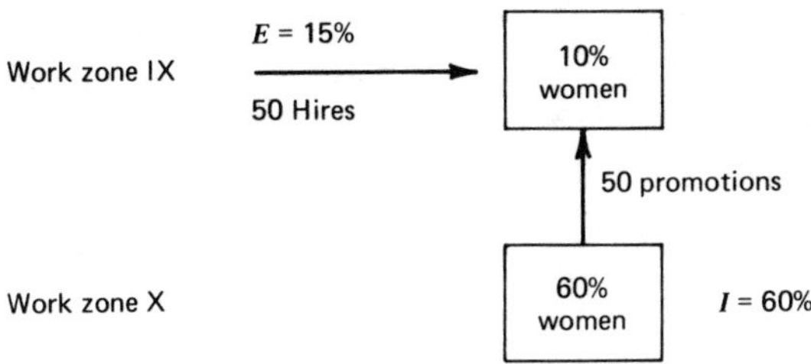

FIGURE 2.

as external hires and how many as promotions from Work Zone X? There are many possible answers.

Suppose that the job-filling manager is able to achieve 15% women out of the 50 external hires. Rounded, this would be eight women hired from external sources. But since the numerical objective calls for 30 women in total, the balance of 22 must be obtained from promotions out of Work Zone X. Since there were 50 promotions, the women's share turns out to be 44% even though their representation in the supply source is 60%.

On the other hand, suppose the job-filling manager is unable to hire any women from external sources. The 30 women needed to satisfy the numerical objective must all come from the internal source in Work Zone X. Since there were 50 promotions, the women's share turns out to be 60%, exactly equal to their representation in the supply source.

The possible combinations of results are almost endless. Later on we can do a generalization which will be a helpful overview of the possible range of results. For the moment, we should note that share of promotions in this example is a *dependent* variable. This is the result of setting numerical objectives on the basis of total additions rather than separately for hires and promotions. In the micro case of a single plant, one could attempt to predetermine promotion share by careful internal market analysis, considering such factors as qualifications, interest, and seniority. At best, there would be considerable imprecision in the result. In the macro approach to a systemic settlement, there is a tradeoff of imprecisions—that associated with specific plant studies vis-a-vis that inherent in reducing the total system to one or more formulas. In the G.E. settlement, the formulas were developed to approximate the flow which can be expected from a truly open nondiscriminatory system. The numerical objectives which result are not quotas but merely a best estimate of what can reasonably be expected to happen. Manageable macro settlements must inevitably contain some compromises and approximations of this nature. They are a basic part of the search for common ground from which to move forward in the EEO arena.

A GENERALIZATION OF THE 0.5I FORMULA

Because share of promotions is a dependent variable, there can be extreme situations where it is too high or too low compared to reality. Its mathematical relationship to the other variables is extremely important and worth examination in detail. On one hand, it could result in expected shares that are unrealistic; on the other, it could result in less than what is actually doable.

Let's generalize the numerical example discussed in connection with Figure 2. Some total number of opportunities for addition to Work Zone IX occur because of losses, growth, and promotions out of the work zone. These total additions are divided into external hires and internal promotions. But the 0.5I formula is applied to total additions, and there is the further option of how to subdivide the women additions between hires and promotions. All of this can be expressed mathematically using the following nomenclature:

- S = fraction of total opportunities for Work Zone IX which are internal promotions independent of race, sex or ethnic considerations.
- I = women percentage representation in the internal market, decimal fraction.
- X_F = fraction of total women additions to Work Zone IX which come from external hiring.
- K = a coefficient which describes women's share of promotions in relationship to their representation in the internal market.
- V_T = total additions to the work zone.

The mathematical relationships are

$$\text{Women Hires} = \text{Women Promotions} + \text{Total Women Additions}$$

$$X_F(.5I)V_T + K \times I \times S \times V_T = (.5I)V_t$$

This expression reduces to:

$$K = \frac{0.5(1 - X_F)}{S}$$

There are limits to the value of X_F. It cannot exceed 1.0, nor can it exceed $\frac{(1 - S)}{.5I}$. These limits merely describe the practical fact that for the numerical objective to be met exactly, 100% of the total need satisfied by external hires is as far as one can go. Similarly, there is some point at which *total* external additions are too low to permit 100% satisfaction of the women's numerical objective by external hires. For example, if there are only 20 external hires in total, but the numerical objective for women turns out to be 30, all of the need cannot be satisfied externally.

A useful way to examine this relationship is to show the values for X_F and S which yield a K value of 1.0. This is shown in Figure 3.

The shaded area shows where unrealistic estimates of the promotion shares expected from a truly open personnel system could possibly arise. For all points in the shaded area, the women's share of promotions must be greater than their representation in the internal market, if the numerical objective is to be met. Similarly, the unshaded area shows the circumstances under which women's share of promotions is something less than their representation in the internal market. For additional perspective, the lines for K values of 0.5 and 0 are shown. As a quick rule of thumb, as long as the total additions (independent of race, sex or ethnic considerations) are divided so that more than half are promotions, the women's share of promotions will be less than their representation in the supplying work zone.

As a numerical example, suppose that for the data in Figure 2, the 100 total additions were divided into 10 external hires and 90 promotions. The numerical objective would still be 30. If three women were hired externally, the value for X_F would be 0.10. The value for

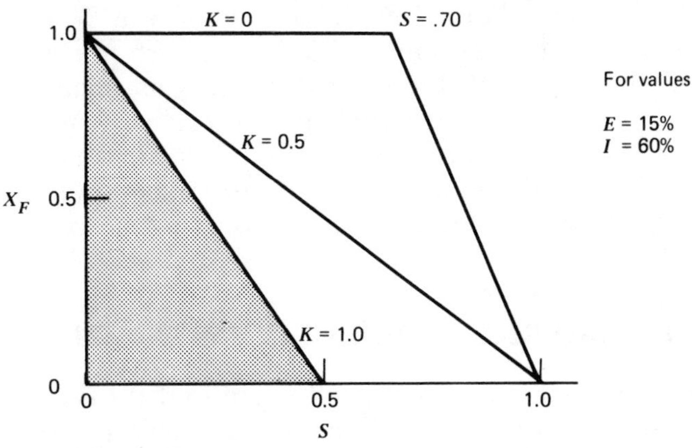

FIGURE 3.

S is 0.9. If this point is located on the graph in Figure 3, it falls in the unshaded portion, roughly on the line where K has a value of only 0.5. Note also that if all total additions come from promotions, women's share of promotions will be half of their representation in the supplying work zone.

Some additional observations can be made based on Figure 3. It seems clear that the $0.5I$ numerical objective was not designed to reduce concentrations of women at entry level. Rather it was designed to improve representation at the next higher level. For those division locations where there are concentrations of women in Work Zone X, the discussion in earlier chapters is relevant. Such concentrations cannot be reduced without attempting to artificially control the women's share of external hires at entry level. This is something of a paradox because, presumably, one of the bases for the Track I charge was observed concentrations of women in Work Zone X (hourly entry level) in some of the light manufacturing operations. If General Electric continues to be an attractive employer for women in Work Zone X in a number of locations (as it historically has been), and if the personnel systems behave as predicted by the formulas, some concentrations of women at entry level will still exist after the five-year life of the settlement. Both the company and the Commission need to remind themselves of this potential reality now so that it will not surface as a surprise at a later date.

It should be observed also that the hiring manager would do well to see that the value for S (the fraction of total additions which are internal promotions) does not fall below 0.5. If it does and external hiring produces few if any women, the K factor falls into the shaded area of Figure 3 and the numerical objective is an unrealistic one.

Also, it has been argued that external hiring practices could deliberately place men in Work Zone IX and women in Work Zone X. The numerical objectives formula discourages such practices. As the relative number of external hires increases (S gets smaller), and the relative number of women external hires decreases (X_F gets smaller), the value of K moves in the direction of the lower left-hand corner of the graph. The formula in itself does not guarantee a nondiscriminatory personnel system, but at least it works in the reinforcement direction.

WHEN NUMERICAL OBJECTIVE = $E + .2I$

If the data displayed in Figure 2 are changed so that I is not 60% but only 40%, the formula $N.O. = E + .2I$ is the applicable one because it yields a higher value than $0.5I$.

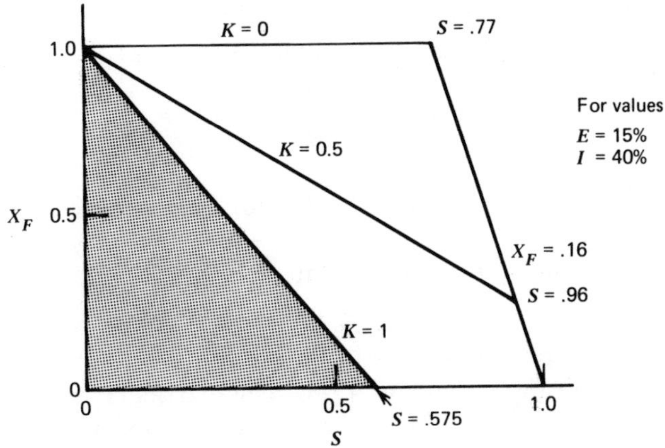

FIGURE 4.

This formula can be generalized to produce a graph similar to that in Figure 3. The general equation is

$$K = \left(\frac{E}{IS} + \frac{.2}{S}\right)(1 - X_F)$$

Note that the ratio $\frac{E}{I}$ is a factor in the equation. There are also limits to the value for X_F. It cannot exceed 1.0 nor can it exceed $\frac{(1 - S)}{E + .2I}$. Figure 4 shows the results of this equation for a value of $\frac{E}{I}$ $= \frac{15}{40} = .375$.

A comparison of Figures 3 and 4 shows only small differences. The shaded area where unrealistic numerical objectives could arise is only slightly larger in Figure 4. The discussion applicable to Figure 3 would be generally applicable in this new set of circumstances.

WHEN NUMERICAL OBJECTIVE = 1.5*E*

If the data displayed in Figure 2 are changed so that *I* is only 15%, the formula *N.O.* = 1.5*E* is the applicable one. The representation of women in Work Zone X is relatively low. This might be the case in a heavy manufacturing operation.

The formula can be generalized to produce a graph similar to those in Figures 3 and 4. The general equation is

$$K = \frac{1.5E(1 - X_F)}{IS}$$

The value of X_F cannot exceed 1.0, nor can it exceed $\frac{(1 - S)}{1.5E}$. Figure 5 shows the results of this equation for a value of $\frac{E}{I} = \frac{15}{15} =$ 1.0.

Note how sharply the results in Figure 5 differ from those for the other formulas in Figures 3 and 4. For this particular set of data, the job-filling manager doesn't have a great deal of unshaded area within which to operate. For example, suppose $I = 15\%$, $E = 15\%$, and 100 total additions are split equally between hires and promotions. The numerical objective is 23% (rounded). The manager can't possible meet the objective without exceeding fair share either externally or internally. From a 15% external supply, the normally expected yield out of 50 hires would be 8 women. Similarly, from a 15% internal supply, the normally expected yield out of 50 promotions would be 8 women. On a combined basis, the manager would have added only 16 women out of a total need of 23. The needed difference can be obtained only by exceeding the normally expected results in one or both of the labor markets.

From this illustration we can see where the convenience and flexibility in setting numerical objectives on a total additions basis can be

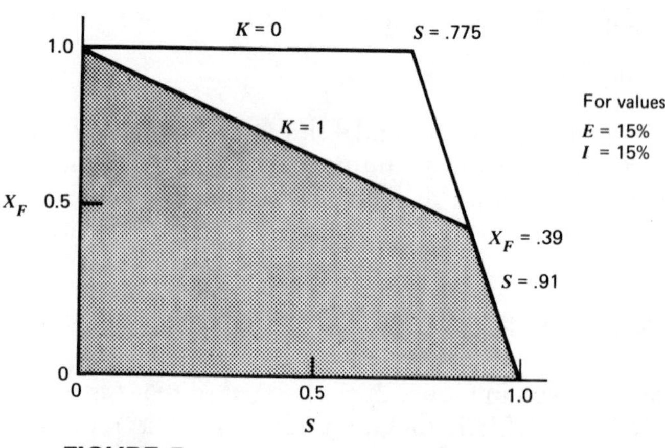

FIGURE 5.

offset by the hazards in letting share become a dependent variable. When the 1.5E formula is operative, the job-filling manager may run into problems from two directions simultaneously—the external market on one hand and the internal market on the other. This example also brings to light the hazard in casually applying affirmative action multipliers to an external labor market. What appears to be a 1.5 multiplier on the external labor supply can in reality be much higher, depending upon how the opportunities are divided between hires and promotions, independent of race, sex or ethnic considerations. For example, if 100 opportunities are equally split between hires and promotions, and the internal supply of women is zero, the manager must actually triple the external market share in order to meet a 1.5E objective. The need would be 23 women out of only 50 external hires, or a 46% share compared to a 15% source.

WHEN ARE NUMERICAL OBJECTIVES NECESSARY?

In the General Electric settlement, a choice of formulas is generally available for each work zone. For example, for women in Work Zones VII through X, the formulas shown in Figure 6 are applicable.

The formula to be used is the one that yields the highest answer for the numerical objective.

In deciding whether or not it is necessary to set a numerical objective, two decision rules (with minor exceptions) are used.

- When the formula 0.5I is the governing one, a numerical objective is necessary only when the women's representation in the work zone is less than 0.5I.

Work Zone	Formula
VII, VIII	$E + .2I$ $2E$ $0.5I$
IX	$E + .2I$ $1.5E$ $0.5I$
X	$1.2E$

FIGURE 6.

Work Zone	% Rep	% E	% I
VII	2	2	4
VIII	4	4	13
IX	13	13	40
X	40	40	—

FIGURE 7.

- When a formula other than $0.5I$ is the governing one, a numerical objective is needed only when the women's representation in the work zone is less than E.

To illustrate the application of these rules, suppose we have the data array for women shown in Figure 7.

No numerical objectives are necessary, because the formula $0.5I$ is not the governing one for any of the work zones, and in each instance the women's representation equals the value for E. If a General Electric division location maintained this distribution throughout the five-year life of the agreement, it would not have to set any numerical objectives. On the other hand, the data display in Figure 8 would require a numerical objective for Work Zone IX, but not for the others.

For Work Zone IX, the $0.5I$ formula is the governing one and the representation is less than $0.5I$. The only difference between Figures 7 and 8 is a 10 percentage point differential for women's representation in Work Zone IX. Yet the division location portrayed in Figure 8 has in reality set into motion a domino effect which, if time permitted, would ultimately require numerical objectives for all four work zones. The manager must set numerical objectives for Work Zone IX until the representation reaches 25%. But when that hap-

Work Zone	% Rep	% E	% I
VII	2	2	4
VIII	4	4	13
IX	13	13	50
X	50	40	—

FIGURE 8.

Work Zone	% Rep	% *E*	% *I*
VII	6.25	2	12.5
VIII	12.5	4	25
IX	25	13	50
X	50	40	—

FIGURE 9.

pens, the internal market for Work Zone VIII is increased so that the $0.5I$ formula is the governing one. Theoretically, numerical objectives would be required until the distribution reaches that shown in Figure 9.

It isn't likely that this theoretical domino effect would prevail within the relatively short time span of a five-year agreement, but the principle still remains the same. Although the option might not really be a practical one, the manager in Figure 8 could theoretically reduce the women's representation in Work Zone X to 40% and avoid the necessity for any further numerical objectives per the rationale for Figure 7.

For the general Electric Company, the disparity in numerical objectives requirements for the managers involved in Figures 7 and 8 is a matter that can be explained and handled internally. It simply is one of the inevitable anomalies that will occur in systemic charge settlements involving companies as diverse and complex as General Electric. The EEO Commission was very careful to point out that this particular settlement is not to be construed as precedent setting. Other employers need to be very careful that they do not base their EEO plans and approaches on the anomalies rather than the substance of the G.E. settlement.

In the micro, nonsystemic view, employers with profiles such as those in Figures 7 and 8 should be reading a signal that some careful analysis of EEO performance and practices is called for. As was discussed earlier, no really valid conclusions can be drawn from static snapshots. But they surely can signal the need for a closer look.

SUMMARY

1. EEO numerical objectives have generally become a way of life for a very large number of employers. They may take the micro form as in the case of local affirmative action plans, or the macro form in the larger corporations either voluntarily or in conciliated response to charges of systemic discrimination. As the EEO Commission continues and most likely expands its systemic thrust, some major corporations will find themselves setting numerical objectives in both the micro and macro modes. The complexity increases by several orders of magnitude as the basis for numerical objectives shifts from the micro to the macro.

2. In either form, the desired outcome of numerical objectives is a change in work force profile in some way or other more favorable to minorities and women. Even in view of this end purpose, share of opportunities is a more rational basis than some forecast of future representation.

3. For private employers, the United States Supreme Court decision in the Weber case has given added impetus to the goal setting process. Whether the issue of reverse discrimination has been put completely to rest is still an unanswered question.

4. The General Electric Company's numerical objectives process detailed in a conciliation agreement with the EEOC is a good example of an effective mutual search for common EEO ground. As complex and diversified as all of the considerations had to be, the Commission and the company arrived at a manageable process which is well founded in carefully done analytical work. Caution needs to be observed in recognizing the customized solution, unique to General Electric and nonprecedent-setting for other employers. The conciliation agreement illustrates some of the compromises inherent in a macro approach. For example, combining hires and promotions and setting numerical objectives on a composite basis has administrative advantages. However, it makes the women-minority share of promotions (or hires) a dependent variable. Ideally, when numerical objectives are based on share of opportunities, promotions and hires should be separate categories. In the practical world at the systemic level, one often has to forego the ideal as in this instance. But composite goal formulas must be very carefully structured, or they may fail to serve their purpose of approximating the flow to be reasonably expected from an open, nondiscriminatory personnel system.

5. A great deal of research needs to be done in the numerical objectives arena to establish meaningful guidelines on when they are needed and what they are expected to accomplish. Mathematical exploration of the General Electric process is helpful in this regard. But that is only one illustration in a vast and complex arena.

CHAPTER TEN

Statistical Disparities

In June, 1977, Justice Potter Stewart delivered the majority opinion of the Supreme Court in the case of Hazelwood School District versus the United States. This opinion is of particular importance for four reasons:

1. It emphasizes the importance of analyzing cases of discrimination on a share of opportunities basis.
2. There is some excellent discussion on appropriate ways to assess labor markets.
3. Some statistical methods for analyzing apparent EEO disparities are discussed in some detail.
4. There is an error (footnoted) in statistical methodology which, although not critical to the decision in the Hazelwood Case, can have serious implications for future cases.

Although the following excerpts from Justice Stewart's opinion are lengthy, they are helpful in gaining perspective on how EEO law is evolving.

QUOTING FROM JUSTICE STEWART*

The petitioner Hazelwood School District covers 78 square miles in the northern part of St. Louis County, Missouri. In 1973 the Attorney General brought this lawsuit against Hazelwood and various of its officials, alleging that they were engaged in a "pattern or practice" of employment discrimination in violation of Title VII of the Civil Rights Act of 1964, as amended. . . . The complaint asked for an

*All case quotations are from B.N.A., Daily Labor Report.

injunction requiring Hazelwood to cease its discriminatory practices, to take affirmative steps to obtain qualified Negro faculty members, and to offer employment and give backpay to victims of past illegal discrimination.

Hazelwood was formed from 13 rural school districts between 1949 and 1951 by a process of annexation. By the 1967–68 school year, 17,550 students were enrolled in the district, of whom only 59 were Negro; the number of Negro pupils increased to 576 of 25,166 in 1972–73, a total of just over 2%.

From the beginning, Hazelwood followed relatively unstructured procedures in hiring its teachers. Every person requesting an application for a teaching position was sent one and completed applications were submitted to a central personnel office, where they were kept on file. During the early 1960s, the personnel office notified all applicants whenever a teaching position became available, but as the number of applications on file increased in the late 1960s and early 1970s, this practice was no longer considered feasible. The personnel office thus began the practice of selecting anywhere from three to ten applicants for interviews at the school where the vacancy existed. The personnel office did not substantively screen the applicants in determining which of them to send for interviews, other than to ascertain that each applicant, if selected, would be eligible for state certification by the time he began the job. Generally, those who had most recently submitted applications were most likely to be chosen for interviews.

Interviews were conducted by a department chairman, program coordinator, or the principal at the school where the teaching vacancy existed. Although those conducting the interviews did fill out forms rating the applicants in a number of respects, it is undisputed that each school principal possessed virtually unlimited discretion in hiring teachers for his school. The only general guidance given to the principals was to hire the "most competent" person available, and such intangibles as "personality, disposition, appearance, poise, voice, articulation, and ability to deal with people" counted heavily. The principal's choice was routinely honored by Hazelwood's superintendent and Board of Education.

In the early 1960s, Hazelwood found it necessary to recruit new teachers, and for that purpose members of its staff visited a number of colleges and universities in Missouri and bordering states. All the institutions visited were predominantly white, and Hazelwood did not seriously recruit at either of the two predominantly Negro four-year colleges in Missouri. As a buyer's market began to develop for public school teachers, Hazelwood curtailed its recruiting efforts. For the 1971–72 school year, 3127 persons applied for only 234 teaching vacancies; for the 1972–73 school year, there were 2373 applications for 282 vacancies. A number of the applicants who were not hired were Negroes.

Hazelwood hired its first Negro teacher in 1969. The number of Negro faculty members gradually increased in successive years: six of 957 in the 1970 school year; 16 of 1107 by the end of the 1972 school year; 22 of 1231 in the 1973 school year. By comparison, according to 1970 census figures, of more than 10,000 teachers employed in that year in the St. Louis area, 15.4% were Negro. That percentage figure included the St. Louis City School District, which in recent years has followed a policy of attempting to maintain a 50% Negro teaching staff. Apart from that school district, 5.7% of the teachers in the county were Negro in 1970.

Drawing upon these historical facts, the Government mounted its "pattern or practice" attack in the District Court upon four different fronts. It adduced evidence of (1) a history of alleged racially discriminatory practices, (2) statistical disparities in hiring, (3) the standardless and largely subjective hiring procedures, and (4) specific instances of alleged discrimination against 55 unsuccessful Negro applicants for teaching jobs. Hazelwood offered virtually no additional evidence in response, relying instead on evidence introduced by the Government, perceived deficiencies in the Government's case, and its own officially promulgated policy "to hire all teachers on the basis of training, preparation, and recommendations, regardless of race, color, or creed."

The District Court ruled that the Government had failed to establish a pattern or practice of discrimination. The court was unpersuaded by the alleged history of discrimination, noting that no dual school system had ever existed in Hazelwood. The statistics showing that relatively small numbers of Negroes were employed as teachers were found nonprobative, on the ground that the percentage of Negro pupils in Hazelwood was similarly small. The court found nothing illegal or suspect in the teacher hiring procedures that Hazelwood had followed. Finally, the court reviewed the evidence in the 55 cases of alleged individual discrimination, and after stating that the burden of proving intentional discrimination was on the Government, it found that this burden had not been sustained in a single instance. Hence, the court entered judgment for the defendants. . . .

The Court of Appeals for the Eighth Circuit reversed. After suggesting that the District Court had assigned inadequate weight to evidence of discriminatory conduct on the part of Hazelwood before the effective date of Title VII, the Court of Appeals rejected the trial court's analysis of the statistical data as resting on an irrelevant comparison of

Negro teachers to Negro pupils in Hazelwood. The proper comparison, in the appellate court's view, was one between Negro teachers in Hazelwood and Negro teachers in the relevant labor market area. Selecting St. Louis County and St. Louis City as the relevant area, the Court of Appeals compared the 1970 census figures, showing that 15.4% of teachers in that area were Negro, to the racial composition of Hazelwood's teaching staff. In the 1972–73 and 1973–74 school years, only 1.4% and 1.8%, respectively, of Hazelwood's teachers were Negroes. This statistical disparity, particularly when viewed against the background of the teacher hiring procedures that Hazelwood had followed, was held to constitute a prima facie case of a pattern or practice of racial discrimination.

In addition, the Court of Appeals reasoned that the trial court had erred in failing to measure the 55 instances in which Negro applicants were denied jobs against the four-part standard for establishing a prima facie case of individual discrimination set out in this court's opinion in *McDonnell Douglas Corp. v. Green*, . . . Applying that standard, the appellate court found 16 cases of individual discrimination, which "buttressed" the statistical proof. Because Hazelwood had not rebutted the Government's prima facie case of a pattern or practice of racial discrimination, the Court of Appeals directed judgment for the Government and prescribed the remedial order to be entered. . . .

We granted certiorari.—U.S.—to consider a substantial question affecting the enforcement of a pervasive federal law. . . .

. . . .

The Court of Appeals totally disregarded the possibility that this prima facie statistical proof in the record might at the trial court level be rebutted by statistics dealing with Hazelwood's hiring after it became subject to Title VII. Racial discrimination by public employers was not made illegal under Title VII until March 24, 1972. A public employer who from that date forward made all its employment decisions in a wholly nondiscriminatory way would not violate Title VII even if it had formerly maintained an all-white work force by purposefully excluding Negroes. For this reason, the court cautioned in the *Teamsters* opinion that once a prima facie case has been established by statistical work force disparities, the employer must be given an opportunity to show "that the claimed discriminatory pattern is a product of pre-Act hiring rather than unlawful post-Act discrimination."

The record in this case showed that for the 1972–73 school year, Hazelwood hired 282 new teachers, 10 of whom (3.5%) were Negroes; for the following school year it hired 123 new teachers, five of whom (4.1%) were Negroes. Over the two-year period, Negroes constituted a total of 15 of the 405 new teachers hired (3.7%). Although the Court of Appeals briefly mentioned these data in reciting the facts, it wholly ignored them in discussing whether the Government had shown a pattern or practice of discrimination. And it gave no consideration at all to the possibility that post-Act data as to the number of Negroes hired compared to the total number of Negro applicants might tell a totally different story.

What the hiring figures prove obviously depends upon the figures to which they are compared. The Court of Appeals accepted the Government's argument that the relevant comparison was to the labor market area of St. Louis County and St. Louis City, in which, according to the 1970 census, 15.4% of all teachers were Negro. The propriety of that comparison was vigorously disputed by the petitioners, who urged that because the City of St. Louis has made special attempts to maintain a 50% Negro teaching staff, inclusion of that school district in the relevant market area distorts the comparison. Were that argument accepted, the percentage of Negro teachers in the relevant labor market area (St. Louis County alone) as shown in the 1970 census would be 5.7% rather than 15.4%.

The difference between these figures may well be important; the disparity between 3.7% (the percentage of Negro teachers hired by Hazelwood in 1972–73 and 1973–74) and 5.7% may be sufficiently small to weaken the Government's other proof, while the disparity between 3.7% and 15.4% may be sufficiently large to reinforce it. In determining which of the two figures—or very possibly, what intermediate figure—provides the most accurate basis for comparison to the hiring figures at Hazelwood, it will be necessary to evaluate such considerations as (i) whether the racially based hiring policies of the St. Louis City School District were in effect as far back as 1970, the year in which the census figures were taken; (ii) to what extent those policies have changed the racial composition of that district's teaching staff from what it would otherwise have been; (iii) to what extent St. Louis' recruitment policies have diverted to the city teachers who might otherwise have applied to Hazelwood; (iv) to what extent Negro teachers employed by the city would prefer employment in other districts such as Hazelwood; and (v) what the experience in other school districts in St. Louis County indicates about the validity of excluding the City School District from the relevant labor market.*

It is thus clear that a determination of the appropriate comparative figures in this case will depend upon further evaluation by the trial court. As this Court admonished in *Teamsters*, "statistics . . . come in infinite variety. . . . (T)heir usefulness depends on all of the surrounding facts and circumstances." . . . Only the trial court is in a position to make the appropriate determination after further findings. And only

*At this point a significant statistical footnote was made.

after such a determination is made can a foundation be established for deciding whether or not Hazelwood engaged in a pattern or practice of racial discrimination in its employment practices in violation of the law.

We hold, therefore, that the Court of Appeals erred in disregarding the post-Act hiring statistics in the record, and that it should have remanded the case to the District Court for further findings as to the relevant labor market area and for an ultimate determination of whether Hazelwood engaged in a pattern or practice of employment discrimination after March 24, 1972. Accordingly, the judgment is vacated, and the case is remanded to the District Court for further proceedings consistent with this opinion. It is so ordered.

FOOTNOTE TO JUSTICE STEWART'S OPINION

The following footnote, among many others, appears in the decision:

A precise method of measuring the significance of such statistical disparities was explained in *Castaneda vs. Partida*. . . . It involves calculation of the 'standard deviation' as a measure of predicted fluctuations from the expected value of a sample. Using the 5.7% figure as the basis for calculating the expected value, the expected number of Negroes on the Hazelwood teaching staff would be roughly 63 in 1972–73 and 70 in 1973–74. The observed number in those years was 16 and 22 respectively. The difference between the observed and expected values was more than six standard deviations in 1972–73 and more than six standard deviations in 1973–74. The Court in *Castaneda* noted that as a general rule for such large samples, if the difference between the expected value and the observed number is greater than two or three standard deviations, then the hypothesis that teachers were hired without regard to race would be suspect.

QUOTING FROM JUSTICE STEVENS' DISSENTING OPINION

Absolute precision in the analysis of market data is too much to expect. We may fairly assume that a nondiscriminatory selection process would have resulted in the hiring of somewhere between the 15% suggested by the Government and the 5.7% suggested by the petitioner, or perhaps 30 or 40 black teachers instead of the 15 actually hired. On that assumption, the Court of Appeals' determination that there were 16 individual cases of discriminatory refusal to hire black applicants in the post-1972 period seems remarkably accurate.

In sum, the Government is entitled to prevail on the present record.

OBSERVATIONS ON THE HAZELWOOD CASE

There are a number of features in the Hazelwood Case that have national implications for the EEO process in the future.

1. The charges were systemic. Instead of singling out specific schools within the district, the United States Government held the school district as an entity responsible for its component parts even though the individual schools had some degree of control over their hiring decisions. In essence, the school district was charged with failing to control the hiring processes with regard to their EEO implications. The analogy to the larger corporations is clear—decentralization is not an excuse for less than acceptable EEO performance.
2. Employment practices were challenged with particular emphasis on the intangibles, such as "personality, disposition, appearance, poise, voice, articulation, and ability to deal with people." We can't tell from Justice Stewart's text whether the instruction to hire the "most competent" person available was also challenged. By implication, it probably was, because a footnote makes reference to the McDonnell Douglas case in which the guidelines for a prima facie case of illegal employment discrimination were outlined:

   a. That (an individual) belongs to a racial minority;
   b. That he applied and was qualified for a job for which the employer was seeking applicants;
   c. That, despite his qualifications, he was rejected;
   d. That, after his rejection, the position remained open and the employer continued to seek applicants of complainant's qualifications.

   Similarly we can't tell from the text what changes in employment practices Hazelwood would have to make in order to be judged nondiscriminatory. The injunction asked that Hazelwood cease its discriminatory practices. Presumably, there was something of a "fishing expedition" that implicitly said stop doing whatever it is that is producing a less than reasonably expected distribution of Negroes in the work force. Ideally, one might expect to be able to review personnel practices independent of the yield of minorities and women and redesign the system (if necessary) to be sure that it is nondiscriminatory. In the practical world at this point in time, that may not be possible. The approach may have to be to estimate a reasonably expected share of opportunities for minorities and women and to evaluate the practices vis-a-vis their actual yield.

3. Justice Stewart pointed out the importance of the share of opportunities concept in contrast to the mere examination of Negro representation in the work force of Hazelwood at the time of the litigation. This is consistent with the conclusions we have drawn from the models in previous chapters. The United States Government's charges were at least partially based on the fact that Negro representation in the district's teaching staff was only 1.8% in the year 1973–74. In response, Justice Stewart stated,

"The Court of Appeals totally disregarded the possibility that this prima facie statistical proof in the record might at the trial court level be rebutted by statistics dealing with Hazelwood's hiring after it became subject to Title VII. Racial discrimination by public employers was not made illegal under Title VII until March 24, 1972. A public employer who from that date forward made all its employment decisions in a wholly nondiscriminatory way would not violate Title VII even if it had formerly maintained an all-white work force by purposefully excluding Negroes."

In effect, an employer cannot be judged discriminatory on the basis of a snapshot of minority and women's representation at any point in time. The important thing is what the employer did with the opportunities that were available.

4. The external labor market was a major issue in the case. Because promotion flow or upward mobility was not a part of the charge, there was no consideration of internal labor markets. In our earlier discussions, we observed that labor market definition involved consideration of qualifications and geographic domain. For the Hazelwood case, qualifications were keyed basically to the teaching credential. An applicant, if selected, would have to be eligible by the time he (sic) began the job. Over and above this requirement, there were some intangibles such as disposition and poise, but these were a part of the selection process and were not reflected in the sizing of the external labor market.

Essentially, both the United States Government and Hazelwood used the bench mark job approach. Employed teachers within a geographic area were the bench mark. From the text, it would appear that unemployed teachers and the new output from schools of education were not taken into account in the numerical determination of the size of the labor market. Although there is reference to Hazelwood's recruiting at colleges and universities in Missouri and bordering states, apparently the real issue was whether or not the St. Louis School District should be considered as part of Hazelwood's external labor market. When it is included, the percentage of Negroes among teachers in the county is 15.4%. Otherwise, the percentage is only 5.7%. Hazelwood argued that, because the City of St. Louis had made special attempts to maintain a 50% Negro teaching staff, inclusion of that school district in the relevant market area distorts the comparison. How legitimate that argument is remains to be judged by the courts.

For the employer in general, the Hazelwood case makes the point that there is such a thing as a relevant external labor market for EEO purposes. It contains the elements of pertinent qualifications and geographic area, and provides a reasonable basis for evaluating EEO external hiring performance. The determination of the minority and women's representation in that labor market can be critical to the judgment of whether or not a prima facie case of illegal employment discrimination exists. If the employer is to remain free of EEO legal entanglements, detailed attention needs to be paid to the identification and assessing of that market. How this is done is a matter of selecting an appropriate analytical procedure on the part of the monitoring agency and employer. But it must be done thoroughly and objectively, almost unrelentingly, until supportable conclusions are reached. One clear message for employers is: Don't settle for the first broad-brush answer. Keep searching until there is solid, in-depth knowledge of the real picture. In the Hazelwood case, four years elapsed with the charges unsettled because at the Supreme Court level it was still necessary for Justice Stewart to suggest the additional work that needed to be done.

Surprisingly, there apparently was no labor market segmentation on either a vertical or horizontal basis. For example, in addition to the teaching credential and the geography, consideration could have been given to grade level (elementary vs. secondary) and subject matter such as mathematics, music, art, physical education, and the social sciences. Generally, such segmentation brings one much closer to the identification of the "real" labor market. It is quite possible that the profile of the teaching work force in the City of St. Louis district, independent of race, sex or ethnic considerations, could be substantially different from that of Hazelwood in terms of both grade level and subject matter. This difference in profile, particularly on a share of opportunities basis, could be more extreme than the 15.4% vs. 5.7% which was a major hang-up in the case.

Finally, with respect to the external labor market, Justice William J. Brennan Jr. added the following to the majority opinion: "Hazelwood reasonably should be given the opportunity to come forward with more focused and specific applicant flow data in the hope of answering the Government's prima facie case. If, as presently seems likely, reliable applicant data is found to be lacking, the conclusion reached by my Brother Stevens will inevitably be forthcoming." The final message to the employer is "don't stop when you think you have defined and sized the external labor market. Cross-check it against applicant flow."

5. Statistical standard deviation was further recognized as one logical basis for evaluating EEO performance. This was a carry over from previous cases, thus reinforcing the use of this statistical technique in settling EEO issues. In view of this, a brief discussion of the standard deviation is appropriate.

STANDARD DEVIATION

During the 1972–73 school year, Hazelwood hired 282 teachers. Ten of these (3.5%) were Negroes. But even if the City of St. Louis district is excluded, Negroes constitute 5.7% of the labor market. Why weren't 5.7% of the hires Negroes? Could the difference between the expected and the actual be the result of random chance, or does it suggest that there is discrimination in the selection process? The standard deviation is a way of addressing that question.

Basically, the standard deviation applies tolerance limits to the hiring results. If the difference between the actual and expected lies beyond these limits, the conclusion is that the results are "suspect" and possibly imply discrimination in the process.

The formula for standard deviation applicable to the Hazelwood case is

$$\sigma = \sqrt{\frac{pq}{N}} \times 100$$

where N is the number of teachers hired.
p is the fraction of Negroes in the supply pool.
q is equal to $(1 - p)$.

For example, in the 1972–73 school year, N has a value of 282 because that is how many teachers were hired. The value for p is the 5.7% of Negoes in the labor market expressed as a decimal fraction.

$$\sigma = \sqrt{\frac{(.057)\ (.943)}{282}} \times 100$$

$$\sigma = 1.4\%$$

The difference between the actual (3.5%) and the expected (5.7%) Negro share is 2.2 percentage points. If we divide the value for a standard deviation into this difference, we get an answer of 1.6. We then say that the actual result is 1.6 standard deviations below the expected. How can this result be translated into something more meaningful?

If we assume a normal distribution in the supply, we can use Figure 1 to determine the probability of getting a result greater than 1.59 below the mean. That answer, from the chart, is .0559. There is roughly a one in twenty chance that the actual hiring result which was 3.5% Negro could have occurred at random. Whether that is sufficiently low to justify a conclusion that discrimination existed is a judgment call. The footnote in the Hazelwood decision states that two or three standard deviations is the point at which the results become suspect. In this case, using two standard deviations as the criterion, Hazelwood's results would be suspect only if they were as low as 2.5% Negro.

Although it is not mentioned in the text, there is also an upper limit beyond which one might argue that reverse discrimination existed. Using two standard deviations for both lower and upper limits, the range of results for which Hazelwood would be safe in both directions would be 2.5% to 8.9% Negro share of hires.

Similarly, we can determine how Hazelwood might be judged if the City of St. Louis district is included in the labor market and the expected Negro share were 15.4%.

$$\sigma = \sqrt{\frac{(.154)\,(.846)}{282}} \times 100$$

$$\sigma = 2.2\%$$

Now the difference between actual (3.5%) and expected (15.4%) is 11.9 percentage points or 5.4 standard deviations and Hazelwood would clearly be suspect. The chances of obtaining this kind of result at random are practically negligible.

We should observe also that the standard deviation applied to applicant flow would contribute additional insights into Hazelwood's EEO performance. Although such data are not available in the text, Justice Brennan's statements make it clear that they are expected to be the next time around on the case.

The Normal Distribution: Probability of a Variable Being More than *k* Standard Deviations Below the Mean

Normal Deviate *k*	.00	.01	.02	.03	.04	.05	.06	.07	.08	.09
.0	.5000	.4960	.4920	.4880	.4840	.4801	.4761	.4721	.4681	.4641
.1	.4602	.4562	.4522	.4483	.4443	.4404	.4364	.4325	.4286	.4247
.2	.4207	.4168	.4129	.4090	.4052	.4013	.3974	.3936	.3897	.3859
.3	.3821	.3783	.3745	.3707	.3669	.3632	.3594	.3557	.3520	.3483
.4	.3446	.3409	.3372	.3336	.3300	.3264	.3228	.3192	.3156	.3121
.5	.3085	.3050	.3015	.2981	.2946	.2912	.2877	.2843	.2810	.2776
.6	.2743	.2709	.2676	.2643	.2611	.2578	.2546	.2514	.2483	.2451
.7	.2420	.2389	.2358	.2327	.2296	.2266	.2236	.2206	.2177	.2148
.8	.2119	.2090	.2061	.2033	.2005	.1977	.1949	.1922	.1894	.1867
.9	.1841	.1814	.1788	.1762	.1736	.1711	.1685	.1660	.1635	.1611
1.0	.1587	.1562	.1539	.1515	.1492	.1469	.1446	.1423	.1401	.1379
1.1	.1357	.1335	.1314	.1292	.1271	.1251	.1230	.1210	.1190	.1170
1.2	.1151	.1131	.1112	.1093	.1075	.1056	.1038	.1020	.1003	.0985

1.3	.0968	.0951	.0934	.0918	.0901	.0885	.0869	.0853	.0838	.0823
1.4	.0808	.0793	.0778	.0764	.0749	.0735	.0721	.0708	.0694	.0681
1.5	.0668	.0655	.0643	.0630	.0618	.0606	.0594	.0582	.0571	.0559
1.6	.0548	.0537	.0526	.0516	.0505	.0495	.0485	.0475	.0465	.0455
1.7	.0446	.0436	.0427	.0418	.0409	.0401	.0392	.0384	.0375	.0367
1.8	.0359	.0351	.0344	.0336	.0329	.0322	.0314	.0307	.0301	.0294
1.9	.0287	.0281	.0274	.0268	.0262	.0256	.0250	.0244	.0239	.0233
2.0	.0226	.0222	.0217	.0212	.0207	.0202	.0197	.0192	.0188	.0183
2.1	.0179	.0174	.0170	.0166	.0162	.0158	.0154	.0150	.0146	.0143
2.2	.0139	.0136	.0132	.0129	.0125	.0122	.0119	.0116	.0113	.0110
2.3	.0107	.0104	.0102	.0099	.0096	.0094	.0091	.0089	.0087	.0084
2.4	.0082	.0080	.0078	.0075	.0073	.0071	.0069	.0068	.0066	.0064
2.5	.0062	.0060	.0059	.0057	.0055	.0054	.0052	.0051	.0049	.0048
2.6	.0047	.0045	.0044	.0043	.0041	.0040	.0039	.0038	.0037	.0036
2.7	.0035	.0034	.0033	.0032	.0031	.0030	.0029	.0028	.0027	.0026
2.8	.0026	.0025	.0024	.0023	.0023	.0022	.0021	.0021	.0020	.0019
2.9	.0019	.0018	.0018	.0017	.0016	.0016	.0015	.0015	.0014	.0014
3.0	.0013	.0013	.0013	.0012	.0012	.0011	.0011	.0011	.0010	.0010

FIGURE 1.

THE FOOTNOTE ERROR IN STATISTICAL METHODOLOGY

The footnote quoted earlier in this chapter also applies the statistical disparity approach to the representation. The arithmetic is correct, but the concept is wrong. In 1972–73, 16 of 1107 teachers were Negroes. The standard deviation can be calculated as:

$$\sigma = \sqrt{\frac{pq}{N}} \times 100$$

$$\sigma = \sqrt{\frac{(.057)\,(.943)}{1107}} \times 100$$

$$\sigma = 0.7\%$$

The shortfall is 5.7 − 1.4 = 4.3%. The representation is slightly more than six standard deviations below the mean expected value. That agrees with the "more than six standard deviations" mentioned in the footnote

But the representation of Negroes in the teaching staff for the 1972–73 school year depends upon a number of variables as was discussed in Chapter Five. Incomplete historical data are available from Justice Stewart's text, but the principle can be easily illustrated. Suppose that in the year 1964, the time of the passage of Title VII into law, the Hazelwood district had 600 teachers none of whom were Negro (the first Negro was hired in 1969). Suppose also that there were no losses during the period from 1964 to the school year 1972–73. The only opportunities for adding Negro teachers would have come from growth. There would have been 1107 minus 600 or 507 new teachers hired during that period. If 5.7% (of these) had been Negroes, their representation in 1973–74 would have been

$$R_m = \frac{.057 \times 507}{1107} = 2.6\%$$

Under these assumptions, it would have been impossible to achieve the 5.7% representation on which the footnote discussion is based.

It is possible to try several reconstructions beyond this first pass, which was based on a growth but no losses assumption. Let's try one where the loss rates are assumed to be 5% per year for the total work

Total Work Force				
Start Year	**Total**	**After Losses**	**Year End Need**	**Number Hires**
1	600	570	642	72
2	642	610	687	77
3	687	653	735	82
4	735	698	786	88
5	786	747	842	95
6	842	800	900	100
7	900	855	963	108
8	963	915	1031	116
9	1031	979	1103	124

FIGURE 2.

force and also 5% per year for Negroes. Between 1964–65 and 1972–73, the growth would be from the assumed 600 up to 1107 for an annualized rate of about 7% per year. If we assume zero Negro representation initially and assign a 5.7% share of annual opportunities, what will be the Negro representation at the end of the ninth year?

We can use the general equation from Chapter Five to derive the answer of 3.7%. However, for purposes of emphasis, a hand-built model as displayed in Figures 2 and 3 may be useful.

The minor difference in the answers obtained from the general algebraic solution and the hand-built model is due to arithmetic rounding. Under the stated conditions, it would have been impossible to achieve a 5.7% representation of Negroes in the Hazelwood work force.

Both examples illustrate the fact that applying the statistical disparity test to representation is not mathematically valid. Representation is a dependent variable. The independent variable is share of hires and that is where the statistical disparity test should be applied. In the Castaneda versus Partida case, it was applied to *share* as indicated by the following excerpt from the Court's opinion:

> If the jurors were drawn randomly from the general population, then the number of Mexican-Americans in the sample could be modeled by binomial distribution. . . . Given that 79.1% of the population is

Negro Work Force

Start Year	Total	Lose	Hires	Net Additions	Total End Year	% Rep
1	0	0	4	4	4	0.6
2	4	0	4	4	8	1.2
3	8	0	5	5	13	1.8
4	13	1	5	4	17	2.2
5	17	1	5	4	21	2.5
6	21	1	6	5	26	2.9
7	26	1	6	5	31	3.2
8	32	2	7	5	36	3.5
9	37	2	7	5	41	3.7

FIGURE 3.

Mexican-American, the expected number of Mexican-Americans among the 870 persons summoned to serve as grand jurors over the 11-year period is approximately 688. The observed number is 339. Of course, in any given drawing some fluctuation from the expected number is predicted. The important point, however, is that the statistical model shows that the results of a random drawing are likely to fall in the vicinity of the expected value. The measure of the predicted fluctuations from the expected value is the standard deviation, defined for the binomial distribution as the square root of the product of the total number in the sample (here 870) times the probability of selecting a Mexican-American (0.79) times the probability of selecting a nonMexican-American. Thus, in this case the standard deviation is approximately 12. As a general rule for such large samples, if the difference between the expected value and the observed number is greater than two or three standard deviations, then the hypothesis that the jury drawing was random would be suspect to a social scientist. The 11-year data here reflect a difference between the expected and observed number of Mexican-Americans of approximately 29 standard deviations.

The implications of applying the statistical disparity test to representation data are disturbing. If that statistical approach is used in future negotiated settlements or additional court decisions, there is considerable risk that justice may not properly be served.

ADDITIONAL APPLICATIONS OF STATISTICAL DISPARITY TESTS

It seems reasonable to expect that the statistical disparity approach illustrated by the Hazelwood case will be widely used in a variety of circumstances in the EEO arena. It is a rational way of taking a quick broad brush reading and can be expected to be applied to cases of promotion share as well as to the hiring process and resulting shares. As minorities become more fully assimilated into the work force as a whole, increased attention will be paid to the issue of upward mobility as discussed in Chapter Seven. Statistical disparity tests can be a useful technique in analyzing upward mobility, but their application is less definitive and considerably more complex than in cases limited strictly to hiring from the external market place. This fact was touched upon in some detail in Chapter Eight. It can now be addressed from a statistical point of view as an off-shoot of the Hazelwood case.

Suppose an employer has an entry level factory work force which consists of 1000 people at the start of the year 1978 and that 25% or 250 are minority. During the year, there are 300 promotions to the next higher job grade. Statistically, one might expect 25% or 75 promotions should go to minorities. But suppose when all the results are in, the actual number of minority promotions is found to be only 60 or 20%. By inspection, this share appears to be much too low. How can it be measured statistically and expressed in standard deviations per the Hazelwood case?

A commonly used approach is to recognize that promotions are being drawn from two populations (minority and other) and to pool the variance. The calculations can be done in the following manner:

n = total number of people in the source population = 1000
n_m = number of minority in the source = 250
n_o = number of others in the source = 750
X = total numer of promotions = 300
X_m = number of minorities promoted = 60
X_o = number of others promoted = 240

$$p = \text{proportion of total people promoted} = \frac{X}{n} = \frac{300}{1000} = .30$$

(Note that pn_m and pn_o must be greater than 5 for this methodology to apply. In this case, the data pass the screening test. pn_m = .30(250) = 75 and pn_o = .30(750) = 225.)

$$p_m = \text{proportion of minorities promoted} = \frac{60}{250} = .240$$

$$p_o = \text{proportion of others promoted} = \frac{240}{750} = .320$$

$$V = \text{pooled variance} = p\ (1 - p)\left(\frac{1}{n_m} + \frac{1}{n_o}\right)$$

$$= .30(.70)\left(\frac{1}{250} + \frac{1}{750}\right) = .00112$$

$$Z = \text{number of standard deviations from the mean}$$

$$= \frac{p_m - p_o}{\sqrt{V}} = \frac{.240 - .320}{\sqrt{.00112}} = \frac{-.08}{.0335} = -2.39$$

The calculations show a result that is between two and three standard deviations from the mean. Per the Hazelwood case, the minority share of promotions is statistically suspect as being too low.

The employer's defense (if there really is one) against this type of statistic is not nearly as clear cut as that in Hazelwood. There, the case was limited to hiring from a population whose skills (certificated teachers or practically so) are clearly definable and generally well understood. But on the lower end of the factory job grade spectrum, the skills demarcations are much more difficult to draw. As people look upward from entry level to the next higher job grade, they usually see a wide array of skills requirements as was discussed in Chapter Eight. Some of these can be acquired by assimilation, such as learning more advanced assembly skills by the experience of doing elementary assembly work. Others cannot be so directly acquired but may call for some experience or training in the operation of machine tools, or reading blueprints, or using precision measuring instruments. So in reality, there may not be just one pool of candidates at entry level from which promotions can be drawn; but perhaps several pools. Often the employer is reluctant to base a defense on this concept because it lays open to challenge the whole job evaluation and pay plan process and can lead to extended arguments over minute details of individual jobs. Yet if there are unfavorable statistical disparities which cannot be explained by a bona fide seniority system, the employer has little choice but to fall back on the multi-pool concept as a basis for defense. Although it seems unfair that a five-minute statistical calculation can trigger weeks and perhaps months of detailed search into personnel files, that is a fact of life in the EEO arena.

In many EEO challenges of promotion share, the real truth probably cannot be found at the initial statistical level. Suppose, to continue with our specific numerical example, all of the 1000 jobs at entry level are in elementary assembly and that half of the promotions are to lathe operator jobs and half are to advanced assembly. Further assume that the lathe jobs legitimately require previous lathe training or experience, but the advanced assembly job skills can be acquired through elementary assembly on-the-job experience. We now have the situation depicted in Figure 4.

Assuming that none of the 1000 people at entry level have acquired lathe skills after being hired by going to off-hours school or other sources of skills acquisition, the only explanation for 150 promotions into lathe jobs is that the promotees brought such skills with them at the time of hire. In times of relatively high unemployment, such a scenario is quite likely. For most people, being underemployed is better than being unemployed. Thus in this very simplified example, the conclusion has to be that there were at least 150 people who had the necessary lathe skills at the time of hire, but because of a tight job market were willing to accept entry level jobs where those skills were neither required nor utilized. The real truth lies not in the initial statistical disparity test but in a search of the 1000 personnel folders of the entry level population.

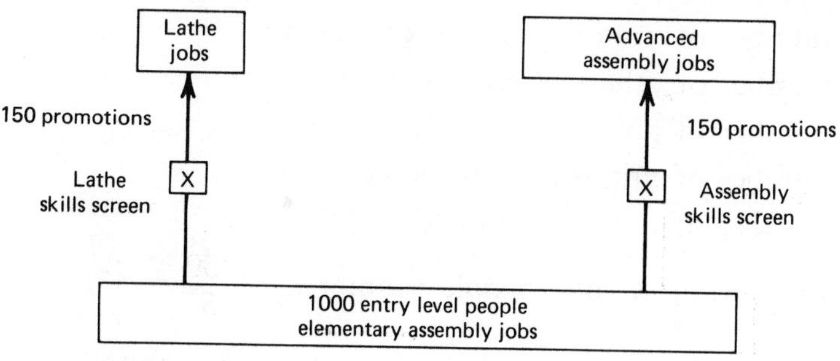

FIGURE 4.

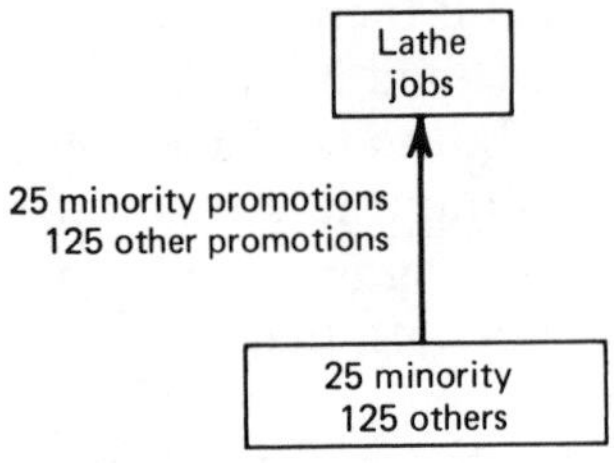

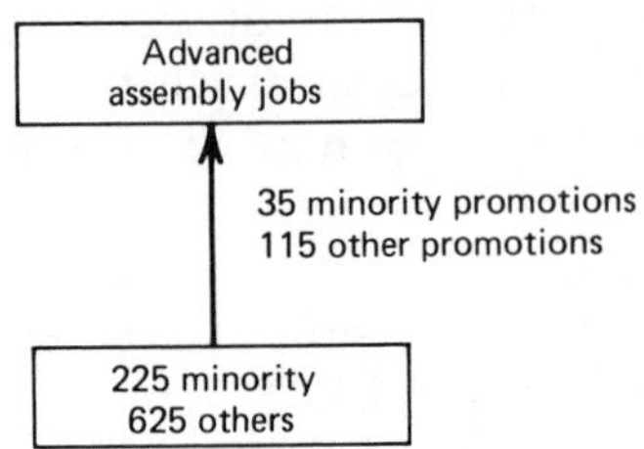

FIGURE 5.

Suppose the search of the folders reveals that 25 minority workers and 125 others actually had the necessary lathe skills at the time of hire. This is not an unreasonable supposition, but a very likely one. Close study of the U.S. Census data for most SMSAs suggests that in a random drawing from the blue collar civilian labor force, there would be a disproportionately higher percentage of nonminorities with higher than entry level skills. (In reality, that's one of the main issues in the EEO arena—the skills distribution of minorities in the civilian labor force are not the same as those of nonminorities and affirmative action is necessary to produce the needed change.)

How does this added information gleaned from the personnel folders change the statistical analysis? Now the situation can be depicted as in Figure 5.

The promotions to the lathe jobs are accounted for, with 16.7% going to minority. Of the 150 promotions to advanced assembly jobs, 35 or 23.3% went to minority from a source population that was 26.5% minority. There is still a statistical disparity, and the test can be reapplied to this segmented population to examine how serious the disparity is:

$$n = \text{number of people in source population} = 850$$

$$n_m = \text{number of minority in source} = 225$$

$$n_o = \text{number of others in source} = 625$$

$$X = \text{number of promotions} = 150$$

$$X_m = \text{number of minorities promoted} = 35$$

$$X_o = \text{number of others promoted} = 115$$

$$p = \text{proportion of total people promoted} = \frac{150}{850} = .176$$

$$p_m = \text{proportion of minorities promoted} = \frac{35}{225} = .156$$

$$p_o = \text{proportion of others promoted} = \frac{115}{625} = .184$$

$$V = \text{pooled variance} = p(1 - p)\left(\frac{1}{n_m} + \frac{1}{n_o}\right)$$

$$= (.176)\,(.824)\left(\frac{1}{225} + \frac{1}{625}\right) = .000876$$

$$Z = \text{number of standard deviations from the mean}$$

$$= \frac{p_m - p_o}{\sqrt{V}} = \frac{.156 - .184}{\sqrt{.000876}} = \frac{-.028}{.0296} = -.95$$

The calculations show a result that is less than one standard deviation from the mean. Per the Hazelwood case, results that are two or three standard deviations from the mean are suspect. By inference, this result might not be construed as suspect.

Standing back from the statistics and looking at absolute numbers instead of percentages, how much shortfall in actual minority promotions corresponds to two and three standard deviations? For the advanced assembly promotions, minorities constitute 26.5% of the source and thus could expect to get that share of the 150 promotions, or an actual 40 (rounded). The table in Figure 6 shows the standard deviations corresponding to actual promotions less than the expected value.

Promotions		Standard Deviations
Minority	Other	From Mean
40	110	.00 (approx)
38	112	.35
36	114	.76
34	116	1.17
32	118	1.57
30	120	1.98
28	122	2.39
26	124	2.80
24	126	3.21

FIGURE 6.

For this particular example, the table shows why two or three standard deviations constitute a reasonable threshold of suspicion. On the other hand, standard deviations less than one would appear to impose an unduly rigorous standard of measurement. However, we have to bear in mind that this example deals with segmented populations analogous to the teacher segment in the Hazelwood case. If the same criteria are used for unsegmented populations, they may too easily and too quickly demonstrate results which are statistically suspect but quite removed from a genuine understanding of what is really taking place in the personnel system.

CHAPTER ELEVEN

Potential Liability and Retro Models

When an employer is charged with EEO discrimination, the first reactions are probably disbelief and shock. When those wear off, a predominant question is: "How much could this cost us?" The answer to that question, the potential dollar liability,* is a major factor in deciding how to deal with the charge. One alternative is to let a judge decide in court whether discrimination existed and what the remedies (including dollars in back pay) should be. The other is to try to negotiate an out-of-court settlement based on paying no more than is really fair or simply minimizing the dollar output. These two alternatives really go hand in hand because good negotiators will not give away the litigation alternative. For either alternative or for deciding which is the better of the two, the employer must have some approximation of potential liability before strategy and tactics can be decided upon. One simply cannot rationally proceed very far without this piece of knowledge. In addition, an estimate of potential liability is useful to management in determining the amount and kinds of company resources appropriate to coping with the charge.

There are a number of possible methodologies for estimating potential liability. To discuss these, some data assumptions are necessary. For simplification, let's use a work force which consists of only four job levels—A, B, C and D. Let's assume we are dealing with a charge of discrimination against women. The end of year 1977 work force distribution related to the charge is shown in Figure 1.

What is the potential liability? Obviously the time frame is an

*Throughout this chapter, the term potential liability refers to back pay or its equivalent resulting from failure to hire and promote minorities and women. The question of wage rate bias is not discussed.

Job Level	Total	No. Women	% Women	Job Rate $/hr
A	200	4	2.0	8.00
B	200	14	7.0	6.00
C	400	80	20.0	4.00
D	800	400	50.0	3.00
Total	1600	498	31.1	

FIGURE 1.

important factor. Does the liability go back into time three years, five years, or all the way to 1964, the year in which Title VII was enacted into law? That is a legal question which depends upon the timing and nature of the particular charge. However, for purposes of illustration, let's assume that the liability period is five years and for each of those years the data display was the same as that in Figure 1. Also, for simplification, let's omit benefits from the estimate; use 2000 for the number of paid working hours in a year; and hold the job rates constant for the five-year period.

We now have a picture that, although greatly simplified, can serve as a useful illustration. It's not difficult to imagine a monitoring agency reviewing the five-year data display, seeing no improvement in the distribution of women, and concluding that the "maldistribution" must be the result of discrimination. A charge is made against the employer, who now must ask: "How guilty am I? What could this cost me in court or in a negotiated settlement?"

The Hazelwood Case (Chapter Ten) is helpful because it points out two bases for judging the presence or absence of discrimination—representation and share of opportunities. The modelling examples previously discussed argue for share of opportunities as the more rational basis for judging possible guilt and potential liability. However, because the representation basis has been advanced and argued from time to time, four examples of the methodology are discussed.

1. Representation Basis—Civilian Labor Force

The contention in this approach is that the distribution of women in the employer's work force should correspond to their representation in the civilian labor force. This latter number is approximately 40%, hence 40% of

Job Level	Total	Number of Women Actual	By CLF	Job Rate $/hr
A	200	4	80	8.00
B	200	14	80	6.00
C	400	80	160	4.00
D	800	400	320	3.00
Total	1600	498	640	

FIGURE 2.

the jobs in each level should be held by women. A display such as Figure 2 is used as the basis for the potential liability calculation.

There are two types of liabilities represented by the data. First of all, there are fewer than 40% women in the total work force—there is a "shortage" liability. Consequently, 142 women are hypothetically added to the work force to bring their overall representation to 40%. Secondly, the incumbent women are concentrated in the lower paying jobs—there is a "distribution" liability. After the shortage of 142 women has been corrected, the total of 640 are redistributed so that each job level contains 40% women.

The next step is to calculate the women's annual payrolls for the actual data and for the hypothetical distribution. The difference between the two is the potential liability for one year. When the arithmetic is done, this comparison turns out to be

- ◆ CLF basis women's payroll = $5,440,000/yr
- ◆ Actual women's payroll = 3,272,000/yr

Difference = $2,168,000/yr

The potential liability is $2,168,000 for one year. However, in structuring the example we assumed a five-year liability period and no changes in job rates, so the total potential liability is $10,840,000.

Expressed more emotionally, the conclusion is that this particular employer has "short-changed" women out of more than ten million dollars over the five-year period.

2. Representation Basis—Average Wages

This approach does not consider whether or not there are fewer women in the work force than there should be. The potential liability is merely based on the difference in average wage rates for men and women.

◆ Average pay rate for men = $4.69/hr

◆ Average pay rate for women = 3.29/hr

Difference = $1.40/hr

For one year, the potential liability would be: 2000 hours × 498 women × $1.40/hr = $1,394,400. Since we assumed a five-year liability period and no changes in job rates, the total potential liability is $6,970,000.

It should be noted that comparing average women's pay to the average for men overstates the potential liability by a considerable amount. In fact, if the employer were to achieve that equality, the total payroll (men and women combined) would have to be increased. A more rational approach would be to make the comparison on the basis of women's average pay versus the average for the total work force. In that case the results would be

◆ Average pay rate for work force = $4.25/hr

◆ Average pay rate for women = 3.29/hr

Difference = $ .96/hr

◆ One-year potential liability = $956,000
◆ Five-year potential liability = $4,780,000

3. Representation Basis—Women Redistributed

This approach is similar to that which uses the civilian labor force as the appropriate bench mark. However, in this methodology shortages of women are not taken into account. Instead, the incumbent women in the work force (31.1% in this example) are hypothetically redistributed so that 31.1% of all jobs at each level are held by women as shown in Figure 3.

Job Level	Total	Number of Women Actual	Number of Women Hypothetical	Job Rate $/hr
A	200	4	62	8.00
B	200	14	62	6.00
C	400	80	124	4.00
D	800	400	250	3.00

FIGURE 3.

When the arithmetic is completed, the results are

- Hypothetical women's payroll = \$4,228,000/yr
- Actual women's payroll = 3,272,000/yr

Difference = \$956,000/yr

For the five-year period, the total potential liability is \$4,780,000. Note that this result is exactly the same as that obtained on the average wage basis when the comparison was made between total work force and women.

4. Representation Basis—External Labor Market

In this approach, the assumption is that women should be distributed in relationship to their representation in the external labor market. The data can be displayed as in Figure 4.

Note there are now fewer women in the hypothetical work force than in the actual. If we use total payroll as a basis for comparison as we did in two of the previous examples, we get the following results:

- "Should be" women's payroll = \$3,096,000/yr
- Actual women's payroll = \$3,272,000/yr

From the payroll point of view, the employer is paying out more dollars to women in the actual case than would be necessary in the hypothetical case. From this view there is no potential liability at all, yet we can easily see that there must be some as reflected by the Women Shortfall column. Shortfall is simply the difference between the hypothetical and actual number of women at each job level. For example, at Job Level A there should be 8 more women than there actually are. Similarly, the shortfall is 15 women at Job Level B and 75 at C. There is no shortfall at Job Level D because the actual number of women exceeds that necessary to equal the 35% in the external labor market.

Where a shortfall exists, each of the "missing" women is assumed to be currently in Job Level D earning \$3.00/hr. The potential liability for one year is:

$$\begin{aligned}\$\text{ potential liability} &= [8(8-3) + 15(6-3) + 75(4-3)]\ 2000 \\ &= \$320{,}000\end{aligned}$$

For the five-year period, the total potential liability is \$1,600,000.

The above result is based upon the assumption that the external labor market has been precisely defined. As we know from the Hazelwood Case

Job Level	Total	No. Women	Ext Mkt E, % Women	No. Women To Equal *E*	Women Shortfall
A	200	4	8	16	8
B	200	14	15	30	15
C	400	80	25	100	75
D	800	400	35	280	
Total	1600	498		426	

FIGURE 4.

and other discussions, precision in the definition of the external labor market is difficult to achieve. When using this particular approach to potential liability estimating, the employer might want to apply a multiplier of 1.5 or so to the answer and express the results as a range, such as $1,600,000 to $2,400,000.

REPRESENTATION BASIS—SUMMARY

The underlying assumption of the representation approach is that at some point a particular distribution of women should have been achieved. The difference between the actual and what should have been is the basis for establishing potential liability. The results of the four different ways of applying this concept are summarized in Figure 5.

The representation-based methodologies have the advantage of simplicity. The necessary data are generally available and the calculations are easy to do. However, the underlying assumption is not valid because the possible distribution to which the actual is being compared depends upon the opportunities for change which were available during the potential liability time period. Share of opportunities is a more rational basis, but it is more complex and requires data that may not always be available.

SHARE OF OPPORTUNITIES BASIS

In this approach, the time frame must be introduced at the outset, because what could have happened in each year depends upon what

Representation Basis
Five-Year Potential Liability

Reference Point	Potential Liability
1. Civilian Labor Force	$10,840,000
2. Average Men's Wages	6,970,000
3. Women Redistributed	4,780,000
4. External Labor Market	1,600,000

FIGURE 5.

Job Level	Hires Into		Promotions Into		Losses From	
	Men	Women	Men	Women	Men	Women
A	4	0	16	0	20	0
B	9	0	35	2	28	2
C	21	2	78	16	64	16
D	178	116			100	100

Data are constant for five years

FIGURE 6.

could have happened in the prior. In effect, one must build a model beginning with the first year of potential liability and project a pro forma distribution for each subsequent year. The projected distribution is the basis for estimating potential liability. In order to construct the model, we need more data than was necessary for the representation-based methodologies.

For purposes of illustration, let's assume personnel records contain the data displayed in Figure 6. All other data will be the same as that used in the representation-based examples.

We also need to make some assumptions for loss rates and for women's share of hires and promotions into each job level.

- Women's share of external hires is equal to their representation in the external labor market as displayed in Figure 4.
- Women's share of promotions is equal to their representation in the supplying job level.
- Loss rates are

Job Level	Total Loss Rate %/yr	Women's Loss Rate %/yr
A	10	10
B	15	15
C	20	20
D	25	25

Actually, the loss rates shown here as assumptions can be derived from the initial distribution data. However, it is best to view them as an assumption because we don't know what they might have been under the circumstances dictated by the model.

When the model is constructed and exercised using the techniques discussed in Chapter Seven, the redistribution which should have occurred for the given data and assumptions is that shown in Figure 7.

Note that over the five-year period, the total number of women on the payroll has been reduced slightly, from 498 to 483. This is the result of assigning women's share of hires equal to their representation in the external labor market. In view of this, the shortfall approach is the best one to use for the potential liability estimate.

When the data in Figure 7 is translated into a shortfall table, the result is the display shown in Figure 8.

A shortfall at Job Level A is worth the annual difference between the $8.00 per hour at that level and the $3.00 per hour rate at Job Level D. Yearly, this is $10,000. Similarly, the annualized value is $6,000 at B and $2,000 at C. When these values are applied to the shortfalls in Figure 8, the potential liability can be determined. The results are shown in Figure 9.

The total potential liability for the five-year period is $1,180,000.

For this particular very simplified example, the result is less than that obtained using any of the representation-based methods of calculation. It is fairly close to that obtained using the external labor market as the reference point (Figure 5), but that will not necessarily always be the case.

One could make some additional refinements in the process used to arrive at Figure 9. For example, something less than a full year's liability charge for each job level could be used, recognizing that all opportunities for change do not occur on the first of each year. But all we are seeking is some order of magnitude number for the potential liability to use as a guideline in developing strategy and tactics. At this point, we could arbitrarily put some tolerance limits on the $1,180,000 result. Maybe the real share of promotions would have been something less than the one assumed. On the other hand, a judge might decide that some higher share should have been used as an affirmative action step. For strategic decision-making purposes, one might view the potential liability as somewhere between $750,000 and $1,500,000 for the five-year period.

This opportunities-based method has an added advantage of identifying where the major potential liability lies. For example, Figure 9

Model for Women

Job Level	Number Start Yr	Lose	Ext Hires	Promotions Into	Promotions Out of	Number End Yr	% Rep
			Year 1973				
A	4	0	0	1	—	5	2.5
B	14	2	1	7	1	19	9.5
C	80	16	6	47	7	110	27.5
D	400	100	103	—	47	356	44.5
			Year 1974				
A	5	1	0	2	—	6	3.0
B	19	3	1	10	2	25	12.5
C	110	22	6	42	10	126	31.5
D	356	89	103	—	42	328	41.0
			Year 1975				
A	6	1	0	2	—	7	3.5
B	25	4	1	12	2	32	16.0
C	126	25	6	39	12	134	33.5
D	328	82	103	—	39	310	38.8
			Year 1976				
A	7	1	0	3	—	9	4.5
B	32	5	1	12	3	37	18.5
C	134	27	6	36	12	137	34.3
D	310	78	103	—	36	299	37.4
			Year 1977				
A	9	1	0	3	—	11	5.5
B	37	6	1	13	3	42	21.0
C	137	27	6	35	13	138	34.5
D	299	75	103	—	35	292	36.5

Women Shortfalls			
	Job Level		
Year	A	B	C
1973	1	5	30
1974	2	11	46
1975	3	18	54
1976	5	23	57
1977	7	28	58

FIGURE 8.

shows that 85% of it is associated with Job Levels B and C. Moreover, as careful study of Figure 7 shows, most of the shortfalls in achievement occur in the promotion stream. If the employer could prove that women's share of promotions should really be less than their representation in the supplying job level because of differential interests and qualifications, there is a chance that the potential liability could be dramatically reduced. This is a leverage point, an area in which the employer should invest some of the resources allocated to coping with the charge. The more the employer knows about causes and effects in this area, the more fruitful the settlement strategy will prove to be.

Potential Dollar Liability (000's)				
			Job Level	
Year	Total	A	B	C
1973	100	10	30	60
1974	178	20	66	92
1975	246	30	108	108
1976	302	50	138	114
1977	354	70	168	116
Total	1180	180	510	490

FIGURE 9.

AN ALTERNATIVE SHARE OF OPPORTUNITIES APPROACH

As an alternative to building a complete model, it is possible to treat each year individually providing some appropriate correction factors are used. Let's start with the year 1973. From the model for that year, the missed opportunities are as shown in Figure 10.

For example, at Job Level B there were five missed opportunities in the promotion stream. For each of these, the dollar value is the yearly difference between $6.00 per hour at B and $4.00 per hour at C—a value of $4,000 for the year. There was also one missed opportunity in external hiring. If we assume that the "missing" woman is employed elsewhere, we can arbitrarily assign the same value to a missed hire as to a missed promotion. This is logical because the external labor market sizing was probably based on employed persons, and we would expect a woman changing jobs to be looking for some increase in pay.

By applying this same logic pattern we used for Job Level B to the other job levels, we can construct the table shown in Figure 11.

If we assume these missed opportunities went uncorrected for the five-year period, we can multiply the results in Figure 11 by a factor of 5.

Now we can do the same thing for the year 1974—build a one-year model, determine the missed opportunities, and translate them into potential liability. However, the correction factor multiplier would be only four instead of five, because we assume the missed opportunities went uncorrected for only four years. In the very simplified

1973 Women Shortfalls

Job Level	External Hires Model	External Hires Actual	Missed Oppor	Promotions Into Model	Promotions Into Actual	Missed Oppor
A	0	0	0	1	0	1
B	1	0	1	7	2	5
C	6	2	4	47	16	31
D	103	116	—	—	—	—

FIGURE 10.

Job Level	Annual Value per Missed Oppor	Number of Misses	Total Potential Liability
A	$4,000	1	$ 4,000
B	4,000	6	24,000
C	2,000	35	70,000
			$98,000

FIGURE 11.

illustration we have been using, we assumed the distribution of people was exactly the same each year. Therefore, it isn't necessary to build any additional one-year models, because each year yields the same results. All we have to do is to use a multiplier of five for 1973, four for 1974, three for 1975, two for 1976, and one for 1977. The results of the appropriate calculations are shown in Figure 12.

This method is not as theoretically correct as a complete model, because it does not take into account how one year's success in promoting women increases the women's internal market for the next year. However, this is compensated for by using the annual multipliers of five, four, three, two, one. Although the approach is a much rougher approximation than a complete model, it has the advantage of being somewhat easier to use. It is generally easier to build five one-year models than one five-year model.

Year	Potential Liability
1973	$ 490,000
1974	392,000
1975	294,000
1976	196,000
1977	98,000
Total	$1,470,000

FIGURE 12.

RETRO MODELS

Most companies could be expected to have historical end-of-year representation data for a fairly long time span. A lesser number could be expected to have complete transaction data to support a share of opportunities analysis. Transaction data includes such things as applicant flow, external hires, promotions, selection ratios, and loss rates.

What can one do, given representation data for two points in time, to reconstruct what might have happened? A retro model, one going backward rather than forward in time, can provide some useful insights.

A single total work force retro model (as in the Hazelwood Case) can be used to illustrate the approach. Assume that end of year data are available for the five-year period of 1973 through 1977 as shown in Figure 13.

There are no promotions into or out of the work force. All additions come from external hiring in a labor market that is 15% minority.

A monitoring agency observes the 8% representation versus the 15% minority in the labor market and concludes that there is a prima facie case of discrimination. Statistically, the minority representation in 1977 is more than six standard deviations less than the mean of 15%, a result which presumably reinforces the conclusion that discrimination exists. As we discussed in Chapter Ten, the employer argues that a more valid measurement would be a statistical disparity test based on share of opportunities over the five-year period. Unfortunately, the data which would help to support the share argument is incomplete. There are some data to suggest that loss rates were

End of Year	Total	Number Minority	% Minority
1972	1000	50	5.0
1973	1000	55	5.5
1974	1000	65	6.5
1975	1000	70	7.0
1976	1000	75	7.5
1977	1000	80	8.0

FIGURE 13.

probably 10% per year for both minorities and total, although it is possible they could have been as low as 5% or as high as 15% and differential as well. What can the employer do?

A retro model offers some interesting possibilities. As a first pass, let's use a 10% per year loss rate for both the minority and the total population. In the no-growth mode, the total opportunities each year are simply 10% of 1000, or 100 external hires annually. In this model, we know what the minority representation must be at the end of each year. What we have to determine is the minority share of opportunities necessary to achieve that after minority losses are taken into consideration. The calculations are shown in tabular form in Figure 14.

The minority share of hires in the model ranges from 12% to 16%.

For 100 annual hires from a labor market that is 15% minority the standard deviation is

$$\sigma = \sqrt{\frac{(.15)\ (.85)}{100}} \times 100 = 3.6\%$$

We can now develop Figure 15 which shows the number of standard deviations from the expected mean that occurred each year.

In view of the two or three standard deviations suggested as a guideline by the U.S. Supreme Court in the Hazelwood Case, there is not much of a prima facie case of discrimination if the model reasonably well approximates what actually happened. However, one single retro model is not enough to prove a point because the assumptions could be too self-serving. Several retro reconstructions are necessary for an objective analysis.

Minority Share

Start Year	Number Minority	Lose	End Year Minority	Needed Hires	% Share
1	50	5	55	10	10
2	55	6	65	16	16
3	65	7	70	12	12
4	70	7	75	12	12
5	75	8	80	13	13

FIGURE 14.

	Minority Share of Hires	
	Total Loss Rate 10%/Yr Minority Loss Rate 10%/Yr	
Year	**% Share**	**Number S.D. From Mean**
1973	10	−1.4
1974	16	+0.3
1975	12	−0.8
1976	12	−0.8
1977	13	−0.6

FIGURE 15.

For a second trial, loss rates of 15% per year for total and minority can be used. The results are shown in Figure 16.

For a third trial, loss rates of 5% per year for total and minority can be used. The results are shown in Figure 17.

When the loss rates are as low as 5%, the number of standard deviations from the mean are all positive. Minority hiring share exceeded the external market in every year.

From the results of the first three retro models it is apparent that

	Minority Share of Hires	
	Total Loss Rate 15%/Yr Minority Loss Rate 15%/Yr	
Year	**% Share**	**Number S.D. From Mean**
1973	8.7	−2.2
1974	12.0	−1.0
1975	10.0	−1.7
1976	10.7	−1.5
1977	10.7	−1.5

FIGURE 16.

Minority Share of Hires		
Total Loss Rate 5%/Yr Minority Loss Rate 5%/Yr		
Year	**% Share**	**Number S.D. From Mean**
1973	16	+0.2
1974	26	+2.2
1975	16	+0.2
1976	18	+0.6
1977	18	+0.6

FIGURE 17.

the worst case could occur when minority loss rate is only 5% per year, but the total loss rate is 15% per year. The results for these assumptions are shown in Figure 18.

In the extreme case of much higher loss rates in total than for minority workers, the number of standard deviations below the mean exceeds a value of three in four of the five years. The converse, where minority loss rate is 15% per year and total loss rate is only 5% per year, is shown in Figure 19.

Minority Share of Hires		
Total Loss Rate 15%/Yr Minority Loss Rate 5%/Yr		
Year	**% Share**	**Number S.D. From Mean**
1973	5.3	−3.3
1974	8.7	−2.2
1975	5.3	−3.3
1976	6.0	−3.1
1977	6.0	−3.1

FIGURE 18.

Minority Share of Hires

Total Loss Rate 5%/Yr
Minority Loss Rate 15%/Yr

Year	% Share	Number S.D. From Mean
1973	26	+2.2
1974	36	+4.1
1975	30	+2.9
1976	32	+3.3
1977	32	+3.3

FIGURE 19.

If the assumptions for Figure 19 describe what actually happened, the minority share of hires would have been high enough to suggest reverse discrimination.

For this example, the results of the five retro models suggest that there is not very much prima facie evidence of discrimination against minorities. The basic issues come down to that of differential loss rates. If management could demonstrate that minority loss rates are generally equal to or larger than those for non-minorities, the prima facie case of discrimination would be extremely weak.

A DUAL APPROACH

An employer needs to develop a dual approach—two strategies as it were—for operating in the EEO arena. The first of these addresses the role of being a good corporate citizen and the extent to which the employer wishes to serve as an agent of change in the social-cultural transformation that is taking place. The strategy can range from doing a great deal in the form of training programs and other services to the national and local communities to operating in a minimal low-profile way. Whether the motivation is social conscience or public relations, or even if there is little motivation at all, the employer's posture should be based on a conscious decision related to short- and long-term business plans. This is particularly true of the larger corporations whose very right to exist is currently being challenged and whose role in society may be subject to much deeper probing in the next decade.

But whatever the good-citizen-oriented strategy may be, it is not a guarantee nor a bulwark against the clearly announced systemic charge thrust of the EEO Commission. The General Electric Company can attest all too well to that fact. Despite its well deserved reputation as a good corporate citizen, an image based upon some very good contributions to EEO progress in such activities as PIMEG, it was the unhappy recipient of a Track I charge of systemic discrimination.

Likewise, the successful passing of Affirmative Action Program reviews is not a guarantee against receiving charges of systemic discrimination nor being named in class action or reverse discrimination law suits. How, then, can an enterprise, public or private, meet its obligation to manage prudently and protect the resources made available to it? An EEO strategy, beyond the socially-culturally oriented one, is needed to protect against the risk of financial losses associated with EEO enforcement activities. This is especially true if one accepts the emerging recognition that EEO will be a major issue in the world of work well into the twenty-first century.

One useful approach is for the employer to ask the question: "What would we do to defend ourselves if we received a charge of systemic discrimination from the Equal Employment Opportunities Commission?" An employer who has answered that question in detail will, in the process, have uncovered most of the elements necessary to a successful strategy. Although on the surface this might seem like an elementary exercise, it does in fact impose a surprisingly strict discipline on the internal review process. In addition to testing the legality and the logic of the internal system for coping with EEO requirements, it puts the data collection and recording processes under intensive scrutiny. The latter is a matter of extreme importance, because good data are a critical element in successfully withstanding challenges in court or in holding the firm po[illegible]tions sometimes needed in negotiations. When the data have be[illegible]ted in advance of a charge, they seem to be more credible [illegible] collected or reconstructed in hindsight. When they a[illegible] a post facto resurrection, they tend to be suspect as [illegible] and too self-serving. And, worst of all, some of th[illegible] may not be retrievable at all.

Regardless of how the defensive strategy mi[illegible] should not be viewed as a one-time, cast-in-c[illegible] law continues to evolve, changes in strategy ar[illegible] have to be made from time to time. It is important that these changes be made in an anticipatory vein. An employer needs to look back to court decisions as a matter of legal precedent but forward when it comes to their implications.

SUMMARY

1. The best way to estimate potential dollar liability is to construct a model that predicts what the distribution of minority and women could have been at the present time, given some initial starting data and a time period. When this "could have been" is compared to the actual distribution, the differences can be translated into potential liability (back pay or its equivalent). The "could have been" distribution is based on determining a reasonable share of hires and promotions for minorities and women, and applying that to the opportunities that were available. If the actual shares for minorities and women were less than what they should have been, the result is shortfalls in representation. Dollar values are assigned to the shortfalls in the different job categories and the total potential liability can be approximated.

2. Potential liability estimates based simply on static snapshots of representation have several weaknesses:

- They do not take into account the opportunities for change that were available.
- They do not impose the discipline of sizing both the external and internal markets.
- They sometimes produce results that are so extreme that they generate polarized positions between the monitoring agency and the employer. This is particularly true when the civilian labor force or average wage rates for minorities and women versus those for others is used as the basis of comparison.
- Although representation-based estimates using the external labor market yield potential liability results which seem reasonable, this is mostly a matter of coincidence. Very often, the mainstream of opportunities lies in the promotion flow where the internal market is the critical factor.

3. When an employer is faced with statistical disparity test results [illegible]d on the representation of minorities and women, an appropriate response is to change the basis of comparison from representation to share of opportunities. Statistical disparity tests applied to a static distribution profile do not prove discrimination nor establish potential dollar liability. In many instances, when such tests are applied on a shares basis, a prima facie case of discrimination which is statistically based will be greatly weakened.

4. In the absence of actual data for a share of opportunities approach, retro models can be helpful. A range of assumptions can be made and a series of models developed to describe a number of possible reconstructions of what actually happened. These reconstructions can form a basis for determining whether discrimination existed and how much the associated dollar liability might be.

5. Models used for purposes of estimating potential liability serve two additional useful purposes:

- They can identify the most troublesome areas and provide helpful clues for the development of strategy and tactics in dealing with a charge of discrimination or planning corrective actions.
- They provide understanding of the dynamics of the work force—a factor of critical importance in how numerical objectives should be set and the degree of commitment to them.

6. An employer needs to develop a dual approach to EEO because there are two possibly contradictory responsibilities. The first is that related to good citizenship and to contributing to EEO progress locally and nationally. The second pertains to protecting the resources of the enterprise, whether public or private, against costly mistakes. These strategies need to be flexibly responsive to the evolving law and the social-cultural transformation that is taking place.

CHAPTER TWELVE

Goals and Timetables in the California Schools

Although the bussing of students to achieve racial integration in the massive Los Angeles City School District has captured the headlines, little has been written about the affirmative action employment plans required of all school districts in the State of California. Yet the story of these plans—how the requirement came to be and how it is being responded to by the individual school districts—is a striking example of the confusion, frustration, and potential litigation that can be generated by well intended but not well thought out regulations.

To fully understand what is happening, one has to work at a level of detail that is burdensome and time consuming. Yet there is little other choice if the weaknesses and distortions in the process—from the State Board of Education to the actual affirmative action plans now being implemented—are to be clearly identified and ultimately corrected. One has to study in sequence,

- The pertinent Administrative Code Chapter,
- The Guidelines for Affirmative Action Employment Programs issued by the State Department of Education,
- Some actual plans from selected school districts.

The reward of genuine understanding is there, but it takes considerable effort to reach it. Bearing in mind that appeal for patience and determination to stay with it, let's get on with the task.

TITLE 5 AFFIRMATIVE ACTION PROGRAMS

Title 5 of the Administrative Code contains the State Board of Education regulations pertaining to primary and secondary schools. In 1974 the following chapter appeared for the first time.

CHAPTER 4. AFFIRMATIVE ACTION EMPLOYMENT PROGRAMS

Detailed Analysis

30. Findings of Fact. The State Board of Education finds and hereby declares that:

(a) In general, California school districts employ a disproportionately low number of racial and ethnic minority teachers and a disproportionately low number of women and members of racial and ethnic minorities in administrative positions.

(b) There is a close correlation between the school assignment of pupils and the school assignment of professional staff of the same racial and ethnic minority groups, i.e., minority staff members tend to be concentrated in ethnically imbalanced schools.

(c) It is educationally sound for the minority student attending a racially impacted school to have available to him the positive image provided by minority teacher, counselor, and administrator. It is likewise educationally sound for the child from the majority group to have positive experiences with minority people which can be provided, in part, by having minority teachers, counselors, and administrators at schools where the enrollment is largely made up of majority-group students. It is also educationally important for students to observe that women as well as men can assume responsible and diverse roles in society.

(d) Past efforts to promote additional action in the recruitment, employment, and promotion of women and minorities have not resulted in a substantial increase in employment opportunities for such persons.

(e) Lessons concerning democratic principles and the richness which racial diversity brings to our national heritage can be best taught by the presence of staffs of mixed races and ethnic groups working toward a common goal.

(f) In order for school districts and offices of county superintendents of schools to increase representation of women and racial and ethnic minority group staff members, there should be policy direction from the State Board of Education which requires such agencies to adopt and implement affirmative action employment plans.

NOTE: Authority cited: Section 152, Education Code; California Fair Employment Practices Act (Sections 1410, et seq.); Titles VI and VII, Civil Rights Act of 1964 (42 U.S.C. 2000(d)-2000(e)-15); Title 45, Code of Federal Regulations (Sections 70.1-70.16); Presidential Executive Order 11246, as amended by Executive order 11375; and the California Code of Fair Practices.

History: 1. New Chapter 4 (§§ 30 through §§ 36) filed 4-17-74; effective thirtieth day thereafter (Register 74, No. 16).

31. Policy. The State Board of Education maintains as its policy to provide equal opportunity in employment for all persons and to prohibit discrimination based on race, sex, color, religion, age, physical handicap, ancestry, or national origin in every aspect of personnel policy and practice in employment, development, advancement, and treatment of employees; and to promote the total realization of equal employment opportunity through a continuing affirmative action employment program.

32. Statement of Intent. The State Board of Education recognizes that it is not enough to proclaim that public employers do not discriminate in employment but that we must also strive actively to build a community in which opportunity is equalized. In adopting this chapter, it is the intent of the State Board of Education to require educational agencies to adopt and implement plans for increasing the numbers of women and minority persons at all levels of responsibility.

33. Definitions. As used in this Chapter: (a) "Affirmative action employment program" means planned activities designed to seek, hire, and promote women and persons of minority racial and ethnic backgrounds. It is a conscious, deliberate step taken by a hiring authority to assure equal employment opportunity for all staff, both certificated and classified.

Such programs require the employer to make additional efforts to recruit, employ and promote members of groups formerly excluded at the various levels of responsibility who are qualified or may become qualified through appropriate training or experience within a reasonable length of time. Such programs should be designed to remedy the exclusion, whatever its cause.

Affirmative action requires imaginative, energetic and sustained action by an employer to devise recruiting, training and career advancement opportunities which will result in increased representation of women and minorities.

(b) "Goals and timetables" means projected new levels of employment of women and minority racial and ethnic groups to be attained on a specific schedule, given the expected turnover in the work force and the availability of persons who are qualified or may become qualified through appropriate training or experience within a reasonable length of time. Goals are not "quotas" or rigid proportions. They should relate both to the qualitative and quantitative needs of the employer.

(c) "Public education agency" means the State Department of Education, each office of the county superintendent of schools, and the governing board of each school district in California except community college districts.

34. Development and Implementation of Programs.* Each public education agency will develop and implement an affirmative action employment program for all operating units and at all levels of responsibility within its jurisdiction. The affirmative action employment program shall have goals and timetables for its implementation. The plan will be a public record within the meaning of the California Public Records Act (Government Code Sections 6250 through 6260).

35. Responsibility of Department. The Department of Education shall develop and disseminate to public education agencies guidelines to assist such agencies in developing and implementing affirmative action employment programs and shall render assistance to such agencies in carrying out the requirement of this chapter.

36. Responsibility of County Superintendent of Schools. Each county superintendent of schools shall render assistance in developing and implementing affirmative action employment programs to elementary school districts under his jurisdiction which had fewer than 901 units of average daily attendance during the preceding fiscal year, and in high school districts under his jurisdiction which had fewer than 301 units of average daily attendance during the preceding fiscal year, and in unified school districts under his jurisdiction which had fewer than 1,501 units of average daily attendance during the preceding fiscal year.

COMMENTS ON TITLE 5

When the State Board of Education issues a findings of fact as sweeping and important as that in Section 30, one would expect to find an in-depth comprehensive study, well supported by data, stating the problem in reasonably precise terms and outlining some

*Later amended to require that the plans be developed no later than January 1, 1976.

fruitful avenues of solution. Yet, according to the Bureau of Intergroup Relations of the State Department of Education, there was no such study. Rather, the findings were reached by consensus of board members, department staff and associates, formal associations of administrators and teachers, and other concerned groups. Had detailed studies been made, a number of potential problems contained in the wording of Title 5 might have been detected and resolved. Instead, the requirement for affirmative action plans was launched more in the form of a statement of social and educational purpose, leaving the realities to the State Department of Education in the formulation of guidelines, and to the school districts in the creation of "imaginative and energetic action" programs. Thus, at the very outset the Board's action in amending Title 5 has three and perhaps four serious shortcomings.

1. The principal thrust is to increase the representation of minority workers and women in those jobs or job groupings in which they are judged to be underrepresented. Yet the basis for making that judgment is not clearly stated. In the findings of fact, there is no indication of what standard the Board used to arrive at its own generic conclusion of underrepresentation. On what bench mark was underrepresentation of minority teachers, for example, based? Minority percentage in the statewide population? Minority percentage in the statewide student population? Or on some relevant labor market? The question remains unanswered at the Title 5 level. As we shall see later, it remains unanswered in the Guidelines from the State Department of Education and is a mixed bag in the various district affirmative action plans.

   This is a matter of critical concern, not only for determining when a goal is necessary, but also for knowing when a representation goal has been reached. Suppose, for example, that a school district has a minority teacher representation of 15%, a minority student population of 25%, a minority labor market of 15%, and the community is 20% minority. Are minorities underrepresented and, if so, at what representation percentage would the intent of the Title 5 regulations be satisfied?
2. The Board, in noting the lack of previous progress in recruitment, employment, and promotion of minorities and women, gave no indication of the size of the perceived shortfalls nor the expected time frame within which acceptable results could be achieved. In fact, without collecting share of opportunity and relevant labor market data and applying that to observed changes in representation, the Board has no basis for judging (other than intuitively) whether the rate of change is good, average, or poor. Analytical models show time

and time again that except in the very early stages of minority and women hiring thrusts, substantial changes in representation are difficult to achieve because of the way in which the dynamics variables are related. If failure to appreciate this fact brings only disappointment, no serious damage is done. But if individual school districts read the judgment of the Board as a signal calling for highly intensified actions and results, they may be unable to comply with the other directive of setting realistic goals.

3. The Board very clearly defines goals as projected new levels of employment to be attained on a specific schedule—in other words, goals based on predicted representation, not on share of opportunities vis-a-vis the relevant labor market. This is not a rational way to set goals. Mathematically, it reverses the dependent and independent variables. It masks the need to do a thorough labor market analysis and is the gateway to potential reverse discrimination charges. The obvious problems of this approach are exacerbated when the representation goal is fairly high and the allowable time frame (five years in the case of the Department of Education Guidelines) is relatively short. As the school district attempts to cope with this approach, estimated share of hires for minority teachers sometimes reach the 50% level in a labor market that may be only 15% or so. When affirmative action multipliers (the multiple of a reasonably expected share, e.g., 15%) reach values of three they are extremely difficult to achieve without challenges of reverse discrimination.

   The rational way to set goals is

   - Segment the work force.
   - Determine the relevant labor markets.
   - Establish a reasonable expectation of yield from the labor market vis-a-vis expected opportunities.
   - Calculate the resulting representation as a dependent variable, using several varying sets of assumptions. If the representation which results is emotionally disappointing, it is nevertheless a reality of nondiscrimination in employment.

Because the findings of fact displayed in Title 5 do not reveal the basis for setting a representation goal, it is possible that some school districts have read the regulations as striving to achieve a minority teacher representation equal to the percentage of minorities in the community or minorities in the student population within a five-year period (per the Guidelies). The discipline of determining the relevant labor market is by-passed, and an arbitrary allocation of share of hires is made for minority teachers—sometimes inordinately high.

4. If the real problem is one of short supply in the relevant labor market, the affirmative action plans of the school districts are not at all likely to produce the accelerated rate of change in representation envisioned by the Board. Valuable time will have been lost in getting to the causes, diagnosis and cure. The perceived disproportionate representation of minorities and women will continue to exist indefinitely if the relevant supply is at a lower level then the Board's vision of equality.

   Supply problems at the professional level where specific credentials based on college education are required cannot be solved by goals and timetables which merely stimulate the dividing up of a shortage. They have to be attacked on a long-range basis by programs of the character of PIMEG (Chapter Three). Exhortation to do more, to be energetic, to be creative is helpful to short-range morale and sometimes to short-range results. But sooner or later, if there is a gap between expectations and supply, the problem has to be faced and solved, preferably sooner than later.

GUIDELINES FOR AFFIRMATIVE ACTION EMPLOYMENT PROGRAMS

As part of the Title 5 regulations, the Board instructed the Department of Education "to develop and disseminate to public education agencies guidelines to assist such agencies in developing and implementing affirmative action employment programs and shall render assistance to such agencies in carrying out the requirements of this chapter." The Department responded to this mandate and issued the Guidelines for Affirmative Action Employment Programs, dated September, 1975.

In early 1979 these Guidelines were being revised as a result of Senate Bill No. 179 (1977) which essentially wrote into law the Title 5 regulations of the Board, adding the Handicapped as a special group. Nevertheless, in effect for what will amount to four years, the initial Guidelines had a profound effect on the affirmative action plans prepared by the school districts. They are a part of the story and are included in Appendix D as a matter of documentation. On the whole, they focus strongly on personnel practices which they assert should be a part of affirmative action. From that point of view alone they are useful and interesting reading.

The Guidelines say relatively little about goals and timetables, shedding not much additional light on how to interpret Title 5. Pertinent excerpts are given below.

Definitions

- Minority Groups—For purposes of these Guidelines, minority groups shall include the following: Native American, Asian, Black, Filipino, and Spanish-surnamed. The above designations do not denote scientific definitions of anthropological origins. For purposes of these Guidelines, an employee may be included in the group with which he or she identifies, appears to belong, or is regarded in the community as belonging.
- Underrepresentation—Those employment situations in which there are significantly fewer persons of a particular grouping (minorities, women, men, etc.) serving at a particular job level or holding a particular kind of position than might be expected when compared to the distribution of that grouping in the available work force.
- Goal—A realistic level of accomplishment which an educational agency establishes for itself and to which the agency commits itself to increase employment opportunities for minorities and women at all levels (established in terms of the number of projected vacancies and the number of applicants who are qualified or qualifiable in the relevant job market).
- Timetable—The maximum time span the agency sets as the long-range and short-range periods for reaching the projected goals, which should be within five years.

Text

Goals and Timetables

Affirmative action programs are designed to eliminate discriminatory employment practices and to achieve a staff that is representative of the multiracial and multicultural society in which the student lives.

Goals, timetables, and affirmative action commitments must be designed to correct any identifiable deficiencies in representation from racial and ethnic minority groups and women at all employment levels within the agency. When deficiencies exist, the agency shall establish and set forth specific goals and timetables. Such goals and timetables shall be documented as part of the agency's written affirmative action program and shall be maintained in the agency's central office. The goals and timetables should be established in terms of the agency's analysis of deficiencies and a projection of anticipated vacancies, expansion, and attrition. Thus, in establishing goals and timetables, the agency should consider the results which could be reasonably expected from its efforts to accomplish the overall goal of the affirmative action program. The educational agency's compliance efforts should be judged by the quality of its affirmative action program and its good-faith efforts exerted toward implementation in conformity with state and federal statutes, regulations, and guidelines.[1]

The following are factors which should be considered in establishing goals and timetables:

1. Selected staff persons, advisory committees, community representatives, site administrators, employee organizations, and support personnel should be involved in the goal-setting process.
2. Goals should be realistic, measurable, and attainable.
3. Goals should be specific for planned results with timetables for completion.
4. Goals are targets that are reasonably attainable by means of applying every good-faith effort to make all aspects of the affirmative action program work. They are not to be confused with rigid quotas which must be met.
5. In setting goals, reference should be made to the State of California Fair Employment Practice Commission guidelines on affirmative action.

COMMENTS ON AFFIRMATIVE ACTION GUIDELINES

In general, a school district does not have much to go on from the written word with respect to goals and timetables. Unquestionably, guidelines by their nature have to be somewhat general and it is impossible to cover all potential questions ahead of time. Yet the vaguer the guidelines, the more open they are to individual interpretations, either by representatives of the State Department of Education or by the individual school districts. When an area as complex as EEO is managed by word of mouth or individual memos and verbal opinions, the result can be confusion and a lack of genuine

[1]The FEPA, Sec. 1410-1432 Calif. Labor Code; Title VII of CRA as amended by the Equal Employment Act of 1972; CRA, Title VI; Higher Ed. Act of 1972, Title IX; Presidential directive (Executive Order 11246), October 13, 1968.

progress toward the envisioned objectives, and worst of all, p litigation. What is missing from both Title 5 and the Guidel clear-cut exposition of the theory of the case. If one exists, it has not been well articulated. The impression is that the State Board of Education moved ahead with an incomplete rationale and left some of the logic pattern to be developed and back-filled at a later date. That task was still not completed at this writing.

The Guidelines are ambiguous. One could interpret the definition of a goal for minority teachers, for example, as being that representation which is equal to the percentage of minorities that could be reasonably expected in the applicant flow from the relevant labor market. There is an implication that a reasonable share of placements for minorities could be established and that, in turn, would lead to the representation goal over a period of time. However, the timetable is arbitrarily set at five years, thus forcing the share of placements to be a dependent variable, or the representation goal to be something less than the relevant labor market. But the concept of relevant market is clearly a factor.

If one moves along to the text, the concept is radically different. There, "affirmative action programs are designed to eliminate discriminatory practices and to achieve a staff that is representative of the multiracial and multicultural society in which the student lives." Thus what started out by definition as a concept of hiring from relevant labor markets reverts to the broader social-educational objective of some kind of parity between minority representation in the work force and their presence in the student population or the community.

In addressing the question of goals and timetables for minority teachers, for example, it is necessary to recognize a four-tiered hierarchy of purpose:

1. To assure that minorities are being hired in close proportion to their presence in the labor market.
2. To achieve a percentage equality between minorities in the teaching work force and their presence in the relevant labor market.
3. To accelerate the process of closing whatever gap may exist between the representation of minorities in the teaching work force and their presence in the relevant labor market—usually by striving for a higher share of hires than would normally be expected.
4. To achieve a percentage equality between minorities in the teaching work force and their presence in some body broader than the relevant labor market such as the community at large.

Purposes 1 and 2 pose no rational nor legal problems.

Purpose 3 begins to introduce possible problems of reverse discrimination. How far can school districts go in applying multipliers to the minority share of hires which could reasonably be expected from a relevant labor market?

Purpose 4 is different in character from employment discrimination in relevant labor markets. It is a social-educational purpose which cannot be fully satisfied if the real problem is not discrimination but a shortage of supply. When it is superimposed on the employment process under the banner of equal employment opportunity, it generates false expectation and diverts energy and resources from the type of thrust necessary to close the gap between the loftier goal and the real world of supply.

Regrettably, the Guidelines do not come to grips with the significance of this four-tiered hierarchy of purposes. The question asked earlier in the chapter remains unanswered by the Guidelines. If a school district has a minority teacher representation of 15%, a minority student population of 25%, a minority labor market of 15%, and the community is 20%, are minorities underrepresented and, if so, at what representation percentage would the intent of the Title 5 regulations be satisfied?

How did the school districts answer this type of question? Let's take a look at a few of the affirmative action plans.

THE SAN LUIS COASTAL UNIFIED DISTRICT PLAN

This plan shows evidence of a very conscientious effort to comply with Title 5 and the Guidelines. In a well structured logic pattern, the steps in the goals and timetables process are:

- Segment the work force into job groupings.
- Define the labor market and determine the percent of minorities and women therein.
- Determine where underrepresentation exists.
- Estimate turnover rates.
- Estimate future growth or reduction in numbers employed.
- Construct a model to predict minority and women representation in the job groupings over a five-year period.

Job Categories for Work Force Analysis

I. Assistant Superintendent
Associate Superintendent
Business Manager
Director (including Classified)
Principal
Superintendent

II. Assistant Director
Assistant Principal
District Librarian
Project Coordinator
Music Coordinator
Cafeteria Manager

III. Counselor
Librarian
MGM Specialist
Music Teacher
Nurse

III. (Continued)
Psychologist
Reading Teacher
Speech Therapist
Work Experience Coordinator

IV. Teachers—Classroom

V. Clerical and Fiscal

VI. Bus Driver
Cafeteria Worker
Instructional Aide
Teacher Clerical Aide

VII. Custodian
Maintenance
Groundsman

FIGURE 1.

Although the logic pattern is sound, the actual goals and timetables for minority hires into certificated nonmanagement positions (essentially teachers) require an inordinately high share vis-a-vis the identified relevant labor market. This can be seen from a step-by-step analysis of the plan.

Figure 1 shows the job categories used in the work force analysis.

Figure 2 shows the further collapsing of the job categories into three major work zones and the distribution therein by race, sex or ethnic categories. As an illustration for reading the display, the lower right-hand corner shows that minorities constitute 2.25% of management, 3.03% of nonmanagement (certificated), and 5.75% of nonmanagement (classified).

For purposes of determining whether there is any underrepresentation, the table displayed in Figure 3 was constructed. (Note the abbreviation Am.F. stands for Filipino-American and Filipino descent.) Mathematically, the display can be followed line by line, much like an IRS 1040 form.

San Luis Coastal Unified School District

Summary of Current Employment
January 20, 1978

Category	Total Employees			Caucasian		
	Male	Female	Total	Male	Female	Total
Management: I & II (includes classified and certificated)	37	9	46	35	9	44
% of I and II	79.78%	20.22%	100%	77.53%	20.22%	97.75%
NonManagement: III & IV (certificated)	199	197	396	192	192	384
% of III and IV	50.35%	49.65%	100%	48.55%	48.47%	97.02%
NonManagement: V, VI & VII (Classified)	103	245	348	94	234	328
% of V, VI, and VII	29.60%	70.40%	100%	27.01%	67.23%	94.24%

Category	Black			Spanish		
	Male	Female	Total	Male	Female	Total
Management: I & II (includes classified and certificated)	1		1			
% of I and II	2.25%		2.25%			
NonManagement: III & IV (certificated)	1		1	6	4	10
% of III and IV	.26%		.26%	1.54%	.92%	2.46%
NonManagement: V, VI & VII (Classified)	2		2	4	5	9
% of V, VI, and VII	.58%		.58%	1.15%	1.44%	2.59%

Category	Asian			American Filipino		
	Male	Female	Total	Male	Female	Total
Management: I & II (includes classified and certificated)						
No. of I and II						
NonManagement: III and IV (certificated)		1	1			
% of III and IV		.26%	.26%			
NonManagement: V, VI and VII (classified)		3	3	1	1	2
% of V, VI & VII		.86%	.86%	.29%	.29%	.58%

Category	American Indian			Total Minorities		
	Male	Female	Total	Male	Female	Total
Management: I & II (includes classified and certificated)				1		1
No. of I and II				2.25%		2.25
NonManagement: III and IV (certificated)				7	5	12
% of II and IV				1.77	1.26	3.0
NonManagement: V, VI & VII (classified)	2	2	4	9	11	20
% of V, VI & VII	.58%	.58%	1.15%	2.59%	3.16%	5.75%

FIGURE 2.

Summary: Underrepresentation as Determined by Ethnic Composition of Staff, Student Body, and Appropriate Labor Market for Each Major Job Group

	Cauc.	Black	Span.	Asian	Am.F.	Am.I.	Total Minority
1. Certificated—Nonmanagement	97.0%	0.3%	2.5%	0.2%	0.0%	0.0%	3.0%
2. Student Body	89.0%	1.4%	5.7%	2.5%	N/A	1.4%	11.0%
3. Line 1 less Line 2		(1.1%)	(3.2%)	(2.3%)	N/A	(1.4%)	(8.0%)
4. Applicable Labor Market (State and County)		2.7%	4.2% ←		4.0%	→	10.9%
5. Line 1 less Line 4		(2.4%)	(1.7) ←		(3.8%)	→	(7.9%)
6. Underrepresentation $\frac{\text{Lines } 3 + 5}{2}$		(1.8%)	(2.0)	N/A	N/A	N/A	(8.0%)
7. Classified—Nonmanagement	94.2%	0.6%	2.6%	0.9%	0.6%	1.2%	5.8%

8.	Student Body	89.0%	1.4%	5.7%	2.5%	N/A	1.4%	11.0%
9.	Line 7 less Line 8		(0.8%)	(3.1)	(1.6)	N/A	(0.2%)	(5.2%)
10.	Applicable Labor Market (County)		1.1%	10.6% ←		2.7%	→	14.4%
11.	Line 7 less Line 10		(0.5%)	(8.0%)	N/A	N/A	N/A	(8.6%)
12.	Underrepresentation $\frac{\text{Lines } 8 + 10}{2}$		(0.7%)	(5.6%)	N/A	N/A	N/A	(6.9%)
13.	Management	97.8%	2.3%	0.0%	0.0%	0.0%	0.0%	2.3%
14.	Student Body	89.0%	1.4%	5.7%	2.5%	N/A	1.4%	11.0%
15.	Line 13 less Line 14		0.9%	(5.7%)	(2.5%)	N/A	(1.4%)	(8.7%)
16.	Applicable Labor Market		N/A	N/A	N/A	N/A	N/A	N/A
17.	Underrepresentation Line 15		0.9%	(5.7%)	(2.5%)	N/A	(1.4%)	(8.7%)

N/A = Not Available
( ) = Negative Number

FIGURE 3.

- Line 1 identifies the job grouping as certificated nonmanagement and shows a 3.0% total minority representation.
- Line 2 shows the student body population contains 11% minority.
- Line 3 compares the first two lines and shows an 8% shortfall between the two.
- Line 4 states that the applicable labor market is 10.9% minority. (This was derived as the average of a State 13.2% and a County 8.6% minority market.)
- Line 5 compares the representation to the applicable labor market and shows a 7.9% shortfall.
- Line 6 averages the shortfalls derived using the student population and applicable labor market as reference standards. The result is an underrepresentation of 8% for total minority.
- Lines 7 through 17 simply repeat the same analytical process for the other two job groupings.

When underrepresentation exists, the next step is to establish corrective goals and timetables. Figure 4 shows the "turnover" data for certificated personnel. These numbers apparently include management as well as nonmanagement people. They also include adult education teachers where the turnover is probably higher than for others. But in any event, the losses in the overall translate into a 7% annual rate.

Figure 5 shows historical and projected employment data.

The school district expects a decline in employment over the five-year period covered by the goals and timetables. Note that adult education teachers are excluded from this projection although they are included in the goals and timetables.

Figure 6 displays the goals and timetables for certificated nonmanagement positions. In the accompanying text, there is the statement that "These goals and timetables are based on a calculation model. . . . The goals and timetables listed would appear to be reasonable and attainable over the five-year period. It is, however, desirable to achieve these goals at the earliest possible date."

COMMENTS ON THE SAN LUIS COASTAL UNIFIED DISTRICT PLAN

First of all, the student population was used as one basis for determining underrepresentation of certificated nonmanagement

Certificated Terminations

	'72–'73	'73–'74	'74–'75	'75–'76	'76–'77	Total
Deaths	2	0	0	1	2	5
Retirement	7	13	6	7	13	46
Other Job	2	5	4	4	8	23
Other Resignation	14	10	18	11	8	61
Totals	25	28	28	23	31	135

FIGURE 4.

Employment 1973–1982										
Job Group	Oct. 1973	Oct. 1974	Oct. 1975	Oct. 1976	Oct. 1977	Oct.* 1978	Oct.* 1979	Oct.* 1980	Oct.* 1981	Oct.* 1982
Non-Management Certificated†	382	357	370	365	374	354	319	315	310	305
Non-Management Classified	228	231	279	289	346	326	293	290	285	280
Certificated Management	35	31	34	39	37	37	33	33	33	32
Classified Management	N/A	N/A	N/A	N/A	9	9	8	8	8	8

*Projected Figures

†Excludes Adult Education Teachers

FIGURE 5.

Employment Goals and Timetables

	1977–78	1978–79	1979–80	1980–81	1981–82	1982–83
Total Minorities	12	13–14	14–17	16–22	20–29	25–36
% Minorities	3.0%	3.2%–3.6%	3.6%–4.5%	4.3%–6.0%	5.6%–8.3%	7.0%–10.6%

Notes: 1. It is desirable that minorities be assigned equitably among the schools of the District.
2. The ultimate goal is to have 10 to 11% of this group composed of minorities.

FIGURE 6.

minorities. Conceptually, it is not a relevant labor market but addresses a social/educational purpose other than employment discrimination. As things turn out, mathematically, the percentage of minorities in the student population is just about equal to that for the average of the State and County relevant labor markets and the use of this basis does not significantly affect the conclusions drawn with respect to underrepresentation for this particular job grouping.

Of greater interest is the hockey stick character of the goals and timetables. As we discussed in Chapter Two, hockey stick projections reflect an optimism that somehow things will be better in the future. Plotting the goals and timetables data for certificated non-management positions, we get the results shown in Figure 7. Even the minimum forecasted representation in the year 1982–83 appears overly optimistic in view of an expected decline in enrollment. The maximum value for representation in that year seems, almost by casual inspection, to be unattainable without assigning an exceptionally high share of placements to minority.

Unfortunately, the plan does not state what the minority share of hires is expected to be for this job grouping. Similarly, the employment levels on which the goals and timetables are based are not stated in the plan. Adult education teachers are included in the goals but excluded from the data in Figure 5. However, there is sufficient data in Figure 6 on which to base some approximate calculations to estimate what share of hires has been allocated in the model to minorities.

Figure 8 approximates the certificated non-management employment levels used for the goals and timetables model. With these numbers and using the 7% annual loss rate derived from Figure 4, it

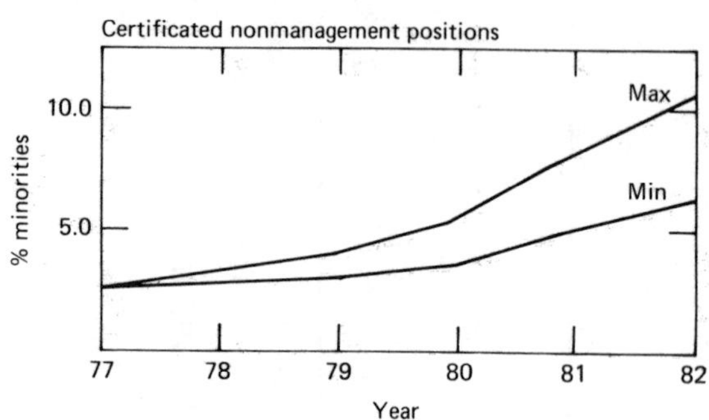

FIGURE 7.

Certificated Nonmanagement Employees	
Year	**Total**
1977–78	396
1978–79	396
1979–80	380
1980–81	370
1981–82	360
1982–83	350

FIGURE 8.

is possible to estimate the annual number of new hires in which minorities are expected to share as shown in Figure 9.

Finally, the necessary minority share can be developed as shown in Figures 10 and 11 in the right column.

What do all of these numbers tell us? First of all, we should note that the results in Figures 10 and 11 are approximations derived from a public document, and they may not describe with precise accuracy the real intent of the school district's plan. It is unfortunate that the written plan did not include specific information on the expected shares of hires. But in the absence of that data, the reconstruction of the model done here is at least one way of searching out the implications of the forecasted representations of minority. The estimated shares create serious doubts about the feasibility of the goals and the wisdom of assigning such high proportions to minority in the model.

Expected New Hires

Year	Vacancies From Losses	Needed Reduction	Expected New Hires
1978–79	28	0	28
1979–80	28	16	12
1980–81	27	10	17
1981–82	26	10	16
1982–83	25	10	15

FIGURE 9.

Minority Shares Model—Minimum Goals

Year	No. Initial Minority	No. Ending Minority	Net Gain Needed	Minority Loss	Needed Minority Hires	% Total Hires
1978–79	12	13	1	1	2	7
1979–80	13	14	1	1	2	17
1980–81	14	16	2	1	3	18
1981–82	16	20	4	1	5	31
1982–83	20	25	5	1	6	40

FIGURE 10.

Minority Shares Model—Maximum Goals						
Year	No. Initial Minority	No. Ending Minority	Net Gain Needed	Minority Loss	Needed Minority Hires	% Total Hires
1978–79	12	14	2	1	3	11
1979–80	14	17	3	1	4	33
1980–81	17	22	5	1	6	35
1981–82	22	29	7	2	9	56
1982–83	29	36	7	2	9	60

FIGURE 11.

For example, if the applicable labor market is 10.9% minority for certificated nonmanagement positions, how realistic are goals that require a minority share allocation as high as 40% to 60%. Attempts to exceed the expected reasonable flow from a labor market by multiples of three or four are cloth from which reverse discrimination suits can be fashioned.

THE SACRAMENTO UNIFIED SCHOOL DISTRICT PLAN

The plan is dated July 19, 1976, and it is a clear, concise plan with very little "boilerplate"—one which lays the important considerations plainly out in the open.

POLICY STATEMENT

The Sacramento City Unified School District believes in a policy which assures that it will not discriminate against any applicant or employee in any employment practice because of race, color, religion, sex, marital status, age, national origin, ancestry, or handicap, and that it will take corrective action to ensure that underrepresentation and/or underutilization will not exist for ethnic minority groups and women at all levels of responsibility.

In addition, the Board of Education is cognizant of the need to provide all students and the community with the opportunity to interact with certificated and classified personnel representing a broad and diverse cross section of the ethnic composition of the community as well as the opportunity to interact with both sexes. This recognizes the educational value of utilizing the unique talents and backgrounds of minorities, women, and persons with handicaps in the Sacramento City Unified School District. In this connection it is important for students to observe that women, minorities, and persons with handicapped conditions can assume responsible and diverse roles in our school system.

The district will promote an active, result-oriented Affirmative Action Program. Further, the Board of Education commits itself to an affirmative action plan which is designed to recruit, employ, and promote minorities and women in all job classifications and levels of responsibility. In order to accomplish this, the Personnel Office will

> seek to achieve minority group and female representation among district employees consistent with their respective percentages in the student population of the Sacramento City Unified School District. The affirmative action program will include specific goals and timetables to be achieved relative to the recruitment, selection, and promotion of minorities and women presently underrepresented or underutilized at various levels of responsibility. Similarly, the district shall take positive steps to employ and advance in employment qualified handicapped persons. The program will also include a plan for semiannual evaluation of the affirmative action program. The goals of this policy will be achieved by filling vacancies as they occur and as new positions are created.
>
> The Affirmative Action policy of the Sacramento City Unified School District embraces placement practices which seek to promote ethnic and sex balance in all schools, offices, and departments. This recognizes the importance of having an integrated work force in order to avoid racial isolation anywhere in the district. Consequently, steps will be taken to correct any racial imbalance prevalent at the local school level.

The sought-for percentage representation for minority teachers, for example, is the percentage of minorities in the student population—a number not contained in the written plan but verbally stated to be 48%. Moreover, racial imbalances will be corrected at the local school level. Thus, labor market data does not appear in the affirmative action plan as it did in the San Luis Coastal district plan.

Figure 12 illustrates the goals and timetables for the job grouping "teachers." Very clearly, the share of vacancies filled is expected to be 50% for minorities although (if the San Luis Coastal data is correct) the statewide market is only 13.2% minority. When the 50% share is fed into a model based upon a loss rate of 7% per year and a decline rate of 2% per year, at the end of the five-year period the minority representation in the "teachers" job grouping turns out to be 26%. Over the time period of the plan, 496 vacancies will be filled, half by minorities, to produce a net increase of 98 minorities and to increase from 19% to 26% their representation on the teaching staff. In the future, the task of further increasing minority representation is a formidable one. If the school district stays with its 50% ultimate goal, it is locked into a 50% minority share of hires well into the next century.

How does the district propose to meet this ambitious goal? The affirmative action plan contains the following statements:

Personnel Service Office
Affirmative Action Program
Proposed Goals and Timetables

Employee Group	Teachers
Includes	Teachers, Adviser Student Activities, Resource, Demonstration, Specialist
	Teacher, Reading, Elementary Special Subjects, Resource Specialists,
	Department Chairman, Speech and Language Specialist.

Current Number of Employees	2067		
Males	767 (37%)	Projected Number of Employees, 1980	1841
Females	1300 (63%)		--------
Minorities	390 (19%)	Five-Year Goal, Minorities	488 (26%)

Average Termination Rate, 1971–75	7%
Estimated Yearly Decline in Positions	2%

	1976	1977	1978	1979	1980
1. Projected Number of Employees	2026	1985	1945	1906	1868
2. Projected Number of Males Remaining in Work Force	713	697	683	670	656
3. Projected Number of Females Remaining in Work Force	1209	1187	1163	1139	1117
4. Projected Numbers of Minorities Remaining in Work Force	363	386	406	424	440
5. Estimated Vacancies	104	101	99	97	95
6. Hiring Goal—Females	0	0	0	0	0
7. Hiring Goal—Minorities	52	51	50	49	48
8. Projected Total—Males	750 (37)	734 (37)	720 (37)	705 (37)	691 (37)
9. Projected Total—Females	1276 (63)	1251 (63)	1225 (63)	1201 (63)	1177 (63)
10. Projected Total—Minorities	415 (20)	437 (22)	456 (23)	473 (25)	488 (26)

Five-year Summary

Vacancies—496
Minority Hiring Goal—250 (50)

FIGURE 12.

RECRUITMENT

1. **A.** Notice of vacancies shall be posted in all schools and offices.
1. **B.** Notice of vacancies shall be issued to public employment agencies, colleges, and organizations serving minorities, women, and persons with handicaps simultaneously when out-of-district applicants can be considered.
2. Notice of vacancies for which out-of-district applicants can be considered will be sent to newspapers, news media, and publications having a large circulation among minorities, women, and persons with handicaps.
3. All available community resources will be used in recruiting applicants for vacancies for which out-of-district applicants can be considered in occupations underrepresented by minorities and women.
4. District employees will be encouraged to refer qualified minorities, women, and persons with handicaps for vacancies being advertised.
5. District employees will be encouraged to inform the Personnel Office of minorities, women, and persons with handicaps who may be interested in employment in the district.
6. An on-going and active working relationship will be established with California community colleges and other California institutions of higher education in an effort to secure applications from minorities, females, and persons with handicaps.
7. Selected target areas will be visited when efforts locally and in California fail to generate a sufficient supply of minority and women applicants.
8. An active applicant file of information will be developed and maintained on minority and women applicants in all employment categories.
9. An active file of information will be maintained on public employment agencies, colleges, and community organizations serving minorities, women, and persons with handicaps.

SELECTION AND EMPLOYMENT

1. Job descriptions and specifications, applications, recruitment materials, and other personnel forms will receive continuous review and scrutiny to eliminate statements and/or questions which indicate a preference for or discrimination against applicants because of ethnicity, sex, marital status, or handicap.
2. All tests used on screening and selecting candidates will be scrutinized for any adverse effects they may have on minorities, women, and persons with handicaps.

3. Evaluation forms used in interviews will be examined in order to ensure that all evaluated areas are job related and are free of minority and sex-biased language.
4. Job descriptions of all classified, administrative, and certificated positions will reflect only those requirements relating to actual job skills performed.
5. A racially and sex balanced corps of interviewers and screening committee members will be trained in: legal requirements, skills of conducting interviews, and screening. These interviews will be utilized at both the certificated and classified levels.
6. Certificated and classified policies, practices, rules, and regulations will be reviewed to identify any action(s) that would have an adverse effect on any member of a protected group.
7. In the selection of district personnel, priority consideration will be given to those applicants who possess qualitative training and experience beyond the minimum qualification standards in the following areas:

   a. Ability to relate to specific students, parents, and community groups;
   b. Experience in working with minority and/or disadvantaged groups;
   c. Experience and training in urban education programs;
   d. Unique job and program related factors; and
   e. Awareness of the changing roles of women in our society.
   f. Ability to relate to persons with handicaps.

8. Except for confidential information, applicants will be advised as to the reasons for rejection upon the applicant's request. Each Sacramento City Unified School District application for employment shall contain a notice to the effect that reasons for rejection will be given the applicant, except for confidential information, upon the written request of the applicant.

STAFF DEVELOPMENT AND PROMOTION

1. In consultation with employees, supervisors will develop realistic career development plans that lead to certification and/or promotion.
2. For those occupations where there are underrepresentation and underutilization of minorities or women, employees will be given the opportunity to develop their potential to assume skilled and/or management level positions through planned, district-sponsored, training programs. Further, positive efforts will be made to include persons with handicaps in such programs.

3. Leadership development programs will be organized for qualifiable persons, with special emphasis on underrepresented groups, interested in leadership and managerial positions.
4. Extensive in-service training workshops for administrators will be conducted centrally regarding affirmative action concepts, implementation, practices, policies, and attendant administrative responsibilities.
5. District administrators will provide on-site affirmative action orientation sessions for their certificated and classified staff members.

From an analytical view, three things are disturbing about the Sacramento City Unified School District's affirmative action plan.

- Although it requires that the personnel process remove all statements and practices which indicate a preference for applicants because of race, sex or ethnic considerations, its thrust clearly is tied to the "protected class." For example, "selected target areas (for recruitment) will be visited when efforts locally and in California fail to generate a sufficient supply of minority and women candidates." Such, of course, is likely to be the case when the labor market is somewhere around 13.2% and the goal is a 50% share of hires.

- The goal is derived from the minority representation in the student population, not from the labor market. It could be argued that the definition of protected class has been shifted from employees to students for social-cultural-educational purposes. Perhaps legally, this is in keeping with Senate Bill 179 (see Appendix E), which defines an affirmative action employment program as "planned activities designed to seek, hire, and promote persons who are underrepresented in the work force compared to their number in the population . . . formerly excluded at the various levels of responsibility who are qualified or may become qualified through appropriate training or experience within a reasonable length of time." There is no further definition of the term "population." Is it state, community, student, or labor market based? In business and industry EEO goals based on Title VII or presidential orders, it is well recognized that women are grossly underrepresented in some job categories such as skilled crafts in comparison to their participation in the total civilian labor force. That is reason enough for the requirement of affirmative action in recruiting, training, et al., but the goals are keyed to labor markets, not to the civilian labor force. It would be an unreal stretch, for example, to set a share of hires for women in crafts at 40% when the availability in the labor market is only 5%. Yet this particular school district has imposed the same kind of unreal stretch in its goal for minority teachers. Equalling the minority representation in the community is a long-range aspiration, not a realistic basis for allocating shares of hires in a five-year affirmative action plan.

- Drifting still further from a basic equal employment opportunity concept, the district states that "priority consideration will be given to those applicants who possess qualitative training and experience beyond the minimum qualification standards in the following areas:

  1. Ability to relate to specific students, parents, and community groups;
  2. Experience in working with minority and/or disadvantaged groups;
  3. Experience and training in urban education programs;
  4. Unique job and program related factors;
  5. Awareness of the changing roles of women in our society;
  6. Ability to relate to persons with handicaps."

One has to seriously question, for example, whether a minimally qualified teacher who can relate well to the community should be given priority consideration over others equally or better qualified. How job related for most teachers are relationships with the community? How job related and measurable is awareness of the changing roles of women in our society? From the logic point of view, the district may be doing some fast foot work. On one hand, "job descriptions will reflect only those requirements relating to actual job skills performed." On the other, priority consideration is given in terms of the six factors quoted above, somewhat in the manner of an escape clause for justifying selections which help to achieve a relatively high goal.

THE SANTA BARBARA SCHOOL AND HIGH SCHOOL DISTRICTS PLAN

The preface to this plan, dated June, 1978, is as follows:

> The purpose of this Affirmative Action Program is to set guidelines for specific and result-oriented procedures to which the Districts commit themselves to apply every good faith effort. The objective of this program is twofold:
>
> **a)** To provide equal employment opportunity
>
> **b)** To increase the utilization of minorities and women at all levels of employment.

This Affirmative Action Program has been developed with the goal of recruiting the best talent available to the Districts.

Following the preface is a statement of the legal basis for the plan.

LEGAL BASIS

A. Laws Covering Discrimination

Over the past few years an increasing number of State and Federal laws have been adopted covering various aspects of racial discrimination. Those of concern to the Santa Barbara School District and the Santa Barbara High School District relate to discrimination in employment, not only as law, but also as to the detrimental effect upon the educational process by underutilization of talent pools due to traditional discrimination patterns.

The applicable laws are Title VII of the Federal Civil Rights Act of 1964, regulations of the Equal Employment Opportunity Commission (EEOC), the California Fair Employment Practices Act (FEPC), various Executive Orders of the President and the U.S. Civil Service Commission. The common objective is to prohibit unfair discrimination in employment based on race, religion, color, creed, national origin or ancestry, sex, age, and handicap. State and Federal agencies have power to enforce the laws, and administrative remedies are provided job applicants who have complaints.

The Courts have pointed the way to provide equal employment opportunity for people who belong to a group protected by the legislation, and the message is clear. Any personnel selection device or employment practice that is based on factors not relevant to job performance must be eradicated; and factors that are job-related must be substituted.

The Courts have repeatedly found that the use of non-job-related factors have the effect of erecting artificial barriers to employment and promotion of persons who, in actuality, may be qualified by experience, potential to learn and improve, and desire to perform. Significant numbers of such excluded persons are members of racial and ethnic groups and women. The laws prohibit non-job-related selection and promotion practices which unfairly exclude a disproportionate number of such persons from employment or promotion.

The various agencies responsible for administering the laws have provided some specific guidelines on employee selection, and these guidelines in themselves have been judged in court to have the effect of law. Those most pertinent to the districts' operation are included below. As significant revisions, additions or modifications are made, the Certificated and Classified Personnel Departments will forward supplements to each school and department in the districts.

B. Illegal Personnel Practices

It is illegal to:

1. Discriminate against individuals engaged in activities supporting the Civil Rights Act.
2. Express preferences or limitations as to race, sex, age, etc. in advertisements of job openings unless the trait is a bona fide occupational qualification. (e.g. actor, actress)
3. Arbitrarily discriminate against individuals over 40 years old, on the basis of age.
4. Maintain separate lines of progression on a seniority system for males and females unless based on genuine occupational qualifications.
5. Have rules against married females if the rules are not equally applied to married males.
6. Refuse to hire a woman because of her sex based on assumptions of the comparative employment characteristics of women in general, e.g., that they have a higher turnover rate than men.
7. Refuse to hire an individual based on stereotyped characterizations of the sexes, e.g., women have better finger dexterity, or males are more aggressive.
8. Refuse to hire an individual because of the preferences of co-workers, employer, clients or customers unless there is a bona fide occupational qualification involved.
9. Use tests to select new employees for jobs into which they are expected to progress rather than for the entry job unless a great majority (at least 50%) of employees on the payroll will reach the higher level job in a reasonable (3-year) period of time.
10. Discriminate against any individual because of membership in the armed forces or in the active reserve, or any social or political affiliation.

C. Scope of the Legislation

The legislation affects the entire gamut of employment practices. Any of the following activities may be scrutinized by the enforcing agencies:

1. Administration of employment practices
2. Advertisement of job openings

3. Employment applications
4. Employment interviews
5. Employment tests
6. Standards for employment
7. Criteria for referral selection
8. Record-keeping on selection criteria and hiring interviews
9. Upgrading and training of employees
10. Promotion, transfer and retention

In this statement, the school district points out that over and above the racial discrimination laws, there is a detrimental effect upon the educational process by underutilization of talent pools due to traditional discrimination patterns. Left unanswered are three major questions: When the personnel system is functioning on a truly nondiscriminatory basis and the natural flow rates of minorities and women are established, how far (if at all) is it necessary to go beyond that natural flow for educational purposes? Relative to the objective of increasing the utilization of minorities and women at all levels of employment, at what point will the objective have been met? If seeking out the best talent available fails to yield some desired increase in minorities and women, what will be the priority?

Later in the plan these questions are answered indirectly in the expression of the goals. Two separate types of schools are included—the elementary and the secondary. The long-range employment goal to be achieved within a period of not more than 10 years is that which (a) for each school reflects at least the ethnic composition of its district, and (b) for each central office reflects the average ethnic composition of the district's student population.

As an illustration, Figure 13 shows the results of a work force analysis for Hispanics in the year 1977–78. For example, the table shows that 8.1% of elementary and 7.3% of secondary classroom teachers are Hispanics. At the unskilled laborers level, 64% of the jobs are held by Hispanics. Once again, we see a typical hierarchy of jobs in which the representation of minorities (in this case Hispanics) is high at the bottom and low at the top. However, the affirmative action goal is described as:

Employment of Hispanics

The Hispanic student population in the elementary district is 44 percent and in the secondary district 20 percent. There should be

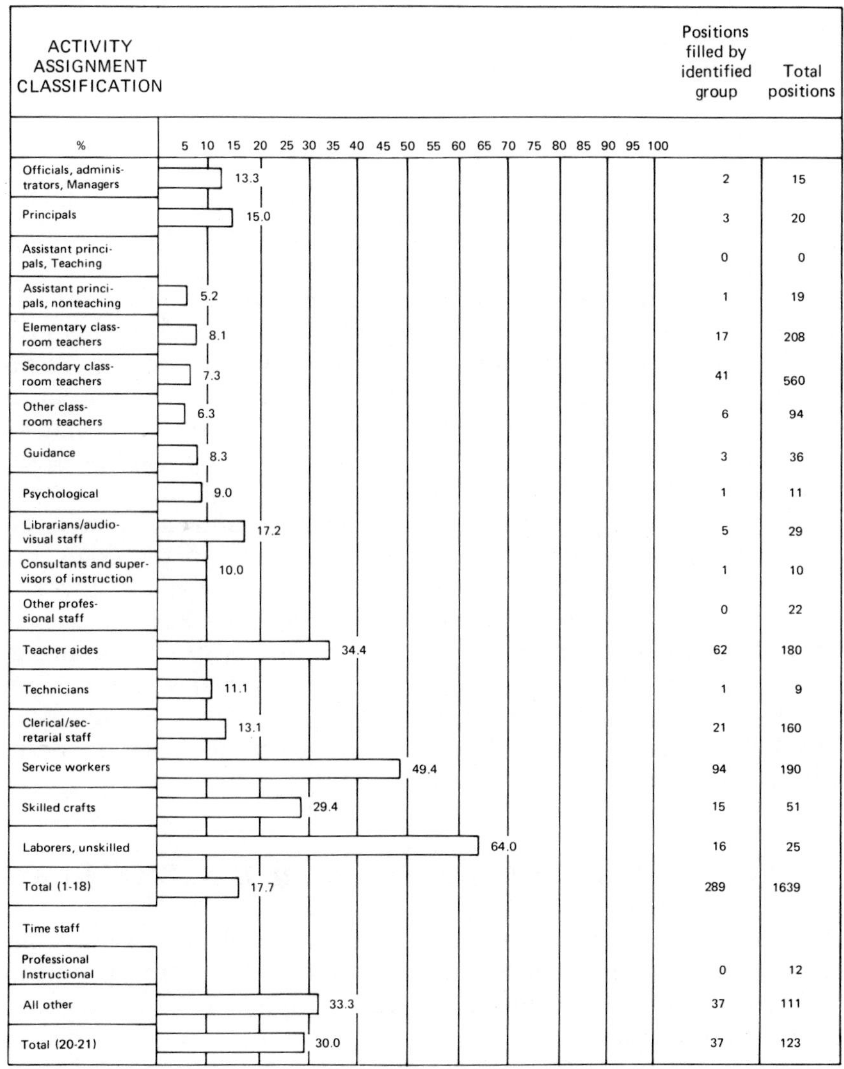

ACTIVITY ASSIGNMENT CLASSIFICATION	%	Positions filled by identified group	Total positions
Officials, administrators, Managers	13.3	2	15
Principals	15.0	3	20
Assistant principals, Teaching		0	0
Assistant principals, nonteaching	5.2	1	19
Elementary classroom teachers	8.1	17	208
Secondary classroom teachers	7.3	41	560
Other classroom teachers	6.3	6	94
Guidance	8.3	3	36
Psychological	9.0	1	11
Librarians/audio-visual staff	17.2	5	29
Consultants and supervisors of instruction	10.0	1	10
Other professional staff		0	22
Teacher aides	34.4	62	180
Technicians	11.1	1	9
Clerical/secretarial staff	13.1	21	160
Service workers	49.4	94	190
Skilled crafts	29.4	15	51
Laborers, unskilled	64.0	16	25
Total (1-18)	17.7	289	1639
Time staff			
Professional Instructional		0	12
All other	33.3	37	111
Total (20-21)	30.0	37	123

FIGURE 13.

proportionate representation in employment classifications (1–18 Table A). This goal will be satisfied if 44 percent of the total classified and certificated staff is Hispanic in the elementary district. The total staff in the secondary district should approximate the Hispanic student population, which is 20 percent. We should reach this goal by 1985.

Referring again to Figure 13 (which is Table A), the total of lines 1 through 18 is 17.7% Hispanic. Although elementary and secondary data cannot be precisely separated, the combined goal is probably 25% to 30% Hispanic representation in 1985 versus only 17.7% in 1977–78. However, by then the surge of elementary students progressing to secondary will further increase the overall target percentage. Whether or not this goal can be met is not nearly as important as its "bottom line" character—a goal based on the total work force rather than segments in the job hierarchy. Assuming validity to the statement in the Legal Basis section of the plan about the detrimental effect upon the educational process by underutilization of talent pools due to traditional discrimination patterns, where in the goals and timetables is the solution to the problem? If in 10 years Hispanics still occupy close to 70% of the unskilled labor jobs, has the detrimental effect of discrimination on the educational process been eliminated? The solution to the disparate distribution of Hispanics very likely is out of the hands of these Santa Barbara School Districts. Nevertheless, it is a deeply rooted problem that lies unattended in the preoccupation with somewhat meaningless goals.

THE GLENDALE UNIFIED SCHOOL DISTRICT PLAN

This plan, in conjunction with its work force analysis and goals and timetables, contains a good summary statement of the problems associated with producing significant changes in minority and women representation.

CONSTRAINTS AND PROBLEMS IN THE IMPLEMENTATION OF AFFIRMATIVE ACTION EMPLOYMENT PROGRAMS IN THE GLENDALE UNIFIED SCHOOL DISTRICT

The Affirmative Action Employment Plan has been developed with the intent of pursuing the goals as specified. The Board of Education of the Glendale Unified School District intends to have the Plan implemented in a manner which will result in an increase in the number of minorities and women in the major employment categories. Achievement of the employment goals, however, is not without constraints that limit the District's ability to implement the affirmative program as prescribed. Included in such constraints are the following:

A. TEACHER TURNOVER

The rate of teacher turnover has declined significantly in the past several years. This change has a marked effect on the number of new teachers that can be brought into the District each year. It is a pronounced problem in those schools which serve a stable attendance area and have long-tenured teachers currently assigned to the staff.

B. CREDENTIAL SYSTEM

The California teacher credentialling system has rigid legal requirements. Generally, the law permits teachers to teach in authorized subject areas only. Minority applicants may have credential teaching authorizations in crowded fields or fields where no or few vacancies exist. Also, state law requires the holding of special credentials for pupil personnel services and administrative positions.

C. COMPETITION

Due to equal opportunity and affirmative action laws, school districts throughout the State are seeking minority applicants. This intense competitive labor market increases the difficulty of school districts in achieving their affirmative action goals.

D. SHORTAGE OF CERTIFICATED MINORITIES

There are indications that there exists a shortage of certificated minorities. This probably is made more extreme by the competition for such personnel.

E. CIVIL SERVICE MERIT SYSTEM

The classified staff of the Gendale Unified School District are hired under Rules and Regulations which provide competitive bases for selection and promotion. The Merit System Rules and Regulations are derived from the California Education Code. Selection procedures limit the flexibility of school district hiring practices.

F. LACK OF COMPREHENSIVE STATISTICAL DATA

There is a lack of useful statistical data regarding the specific occupational skills of minorities and women available in the unemployed work force. This lack of adequate information is particularly noticeable for certificated personnel.

G. SINGLE CAREER POSITIONS

A number of positions in the school district are singular positions, i.e., the particular position is held by only one person. Also, these positions typically experience very slow turnover. The incumbents tend to be career oriented in these specialized areas. Such single career positions do not lend themselves well to the affirmative action goal setting process.

H. PROMOTIONAL POLICY

Board Policy 4116a provides that ". . . When promotional opportunities arise, vacancies will be filled by the best qualified candidates available. . . ." The policy also provides for the screening and interviewing of promotional candidates by a representative committee of teachers and administrators. This committee recommends ". . . the best candidates to the Superintendent. . . ." who recommends him/her to the Board of Education for final approval and appointment.

I. DECLINING ENROLLMENT

Enrollment projections for the five-year period 1976–77/1980–81 show a significant decline at all levels of instruction. Due to the direct relationship of student enrollment to staffing patterns, it is projected that the school staff, particularly certificated, will decline proportionately.

J. UPWARD MOBILITY, CERTIFICATED

The retirement pattern of the certificated staff presents some problems regarding upward mobility in the administrative hierarchy. Projected retirements in the administrative categories show only a minimum of vacancy potential in the five year period 1976–77/1980–81.

Before a detailed work force analysis and the development of goals and timetables, the plan makes three significant statements:

- Representation of minorities and women will be increased in those employment categories where minorities and women are underrepresented and are available in the relevant job market.
- The primary purpose of the Glendale Unified School District is the educational welfare of its children. For this reason, it is imperative that the employment system have as its goal the recruiting, hiring, retaining, and promoting of the best possible qualified teachers, administrators, classified, and support per-

sonnel. The Affirmative Action Program is not intended to constitute a justification for the lowering of qualification standards.

- In addition to the federal and state laws and regulatory guidelines which mandate that local public school agencies develop and implement affirmative action plans, there are sound educational bases for such actions. It is educationally important for all children to enjoy cultural enrichment, including having positive experiences with persons from diverse racial and ethnic backgrounds. It is equally important for children to observe that women as well as men can assume responsible roles in society. For the minority child, it is especially desirable to have the positive image provided by competent minority teachers, counselors, and administrators. It is likewise educationally desirable for the child from the majority group to have positive experiences with minority group members at all levels within the school setting.

The pursuit of the educational goals of the Glendale Unified School District can be enhanced through the implementation of the equal opportunity and affirmative action programs.

Against the foregoing backdrop, the plan proceeds with a utilization analysis. For certificated personnel the results are:

- Of 403 elementary teachers K–6, 19 are minority (4.7%).
- Of 477 secondary classroom teachers, 13 are minority (2.7%).
- Of 117 other certificated teachers, 8 are minority (6.8%).

In keeping with the earlier statement that underrepresentation would be judged on the basis of relevant labor market, the plan struggles unsuccessfully to define and size that market. There are analyses of the labor forces in the City of Glendale, and in Los Angeles County, resulting in the conclusion that the data are too old and do not contain sufficient segmentation to focus on certificated personnel. There is also a study of enrollments and racial-ethnic composition in the independent colleges of Southern California which offer teacher preparation credential programs. No conclusion is drawn from the data; the search for the relevant labor market dwindles away at that point.

The next step is to develop the expected number of vacancies to be filled over the five-year period of the plan. The final step is to state the goals and timetables, as shown in Figure 14.

Goals—Certificated Staff
Five-Year Period, 1976–77/1980–81

Employment Categories	Number of Personnel 1975–1976: Total	Females	Minorities M/F	Projected Vacancies Five Year Period 1976–77/1980–81	Goals: To Maintain Present Proportionate Level Plus Additional Minorities/Females
Teachers:					
Elementary K-6	403	362	19	35	18 minorities M/F
Secondary 7–12	477	219	13	34	17 minorities M/F
Other Certificated	117	97	8	8	4 minorities M/F
Pupil Personnel Services:					
Counselors	22	13	1	3	2 minorities M/F
Psychometrists	—	—	—	—	*
Psychologists	9	6	—	—	*
Administration:					
Category A	12	7	2	1	*
Category B	14	6	—	2	1 Minority M/F 1 Female
Category C	38	12	2	2	1 minority M/F 1 Female
Category D	8	—	—	—	*

NOTE: *No vacancies are projected for these employment categories for the five-year period 1976–1977/1980–81. If vacancies occur in those categories in which no or only one vacancy is projected for the five-year priod, the filling of such positions will be reviewed within the context of the intent and goals of the Affirmative Action Employment.

FIGURE 14.

The expected minority share of opportunities in the certificated teacher category is 50%. There is also an affirmative retention goal of retaining the present proportionate level of minorities; that is, equal turnover rates for minorities and for the teaching staff as a whole.

In principle, at least, this district keyed its goals to a relevant labor market, even though it was unable to arrive at a satisfactory definition or sizing. In practice, it may have felt considerable pressure for high shares of opportunities for minorities on the basis of student and community population. In March, 1976, the elementary school population was approximately 25% minority and on a growth curve. The 1970 census data show 18.4% minority in the City and 16.7% minority in the labor force.

Even if the Glendale Unified School District meets its share of hires goal and is successful in affirmative retention, only a modest improvement in minority representation will occur over the five-year period of the plan. On the whole, whatever undesirable things might be read from the certificated teachers numerical profile at the start of the plan will still be read at the end of the five years. That is the reality for this school district regardless of aspirations and exhortation to accomplish more.

THE BASIC PROBLEM

It seems clear enough that the State of California is using the banner of Equal Employment Opportunity to address social-educational purposes well beyond the issue of employment discrimination. Although EEO case law is still evolving, a basic logic pattern has already come into reasonably sharp focus:

- Segment the work force.
- Determine the relevant labor markets (external and internal) for the segments.
- Compare the representation of minorities (for exa[illegible] [illegible]g-
  ments with that in the labor market to determine i[illegible]
  resentation.
- Where underrepresentation exists, take approp[illegible]
  toward the objective of reaching an appro[illegible]
  equality with the relevant labor market.
- In the overall, purge the personnel syste[illegible]
  practices which may exist. Likewise striv[illegible]
  has no race, sex or ethnic overtones.

The State of California has moved far afield from this relatively simple logic pattern. In the quest for objectives not directly related to employment discrimination, the student population has been substituted for the relevant labor market. The result is the confusion and inconsistency reflected in the four affirmative action plans that were discussed. When the minority student population exceeds the general availability of certificated minority teachers, whatever real underrepresentation exists will be magnified by the irrelevant comparison basis. The artificially high gap calls for inordinately high shares of hires for minority if more than minimal improvements in representation are to be achieved. Rationalization for these high shares takes strange forms, such as minimally qualified teachers being given priority in hiring on the basis of their ability to relate to the community. Even when buttressed by such rationalizations, goals that allocate 50% shares to minorities are generally unattainable without high risk of reverse discrimination charges. Whatever direction the State may take in revising its Guidelines for Affirmative Action Employment Programs, it has already left a trail of confusion and false expectations while proclaiming a realistic results-oriented approach.

THE TIP OF THE ICEBERG

Because they are public documents, affirmative action plans in the California schools are readily accessed and openly quotable. What they reveal is illustrative of the broader EEO arena where the documentation is not generally available because of confidentiality but where the same kind of things are taking place. As the EEO process moves in stages from the law, to presidential orders, to regulatory agencies, and to monitoring agencies in the field, objectives beyond stamping out discriminatory personnel practices and righting past wrongs creep into the system. The logic pattern which can work in fairness to all is shunted aside and replaced by seat-of-the-pants negotiations which, if employers are correct in their statements, take place in a "gun at the head" atmosphere. What is so often produced in business and industry are unachievable goals which later require incredible inputs of energy to explain why they were missed. Too often in the EEO arena the search for realities stops at a very shallow level, unduly influenced by intuitive expectations and objectives not directly related to employment discrimination.

CHAPTER THIRTEEN

Pitfalls and Programs

When an EEO monitoring agency makes a charge of discrimination against an employer, it sets in motion a process that contains many pitfalls. This is particularly true if the charge is based on prima facie evidence of disparate representation of minorities and women in the employer's work force. Faced with such a charge, the employer has only two viable options—negotiate a settlement or let a judge decide the merits of the case in a court of law. Generally, the decision will be to negotiate, because the risks are more controllable at a conference table than in a courtroom. When the settlement has been reached, the agreement typically has four major features:

1. No admission of guilt on the part of the employer.
2. Some back pay and perhaps forward pay in the form of promotion bonuses.
3. Redesign of the personnel system to remove any discriminatory impediments to the hiring and promotion of minorities and women, such as unvalidated tests or light versus heavy blue collar work.
4. Numerical objectives for five years into the future.

The numerical objectives may, in one form or another, attempt to accelerate changes in minority and women representation in the work force beyond the rate at which they have historically occurred.

The following discussion of possible pitfalls is not intended to discredit the process but to help it function more effectively. If these pitfalls can be avoided, the real objective of improving the work force status of minorities and women can much more readily be attained.

PROCESS PITFALLS

1. *Prima Facie Evidence*—As we discussed in Chapters Ten and Eleven, a prima facie case based on representation of minorities and women in the work force can be misleading. The representation in any year depends upon the opportunities for change that occurred and how they were utilized. The Equal Employment Opportunity Commission does not collect opportunities data in its routine reporting system. It collects representation data based upon nine work categories related to the way census data are compiled. At the outset, the Commission runs some risk of missing the guilty and charging the innocent simply because it does not have share of opportunities data. It also starts off at a considerable negotiations disadvantage. The chances are high that the ultimate agreement will be based on a share of opportunities concept. Unless the Commission very early develops its negotiations strategy on this basis, it can collect the wrong kind of data in its requests for additional information from the employer. Instead of bringing to bear the really critical data necessary to support the charge, the Commission can become mired in a mass of irrelevant information.
2. *External Market Bench Marks*—As we discussed in Chapter Seven, equalling the minority and women representation in the relevant external market is not sufficient proof that an employer is nondiscriminatory. This is particularly true where substantial internal markets exist. An employer who places too much confidence in the external market bench mark faces two potential problems.

    - If insufficient attention has been paid to the internal market, discriminatory personnel practices can continue to exist. As a result, if a charge is received, the risk of vulnerability on the part of the employer can be very high. Once the prima facie evidence has been set aside, the really critical factor is whether the charging agency can prove the existence of discriminatory practices. If it can, the employer is in deep trouble. This actually could have been avoided.
    - If a charge is received, the employer may overconfidently base his defense on the external market bench mark approach. In reality, the more quickly he or she gets to a full understanding of the size and dynamics of the internal market and the character of the related personnel practices, the better the chances for a successful defensive strategy.

3. *Redesigned Personnel Systems*—When the personnel system has been redesigned and purged of any discriminatory practices, it will produce some natural flow of people. The minority and women share of this natural flow can be disappointingly low. This will happen when the

real causes of disparate representation or disparate share are in whole or part not the result of discrimination but of other factors. For example, if women in entry level jobs are generally not interested in bidding for and accepting higher level jobs, little upward mobility will occur. Unless the root causes for this are identified during the negotiations, programs for corrective actions will not be a part of the agreement. Without such programs, the "futures" part of the agreement will fall short of what it was expected to accomplish. It is quite possible that the profile of women in the work force which triggered the charge initially will not be significantly changed during the five-year life of an agreement.

Unfortunately, in an atmosphere of "charge and response" with the threat of litigation always in the background, it is difficult to get much mutual agreement on root causes. There is considerable risk that the "futures" part of an agreement will be somewhat superficial. In fact, unless root causes are identified and acted upon, the agreement may simply delay the inevitable tasks that have to be undertaken for genuine redistribution of minorities and women in the work force.

4. *Numerical Objectives and Reverse Discrimination*—The most serious risk situation occurs when numerical objectives have been set on the basis of forecasted representation. The numerous models discussed in earlier chapters have demonstrated that representation should be the dependent variable. A commitment to a representation goal or objective can sometimes translate into an exceptionally high share of opportunities for minorities and women. Inadvertently, the representation numerical objective may put the employer in the position of missing goals by wide margins.

   If numerical objectives are based on share of opportunities, the changes in minority and women representation over the life of the agreement may be disappointingly small. Five years on a "fair share" basis is generally not long enough to produce substantial changes. The models repeatedly show that actual results will generally fall short of intuitive expectations. When this is perceived, there is a temptation to accelerate the results by using an affirmative action factor. For example, if the external and internal labor market analysis shows that a minority "fair share" of opportunities should be 20%, the numerical objective might be set at 1.5 times that value or 30%. Generally, monitoring agencies have argued that affirmative action factors are a logical "future" remedy for past wrongs. The judgment of the courts with respect to the issue of affirmative action factors is not yet completely clear. Meanwhile, the employer has no way of knowing how much affirmative action is legally too much. Whatever the numerical objectives may be, they must be designed in a rational way and capable of withstanding a test in court.

There is one additional pitfall in the numerical objectives part of an agreement. Generally, they tend to obscure the usefulness of lateral movements in positioning minorities and women for subsequent promotions. As we discussed in Chapter Eight, lateral movements can be an important key to upward mobility. Unless lateral movements are provided for in the agreement, their potential contribution to the redistribution of minorities and women may be lost.

5. *Back Pay Liability*—In a large scale negotiated agreement, the dollars that the employer commits will almost always be based on compromises. Not all of the necessary data will be available and history is difficult to reconstruct. However, two extremes need to be avoided. One is to bench mark against some hypothetical redistribution equal to the civilian labor force or the percent of women and minorities in the employer's work force. In this approach, the difference between the hypothetical and the actual distribution determines the amount of back pay to be awarded. As discussed in Chapter Eleven, this approach has more emotional appeal than logic to support it. The other extreme is to determine missed opportunities, on a year-by-year basis, by comparing actual shares of hires and promotions to what might have been achieved in the given external and internal labor markets. Although this approach seems logical, the fallacy lies in treating each year of the liability period on a free-standing basis. This approach will understate liability because it fails to recognize the growth in the internal market that would have occurred if earlier opportunities had not been missed. That growth would have increased the "fair share" of promotions for minorities and women year-by-year and needs to be taken into account.

   The best approach, complex though it may be, is to use a model to make some reasonable estimate of what might have been achieved with the available opportunities and labor markets. A comparison of what might have been with actual results yields a rational estimate of back pay liability.

6. *Implementation*—There is great temptation, once an agreement has been reached, to view the EEO issue as settled and that all that remains is the implementation. This can be a serious mistake. The EEO issue will probably not be settled within the next two decades. A five-year agreement is a relatively small accomplishment when compared to the total task that lies ahead. The EEO arena is a new and evolving one in which there is still much to be learned and done. Monitoring agencies and employers alike would do well to maintain an anticipatory capability. In the case of the employer, this need not be a large commitment of resources, perhaps just enough to prevent surprises. For the monitoring agencies, particularly the Equal Employment Opportunity Commission, the responsibility is far more substantial. In the long run, the "futures" part of major agreements may well be the most important thing of all. Yet at this point in time,

the "futures" element in the EEO arena is probably the least understood.

A CREDENTIALS STRATEGY

For many occupations there are legally mandated requirements. A person who does not have the necessary credential cannot lawfully practice the occupation. Although we tend to think of credentials at the professional level, such as medicine and law, they are fairly pervasive at all levels in the American work force. The list of occupations that require legally mandated credentials is a long one—and appears to be getting longer each year. From time to time, the need for and the details of the requirements are challenged. But in the main, the credentials have their roots in public health, safety, and well being and successfully withstand most challenges. For minorities and women, the message is clear. Unless they take the necessary steps to acquire the credentials, they are foreclosed from practicing certain occupations.

In many cases where credentials are not legally mandated, they exist by general consensus. These consensus credentials are reflected in many ways in job descriptions, position guides, or whatever documents specific employers use in describing their job requirements. For example, although some jobs in engineering require legally mandated professional registration, many others do not. For the bulk of engineering jobs in industry, the baccalaureate degree is the usual credential. There is widespread agreement on the need for the degree—it is a consensus credential. In fact, in recent years, the trend is toward the advanced degree as a basic requirement for the more complex engineering work.

Consensus credentials are obviously more vulnerable to challenge than those which are legally mandated. It is often argued that many so-called engineering jobs do not really require an engineering degree. Certainly the argument is a valid one in a number of instances. Similarly, the argument that a Ph.D. is not always really necessary to perform successfully as a university teacher has considerable merit. However, a minority and women EEO strategy based upon waiving the Ph.D. requirement would not be a very successful one. A strategy of challenging job requirements might be more successful in engineering or in skilled crafts or a number of other areas. But in general, the yield is small in comparison to the input energy required. Such a strategy only nibbles at the edges of the real problem. It is a "tearing down" approach, useful only in obtaining limited short-term results.

A more effective long-range strategy is to help minorities and women obtain the qualifications necessary to compete effectively in the market place. This strategy by no means suggests an easing of efforts to eliminate discriminatory personnel practices. The more obvious "over-requirements" for jobs can be identified and remedied with a relatively small amount of effort. But beyond the obvious, there is a vast gray area where a job requirements validation approach is a high energy input/low yield proposition. A much better approach in general is to say on behalf of minorities and women: "Help us identify the steps we must take to qualify for a hire or a promotion—and help us find ways to take those steps." That is the fruitful way to approach the upward mobility problem.

PIMEG, which was discussed in Chapter Three, is based upon this more positive strategy. Before the launching of PIMEG, there was considerable in-depth discussion of possible strategies. One alternative was an intensive within-the-company drive to find jobs then held by engineering degreed people which could possibly be held by non-degreed minority. That would have been an awesome task, involving tens of thousands of jobs, and with prospects for success relatively low. In general, the company had already done nearly all it could along this avenue. Further massive efforts would have had a relatively small yield in comparison to attacking the real supply problem at its root causes.

The credentials strategy has the added advantage of focusing attention on the hierarchical input distribution of minorities and women to the work force. This is true for a single company, and particularly so for an SMSA. Aside from migration into the SMSA or the filling of jobs with people from other regions, the input to the SMSA is the output from its own school systems. If the hierarchical output of minorities and women from the school systems into the general work force is badly skewed toward the lower, less skilled levels, the SMSA as a whole will have pervasive upward mobility problems. In fact, between the school systems and the employers, an SMSA has considerable control over its own EEO destiny.

PROGRAMS IN AN SMSA

If the long-range EEO objective is to redistribute minorities and women in the work force, eliminating discriminatory personnel practices is only one step in the process. Suppose that we accept redistribution as a national objective. Further suppose that there are other factors besides discriminatory personnel practices which are impediments to the redistribution objective. What happens next if, after discriminatory practices have been purged, the hoped for redistribution is proceeding at a snail's pace or not at all? Now the problem is no longer one of discrimination. Unless programs for additional changes in distribution are put into action, the objective cannot be met. Where will the initiative come from and what should those programs be?

The question of why employers should really care about redistribution of minorities and women has not been fully explored and documented. As long as the issue is a legal one, the need to care is obvious. But when the legal issues have been resolved, the only other motivators for care are profitability and what is sometimes called social conscience. How powerful these motivators might be remains to be seen. The evidence of PIMEG suggests that when the package is right, industry will respond. It will work effectively and enthusiastically toward the objective of a more equitable distribution of minorities in the work force. But one of the major problems is finding the right packages—the programs that will really produce a "turn on."

One approach which offers interesting possibilities is to use the SMSA as the basic building block for local and national programs. Off hand, one might think of an SMSA as simply a convenient categorization for recording census data. However, the concept goes deeper than that. By definition, an SMSA is a market place where many common interests come together. It is an economic community where the well being of many people is closely interwoven. Perhaps, above all else, it is admirably suited to a systems approach. If EEO is approached on an employer-by-employer or industry-by-industry basis, the synergism of a systems approach can be lost, and the results can sometimes even be counterproductive.

The EEO dynamics of an SMSA have not been thoroughly studied. Although such a study is a large task, it is not an unmanageable one. In fact, an SMSA can be modelled in the same way that a model can be built for any single employer. It can be segmented vertically and horizontally, upward mobility trails can be mapped, and the impact of programs can be examined and evaluated before they are selected and implemented. Probably the best approach would be to build several models and connect them together. Some typical ones would be:

- Economic forecast
- Employed labor force
- Unemployed labor force
- School systems (including universities)

These models would help to identify the real leverage points for EEO programs aimed at redistribution of minorities and women. As an interesting spin-off, they could provide additional insights into economic health and prosperity for the SMSA.

There is an exciting opportunity for a pilot study of a selected SMSA to develop methodologies applicable to most or all of the others. A highly capable study team might be able to learn more about the real problems and solutions in the EEO arena than has been learned to date on the empirical trial and error basis. Moreover, the transferable methodology would accelerate the learning process and the development of programs in the other SMSA's.

If there is any doubt that programs are needed to meet a redistribution objective, one more look at the data in Appendix B should dispel that doubt. Three SMSA's are shown, but for simplification, just look at the first two—Baltimore, and Washington, D.C.-Md.-Va. As one might expect, the economies of the two have a different emphasis. For example, 31% of the Baltimore SMSA jobs are in the blue collar category (crafts, operatives, and laborers); the corresponding number for Washington is 16%. Conversely, Baltimore has only 51% white collar (professional, managerial, sales, and office and clerical) compared to Washington's 68%. But in either case, the distribution of women is considerably different from that for men. When looking at the data, do so in detail because aggregations can too easily mask the real areas of program need. Look at a job listing, mentally picture what the job requires in skills, estimate whether pay is relatively high or low, and then examine the relative share of men-women incumbents. Without models, or charts, or statistical analysis, it is obvious that the women's share of the better jobs is relatively low. (This same exercise can be repeated for minorities with generally the same results.) Then, recall the time frame necessary for change as illustrated in a number of earlier models. It seems clear that a systematic approach of carefully considered programs is the best way to tackle the extremely formidable task of achieving significant redistributions of minorities and women.

A FINAL WORD

There is a temptation to conclude with a plea for better articulation of national EEO goals and an array of federal and state programs to help in meeting them. That would not be in keeping with a theme of realism, nor would it be a very productive contribution at this point in time. At the moment, we don't really understand the EEO problem sufficiently to design any massive programs to solve it. It is obvious that minorities and women are not distributed throughout the work force in proportions anywhere near their overall representation. One doesn't need an articulation of national goals to recognize that fact. Something needs to be done to improve distribution and, as a nation, we need to get on with the task. How we do so is the critical factor for the future. We can mess it up in several ways:

- By assuming that all of the unsatisfactory distribution is the result of historical and on-going discrimination.
- By creating expectation levels that are grossly incompatible with what the real dynamics can produce.
- By trying to do too much in too short a time.
- By failing to seek out and implement programs that have high enough leverage to produce significant results.

In short, we must be sure not to fly by the seat of our pants, but in the most carefully instrumented ways we can devise. How far we can get by the year 2000 remains to be seen. But the journey will be less frustrating, and the results more rewarding if we stay on a well conceived, well charted course.

APPENDIX A

APPENDIX A
Values for α (Chapter Four)

$\alpha = 1 + (1 - L) + (1 - L)^2 + \ldots (1 - L)^{n-1}$
L = Annual loss rate, decimal fraction
n = Number of years considered

n \ L	.01	.02	.03	.04	.05	.06	.07	.08	.09	.10	.11	.12	.13	.14	.15	.20	.25
1	1.000	1.000	1.000	1.000	1.000	1.000	1.000	1.000	1.000	1.000	1.000	1.000	1.000	1.000	1.000	1.000	1.000
2	1.990	1.980	1.970	1.960	1.950	1.940	1.930	1.920	1.910	1.900	1.890	1.880	1.870	1.860	1.850	1.800	1.750
3	2.970	2.940	2.911	2.882	2.853	2.824	2.795	2.766	2.738	2.710	2.682	2.654	2.627	2.600	2.573	2.440	2.313
4	3.940	3.882	3.824	3.766	3.710	3.654	3.600	3.545	3.492	3.439	3.387	3.336	3.286	3.236	3.187	2.952	2.734
5	4.901	4.804	4.709	4.616	4.524	4.435	4.347	4.262	4.177	4.095	4.015	3.936	3.858	3.783	3.709	3.362	3.051
6	5.852	5.708	5.568	5.431	5.298	5.169	5.043	4.921	4.801	4.686	4.573	4.463	4.357	4.253	4.152	3.689	3.288
7	6.794	6.594	6.401	6.214	6.033	5.859	5.690	5.527	5.369	5.217	5.070	4.928	4.790	4.658	4.529	3.951	3.466
8	7.726	7.462	7.209	6.965	6.732	6.507	6.292	6.085	5.886	5.695	5.512	5.336	5.168	5.006	4.850	4.161	3.560
9	8.648	8.313	7.992	7.687	7.395	7.117	6.851	6.598	6.356	6.126	5.906	5.696	5.496	5.305	5.123	4.329	3.700
10	9.562	9.146	8.753	8.379	8.025	7.690	7.372	7.070	6.784	6.513	6.256	6.013	5.781	5.562	5.354	4.463	3.775
11	10.467	9.963	9.490	9.044	8.624	8.228	7.856	7.505	7.174	6.862	6.568	6.291	6.030	5.783	5.551	4.571	3.831
12	11.362	10.764	10.205	9.682	9.193	8.735	8.306	7.904	7.528	7.176	6.846	6.536	6.246	5.974	5.718	4.656	3.874
13	12.248	11.549	10.900	10.295	9.733	9.211	8.725	8.272	7.851	7.458	7.093	6.752	6.434	6.137	5.861	4.725	3.905
14	13.126	12.318	11.572	10.883	10.246	9.658	9.114	8.610	8.144	7.712	7.312	6.942	6.597	6.278	5.981	4.780	3.929
15	13.995	13.071	12.225	11.448	10.734	10.079	9.476	8.921	8.411	7.941	7.508	7.109	6.740	6.399	6.084	4.824	3.947
16	14.855	13.810	13.158	11.900	11.197	10.474	9.813	9.208	8.654	8.147	7.682	7.256	6.864	6.503	6.172	4.859	3.960
17	15.706	14.534	13.772	12.510	11.638	10.845	10.126	9.471	8.875	8.332	7.837	7.385	6.971	6.593	6.246	4.887	3.970
18	16.549	15.243	14.368	13.010	12.056	11.195	10.417	9.713	9.076	8.499	7.975	7.499	7.065	6.670	6.309	4.910	3.978
19	17.384	15.938	14.946	13.489	12.453	11.523	10.688	9.936	9.259	8.649	8.098	7.600	7.146	6.736	6.363	4.928	3.983
20	18.210	16.619	15.507	13.950	12.830	11.832	10.940	10.141	9.426	8.784	8.207	7.688	7.217	6.793	6.408	4.942	3.988

Example: Loss rate = 5% per year
$L = .05$
$n = 15$
$\alpha = 10.734$

Values for $(1 - L)^n$

L = Annual loss rate, decimal fraction
n = Number of years considered

n\L	.01	.02	.03	.04	.05	.06	.07	.08	.09	.10	.11	.12	.13	.14	.15	.20	.25
1	.9900	.9800	.9700	.9600	.9500	.9400	.9300	.9200	.9100	.9000	.8900	.8800	.8700	.8600	.8500	.8000	.7500
2	.9801	.9604	.9409	.9216	.9025	.8836	.8649	.8464	.8281	.8100	.7921	.7744	.7569	.7396	.7225	.6400	.5625
3	.9703	.9412	.9127	.8847	.8574	.8306	.8044	.7787	.7536	.7290	.7050	.6815	.6585	.6361	.6141	.5120	.4219
4	.9606	.9224	.8853	.8493	.8145	.7807	.7481	.7164	.6857	.6561	.6274	.5997	.5729	.5470	.5220	.4096	.3164
5	.9510	.9039	.8587	.8154	.7738	.7339	.6957	.6591	.6240	.5905	.5584	.5277	.4984	.4704	.4437	.3277	.2375
6	.9415	.8858	.8330	.7828	.7351	.6899	.6470	.6064	.5679	.5314	.4970	.4644	.4336	.4046	.3771	.2621	.1780
7	.9321	.8681	.8080	.7514	.6983	.6485	.6017	.5578	.5168	.4783	.4423	.4087	.3773	.3479	.3206	.2097	.1335
8	.9227	.8508	.7837	.7214	.6634	.6096	.5596	.5132	.4703	.4305	.3937	.3596	.3282	.2992	.2725	.1678	.1001
9	.9135	.8337	.7602	.6925	.6302	.5730	.5204	.4722	.4279	.3874	.3504	.3165	.2855	.2573	.2316	.1342	.0751
10	.9044	.8171	.7374	.6648	.5987	.5386	.4840	.4344	.3894	.3487	.3118	.2785	.2484	.2213	.1969	.1074	.0563
11	.8953	.8007	.7153	.6382	.5688	.5063	.4501	.3996	.3544	.3138	.2775	.2451	.2161	.1903	.1673	.0859	.0422
12	.8864	.7847	.6938	.6127	.5404	.4759	.4186	.3677	.3225	.2824	.2470	.2157	.1880	.1637	.1422	.0687	.0317
13	.8775	.7690	.6730	.5882	.5133	.4474	.3893	.3383	.2935	.2542	.2198	.1898	.1636	.1408	.1209	.0550	.0238
14	.8687	.7536	.6528	.5647	.4877	.4205	.3620	.3112	.2670	.2288	.1956	.1670	.1423	.1211	.1028	.0440	.0178
15	.8601	.7386	.6333	.5421	.4633	.3953	.3367	.2863	.2430	.2059	.1741	.1470	.1238	.1041	.0876	.0352	.0134
16	.8515	.7238	.6143	.5204	.4401	.3716	.3131	.2634	.2211	.1853	.1550	.1293	.1077	.0895	.0743	.0281	.0100
17	.8429	.7093	.5958	.4996	.4181	.3493	.2912	.2423	.2012	.1668	.1379	.1138	.0937	.0770	.0631	.0225	.0075
18	.8345	.6951	.5780	.4796	.3972	.3283	.2708	.2229	.1831	.1501	.1227	.1016	.0815	.0662	.0536	.0180	.0056
19	.8262	.6812	.5606	.4604	.3774	.3086	.2519	.2051	.1666	.1351	.1092	.0881	.0709	.0569	.0456	.0144	.0042
20	.8179	.6676	.5438	.4420	.3585	.2901	.2342	.1887	.1516	.1216	.0982	.0776	.0617	.0490	.0388	.0115	.0032

Example: Loss rate = 5% per year

$$L = .05$$
$$n = 15$$
$$(1 - L)^n = .4633$$

Values for $(1 + i)^n$

n \ i					*i* = Annual growth rate, decimal fraction					
	.01	.02	.03	.04	.05	.06	.07	.08	.09	.10
1	1.010	1.020	1.030	1.040	1.050	1.060	1.070	1.080	1.090	1.100
2	1.020	1.040	1.061	1.082	1.103	1.124	1.145	1.166	1.188	1.210
3	1.030	1.061	1.093	1.125	1.158	1.191	1.225	1.260	1.295	1.331
4	1.041	1.082	1.126	1.170	1.216	1.262	1.311	1.360	1.412	1.464
5	1.051	1.104	1.159	1.217	1.276	1.338	1.403	1.469	1.539	1.611
6	1.062	1.126	1.194	1.265	1.340	1.419	1.501	1.587	1.677	1.772
7	1.072	1.149	1.230	1.316	1.407	1.504	1.606	1.714	1.828	1.949
8	1.083	1.172	1.267	1.369	1.477	1.594	1.718	1.851	1.993	2.144
9	1.094	1.195	1.305	1.423	1.551	1.689	1.838	1.999	2.172	2.358
10	1.105	1.219	1.344	1.480	1.629	1.791	1.967	2.159	2.367	2.594
11	1.116	1.243	1.384	1.539	1.710	1.898	2.105	2.332	2.580	2.853
12	1.127	1.268	1.426	1.601	1.796	2.012	2.252	2.518	2.813	3.138
13	1.138	1.294	1.469	1.665	1.886	2.133	2.410	2.720	3.066	3.452
14	1.149	1.319	1.513	1.732	1.980	2.261	2.579	2.937	3.342	3.797
15	1.161	1.346	1.558	1.801	2.079	2.397	2.759	3.172	3.642	4.177
16	1.173	1.373	1.605	1.873	2.183	2.540	2.952	3.426	3.970	4.595
17	1.184	1.400	1.653	1.948	2.292	2.693	3.159	3.700	4.328	5.054
18	1.196	1.428	1.702	2.026	2.407	2.854	3.380	3.996	4.717	5.560
19	1.208	1.457	1.754	2.107	2.527	3.026	3.617	4.316	5.142	6.116
20	1.220	1.486	1.806	2.191	2.653	3.207	3.870	4.661	5.604	6.727

Example: Growth rate = 5% per year

$i = .05$

$n = 15$ years

$(1 + i)^n = 2.079$

APPENDIX B

Table 171. Detailed Occupation of Employed Persons by Residence, Race, and Sex: 1970—Continued

[Data based on sample, see text. For meaning of symbols, see text]

The State Standard Metropolitan Statistical Areas of 250,000 or More	Standard metropolitan statistical areas					
	Baltimore		Washington, D.C.—Md.—Va.		Wilmington, Del.—N.J.—Md.	
	Male	Female	Male	Female	Male	Female
Total employed, 16 years old and over	**498 091**	**312 454**	**675 813**	**503 177**	**122 376**	**69 685**
Professional, technical, and kindred workers	**79 196**	**49 395**	**189 330**	**106 887**	**24 342**	**12 073**
Accountants	5 754	2 100	12 716	5 363	1 916	356
Architects	562	23	2 097	93	134	19
Computer specialists	3 008	719	11 610	3 634	624	199
Computer programers	1 621	549	5 763	2 440	380	155
Computer systems analysts	1 221	147	5 266	1 075	217	38
Computer specialists, n.e.c.	166	23	581	119	27	6
Engineers	15 673	285	32 148	1 045	5 230	28
Aeronautical and astronautical	318	—	1 207	11	146	—
Chemical	514	9	432	30	1 961	12
Civil	2 358	14	4 674	55	550	7
Electrical and electronic	4 887	139	10 990	112	462	5
Industrial	2 338	49	4 676	667	532	—
Mechanical	2 157	29	3 699	51	816	—
Metallurgical and materials	105	5	154	11	40	—
Mining	6	—	104	—	—	—
Petroleum	5	—	115	—	21	—
Sales	704	5	665	5	111	—
Engineers, n.e.c.	2 281	35	5 432	103	591	4
Farm management advisors	13	—	19	31	24	—
Foresters and conservationists	90	17	296	19	45	5
Home management advisors	—	15	8	140	—	19
Lawyers and judges	3 031	170	14 122	1 115	640	23
Judges	126	6	241	20	42	—
Lawyers	2 905	164	13 881	1 095	598	23

Librarians, archivists, and curators	277	1 016	1 547	3 374	45	307
Librarians	226	1 001	1 082	3 178	34	293
Archivists and curators	51	15	465	196	11	14
Mathematical specialists	709	276	3 031	1 557	90	19
Actuaries	33	19	68	24	26	—
Mathematicians	352	54	1 035	306	30	—
Statisticians	324	203	1 928	1 227	34	19
Life and physical scientists	2 083	377	8 582	1 527	1 876	203
Agricultural	68	5	592	47	24	—
Atmospheric and space	40	—	474	21	7	—
Biological	285	180	1 294	623	91	37
Chemists	1 216	153	2 070	562	1 660	159
Geologists	41	—	690	82	11	—
Marine	41	5	641	44	6	—
Physicists and astronomers	383	18	2 647	140	71	3
Life and physical, n.e.c.	9	16	174	8	6	4
Operations and systems researchers and analysts	1 495	237	4 591	965	203	26
Personnel and labor relations workers	2 675	1 405	6 811	4 341	627	224
Physicians, dentists, and related practitioners	5 767	660	8 313	1 024	1 017	100
Chiropractors	59	7	31	—	25	—
Dentists	705	20	1 461	56	192	12
Optometrists	92	—	117	11	20	—
Pharmacists	1 030	142	1 195	212	177	27
Physicians, medical and osteopathic	3 666	484	5 109	711	562	61
Podiatrists	60	—	82	4	20	—
Veterinarians	135	7	303	18	21	—
Health practitioners, n.e.c.	20	—	15	12	—	—
Registered nurses, dieticians, and therapists	688	9 318	761	14 150	110	2 432
Dietitians	72	365	22	564	5	102
Registered nurses	324	8 464	321	12 628	46	2 242
Therapists	292	489	418	958	59	88
Health technologists and technicians	1 040	2 389	1 904	2 945	100	427
Clinical laboratory technologists and technicians	468	1 160	835	1 388	30	258
Dental hygienists	—	43	15	392	—	24
Health record technologists and technicians	21	150	18	249	—	33
Radiologic technologists and technicians	121	483	166	405	11	55
Therapy assistants	27	36	41	8	8	—
Health technologists and technicians, n.e.c.	403	517	829	503	51	57

Table 171. (Continued)

The State Standard Metropolitan Statistical Areas of 250,000 or More	Standard metropolitan statistical areas					
	Baltimore		Washington, D.C.—Md.—Va.		Wilmington, Del.—N.J.—Md.	
	Male	Female	Male	Female	Male	Female
Religious workers	1 893	244	2 468	540	477	70
Clergymen	1 746	40	2 118	58	447	12
Religious workers, n.e.c.	147	204	350	482	30	58
Social scientists	1 186	273	8 117	2 006	574	31
Economists	714	59	6 004	1 104	486	19
Political scientists	—	—	270	88	6	—
Psychologists	255	162	741	419	48	12
Sociologists	15	15	73	54	10	—
Urban and regional planners	184	17	293	60	24	—
Social scientists, n.e.c.	18	20	736	281	—	—
Social and recreation workers	1 495	2 430	2 179	3 395	234	405
Social	1 058	2 096	1 513	2 813	143	348
Recreation	437	334	666	582	91	57
Teachers, college and university	2 731	1 112	5 410	2 711	852	395
Biology	98	58	202	88	44	18
Chemistry	109	17	186	66	107	10
Engineering	116	12	290	36	62	7
Physics	128	—	268	30	44	12
Other life and physical sciences	29	5	48	4	32	—
Mathematics	170	43	404	117	47	13
Economics	46	5	157	38	33	—
English	177	157	358	363	42	38
History	82	24	257	135	34	10
Miscellaneous social sciences	177	64	386	190	55	5
Other specified teachers	891	413	1 425	982	196	194
Not specified teachers	708	314	1 429	662	156	88

Teachers, except college and university	7 559	19 212	10 396	33 736	2 143	4 823
Adult education	316	288	663	865	82	35
Elementary school	2 150	11 477	2 555	19 181	659	2 706
Prekindergarten and kindergarten	14	1 145	31	2 650	—	395
Secondary school	4 587	5 188	6 313	8 932	1 321	1 399
Teachers, except college and university, n.e.c.	492	1 114	834	2 108	81	288
Engineering and science technicians	9 107	877	13 772	2 376	4 401	631
Agriculture and biological, except health	186	88	216	172	57	13
Chemical	611	113	422	139	1 868	298
Draftsmen	3 270	151	4 647	846	723	37
Electrical and electronic engineering	2 184	129	4 564	401	259	7
Industrial engineering	228	35	100	28	76	15
Mechanical engineering	218	10	89	6	53	—
Mathematical	—	6	9	4	—	—
Surveyors	674	19	796	26	153	7
Engineering and science, n.e.c.	1 736	326	2 929	754	1 212	254
Technicians, except health, and engineering and science	1 327	231	4 361	701	298	33
Airplane pilots	182	—	1 113	11	110	—
Air traffic controllers	144	27	1 476	127	19	—
Embalmers	59	—	48	5	9	—
Flight engineers	10	—	95	5	27	—
Radio operators	298	50	353	40	41	8
Tool programers, numerical control	41	4	58	38	—	—
Technicians, n.e.c.	593	150	1 218	475	92	25
Vocational and educational counselors	601	524	1 510	1 145	180	112
Writers, artists, and entertainers	5 782	2 256	16 553	8 511	1 196	459
Actors	62	48	147	114	4	—
Athletes and kindred workers	513	133	588	268	109	62
Authors	400	55	1 390	661	41	12
Dancers	11	113	15	123	—	9
Designers	915	165	1 208	431	179	24
Editors and reporters	780	531	4 934	3 830	229	127
Musicians and composers	617	376	832	494	84	111
Painters and sculptors	695	384	1 615	946	172	70
Photographers	610	79	1 609	214	141	14
Public relations men and publicity writers	632	229	2 214	679	140	14

Table 171. (Continued)

The State Standard Metropolitan Statistical Areas of 250,000 or More	Standard metropolitan statistical areas					
	Baltimore		Washington, D.C.—Md.—Va.		Wilmington, Del.—N.J.—Md.	
	Male	Female	Male	Female	Male	Female
Radio and television announcers	109	5	443	64	55	—
Writers, artists, and entertainers, n.e.c.	438	138	1 558	687	42	16
Research workers, not specified	1 213	456	5 845	2 972	566	50
Professional, technical, and kindred workers—allocated	3 437	2 773	10 163	7 471	740	677
Managers and administrators, except farm	**51 551**	**10 154**	**96 004**	**23 916**	**12 541**	**2 082**
Assessors, controllers, and treasurers; local public administration	151	13	63	36	55	11
Bank officers and financial managers	2 214	539	4 415	1 043	626	113
Buyers and shippers, farm products	72	—	45	—	14	—
Buyers, wholesale and retail trade	1 235	545	1 338	825	226	93
Credit men	489	111	450	122	115	44
Funeral directors	193	44	258	23	107	—
Health administrators	673	377	1 357	716	64	53
Construction inspectors; public administration	318	—	519	4	37	—
Inspectors, except construction; public administration	1 106	140	1 795	283	118	5
Federal public administration and postal service	677	107	1 469	265	34	5
State public administration	224	21	48	—	66	—
Local public administration	205	12	278	18	18	—
Managers and superintendents, building	515	189	1 481	1 456	141	41
Officers, pilots, and pursers; ship	335	10	84	—	75	—
Officials and administrators; public administration, n.e.c.	3 599	750	23 840	5 457	315	79
Federal public administration and postal service	2 583	475	22 758	5 122	159	23
State public administration	492	107	243	68	116	20
Local public administration	524	168	839	267	40	36
Officials of lodges, societies, and unions	448	49	1 863	457	123	42
Postmasters and mail superintendents	115	71	185	24	56	17
Purchasing agents and buyers, n.e.c.	1 680	236	2 610	826	454	45

Railroad conductors	519	—	206	5	283	—
Restaurant, cafeteria, and bar managers	2 380	1 201	3 067	1 284	515	245
Sales managers and department heads, retail trade	1 708	671	2 710	938	434	181
Sales managers, except retail trade	2 320	64	3 256	155	722	18
School administrators, college	212	126	437	222	62	12
School administrators, elementary and secondary	1 055	712	1 394	1 244	321	124
Managers and administrators, n.e.c., salaried	23 387	3 027	34 148	6 633	5 984	673
Construction	3 054	89	4 464	127	724	28
Manufacturing	5 792	237	3 740	402	1 992	59
Transportation	1 527	189	1 437	328	339	54
Communications, and utilities and sanitary services	845	159	1 786	283	130	20
Wholesale trade	1 939	180	2 407	234	379	35
Retail trade	4 922	828	7 877	1 548	1 359	251
Hardware, farm equipment, and building material retailing	338	19	478	18	75	15
General merchandise stores	748	165	845	400	246	69
Food stores	1 104	166	1 643	261	242	46
Motor vehicles and accessories retailing	688	40	1 100	40	221	7
Gasoline service stations	490	5	896	33	164	—
Apparel and accessories stores	347	169	606	274	77	30
Furniture, home furnishings, and equipment stores	260	35	640	111	71	11
Other retail trade	947	229	1 669	411	263	73
Finance, insurance, and real estate	1 796	307	2 295	608	343	34
Business and repair services	1 361	224	3 392	586	280	32
Personal services	628	276	1 412	439	163	66
All other industries	1 523	538	5 338	2 078	275	94
Managers and administrators, n.e.c., self-employed	4 869	867	5 656	878	1 289	179
Construction	989	4	1 377	19	249	7
Manufacturing	378	24	253	19	87	6
Transportation	110	6	162	24	5	16
Communications, and utilities and sanitary services	21	—	23	4	4	—
Wholesale trade	301	21	262	35	58	—
Retail trade	2 260	592	2 103	311	716	111
Hardware, farm equipment, and building material retailing	121	10	104	—	64	—
General merchandise stores	67	53	73	31	17	5

Table 171. (Continued)

The State Standard Metropolitan Statistical Areas of 250,000 or More	Standard metropolitan statistical areas					
	Baltimore		Washington, D.C.—Md.—Va.		Wilmington, Del.—N.J.—Md.	
	Male	Female	Male	Female	Male	Female
Food stores	718	299	319	74	160	53
Motor vehicles and accessories retailing	93	—	123	5	23	—
Gasoline service stations	681	2	737	23	230	12
Apparel and accessories stores	92	28	121	48	30	10
Furniture, home furnishings, and equipment stores	163	31	124	19	36	—
Other retail trade	325	169	502	111	156	31
Finance, insurance, and real estate	145	20	227	54	15	5
Business and repair services	237	40	522	166	66	—
Personal services	274	95	461	165	65	22
All other industries	154	65	266	81	24	12
Managers and administrators, except farm—allocated	1 958	412	4 827	1 285	405	107
Sales workers	**33 225**	**23 664**	**43 740**	**30 864**	**6 970**	**5 339**
Advertising agents and salesmen	367	114	589	172	86	14
Auctioneers	13	5	17	—	5	6
Demonstrators	15	302	66	396	6	77
Hucksters and peddlers	262	751	278	902	25	187
Insurance agents, brokers, and underwriters	4 110	587	4 463	823	811	60
Newsboys	627	47	1 396	69	110	11
Real estate agents and brokers	1 303	964	3 317	2 461	287	176
Stock and bond salesmen	689	69	1 308	239	156	10
Salesmen and sales clerks, n.e.c.	24 187	19 144	29 248	22 915	5 167	4 442
Sales representatives, manufacturing industries	3 921	411	3 505	449	835	68
Sales representatives, wholesale trade	6 536	408	6 836	427	1 004	68
Sales clerks, retail trade	8 630	16 882	11 631	19 864	2 021	3 975
Salesmen, retail trade	3 373	486	4 637	703	1 069	178
Salesmen of services and construction	1 727	957	2 639	1 472	238	153
Sales workers—allocated	1 652	1 681	3 058	2 887	317	356

Clerical and kindred workers	**47 494**	**120 435**	**78 084**	**232 509**	**8 716**	**26 107**
Bank tellers	244	1 985	816	2 945	119	571
Billing clerks	272	1 134	178	768	36	162
Bookkeepers	2 749	9 927	5 446	15 491	801	2 340
Cashiers	1 894	7 794	3 732	10 443	331	1 857
Clerical assistants, social welfare	6	21	24	36	—	—
Clerical supervisors, n.e.c.	1 274	845	4 176	2 798	133	73
Collectors, bill and account	472	262	512	239	56	30
Counter clerks, except food	546	1 622	1 116	2 162	183	406
Dispatchers and starters, vehicle	741	111	658	143	135	6
Enumerators and interviewers	107	366	220	417	19	70
Estimators and investigators, n.e.c.	3 290	2 552	3 614	2 244	499	241
Expediters and production controllers	2 254	962	1 175	641	423	92
File clerks	1 479	5 241	2 897	7 857	82	738
Insurance adjusters, examiners, and investigators	947	311	973	495	115	35
Library attendants and assistants	412	935	927	2 300	31	259
Mail carriers, post office	2 572	151	4 362	183	572	42
Mail handlers, except post office	981	701	3 079	1 238	175	201
Messengers, including telegraph, and office boys	472	89	1 430	258	70	26
Meter readers, utilities	298	12	314	10	71	—
Office machine operators	2 025	6 323	4 278	6 947	460	1 074
Bookeeping and billing machine	123	683	187	677	22	151
Calculating machine	36	559	29	252	12	24
Computer and peripheral equipment	1 299	720	2 642	900	266	89
Duplicating machine	100	152	358	254	37	39
Keypunch	287	3 741	576	4 321	79	695
Tabulating machine	32	36	43	43	11	18
Office machine, n.e.c.	148	432	443	500	33	58
Payroll and timekeeping clerks	789	1 353	515	1 799	144	182
Postal clerks	2 011	932	5 045	3 076	388	203
Proofreaders	191	245	513	424	32	34
Real estate appraisers	200	10	361	38	46	—
Receptionists	126	2 678	520	5 423	18	630
Secretaries	718	27 851	1 724	78 458	159	7 866
Shipping and receiving clerks	3 800	508	1 947	426	691	193
Statistical clerks	1 406	2 762	2 566	5 342	221	334

Table 171. (Continued)

The State Standard Metropolitan Statistical Areas of 250,000 or More	Standard metropolitan statistical areas					
	Baltimore		Washington, D.C.—Md.—Va.		Wilmington, Del.—N.J.—Md.	
	Male	Female	Male	Female	Male	Female
Stenographers	91	1 513	254	2 937	15	635
Stock clerks and storekeepers	4 387	1 304	5 299	1 827	901	220
Teacher aides, except school monitors	59	1 554	224	1 351	27	380
Telegraph operators	25	54	41	44	4	13
Telephone operators	223	4 592	471	7 176	43	756
Ticket, station, and express agents	511	148	1 363	1 147	69	21
Typists	1 047	15 236	2 432	29 395	121	2 521
Weighers	599	224	70	106	71	56
Miscellaneous clerical workers	2 544	3 767	3 443	6 865	434	625
Not specified clerical workers	3 060	8 168	4 327	13 188	569	1 744
Clerical and kindred workers—allocated	2 672	6 192	7 042	15 872	452	1 471
Craftsmen and kindred workers	**112 163**	**5 419**	**108 291**	**5 643**	**27 909**	**823**
Automobile accessories installers	88	7	75	—	22	—
Bakers	963	299	759	425	179	79
Blacksmiths	143	5	21	9	44	—
Boilermakers	409	9	158	3	94	5
Bookbinders	243	340	867	562	—	17
Brickmasons and stonemasons	2 314	20	2 909	38	639	5
Bulldozer operators	948	16	438	6	178	—
Cabinetmakers	535	40	629	18	118	—
Carpenters	8 923	109	8 132	106	2 196	18
Carpet installers	345	5	614	4	85	—
Cement and concrete finishers	837	2	1 021	5	200	4
Compositors and typesetters	1 875	263	3 260	308	267	16
Cranemen, derrickmen, and hoistmen	3 329	30	638	5	456	—
Decorators and window dressers	417	338	639	454	91	89
Dental laboratory technicians	233	57	316	84	30	5

Electricians	5 632	131	4 708	76	1 804	12
Electric power linemen and cablemen	956	23	849	17	249	—
Electrotypers and stereotypers	82	—	174	—	34	—
Engravers, except photoengravers	65	32	187	63	15	—
Excavating, grading, and road machine operators; except bulldozer	1 578	17	2 009	14	480	3
Floor layers, except tile setters	243	8	516	4	59	—
Foremen, n.e.c.	15 538	1 214	10 280	1 235	4 523	224
Construction	1 706	6	2 165	17	532	—
Manufacturing	9 012	635	2 007	289	2 978	136
Durable goods	6 369	188	731	65	1 077	28
Nondurable goods, including not specified manufacturing	2 643	447	1 276	224	1 901	108
Transportation, communications, and other public utilities	1 641	64	1 686	92	269	5
All other industries	3 179	509	4 422	837	744	83
Forgemen and hammermen	96	6	19	14	17	—
Furniture and wood finishers	192	26	228	14	41	9
Furriers	13	5	40	4	—	—
Glaziers	253	6	408	—	74	4
Heat treaters, annealers, and temperers	178	4	—	—	20	—
Inspectors, scalers, and graders; log and lumber	25	5	—	—	10	—
Inspectors, n.e.c.	1 593	169	997	60	388	17
Construction	291	7	360	6	88	—
Railroads and railway express service	245	—	81	—	97	—
Jewelers and watchmakers	278	10	208	15	32	4
Job and die setters, metal	450	9	11	3	27	—
Locomotive engineers	428	6	167	—	109	—
Locomotive firemen	92	—	25	5	21	2
Machinists	4 354	118	1 298	60	1 112	16
Mechanics and repairmen	23 180	504	23 747	455	6 017	85
Air conditioning, heating, and refrigeration	1 553	19	2 306	27	379	7
Aircraft	540	11	959	9	352	6
Automobile body repairmen	962	26	1 096	15	203	6
Automobile mechanics	7 343	129	8 600	143	2 121	22
Data processing machine repairmen	417	—	970	20	98	6
Farm implement	250	—	152	—	76	—
Heavy equipment mechanics, including diesel	5 943	82	2 985	59	1 201	18

Table 171. (Continued)

The State Standard Metropolitan Statistical Areas of 250,000 or More	Standard metropolitan statistical areas					
	Baltimore		Washington, D.C.—Md.—Va.		Wilmington, Del.—N.J.—Md.	
	Male	Female	Male	Female	Male	Female
Household appliance and accessory installers and mechanics	1 233	26	1 529	23	288	—
Loom fixers	21	—	7	—	23	—
Office machine	470	6	721	17	96	4
Radio and television	1 389	129	1 816	30	297	4
Railroad and car shop	291	—	340	—	226	6
Miscellaneous mechanics and repairmen	1 875	72	1 756	90	487	6
Not specified mechanics and repairmen	893	4	510	22	170	—
Millers; grain, flour, and feed	30	—	24	—	—	—
Millwrights	1 133	10	69	—	594	10
Molders, metal	369	14	6	10	73	—
Motion picture projectionists	104	7	157	18	16	—
Opticians, and lens grinders and polishers	269	32	334	41	62	—
Painters, construction and maintenance	3 843	94	4 974	126	942	23
Paperhangers	140	5	151	—	9	—
Pattern and model makers, except paper	373	6	275	8	40	—
Photoengravers and lithographers	398	27	781	74	41	—
Piano and organ tuners and repairmen	67	—	109	14	11	—
Plasterers	272	—	436	12	109	—
Plumbers and pipe fitters	4 649	52	4 319	82	1 721	15
Power station operators	179	5	90	5	105	—
Pressmen and plate printers, printing	2 231	156	3 699	262	248	19
Rollers and finishers, metal	487	4	9	—	14	—
Roofers and slaters	579	16	691	15	135	6
Sheetmetal workers and tinsmiths	2 048	27	2 143	11	490	—
Shipfitters	455	12	14	—	51	—
Shoe repairmen	268	106	313	2	43	4

Sign painters and letterers	197	25	164	20	47	—
Stationary engineers	2 360	20	3 338	26	546	5
Stone cutters and stone carvers	5	—	51	—	—	—
Structural metal craftsmen	1 091	22	649	5	373	4
Tailors	793	375	353	114	80	42
Telephone installers and repairmen	2 373	51	5 205	101	503	16
Telephone linemen and splicers	380	6	728	8	115	5
Tile setters	310	—	657	3	60	—
Tool and die makers	1 080	41	173	5	166	4
Upholsterers	608	52	416	20	114	9
Craftsmen and kindred workers, n.e.c.	1 147	75	504	28	246	8
Former members of the Armed Forces	...	...	...	...	...	...
Craftsmen and kindred workers—allocated	7 097	340	11 112	567	1 324	39
Operatives, except transport	**60 322**	**36 840**	**27 065**	**14 134**	**17 964**	**7 043**
Asbestos and insulation workers	337	—	423	—	167	—
Assemblers	4 359	3 550	492	1 122	2 747	751
Blasters and powdermen	53	4	11	5	—	—
Bottling and canning operatives	424	335	46	14	38	73
Chainmen, rodmen, and axmen; surveying	145	10	205	—	58	—
Checkers, examiners, and inspectors; manufacturing	3 252	2 401	598	759	1 132	992
Clothing ironers and pressers	649	1 746	312	1 246	32	274
Cutting operatives, n.e.c.	1 324	335	269	27	239	89
Dressmakers and seamstresses, except factory	53	1 015	75	1 391	4	258
Drillers, earth	247	15	151	11	29	5
Dry wall installers and lathers	447	5	685	5	157	—
Dyers	32	6	5	4	88	—
Filers, polishers, sanders, and buffers	583	34	147	5	167	11
Furnacemen, smeltermen, and pourers	1 243	36	33	—	63	5
Garageworkers and gas station attendants	3 428	39	4 984	94	927	4
Graders and sorters, manufacturing	46	167	63	18	21	45
Produce graders and packers, except factory and farm	42	68	22	7	—	6
Heaters, metal	136	—	—	—	20	—
Laundry and drycleaning operatives, n.e.c.	540	876	762	1 391	103	216
Meat cutters and butchers, except manufacturing	1 849	130	2 283	87	353	19
Meat cutters and butchers, manufacturing	407	55	75	—	8	22
Meat wrappers, retail trade	22	606	63	718	5	129

Table 171. (Continued)

The State Standard Metropolitan Statistical Areas of 250,000 or More	Standard metropolitan statistical areas: Baltimore		Washington, D.C.—Md.—Va.		Wilmington, Del.—N.J.—Md.	
	Male	Female	Male	Female	Male	Female
Metal platers	245	4	58	3	11	3
Milliners	—	31	—	66	—	—
Mine operatives, n.e.c.	142	25	125	18	16	—
Mixing operatives	887	13	79	5	265	17
Oilers and greasers, except auto	599	13	150	—	129	—
Packers and wrappers, except meat and produce	2 233	4 797	859	948	456	577
Painters, manufactured articles	1 015	75	314	21	404	23
Photographic process workers	239	207	867	548	66	51
Precision machine operatives	2 660	269	247	16	435	41
Drill press operatives	388	47	40	16	57	15
Grinding machine operatives	822	44	39	—	133	—
Lathe and milling machine operatives	986	74	130	—	179	26
Precision machine operatives, n.e.c.	464	104	38	—	66	—
Punch and stamping press operatives	614	328	74	25	47	62
Riveters and fasteners	86	67	9	4	17	18
Sailors and deckhands	506	—	66	—	91	—
Sawyers	462	31	89	—	54	10
Sewers and stitchers	564	7 316	87	820	34	996
Shoemaking machine operatives	166	278	10	—	5	5
Solderers	56	396	28	40	28	12
Stationary firemen	914	46	782	—	325	6
Textile operatives	385	338	36	34	301	253
Cording, lapping, and combing operatives	17	14	6	—	15	6
Knitters, loopers, and toppers	4	5	5	—	23	16
Spinners, twisters, and winders	67	86	10	12	22	64
Weavers	46	49	10	5	4	16
Textile operatives, n.e.c.	251	184	5	17	237	151

Welders and flamecutters	5 055	458	1 595	47	1 368	44
Winding operatives, n.e.c.	332	170	41	36	84	135
Miscellaneous and not specified operatives	18 829	7 186	6 106	2 021	6 365	1 277
Occupation:						
Machine operatives, miscellaneous specified	6 785	2 600	1 718	541	2 228	572
Machine operatives, not specified	4 676	2 117	1 023	672	2 435	188
Miscellaneous operatives	5 095	1 706	2 891	640	1 128	349
Not specified operatives	2 273	763	474	168	574	168
Industry:						
Manufacturing	15 675	6 304	2 259	1 097	5 722	1 152
Durable goods	9 879	2 682	744	360	1 540	417
Lumber and wood products, except furniture	155	48	13	5	20	—
Furniture and fixtures	262	180	33	10	19	12
Stone, clay, and glass products	1 073	192	180	28	334	86
Primary metal industries	3 628	98	52	5	298	53
Blast furnaces, steel works, and rolling and finishing mills	2 878	37	8	5	77	—
Fabricated metal industries, including not specified metal	1 063	421	49	5	116	32
Machinery, except electrical	874	276	104	51	87	5
Electrical machinery, equipment, and supplies	1 503	1 106	142	208	73	194
Transportation equipment	926	73	19	4	376	11
Motor vehicles and motor vehicle equipment	269	55	—	—	265	11
Professional and photographic equipment, and watches	33	49	27	6	10	5
Ordnance	16	16	9	8	10	14
Miscellaneous manufacturing industries	292	210	108	30	193	5
Durable goods—allocated	54	13	8	—	4	—
Nondurable goods	5 711	3 549	1 474	715	4 141	728
Food and kindred products	1 384	547	348	40	159	210
Tobacco manufactures	—	—	—	—	—	—
Apparel and other fabricated textile products	243	659	—	5	23	78
Paper and allied products	1 136	875	41	81	364	64
Printing, publishing, and allied industries	509	426	908	528	57	40
Chemicals and allied products	1 427	287	138	20	2 398	84
Petroleum and coal products	104	14	—	—	259	—

Table 171. (Continued)

The State Standard Metropolitan Statistical Areas of 250,000 or More	Standard metropolitan statistical areas					
	Baltimore		Washington, D.C.—Md.—Va.		Wilmington, Del.—N.J.—Md.	
	Male	Female	Male	Female	Male	Female
Rubber and miscellaneous plastic products	815	610	24	26	705	140
Leather and leather products	53	119	10	9	162	106
Nondurable goods—allocated	40	12	5	6	14	6
Not specified manufacturing industries	85	73	41	22	41	7
Nonmanufacturing industries	3 154	882	3 847	924	643	125
Construction	408	12	377	5	46	7
Transportation, communications, and other public utilities	607	34	768	20	135	4
Wholesale and retail trade	1 105	429	767	201	251	44
Business and repair services	421	65	671	81	135	17
Public administration	299	50	735	305	11	—
All other industries	314	292	529	312	65	53
Operatives, except transport—allocated	4 715	3 359	3 739	2 578	1 105	614
Transport equipment operatives	**31 246**	**1 736**	**32 565**	**2 551**	**5 943**	**450**
Boatmen and canalmen	67	19	5	9	29	5
Bus drivers	1 955	1 034	3 624	1 467	285	299
Conductors and motormen, urban rail transit	9	—	23	5	—	—
Deliverymen and routemen	6 245	125	6 012	247	1 157	24
Fork lift and tow motor operatives	2 856	60	574	5	564	4
Motormen; mine, factory, logging camp, etc.	86	10	—	—	—	—
Parking attendants	379	6	764	9	68	6
Railroad brakemen	679	8	230	—	141	—
Railroad switchmen	209	—	58	—	42	6
Taxicab drivers and chauffeurs	3 973	154	5 231	288	306	28
Truck drivers	12 445	155	10 994	147	2 947	31
Transport equipment operatives—allocated	2 343	165	5 050	374	404	47
Laborers, except farm	**34 191**	**2 532**	**31 767**	**2 362**	**6 612**	**449**
Animal caretakers, except farm	250	126	597	179	81	41
Carpenters' helpers	700	—	762	4	57	—

Construction laborers, except carpenters' helpers	5 994	126	6 966	127	1 276	10
Fishermen and oystermen	191	5	10	—	28	—
Freight and material handlers	5 337	296	3 467	229	1 071	44
Garbage collectors	815	17	1 197	18	164	5
Gardeners and groundskeepers, except farm	2 245	79	3 299	101	651	3
Longshoremen and stevedores	1 685	24	43	—	96	—
Lumbermen, raftsmen, and woodchoppers	132	5	44	6	36	—
Stock handlers	4 416	909	4 554	634	878	166
Teamsters	9	5	9	10	14	—
Vehicle washers and equipment cleaners	875	96	848	101	217	11
Warehousemen, n.e.c.	1 262	33	1 157	41	176	—
Miscellaneous and not specified laborers	6 451	625	3 259	479	1 101	128
Occupation:						
Miscellaneous laborers	2 338	232	993	104	310	38
Not specified laborers	4 113	393	2 266	375	791	90
Industry:						
Manufacturing	3 559	349	356	43	563	72
Durable goods	2 819	235	128	11	229	13
Lumber and wood products, except furniture	81	3	6	2	—	—
Furniture and fixtures	18	29	—	—	—	—
Stone, clay, and glass products	264	29	54	—	29	—
Primary metal industries	1 655	25	—	—	48	4
Blast furnaces, steel works, and rolling and finishing mills	1 454	15	—	—	36	—
Fabricated metal industries, including not specified metal	236	91	27	—	26	—
Machinery, except electrical	85	5	13	—	14	5
Electrical machinery, equipment, and supplies	33	31	—	—	4	4
Transportation equipment	395	5	9	—	56	—
Motor vehicles and motor vehicle equipment	78	—	—	—	50	—
Professional and photographic equipment, and watches	4	6	19	—	—	—
Ordnance	7	—	—	—	—	—
Miscellaneous manufacturing industries	17	6	—	9	44	—
Durable goods—allocated	24	5	—	—	8	—
Nondurable goods	704	114	213	32	325	59
Food and kindred products	299	18	73	5	21	5
Tobacco manufactures	—	—	7	—	—	—

Table 171. (Continued)

The State Standard Metropolitan Statistical Areas of 250,000 or More	Standard metropolitan statistical areas					
	Baltimore		Washington, D.C.—Md.—Va.		Wilmington, Del.—N.J.—Md.	
	Male	Female	Male	Female	Male	Female
Textile mill products	21	—	—	—	19	5
Apparel and other fabricated textile products	5	12	5	4	6	—
Paper and allied products	83	10	6	—	27	21
Printing, publishing, and allied industries	38	6	94	19	5	—
Chemicals and allied products	172	40	11	4	151	14
Petroleum and coal products	16	—	7	—	12	—
Rubber and miscellaneous plastic products	41	25	—	—	55	—
Leather and leather products	14	3	4	—	29	14
Nondurable goods—allocated	15	—	6	—	—	—
Not specified manufacturing industries	36	—	15	—	9	—
Nonmanufacturing industries	2 892	276	2 903	436	538	56
Transportation, communications, and other public utilities	1 225	23	1 056	61	160	5
Wholesale and retail trade	716	90	457	52	195	17
Business and repair services	158	33	113	26	33	5
Public administration	264	25	562	76	28	5
All other industries	529	105	715	221	122	24
Laborers, except farm—allocated	3 829	186	5 555	433	766	41
Farmers and farm managers	**2 834**	**432**	**1 713**	**255**	**1 326**	**115**
Farmers, owners and tenants	2 220	221	1 083	128	1 092	84
Farm managers	220	—	279	7	109	4
Farmers and farm managers—allocated	394	211	351	120	125	27
Farm laborers and farm foremen	**2 611**	**487**	**2 728**	**488**	**1 115**	**149**
Farm foremen	99	26	165	37	11	4
Farm laborers, wage workers	1 913	250	1 940	209	887	60
Farm laborers, unpaid family workers	228	117	109	44	64	73
Farm service laborers, self-employed	—	—	5	6	—	—
Farm laborers and farm foremen—allocated	371	94	509	192	153	12

APPENDIX C

WILLIAM H. BROWN, III
Charging Party,

v.

EEOC Charge No.
TNP 4C-2000

GENERAL ELECTRIC COMPANY, et. al.
Respondents.

CONCILIATION AGREEMENT

A member of the Equal Employment Opportunity Commission on August 31, 1973, pursuant to Title VII, Section 706 (a) and (b) of the Civil Rights Act of 1964, as amended, 42 U.S.C. 2000 (e) et sec., charged General Electric Company with discrimination in violation of Sections 703 (a), (d) and 704 (b) of the Civil Rights Act of 1964, as amended. The Equal Employment Opportunity Commission served the charge on General Electric Company and investigated the alleged discriminatory practice. The Equal Employment Opportunity Commission and General Electric Company have held pre-determination settlement conferences pursuant to Section 706 (b) of the Civil Rights Act of 1964, as amended which have culminated in this Conciliation Agreement.

I. DEFINITIONS

For the purposes of this Agreement, the following definitions apply:

A. The term "Company" shall refer to General Electric Company's operations in the United States of America, but shall not apply to any subsidiary or affiliated company.

B. The term "Commission" shall refer to the Equal Employment Opportunity Commission.

C. The term "minority" shall include those racial and ethnic groups referred to and defined in Appendix 4 of the "Instruction Booklet," as amended by the Commission on July 14, 1977 for use in the preparation of EEO-1 Reports required by the Commission.

D. The term "Work Zones" shall refer to groupings of jobs agreed to between the Commission and the Company designed to described both the hierarchy of skills and significant differences in pay and skill levels at a given Company location.

E. The term "location" shall refer to a plant, office or other Company facility with clearly defined boundaries making it geographically distinct from another location.

F. The term "Division location" shall refer to that portion of a location as defined above that encompasses employees of only one organizational entity referred to as a Division or equivalent in the Company's Organization Directory.

II. GENERAL PROVISIONS

A. This Agreement finally resolves between the Commission and the Company all issues of discriminatory acts or practices raised by Commissioner's Charge TNP 4C-2000 as well as any future effect of the alleged acts or practices raised by the Charge.

B. The Commission and Company have reached this Agreement after extensive negotiations and conciliation in a mutual effort to avoid costly and protracted further administrative processing and litigation. The Commission and the Company recognized the difficulty of resolving issues raised by the Charge in light of the scope of the Charge and size, complexity and diversity of the Company's operations. In recognition of the Company's size, complexity and diversity, the Commission focused its investigation upon general allegations in the Charge which were believed to be characteristic of industrial relations practices at many of the Company's facilities. The parties agree that resolution of the nation-wide Charge by the implementation of the procedures set forth below is proper and appropriate.

C. This Agreement applies to all locations of the General Electric Company within the United States, except those owned either in whole or in part by a subsidiary of the General Electric Company, and those Company locations which are subject to federal court consent decrees under Title VII of the Civil Rights Act of 1964, as amended, as of the effective date of this Agreement. At those locations covered by pre-existing federal court consent decrees the provisions of this Agreement shall be applicable insofar as they do not conflict with or differ from the provisions of such existing current decrees.

D. The Company expressly denies that any of its actions, omissions, programs or practices are in violation of Title VII of the Civil Rights Act of 1964, as amended or of any other equal employment law, regulation or order and expressly denies that it has any liability under any such law, regulation or order.

E. The Company and the Commission recognize that a number of labor unions currently possess rights under the National Labor Relations Act to bargain collectively on behalf of designated employees at certain Company locations, and that this Agreement is not intended to impinge upon or affect in any way the collective bargaining rights of those unions. In addition, the Company the Commission agree that nothing in this Agreement is in conflict with or in derogation of any provision of the present collective bargaining agreements between the Company and the unions certified or recognized to represent Company employees.

III. CORPORATE EQUAL OPPORTUNITY COMMITMENT

A. The provisions of this Agreement rest on and stem from the General Electric Company's longstanding policy to provide employment, training, compensation, promotion and other conditions of employment without regard to race, color, national origin or sex, as well as on the Company's plans, both existing and to be implemented pursuant to the terms of this Agreement, to enhance equal employment opportunity.

B. The Company reiterates its policy by agreeing that its officers, agents and employees will not engage in any act, omission, program or practice which unlawfully discriminates against any individual at any of the Company's locations covered by this Agreement because of the individual's race, sex or national origin and will not:

1. Fail or refuse to hire or promote; discharge any individual; or otherwise discriminate against any individual with respect to compensation, terms conditions or privileges of employment, because of such individual's race, sex or national origin; or

2. Limit, segregate or classify its employees in any way which would deprive or tend to deprive any individual of employment opportunities or otherwise adversely affect an individual's status as an employee, because of the individual's race, sex or national origin.

IV. AFFIRMATIVE ACTIONS

The Company agrees that its policy on and commitment to equal employment opportunity will best be demonstrated by re-emphasizing and continuing or initiating affirmative actions designed to achieve that end.

The Company agrees that it will undertake or continue, and complete the affirmative actions listed below and described in Paragraphs V-X.

1. Wage Structure Modifications
2. Promotion Incentives
3. Open Promotion Systems
4. Hourly Employee Training
5. Employment Procedures
6. Management Education

V. WAGE STRUCTURE MODIFICATIONS

A. The Company will initiate and/or complete the modifications with regard to hourly wage structures listed in Appendix A by increasing the compensation levels as listed in that Appendix.

B. 1. The Company agrees to make a special lump sum payment to all present employees, including inactive employees with protected service as of the effective date of this Agreement, who for any period beginning not earlier than July 1, 1975, up to the date of each job rate adjustment, were regularly assigned to any of the jobs whose rates have been, or are to be adjusted pursuant to subparagraph (A) of this Paragraph.

The amount of each such employee's special payment will be calculated by determining the difference between the hourly rate actually paid for time worked on a job later adjusted as specified, and the hourly rate which would have been paid had a similar adjustment been made effective at the beginning of each work week beginning not earlier than July 1, 1975. That difference will be multiplied by forty (40) times the number of work weeks during which the employee was regularly assigned to the job.

2. No portion of any payment made pursuant to subparagraph (B)(1) above shall be included by the Company in any compensation base for computing benefits available to any employee.

3. A lump sum payment computed and paid in accordance with the terms of this Agreement will constitute the full payment for increased wages which would have been paid between July 1, 1975 and the effective dates of the adjustments made pursuant to subparagraph (A) of this Paragraph.

C. In order to receive such lump sum payment, each affected employee shall be required to execute a release, a copy of which is attached as Appendix B. If an affected employee does not execute such a release, such employee shall not be entitled to receive any lump sum payment under this paragraph and the Company shall be relieved of all liability with respect to payment of the lump sum otherwise payable to the employee under this Agreement.

D. The Company estimates that the ongoing increased costs in wages and benefits, associated with re-evaluations specified in subparagraph (A) will total one million, one hundred thousand dollars ($1,100,000) annually. The Company's good faith estimate which has been reviewed by the Commission is that the total cost of implementing this paragraph, from July 1, 1975 to April 1, 1982, including lump sum special payments, is approximately seven million, four hundred thousand dollars ($7,400,000).

VI. PROMOTION INCENTIVE PROGRAM

A. The Company will establish a Promotion Incentive Program as an affirmative action designed to provide an incentive for female and minority male employees to seek and accept promotions into higher Work Zones.

B. The Company hereby makes a financial commitment of ten million, six hundred thousand dollars (10,600,000) which shall be available for payments under the Program. Any employee who is eligible for a Promotion Incentive Bonus under the conditions of the Promotion Incentive Program as set forth below will be paid the appropriate Bonus. No portion of any Bonus paid pursuant to this Paragraph shall be included by the Company in any compensation base for computing benefits available to any employee.

C. A Promotion Incentive Bonus will be paid to an eligible female or minority male employee who achieves a promotion to a higher rated position within a higher Work Zone, provided, however, that the employee has not previously held that position. A promotion from Work Zone II to Work Zone I does not qualify an individual for a Bonus.

D. The amount of such Bonuses shall be based upon the Work Zone within which the new position is included as set forth below:

New Work Zone	Amount of Bonus
Work Zone I	$800
II	800
III	500
IV	500
V	500
VII	800
VIII	800
IX	500

E. Promotions occurring on or after April 1, 1976 and which otherwise qualify an eligible female or minority male employee for Bonus payment will be subject to this Paragraph.

F. To be eligible for a Promotion Incentive Bonus, a female or a male minority employee must satisfy each of the following eligibility standards:

1. Be actively employed or on inactive status with protected service, as established by existing local practice, as of the effective date of this Agreement to receive Bonuses for promotion from April 1, 1976 to the effective date of this Agreement and be otherwise eligible for a Promotion Bonus; and

2. Have continuous service with the Company at the time of promotion as follows:

   a. for promotion to positions within Work Zones I and II, three (3) or more years.

   b. for promotion to positions within Work Zones III, IV and V, two (2) or more years.

   c. for promotion to positions within Work Zones VII and VIII, one (1) or more years.

   d. for promotion to positions within Work Zone IX, six (6) or more months; and

3. Complete six months satisfactory performance following the promotion, or attain Job Rate on the new job as established locally by existing compensation practices, if Job Rate is attained in less than six months; and

4. An individual may be awarded a Bonus only for the first promotion which qualifies for a Bonus under this Paragraph.

G. An individual who has received back pay and/or individual monetary relief under a prior settlement agreement, conciliation agreement, or consent decree shall be eligible to receive additional relief with respect to the same claim of discrimination as a result of this Paragraph, only to the extent that the total amount of prior monetary relief and the Bonus provided hereunder does not exceed the amount of Bonus to which the employee is entitled under this Paragraph.

H. In order to receive a Bonus payment, each affected employee shall be required to execute a release, a copy of which is attached as Appendix C. If an eligible employee fails to execute such release, the employee shall not be entitled to a Bonus payment under this Paragraph and the Company shall be relieved of all liability to the employee with respect to the Promotion Incentive Bonus otherwise payable to the employee under this Paragraph; however the amount of the Bonus otherwise payable for that promotion to the employee will not be deducted from the $10,600,000 commitment.

I. The Company at each of its facilities will communicate the terms and conditions of the Promotion Incentive Program to those employees who have qualified or may at some time in the future qualify for a Bonus under the Program. The communication will include, but not be limited to, such matters as eligibility, pay grades or levels included within each Work Zone, and amount of promotion Bonuses.

J. The Promotion Incentive Program will continue during the term of this Agreement or until Bonus payments actually made pursuant to this paragraph equal the $10,600,000 commitment, whichever occurs first. In no event shall the Company's liability under the Promotion Incentive Program exceed the $10,600,000 commitment.

K. If less than $10,600,000 in Promotion Incentive Payments has been disbursed at the expiration of this Agreement, the remainder will be disbursed consistent with the purposes of this Agreement by mutual agreement between the Company and the Commission.

VII. OPEN SYSTEMS: PROMOTIONS AND JOB POSTING

A. The Company shall implement Open Promotion Systems at all locations in order to ensure that employees have an equal opportunity to request consideration for open jobs, as defined in subparagraph (E)(3) below, to be filled by promotion. Such Systems will be maintained for all hourly rated and non-exempt salaried jobs and all exempt salaried jobs through exempt salary Position Level 9. The purpose of Open Promotion Systems is to enable an employee at any Company location to register a desire to be considered for hourly or non-exempt jobs at that location when such jobs are to be filled by promotion, and to enable an employee to register a desire to be considered for exempt jobs within the employee's division at that location, when such jobs are to be filled by promotion.

B. Job Posting shall continue, in accordance with applicable location procedures, to provide the most commonly used, but not exclusive mechanism by which employees are advised of jobs to be filled by promotion.

C. Any Open Promotion System involving employees represented by a union certified or recognized by the National Labor Relations Board is subject to negotiations with the collective bargaining representative.

D. Each Company location will have a written document which describes its Open Promotion System, and which provides an opportunity for employees to express their interests in, and be considered for, promotions to job openings without regard to race, sex, or national origin.

E. Open Promotion Systems will vary by location because of significant differences in such factors as size, organizational complexity, product, union representation status and geographic dispersion. However, all Systems at all locations shall contain the following common elements:

1. Provision that employees shall have the opportunity to request consideration for promotion to open positions within their present pay category or any other pay category (hourly, non-exempt and exempt salaried), by requesting consideration for any specific opening, notice of which is posted or published and/or by nominating themselves for consideration for promotion in advance of a specific opening.

2. Communication regarding the system in effect at each location including:

a. Formal notification to employees that written documentation of the procedure will be available upon request.

b. Communication to all employees at least annually, of the provisions of the Open Promotion System, including the date on which self-nomination applications are no longer valid, and the availability of such job information as job titles, duties and pay codes at the employment office or other suitable location.

c. Orientation for Managers on the provisions of the Open Promotion System in effect in their division and location.

d. Notification to unsuccessful job candidates.

3. An open job shall be defined as a job vacancy to be filled by promotion of present employees, but will not include the following:

a. Recalls, or placements occasioned by downgrades, lack of work, or returns to previously held classifications.

b. Returns to active payroll from illness or injury, maternity, military or personal leave.

c. Positions filled as a result of a consolidation or reorganization of components.

d. Normal step increases of employees within hourly or non-exempt salaried jobs, or level increases within an exempt job hierarchy as predetermined experience and level of contribution objectives are met.

e. Re-evaluation of existing positions.

f. Positions temporarily opened for summer or co-op students or which are not expected to continue beyond six months' duration.

g. Rotational assignments filled by participants of a recognized corporate or local training program. The filling of an initial assignment into a program does constitute filling an open position.

4. Hiring and promotion decisions, including management decisions and employment office decisions, will be reviewed by an individual other than the hiring or promotion authority to ensure that such decisions were appropriate.

F. Open Promotion Systems are not intended to, nor shall they be construed to alter any Company obligation or right to fill openings by methods other than promotion, or to limit the right of an employee to protest a selection decision in accordance with established local practices.

G. If, for a given year, a division location's actual results do not meet the numerical objective established pursuant to Paragraph XI of this Agreement for a Work Zone or Work Zones, the Company will determine whether the division location has a primary job posting practice for the applicable Work Zone(s). If the division location does not have primary job posting for the jobs in the Work Zone(s) where the numerical objective was not met, primary job posting for at least the jobs in that Work Zone(s) will be implemented by the end of the year in which the numerical objectives results were reported, as long as primary job posting is not in conflict with, or in derogation of applicable collective bargaining agreements. Primary job posting implemented pursuant to this subparagraph will continue for at least twelve (12) months or until the numerical objectives in the applicable Work Zone(s) have been met.

VIII. HOURLY EMPLOYEE TRAINING

A. The Company and Commission agree that formal training would enable persons with that training to compete for promotion and/or placement into certain higher-rated hourly jobs in Work Zones VII and VIII. In addition, the parties agree that by encouraging qualified females and minority males to participate in such formal training programs, the number of qualified females and minority males competing for jobs in Work Zones VII and VIII can reasonably be expected to increase.

B. WORK ZONE VIII TRAINING

1. Within twelve (12) months after the effective date of this Agreement, the Company will implement training in selected Company components at a total level of 500 trainees entering annually. The level of 500 trainees entering annually is based on a forecast of no hourly employment growth during the term of this Agreement, and an annual loss rate of 15% in aggregate Work Zone VIII employment at approximately 35 Company components with a Work Zone VIII population of 150 or more. The Company retains the right to cease training in a location and/or start in another location based on local employment needs, as long as the objective of 500 entering trainees annually is achieved.

2. Training opportunities will be publicized and open to all qualified employees and applicants for employment through self-nomination and application procedures.

3. Training will consist of training room activity, related classwork and on-the-job experience. Training time will vary depending on the training provided and the skill levels of entering trainees, but is estimated to range from two to six months, or an average of approximately three months. All training during normal work hours will be paid at wage rates established pursuant to existing and applicable local procedures.

4. The objective for female entry into Work Zone VIII training for each of the components where training is expected to take place is the female participation rate in the local Experienced Manufacturing Civilian Labor Force, according to local 1970 SMSA (Table #185) census data, or 18%, whichever is greater. (This averages to approximately 30% female entry. If the assumed level of training needs changes in one or more of the components, the average female entry percentage may also change.) The objective for minority male entry to training is 12%. The Company will actively encourage qualified females and minority males to seek admittance to such programs in a good faith effort to meet the numerical objectives.

C. WORK ZONE VII (APPRENTICE) TRAINING

1. Within twelve (12) months after the effective date of this Agreement, apprentice training will be increased to a level of 1,000 apprentices. Representative jobs for which this apprentice training will be provided include, but are not limited to, tool and die maker, electrician, maintenance mechanic and engineering drafter.

2. Training will take place on the job and in an apprentice shop and will be supplemented by related classroom studies. Training time will range from three to four years.

3. The objective for filling apprentice program openings will be 15% for females, (but not less than 10% females at any location having 10 or more apprentices) and 12% for minority males. The Company will make a good faith effort to meet the numerical objectives established for female and minority male entry into apprentice training through additional advertising, recruiting and counseling.

D. TRAINING COSTS

The Company's good faith estimate which has been reviewed by the Commission is that the compensation costs for female and minority male hourly trainees and apprentices, and for the instructors employed to provide the additional training required by this Paragraph will total nine million, nine hundred thousand dollars ($9,900,000). The Company will bear the new and increased costs associated with implementing the provisions of this Paragraph.

The Company in good faith estimates that the additional efforts designed to recruit female and minority male hourly trainees and apprentices will cost five hundred thousand dollars ($500,000).

IX. EMPLOYMENT PROCEDURES

A. The Company shall maintain in each location's hiring area information on job titles, summary of duties, and pay codes for the types of jobs available for external hire so that such information can be reviewed by all job applicants.

B. When an open position is to be filled by hiring, the hiring official will consider first those persons whose applications are on file. All applications shall remain on file for one year.

C. The Company agrees to carefully review the use of tests at all Company locations and to refrain from utilizing tests which are non job-related.

D. The Company will determine whether any job related pre-employment test has an adverse impact on the selection of persons of any one race, ethnic or sex group and if an adverse impact is found, the Company will either validate such test in accordance with "Technical Standards for Validity Studies", Part II of the Proposed Uniform Guidelines for Employee Selection Procedures as they are finalized, or discontinue its use.

X. MANAGEMENT EDUCATION

A. The Company understands that successful implementation and completion of the foregoing affirmative actions depend, in part, on managers' knowledge and understanding. The Company agrees that it will communicate the essential terms of this Agreement to all managers and supervisors through a specific program designed for local adaptation and implementation at all Company locations.

B. The Company's good faith estimate which has been reviewed by the Commission is that such a communication and education program will cost five hundred thousand dollars ($500,000).

XI. NUMERICAL OBJECTIVES

A. Definitions - The definitions below are intended to apply for purposes of this Paragraph of this Agreement, and apply to the establishment of numerical objectives for this Company only.

1. Aggregation is defined as the process for determining the Company's numerical objective for each Work Zone by accumulating through a population-weighting method the numerical objectives for each applicable division location.

2. External Labor Market (E) is defined as the percentage of females or minority males in the occupations appearing in census or other accepted public data who have skills representative of those necessary to perform work within a specified Work Zone. The External Labor Markets for each Work Zone are specified in this Agreement, subparagraphs E and F of this paragraph and Appendices D and E.

3. Internal Labor Market (I) is defined as the percentage of females or minority males in that portion of the workforce from which promotions to a higher

Work Zone are normally expected to come. The procedure for determining the Internal Labor Markets for each Work Zone is set forth below in subparagraph G of this paragraph.

4. Opportunity is defined as an open position, as defined in Paragraph VII(E)(3), in any Work Zone that is filled through external hiring or by promoting an employee from a lower Work Zone. An opportunity can occur more than once in a calendar year for the same job if turnover takes place.

5. Numerical Objective is defined as the percentage of opportunities in a Work Zone which the Company will attempt to fill with females or minority males.

6. Representation is defined as the percentage of females or minority males in the Work Zone population.

B. Annual Numerical Objectives

1. The Company will establish annual numerical objectives for filling opportunities with females and minority males for Work Zones I, II, III, V, VII, VIII, IX and X. The numerical objectives will be established by application of agreed upon formulas and decision rules set forth below in subparagraph C of this paragraph.

The Company's numerical objectives for each Work Zone will be established by aggregating numerical objectives for each Work Zone for each division location which has one hundred (100) or more employees at the end of the third quarter of the year preceding the year for which the numerical objectives are being established.

2. The Company will apply reasonable, good faith efforts to meet any annual numerical objectives established as described herein. Differences between actual results and the numerical objective process-determined expectations will not determine compliance or non-compliance with this Agreement. Such differences will afford a basis for the review of the Company's good faith efforts to successfully fulfill its affirmative action commitments herein described and serve as a guide to the Company and the Commission in ongoing review of such affirmative actions regarding equal employment opportunity.

C. Work Zone Formulas

1. The formulas for determining numerical objectives for females and minority males in each of the eight Work Zones for which such objectives are to be established are set forth below, with exceptions noted in subparagraphs (2-4) of this Paragraph.

FORMULAS FOR NUMERICAL OBJECTIVES

WORK ZONE	FEMALES		MINORITY MALES	
I	largest of	E + .2I	larger of	E + .2I
	or	1.2E	or	1.9E
	or	.5I		
II	largest of	E + .2I	larger of	E + .2I
	or	1.2E	or	2.3E
	or	.5I		
III	largest of	E + .2I	larger of	E + .2I
	or	1.2E	or	1.2E
	or	.5I		
V	largest of	E + .2I	larger of	E + .2I
	or	1.2E	or	1.2E
	or	.5I		
VII	larger of	2E	largest of	E + .2I
	or	.5I	or	1.2E
				.5I
VIII	larger of	2E	largest of	E + .2I
	or	.5I	or	1.2E
			or	.5I
IX	larger of	1.5E	largest of	E + .2I
	or	.5I	or	1.2E
			or	.5I
X		1.2E		1.2E

2. Company numerical objectives for minority males for Work Zones I and II will be 6% and 7% respectively in each year of this Agreement, or the numerical objectives produced by the formula, whichever is higher for the respective Work Zones.

3. The formula for establishing the numerical objective for females in Work Zone X will be .5 E for the following division locations:

Schenectady, NY	- All Divisions of the Turbine Business Group
Lynn, MA	- All Divisions of the Turbine and Aircraft Engine Business Groups
Erie, PA	- Transportation Systems Business Division
Pittsfield, MA	- Large Transformer Business Division
Hickory, NC	- Switchgear & Distribution Transformer Division
Philadelphia, PA	- Switchgear & Distribution Transformer Division
Evendale, OH	- All Divisions of the Aircraft Engine Business Group
Rome, GA	- Large Transformer Business Division
Charleston, SC	- Large Steam Turbine - Generator Division

South Portland, ME   Large Steam Turbine - Generator Division

4. The numerical objective for minority males for Work Zone X shall be 1.2 times the percentage of males in the external male labor market and shall be a percentage of opportunities filled by males in Work Zone X.

D. WORK ZONES

1. The exempt salaried workforce will be divided into Work Zones according to established Company Position Levels.

a. Work Zone I contains Managers and Professionals in exempt Position Levels 7-9.

b. Work Zone II contains First Level Managers and Professionals in exempt Position Levels 1-6.

2. The non-exempt salaried workforce will be divided into Work Zones as follows:

a. Work Zone III - Skilled Technicians

Work Zone III contains the Skilled Technicians jobs determined by establishing the pay symbol in the EEO-1 Report Technicians category which marks the point at which there is an appreciable change in skill levels. That pay symbol or its equivalent and all pay symbols above it in the EEO-1 Report Technician category constitute Work Zone III. The pay symbol(s) which define the lower boundary of Work Zone III is determined by referring to jobs in the EEO-1 Report Technicians category and grouping those jobs which require skills equal to or greater than Engineering Technicians, Designer and Development Technicians.

b. Work Zone IV - Other Technicians

Work Zone IV contains the balance of the Technicians' jobs in the EEO-1 Report Technicians category not included in Work Zone III, Skilled Technicians.

c. Work Zone V - Clerical and Administrative

Work Zone V contains the Clerical and Administrative jobs determined by establishing the pay symbol in the EEO-1 Report Office and Clerical Category which marks the point at which there is an appreciable change in skill levels. That pay symbol or its equivalent, and all above it in the EEO-1 Report Sales Workers and Office and Clerical Categories, constitute Work Zone V. The pay symbol(s) which define the lower boundary of Work Zone V are determined by referring to jobs in the EEO-1 Report Sales Workers and Office and Clerical Categories and grouping those jobs which require skills equal to or greater than Material Control Clerk, Production Control Clerk, and Manufacturing Expediter.

d. Work Zone VI - Other Clerical

Work Zone VI contains the balance of the Clerical Administrative jobs in the EEO-1 Report Sales Workers and Office and Clerical Categories not included in Work Zone,V Clerical and Administrative.

3. The hourly workforce will be divided into Work Zones as follows:

a. Work Zone VII - Apprenticed and Equivalent Crafts

Work Zone VII contains the Apprenticed and Equivalent Crafts jobs determined by establishing the pay symbol in the EEO-1 Report Craft Workers category which marks the point at which there is an appreciable change in skill levels. That pay symbol, or its equivalent, and all above it in the EEO-1 Report Craft Workers, Operatives, Laborers and Service Workers categories constitute Work Zone VII. The pay symbol(s) which define the lower boundary of Work Zone VII are determined by referring to jobs in the EEO-1 Report Craft Workers, Operatives, Laborers and Service Workers categories and grouping those jobs which require skills equal to or greater than the skill level of First Class Electricians, Plumbers, Millwrights, Sheetmetal Smiths and Tool and Die Makers.

b. Work Zone VIII - Other Crafts

Work Zone VIII contains the Other Crafts jobs determined by establishing the pay symbol(s) which is the lower boundary of the traditional jobs in the EEO-1 Report Craft Workers category. That pay symbol or its equivalent, and all above it in the Craft Workers, Operatives, Laborers and Service Workers categories up to the lowest pay symbol of Work Zone VII, Constitute Work Zone VIII.

c. Work Zone IX - Semi-Skilled Operatives

Work Zone IX contains the Semi-Skilled jobs determined by establishing the pay symbol in the EEO-1 Report Operatives, Laborers and Service Workers categories which marks the point at which there is an appreciable change in skill levels. That pay symbol, or its equivalent, and all above it in the EEO-1 Report Craft Workers, Operatives, Laborers and Service Workers categories, up to the lowest pay symbol of Work Zone VIII, constitute Work Zone IX. The pay symbol(s) which define the lower boundary of Work Zone IX are determined by referring to jobs in the EEO-1 Report Craft Workers, Operatives, Laborers and Service Workers categories and grouping those jobs which require skills equal to or greater than Precision Machine Operators, Hand-held Welders and Flame Cutters.

d. Work Zone X - Entry Level Operatives

Work Zone X contains the balance of the jobs in EEO-1 Report Operatives, Laborers and Service Workers categories not included in the other Work Zones.

4. If there is a conflict between the Company's workforce category (exempt, non-exempt, hourly) and the category in which a job is reported in the EEO-1 Report, the following rules shall apply:

a. Exempt salaried jobs will be contained in Work Zone I or Work Zone II.

b. Non-exempt salaried jobs classified as Craft Workers, Operatives, Laborers or Service Workers on the EEO-1 Report will be contained in Work Zone VII, VIII, IX OR X as appropriate, without regard to status as a non-exempt job.

c. Hourly jobs classified as Technicians, Sales Workers or Office and Clerical on the EEO-1 Report will be contained in Work Zone III, IV, V or VI as appropriate without regard to status as an hourly job.

E. EXTERNAL LABOR MARKET - WORK ZONES I and II

The External Labor Markets (E) for Work Zones I and II are constructed for each division location separately for females and minority males as follows:

1. Divide the total population of the division location's Position Level (PL) 1-14 population into the following segments defined by education and work function:

a. Technical Degreed
   1. Engineering and Technology Degreed
   2. Other Technical Degreed (Physical Science and Mathematics)

b. Non-Technical Degreed

c. Non-Degreed (Associate Degrees included)
   1. Engineering
   2. Marketing
   3. Manufacturing
   4. Finance
   5. Employee Relations and Others

2. The representation of females and minority males within each segment of the External Labor Market has been calculated for each location and is set forth in Appendix E for the Engineering and other Technical Degreed population, and for the Non-Technical Degreed population, and in Appendix D for the Non-Degreed population.

3. Calculate separately the percentage of the PL 1-14 population for Technical Degrees, Non-Technical Degrees and Non-Degreed.

4. Calculate separately the percentage of the Technical Degree holders who possess an Engineering or Other Technical degree.

5. Multiply separately the External Labor Market representation of females and minority males (Appendix E) possessing Engineering and Other Technical Degrees (see Step 2) by the percentage obtained in Step 4.

6. Add the results of Step 5 separately for females and minority males, and multiply by the percentage of the PL 1-14 population possessing a Technical Degree (see Step 3).

7. Multiply separately the External Labor Market representation of females and minority males possessing Non-Technical Degrees (see Step 2) by the percentage of the PL 1-14 population possessing a Non-Technical Degree (see Step 3).

8. Calculate separately the percentage of the Non-Degreed PL 1-14 population who work in each of the following functions: Engineering, Marketing, Manufacturing, Finance, Employee Relations and others.

9. Multiply separately the External Labor Market representation of Non-Degreed females and minority males by function by the corresponding percentage obtained in Step 8.

10. Add the results obtained in Step 9 separately for females and minority males and multiply the sum by the percentage of the PL 1-14 population who are Non-Degreed.

11. Add the results of Steps 6, 7 and 10 separately for females and minority males.

F. EXTERNAL LABOR MARKET - HOURLY AND NON-EXEMPT SALARIED WORK ZONES III, V, VII, VIII, IX AND X JOBS

The procedure to determine the External Labor Market for Work Zones III, V, VII, VIII, IX and X jobs is as follows:

1. Occupation titles relevant to the type of work and level of skill for Work Zones III, V, VII, VIII, IX and X are used in conjunction with local SMSA data for each location to dtermine the External Labor Market for females and minority males.

2. The External Labor Markets for each of these Work Zones is identified by location in Appendix D.

G. INTERNAL LABOR MARKET

The procedure for determining the Internal Labor Market (I) is as follows:

1. Work Zones IV, VI and X are entry level Work Zones, and therefore no Internal Labor Market is specified.

2. The representation of females or minority males in Position Levels 5 and 6 are the Internal Labor Markets for Work Zone I for purposes of establishing numerical objectives for Work Zone I.

3. The representation of females or minority males in Work Zones III, V, VII, VIII and IX are the Internal Labor Markets for Work Zone II for purposes of establishing numerical objectives for Work Zone II.

4. The Internal Labor Markets for Work Zones III, V, VII, VIII and IX shall be the representation of females or minority males in the three highest pay symbols or equivalent in the next lower Work Zone.

5. When the population of that portion of the work force from which the Internal Labor Market for any Work Zone is derived is less than one-sixth of the population of the Work Zone for which it is the source, the value of (I) will be zero.

H. AGGREGATION

1. The aggregation process will be as follows:

a. For each Work Zone for each division location, the Company will:

1. Determine the population in the Work Zone.
2. Determine separately the numerical objective for females and minority males.
3. Multiply the population by the numerical objective.
4. Sum the results from Step 3 for all division locations.
5. Sum the total population for all division locations.
6. Divide the result from Step 4 by the result from Step 5.
7. The result from Step 6 is the aggregate numerical objective for the Company.

2. However, the procedure for aggregating the numerical objective for minority males in Work Zone X will be the same as subparagraph H(1)(a) above except that male population will be used instead of total population.

3. The procedure for determining if a division location numerical objective is required for aggregation purposes is as follows:

a. A numerical objective for females in a Work Zone will be required when the applicable formula for the Work Zone is E + . 2 I, 1.5 E, 2.0 E, and 1.2 E, and the representation of females in the Work Zone is less that the External Labor Market (E) for that Work Zone.

b. A numerical objective for females in a Work Zone will be required when the applicable formula for the Work Zone is .5 I or .5 E and the female representation in the Work Zone is less than. 51 or .5 E respectively.

c. A numerical objective for minority males in a Work Zone will be required when the applicable formula for the Work Zone is E + .2 I or 1.2 E and the minority male representation in the Work Zone is less than the External Labor Market (E) for that Work Zone.

d. A numerical objective for minority males in a Work Zone will be required when the applicable formula for the Work Zone is 1.9 E and the minority male representation in the Work Zone is less than 1.9 E for that Work Zone.

e. A numerical objective for minority males in a Work Zone will be required when the applicable formula for the Work Zone is 2.3 E and the minority male representation is less than 2.3 E for that Work Zone.

f. A numerical objective for minority males in a Work Zone will be required when the applicable formula for the Work Zone is .5 I and the minority male representation is less than .5 I for that Work Zone.

g. A numerical objective for minority males in Work Zone X will be required when the representation of minority males to total males in the Work Zone is less than the External Labor Market percentage of minority males to total males.

4. When a numerical objective is not required, determine the value substituted for the numerical objective for aggregation purposes as follows:

a. When a minority male or female numerical objective is not required and the applicable formula is E + .2 I, 1.5 E, 2.0 E, or 1.2 E, substitute E for aggregation purposes only for the applicable Work Zone(s).

b. When a minority male or female numerical objective is not required and the formula is .5 E, 1.9 E, 2.3 E or .5 I, the applicable formula will be used for aggregation purposes only, for the Work Zone(s).

c. When a minority male numerical objective is not required in Work Zone X, the External Labor Market ratio of minority males to total males will be used for aggregation purposes only for Work Zone X.

XII. INDIVIDUAL COMPLAINT RESOLUTION

A. Any currently pending charge which has not been designated as either suitable or unsuitable as of the effective date of this Agreement will be identified and designated by the Commission as suitable or unsuitable within thirty (30) days following the effective date of this Agreement.

B. Following the effective date of this Agreement, unresolved charges, designated as unsuitable will be returned promptly to the appropriate District Offices with Commission instructions to pursue expeditious settlement and/or processing in accordance with existing Commission regulations. In addition, District Offices will be instructed to issue right-to-sue letters with respect to all unsuitable charges filed prior to the date of this Agreement and listed in Appendix F, which may be supplemented by agreement of the Company and Commission, which have not been settled within one hundred and twenty (120) days following the date of Agreement. The 120 day time period can be extended by mutual agreement between the Company and the Commission.

C. Following the effective date of this Agreement, remaining unresolved charges, designated as suitable, and listed in Appendix G which may be supplemented by agreement of the Company and Commission will be discussed by designated headquarters representatives of the Company and the Commission in an attempt to reach a negotiated settlement for each charge. Within 120 days following the effective date of this Agreement, a notice of right-to-sue will be issued for those charges which cannot be resolved through this procedure. The 120 day time period can be extended by mutual agreement between the Company and the Commission.

D. The execution of this Agreement is intended to resolve between the Commission and the Company all allegations of systemic or class discrimination inherent in all charges pending as of the effective date of this Agreement, which have been, or are eventually designated as "suitable."

The Commission will not file suit during the term of this Agreement on the basis of any issue raised in any charge which is raised by Commissioner's Charge TNP 4C-2000.

E. The Company agrees to commit one million dollars ($1,000,000) to be available for use by the Company and the Commission in their efforts to resolve charges, both suitable and unsuitable, filed prior to the effective date of this Agreement, listed in Appendices F and G which may be supplemented by agreement of the Company and the Commission. If less than $1,000,000 is paid to charging parties in resolution of these charges, the remainder will be disbursed by mutual agreement between the Company and the Commission.

XIII. COMPLIANCE REVIEW PROCEDURES

A. Personnel

1. The Commission will designate an employee as the Compliance Review Official (CRO). The Company will deliver all reports and other information required to be supplied under this Agreement to the CRO.

2. The Company will designate an employee as its Compliance Review Representative (CRR).

3. Either the CRO or the CRR may request a meeting with the other for purposes related to compliance with the terms of this agreement, including, but not limited to clarification of reports and/or information, review of events unforeseen by either party which could impact upon the Agreement, or discussion of matters of mutual concern.

B. Procedures

1. The procedure set forth below will be followed in the event that the CRO has reason to believe that a provision or provisions of this Agreement have been violated. In general, such a belief can result from one or more of the following:

a. Review of data supplied to the Commission by the Company pursuant to the reporting provisions of this Agreement.

b. A written claim filed with the Commission by any person alleging that this Agreement, or a portion thereof has been, or is being violated by the Company.

c. Notification to the CRO by a Regional or District Office of the Commission that a charge of discrimination filed with that Region or Office involves alleged violation of provisions of this Agreement.

2. Data Reporting by Company

If the review of data supplied to the Commission by the Company pursuant to any of the reporting or informational provisions of this Agreement indicates to the Commission the possibility that the terms of this Agreement are being violated, the following procedure will be followed:

a. The CRO will notify the CRR of the potential violation of this Agreement, and the CRR shall have the opportunity to submit the Company position with respect to the potential violation within a reasonable period of time.

b. After reviewing any statements or evidence presented by the CRR, the CRO will deliver to the CRR, the Commission's written position concerning the alleged violation and will meet with the CRR in an attempt to resolve the matter by informal discussion.

c. If such attempts at informal resolution are not successful, the CRO shall issue to the CRR a written notification that the Commission will seek judicial relief from the alleged violation or violations not earlier than thirty (30) days from the date of the receipt of notification by the CRR.

3. Claims of Breach

Written claims that any provision of this Agreement has been violated will be processed according to the following procedure:

a. The CRO will give written notice to the CRR of the pendency of the claim.

b. Investigation of the claim by the CRO will be conducted in cooperation with the CRR. The CRO's written conclusions regarding the claim will be delivered to the CRR at the conclusion of the investigation.

c. Informal discussion of the matter will be undertaken by the CRO and CRR, if adverse conclusions are issued under (b) above.

d. If informal discussion fails to resolve the allegations of violation, the CRO shall issue to the

CRR a written notification that the Commission will seek judicial relief from the alleged violation or violations not earlier than thirty (30) days from the date of receipt of the notification by the CRR.

4. Regional and District Office Notification
Notification to the CRO by a Regional or District Office of the Commission alleging a violation of the Agreement will be processed by the CRO in accordance with the following procedure:

a. If the CRO, after receiving the notification from the District or Regional Office, determines that the charge involves an allegation that this Agreement has been violated, the CRO will give written notice of that fact to the CRR.

b. Investigation of the claim of breach by the CRO will be conducted in cooperation with the CRR. The CRO's written conclusions regarding the claim will be delivered to the CRR at the conclusion of the investigation.

c. Informal discussion of the matter will be undertaken by the CRO and CRR, if adverse conclusions are issued under (b) above.

d. If informal discussion fails to resolve the allegations of violations, the CRO shall issue to the CRR a written notification that the Commission will seek judicial relief from the alleged violation or violations not earlier than thirty (30) days from the date of receipt of notification by the CRR.

5. Charges of Retaliation
Charges alleging retaliation will be processed pursuant to exising Commission procedures, and shall not be subject to the conditions recited above.

XIV. REPORTING PROCEDURES

A. Pursuant to this Agreement, the Company through its designated Compliance Review Representative (CRR), will submit to the Commission's Compliance Review Official (CRO) the written reports described herein at the times specified.

Upon request to the Company, the Commission will have access to all documents used by the Company to calculate any of the Numerical Objectives and to compile all reports required under this Agreement for the purpose of auditing Company reports. The data will be made available at an agreed upon time and place, but will remain in the possession of the Company. Due dates for Reports required by this Agreement may be changed by mutual agreement between the Company and Commission.

B. WAGE STRUCTURE REPORTS

1. Within 90 days following the effective date of this Agreement, the Company will provide a report, a form for which is attached as Appendix H, to the CRO with respect to the completed adjustments of wage rates resulting from the application of Paragraph V(A).

2. By April 1, 1979, the Company will provide a report, a form for which is attached as Appendix H, to the CRO with respect to the remaining adjustments pursuant to Paragraph V(A) and not reported pursuant to subparagraph (B)(1) of this Paragraph.

3. By April 1, 1979 the Company will provide a report, a form for which is attached as Appendix J, to the CRO with respect to the lump sum payments made in accordance with Paragraph V(B).

4. The Company shall maintain copies of Releases and other documents which reflect the calculations for lump sum payments, which upon request of the Commission will be subject to inspection by the Commission at an agreed upon time and place.

C. PROMOTION INCENTIVE REPORTS

Six months following the effective date of this agreement the Company will provide a report, a form for which is attached as Appendix K, to the CRO with respect to promotion incentive bonuses paid for the period from April 1, 1976 through December 31, 1977. Thereafter throughout the term of this Agreement, an annual report for each year of the term of this Agreement will be provided to the CRO by April 1st of the year following the year covered by the report.

D. OPEN SYSTEMS REPORTS

1. By April 1st of each year during the term of this Agreement, the Company will provide a report, a form for which is attached as Appendix L, to the CRO with respect to the operation of Open Promotion Systems during the prior year.

2. By April 1st of the first year of this Agreement and annually thereafter, the Company will report to the Commission that it has received, reviewed and retained information from each location of 100 or more hourly employees which summarizes by sex the job classification and pay rate for employees newly hired into Work Zones IX and X during the previous calendar year in order to allow the Company and management of each location to monitor compliance with the open employment procedures set forth in Paragraph IX of this Agreement.

3. By April 1st of the first year of this Agreement and annually thereafter, the Company will report to the Commission that it has received, reviewed and retained workforce statistics from each location of 100 or more hourly employees showing the population by sex of each job classification in Work Zones VII, VIII, IX and X in order to allow the Company and management of each location to monitor compliance with the open employment procedures set forth in Paragraph IX of this Agreement.

E. HOURLY TRAINING REPORTS

By April 1, 1979 the Company will provide a report, a form for which is attached as Appendix M, to the CRO with respect to the level of Work Zone VII apprentice training Company-wide, and identification of the locations where Work Zone VIII training will take place. By April 1, 1980 and annually thereafter, the Company will provide a report, a form for which is attached as Appendix M, to the CRO with repsect to training programs for the previous calendar year.

F. MANAGEMENT EDUCATION REPORT

Six months following the effective date of the Agreement the Company will provide a report to the CRO summarizing the content of the Management Education Program and the number of Company managers who participated in the program.

G. NUMERICAL OBJECTIVE REPORTS

1. By April 1, 1979 and annually thereafter the Company will provide a report, a form for which is attached as Appendix N, to the CRO with respect to numerical objectives established for the year of the report.

2. By April 1, 1980 and annually thereafter, the Company will provide a report, a form for which is attached as Appendix O, with respect to actual achievement of numerical objectives for the year covered by the report.

XV. ADDITIONAL TERMS

A. Duration

This Conciliation Agreement shall become effective as of June 15, 1978, and remain in effect for a period of five years; provided, however, that any portion or obligation hereof which will have been completely performed by an interim date during the term of this Conciliation Agreement shall terminate as of that interim date, and provided that the obligations under Paragraph XI shall continue in effect through the calendar year 1983 and that the report associated with the obligations under Paragraph XI will be due on April 1, 1984.

B. Enforceability

This Agreement is entered into by both the Company and the Commission freely and openly and after an extensive period of conference and conciliation. It is the intention of the Company and the Commission that this Agreement shall be specifically enforceable in United States District Courts as an action initiated pursuant to Title VII, 42 U.S.C. Section 200 (e). The Company agrees that in the event that the Commission initiates an action under Title VII to enforce any term or terms of this Agreement, the Company shall consent to subject matter and personal jurisdiction of the United States District Court.

FOR THE COMPANY:	FOR THE COMMISSION:
Walter A. Schlotterbeck Senior Vice President, General Counsel and Secretary	Abner W. Sibal General Counsel
Frank P. Doyle Vice President, Corporate Employee Relations	Leonard M. Mazor Trial Attorney
David J. Dillon Manager, Compliance Systems and Programs	
Thomas F. Hilbert, Jr. Labor Relations Counsel	
Jerome W. Gerbereux Consultant, Compliance Projects	

Date June 15, 1978

APPENDIX B

RELEASE

(Wage Structure)

In consideration of payment by General Electric Company of $________ to (name) ________ the undersigned, according to the terms of a document entitled Conciliation Agreement hereby releases and forever discharges General Electric Company, its officers, employees, agents, successors and assigns from all claims, actions and causes of action which the undersigned may have on behalf of himself/herself and/or others, known or hereafter discovered by the undersigned, on account of, or connected with or resulting from any violations by General Electric Company based on sex with respect to rates of pay occurring on or before the date of the execution of this release, of any equal employment opportunity laws, ordinances, regulations or orders; including, but not limited to, Title VII of the Civil Rights Act of 1964, as amended, 42 USC §2000(e) et seq., the Civil Rights Act of 1966, 42 USC at 1981, et seq., Executive Order 11246, as amended, and the United States Constitution.

If the undersigned has filed a lawsuit or an outstanding charge with the Commission or any other agency pertaining to matters covered by this release, the undersigned will promptly request withdrawal of the lawsuit or charge.

The undersigned understands that he has the right to consult an attorney of his choice and/or the EEOC's compliance review official regarding the case, its settlement and this release; and knowing and understanding so, the undersigned as his own act voluntarily accepts the above sum in full settlement hereof without duress, coercion, undue influence or otherwise.

EXECUTED in multiple copies, each having equal effect as an original, this ______ day of ________, 197__.

____

THE STATE OF ____________

COUNTY OF ____________

BEFORE ME, the undersigned authority, on this day personally appeared ____________, known to me to be the person whose name is subscribed to the foregoing instrument and acknowledged to me that the same was his act and that he executed the same knowingly and voluntarily for the purposes and considerations therein expressed.

GIVEN UNDER MY HAND AND SEAL OF OFFICE this the ______ day of ________, A.D. 197__.

Notary Public in and for

____

APPENDIX C

RELEASE

(Promotion Incentive Program)

In consideration of payment by General Electric Company in the sum of $________ to (name) ________, the undersigned, according to the terms of a document entitled Conciliation Agreement hereby releases and forever discharges General Electric Company, its officers, employees, agents, successors and assigns from all claims, actions, and causes of action which the undersigned may have on behalf of himself/herself and/or others, known or hereafter discovered by the undersigned, on account of or connected with or resulting from any violations, by General Electric Company relating to hiring, job assignments, promotion, demotion, upgrading, downgrading, transfer, job opportunities, job qualifications, selection requirements and standards, compensation levels, except for the matters dealt with under Section IV, Wage Structure Modification of the Conciliation Agreement between EEOC and the General Electric Company, lay-off, recall, training, training opportunities, or the limitation, segregation, or classification of employees in any way which would deprive or tend to deprive any individual of employment opportunities or otherwise adversely affect his status as an employee, occurring on or before the date of the execution of this release, of any equal employment opportunity laws, ordinances, regulations or orders; including, but not limited to, Title VII of the Civil Rights Act of 1964, as amended, 42 USC §2000(e) et seq., the Civil Rights Act of 1966, 42 USC §1981, et seq., Executive Order 11246, as amended, and the United States Constitution.

If the undersigned has filed a lawsuit or an outstanding charge with the Commission or any other agency pertaining to matters covered by this release, the undersigned will promptly request withdrawal of the lawsuit or the charge.

The undersigned understands that he has the right to consult an attorney of his choise and/or the EEOC's Compliance Review Official regarding this release; and knowing and understanding so, the undersigned as his own act voluntarily accepts the above sum in full settlement hereof without duress, coercion, undue influence or otherwise.

EXECUTED in multiple copies, each having equal effect as an original, this __________ day of __________, 197_.

____

THE STATE OF ______________

COUNTY OF ______________

BEFORE ME, the undersigned authority, on this day personally appeared________ ____________, known to me to be the person whose name is subscribed to the foregoing instrument and acknowledged to me that the same was his act and that he executed the same knowingly and voluntarily for the purposes and considerations therein expressed.

GIVEN UNDER MY HAND AND SEAL OF OFFICE this the __________ day of ____________________, A.D. 197_.

____
Notary Public in and or
____

APPENDIX D

03/17/78 EXTERNAL PERCENT FEMALES AND PERCENT MINORITY MALES BY WORK ZONE AND LOCATION

		REPRESENTATION IN EXTERNAL NON-DEGREED COUNTERPARTS TO BE WEIGHTED BY THE INTERNAL PROFILE FOR DETERMINING THE EXTERNAL LABOR MARKET FOR WORK ZONES I AND II.					EXTERNAL LABOR MARKETS FOR WORK ZONES:					
		ENG'R	MKTG	FIN	MFG	REL & OTH	III	V	VII	VIII	IX	X*
MORGAN, AL	FEM	3.8	4.9	32.5	14.3	14.3	3.8	29.3	1.1	5.4	7.1	20.7
01 0103	MM	1.0	0.	0.	0.	0.	1.0	1.5	1.3	4.0	2.4	7.6
HOUSTON, AL	FEM	0.	0.	24.6	0.	0.	0.	13.6	0.	2.5	0.	40.4
01 0069	MM	0.	0.	0.	0.	0.	0.	29.5	11.5	15.3	6.0	34.2
TUCSON, AZ	FEM	10.9	8.5	31.1	14.8	14.8	10.9	19.9	1.7	1.3	7.2	14.9
8520	MM	15.1	9.1	6.4	21.9	21.9	15.1	22.2	21.7	23.0	35.1	45.9
FORT SMITH, AR-OK	FEM	3.9	7.4	23.3	9.2	9.2	3.9	14.7	1.4	2.9	10.2	29.7
2720	MM	0.	1.6	3.8	0.	0.	0.	3.3	0.6	4.4	1.7	4.3
CRAIGHEAD, AR	FEM	20.0	0.	20.0	16.7	16.7	20.0	11.2	0.	3.6	4.8	35.4
05 0031	MM	0.	0.	0.	0.	0.	0.	0.	0.	0.	0.	5.7
ANAHEIM-SANTA ANA-GARDEN	FEM	8.0	5.4	25.2	7.7	7.7	8.0	22.9	2.1	2.0	7.2	27.9
0360	MM	9.1	3.7	4.3	8.0	8.0	9.1	10.9	8.4	9.7	13.0	20.2
SAN FRANCISCO-OAKLAND, C	FEM	13.7	9.3	26.3	12.0	12.0	13.7	21.8	1.7	1.5	5.9	20.
7360	MM	11.2	6.2	6.3	12.2	12.2	11.2	20.0	16.5	19.4	27.7	34.2
BAKERSFIELD, CA	FEM	8.7	8.3	40.0	4.4	4.4	8.7	32.3	2.3	1.4	0.9	9.6
0680	MM	8.8	1.8	6.8	9.6	9.6	8.8	8.2	9.6	11.1	16.2	22.1
LOS ANGELES-LONG BEACH,	FEM	10.3	10.7	29.3	12.6	12.6	10.3	21.5	2.0	2.4	8.5	27.2
4480	MM	16.3	7.3	7.3	16.6	16.6	16.3	24.6	19.8	24.2	31.9	41.9
ONTARIO, CA	FEM	5.4	9.2	34.2	9.0	9.0	5.4	21.9	1.4	1.8	4.1	19.9
7280	MM	9.7	1.9	3.3	12.5	12.5	9.7	15.8	15.0	14.7	23.4	31.5
SAN JOSE, CA	FEM	13.5	5.1	27.0	11.1	11.1	13.5	22.4	1.2	1.7	6.8	31.3
7400	MM	11.4	9.0	5.0	12.8	12.8	11.4	13.5	13.5	16.9	26.1	32.2
SANTA BARBARA-SANTA MARI	FEM	14.0	7.8	36.5	18.6	18.6	14.0	22.7	2.0	2.3	8.6	26.2
7480	MM	6.7	4.3	0.9	10.3	10.3	6.7	13.7	11.7	20.9	29.2	30.0
DENVER-BOULDER CO	FEM	10.2	6.4	30.0	8.1	8.1	10.2	22.7	0.7	1.9	7.2	21.8
2080	MM	8.2	3.7	4.4	7.7	7.7	8.2	13.3	9.2	10.7	17.4	24.8
BRIDGEPORT, CT	FEM	5.9	14.4	17.1	5.6	5.6	5.9	20.6	1.9	4.0	15.8	38.7
1160	MM	2.9	3.9	0.9	3.7	3.7	2.9	7.8	2.3	9.1	17.4	18.0
NEW BRITAIN, CT	FEM	9.5	7.1	28.6	7.6	7.6	9.5	14.8	3.2	5.0	19.1	39.3
5440	MM	1.2	6.4	0.	2.9	2.9	1.2	3.9	0.4	3.7	4.0	11.6
HARTFORD, CT	FEM	11.7	8.8	25.2	4.7	4.7	11.7	17.6	1.4	3.9	14.1	29.8
3280	MM	3.5	1.7	1.2	1.9	1.9	3.5	5.4	2.1	6.2	7.6	17.9
WASHINGTON, DC-MID-VA	FEM	14.6	11.4	29.7	19.5	19.5	14.6	25.6	1.5	2.0	3.3	16.
8840	MM	13.4	4.9	6.5	8.4	8.4	13.4	30.8	11.4	19.3	15.5	49.2

* FOR WORK ZONE X ONLY, MINORITY MALE % IS BASED ON POPULATION OF MINORITY MALES TO TOTAL MALES.

03/17/78 EXTERNAL PERCENT FEMALES AND PERCENT MINORITY MALES BY WORK ZONE AND LOCATION

		REPRESENTATION IN EXTERNAL NON-DEGREED COUNTERPARTS TO BE WEIGHTED BY THE INTERNAL PROFILE FOR DETERMINING THE EXTERNAL LABOR MARKET FOR WORK ZONES I AND II.					EXTERNAL LABOR MARKETS FOR WORK ZONES:					
		ENGR	MKTG	FIN	MFG	REL & OTH	III	V	VII	VIII	IX	X*
VOLUSIA, FL 12 0127	FEM	7.4	0.	33.8	7.7	7.7	7.4	16.7	4.4	2.4	0.	29.0
	MM	2.3	0.	2.8	7.7	7.7	2.3	5.5	4.0	4.1	0.	28.1
GAINESVILLE, FL 2900	FEM	13.4	11.9	28.8	0.	0.	13.4	14.9	2.1	1.8	20.2	19.7
	MM	5.9	0.	4.3	6.5	6.5	5.9	18.9	3.9	20.8	11.2	40.7
JACKSONVILLE, FL 3600	FEM	12.6	8.8	27.6	7.4	7.4	12.6	20.0	1.2	1.8	1.9	19.5
	MM	6.6	2.0	4.3	7.7	7.7	6.6	17.3	4.7	8.7	11.0	42.2
MIAMI, FL 5000	FEM	14.2	12.1	22.5	22.0	22.0	14.2	21.8	1.7	2.4	6.7	26.4
	MM	32.2	17.5	20.2	30.4	30.4	32.2	38.5	18.7	29.3	48.0	64.1
ORLANDO, FL 5960	FEM	6.0	9.0	26.9	8.9	8.9	6.0	22.0	2.4	2.6	5.3	24.4
	MM	4.1	1.7	1.7	4.2	4.2	4.1	11.1	3.2	5.4	5.3	28.0
PINELLAS, FL 12 0103	FEM	9.6	1.6	27.6	10.4	10.4	9.6	21.9	1.1	1.3	9.1	25.4
	MM	1.6	1.1	1.3	3.2	3.2	1.6	6.3	4.8	3.1	8.7	16.0
TAMPA-ST. PETERSBURG, FL 8280	FEM	11.4	7.3	25.6	11.2	11.2	11.4	21.8	2.0	1.7	5.0	26.5
	MM	7.4	6.1	6.7	9.3	9.3	7.4	13.7	10.4	10.8	13.4	30.2
ATLANTA, GA 0520	FEM	12.2	4.8	35.9	9.9	9.9	12.2	20.9	2.4	1.5	4.9	23.2
	MM	4.9	2.7	2.2	4.1	4.1	4.9	23.2	4.7	10.7	20.5	38.5
FLOYD, GA 13 0115	FEM	13.7	0.	15.7	0.	0.	13.7	13.3	0.9	3.2	2.3	25.4
	MM	4.8	0.	0.	0.	0.	4.8	9.4	2.4	7.6	2.3	15.2
CHICAGO, IL 1600	FEM	10.7	7.9	21.9	9.7	9.7	10.7	19.2	1.4	2.4	11.7	33.
	MM	8.1	3.0	3.6	8.4	8.4	8.1	17.3	6.6	15.0	22.2	33.5
BLOOMINGTON-NORMAL, IL 1040	FEM	21.0	8.0	28.7	4.1	4.1	21.0	19.2	0.9	3.7	8.7	32.8
	MM	1.4	4.8	0.	0.	0.	1.4	0.9	0.6	1.1	5.1	4.2
VERMILION, IL 17 0183	FEM	8.3	0.	25.5	22.2	22.2	8.3	12.6	0.6	5.4	8.0	34.6
	MM	0.	0.	0.	0.	0.	0.	3.2	1.6	2.9	4.2	7.1
DEKALB, IL 17 0037	FEM	12.5	9.1	38.7	10.7	10.7	12.5	15.7	0.	6.7	3.4	38.6
	MM	0.	0.	0.	0.	0.	0.	2.4	0.	0.	0.	3.5
COLES, IL 17 0029	FEM	8.5	23.1	25.9	40.0	40.0	8.5	16.9	0.	1.1	11.6	49.3
	MM	0.	0.	0.	0.	0.	0.	0.	0.	0.	0.	1.3
GRUNDY, IL 17 0063	FEM	9.1	0.	24.6	0.	0.	9.1	15.9	2.6	0.	10.8	37.0
	MM	0.	0.	0.	0.	0.	0.	0.	0.	0.	3.0	0.
WHITESIDE, IL 17 0195	FEM	0.	0.	27.1	7.1	7.1	0.	2.4	0.	2.1	30.0	28.3
	MM	6.1	0.	0.	0.	0.	6.1	0.	1.1	2.5	1.7	11.7
MONROE, IN 18 0105	FEM	20.6	23.8	26.5	10.7	10.7	20.6	8.4	0.	4.5	9.5	40.8
	MM	3.1	0.	0.	0.	0.	3.1	0.	0.	0.6	0.	0.3
ADAMS, IN 18 0001	FEM	13.8	0.	58.6	0.	0.	13.8	20.0	0.	4.2	4.9	38.1
	MM	0.	0.	0.	0.	0.	0.	0.	5.6	0.	7.8	2.7
EVANSVILLE, IN-KY 2440	FEM	7.3	2.6	22.3	5.6	5.6	7.3	15.3	1.2	2.5	5.9	24.0
	MM	1.8	1.1	0.5	0.2	0.2	1.8	6.1	0.9	2.8	4.3	7.4
FORT WAYNE, IN 2760	FEM	6.9	7.5	18.2	4.2	4.2	6.9	22.8	2.4	5.3	10.4	30.[illegible]
	MM	2.3	2.5	0.8	2.8	2.8	2.3	4.0	1.4	5.8	9.1	13.3
GREEN, IN 18 0055	FEM	0.	0.	19.2	0.	0.	0.	23.5	2.7	24.3	11.3	31.8
	MM	0.	0.	0.	0.	0.	0.	0.	0.	0.	0.	0.
INDIANAPOLIS, IN 3480	FEM	8.6	4.7	30.2	6.6	6.6	8.6	21.9	1.3	2.5	7.1	29.0
	MM	4.2	1.2	2.4	3.2	3.2	4.2	8.2	3.8	6.4	8.8	17.7
PERRY, IN 18 0123	FEM	0.	0.	13.2	0.	0.	0.	17.9	0.	9.7	35.4	48.7
	MM	0.	0.	0.	0.	0.	0.	0.	0.	0.	0.	0.

* FOR WORK ZONE X ONLY, MINORITY MALE E IS BASED ON POPULATION OF MINORITY MALES TO TOTAL MALES.

03/17/78 EXTERNAL PERCENT FEMALES AND PERCENT MINORITY MALES BY WORK ZONE AND LOCATION

Location		REPRESENTATION IN EXTERNAL NON-DEGREED COUNTERPARTS TO BE WEIGHTED BY THE INTERNAL PROFILE FOR DETERMINING THE EXTERNAL LABOR MARKET FOR WORK ZONES I AND II.					EXTERNAL LABOR MARKETS FOR WORK ZONES:					
		ENGR	MKTG	FIN	MFG	REL & OTH	III	V	VII	VIII	IX	X*
DESMOINES, IA	FEM	3.0	9.7	36.5	28.6	28.6	3.0	24.0	1.3	3.6	8.6	49.2
19 0057	MM	0.	0.	0.	0.	0.	0.	9.2	0.	0.	1.4	2.7
CARROLL, IA	FEM	0.	17.2	79.6	0.	0.	0.	0.	10.8	0.	0.	18.9
19 0027	MM	0.	0.	0.	0.	0.	0.	0.	0.	0.	0.	0.
COWLEY, KS	FEM	20.4	0.	24.8	0.	0.	20.4	6.0	3.6	3.9	0.	21.8
20 0035	MM	0.	0.	0.	0.	0.	0.	4.0	4.8	5.4	0.	8.7
KANSAS CITY, MO-KS	FEM	14.7	6.6	39.8	10.1	10.1	14.7	24.2	1.4	1.8	6.6	26.3
3760	MM	5.2	1.0	1.1	4.6	4.6	5.2	7.1	3.9	6.0	10.6	20.9
FRANKLIN, KY	FEM	26.6	0.	45.0	0.	0.	26.6	17.3	2.6	2.6	42.6	40.5
21 0073	MM	0.	0.	0.	0.	0.	0.	2.6	0.	3.2	0.	1.9
LEXINGTON-FAYETTE, KY	FEM	13.0	8.3	32.1	8.5	8.5	13.0	21.7	1.3	4.1	18.4	27.5
4280	MM	0.5	2.3	0.	3.5	3.5	0.5	6.2	3.2	5.4	13.0	21.1
LOUISVILLE, KY-IN	FEM	14.5	5.8	22.1	4.9	4.9	14.5	18.3	0.8	1.4	4.4	24.[illegible]
4520	MM	2.6	1.0	1.0	3.2	3.2	2.6	6.2	2.0	4.1	6.2	16.4
HOPKINS, KY	FEM	0.	00.0	0.	12.5	12.5	0.	24.0	2.3	5.3	4.0	20.2
21 0107	MM	0.	0.	0.	0.	0.	0.	8.3	0.	0.	0.	8.4
OWENSBORO, KY	FEM	15.8	11.0	15.4	10.1	10.1	15.8	18.6	1.1	2.0	38.3	39.4
5990	MM	0.	0.	0.	1.2	1.2	0.	3.4	2.0	1.7	0.	6.4
ALLEN, KY	FEM	0.	0.	00.0	0.	0.	0.	20.2	0.	0.	0.	46.7
21 0003	MM	0.	0.	0.	0.	0.	0.	0.	0.	0.	0.	0.
PULASKI, KY	FEM	21.7	0.	36.8	33.3	33.3	21.7	0.	0.	3.0	15.7	20.4
21 0199	MM	0.	0.	0.	0.	0.	0.	0.	0.	1.4	0.	2.2
SHREVEPORT, LA	FEM	7.5	8.7	23.3	10.6	10.6	7.5	18.4	1.3	1.7	6.2	23.5
7680	MM	5.4	0.	1.0	5.1	5.1	5.4	30.6	4.7	19.0	17.1	54.6
LEWISTON-AUBURN, ME	FEM	17.3	9.8	18.3	18.0	18.0	17.3	15.4	5.1	2.8	19.9	47.6
4240	MM	0.	0.	0.	0.	0.	0.	0.	2.0	0.	0.	0.2
PENOBSCOT, ME	FEM	14.9	9.5	15.4	14.3	14.3	14.9	11.6	0.7	1.1	3.5	25.8
23 0019	MM	0.	0.	0.	0.	0.	0.	0.	0.6	0.4	0.	0.
PORTLAND, ME	FEM	12.7	4.1	22.6	7.3	7.3	12.7	12.3	4.4	1.6	6.5	32.4
6400	MM	0.	0.	0.	1.4	1.4	0.	0.	0.	0.6	0.	0.1
BALTIMORE, MD	FEM	8.5	9.5	26.7	7.5	7.5	8.5	21.0	1.8	2.2	8.6	24.4
0720	MM	7.9	3.7	2.3	7.4	7.4	7.9	16.9	7.9	10.1	20.7	37.6
BOSTON MA	FEM	13.0	8.1	21.9	11.2	11.2	13.0	15.8	1.5	2.5	8.8	31.
1120	MM	4.5	1.4	1.7	2.1	2.1	4.5	4.4	2.5	4.7	7.5	7.9
FITCHBURG-LEOMINSTER, MA	FEM	5.6	15.5	15.1	13.2	13.2	5.6	14.2	1.5	1.1	12.3	34.3
2600	MM	0.9	0.	0.	2.6	2.6	0.9	0.6	1.0	0.4	0.	3.3
LOWELL, MA-NH	FEM	11.0	7.9	36.0	8.7	8.7	11.0	13.2	2.5	2.5	15.3	40.4
4560	MM	0.4	0.	0.	1.5	1.5	0.4	0.7	0.	0.	2.6	1.8
PITTSFIELD, MA	FEM	6.6	18.9	27.6	5.6	5.6	6.6	9.0	1.6	0.5	5.1	23.3
6320	MM	1.0	0.	0.	0.8	0.8	1.0	0.9	0.9	1.1	1.9	3.1
DETROIT, MI	FEM	4.9	6.6	23.5	3.3	3.3	4.9	14.9	1.2	1.7	6.3	18.9
2160	MM	4.3	2.6	3.0	6.4	6.4	4.3	12.1	5.5	12.5	21.2	30.[illegible]
GRAND RAPIDS, MI	FEM	9.9	6.7	21.3	4.4	4.4	9.9	14.1	1.0	2.4	11.2	29.8
3000	MM	2.6	0.	1.2	2.5	2.5	2.6	2.6	1.1	1.9	5.4	8.5
BLUE EARTH, MN	FEM	10.1	5.8	12.1	0.	0.	10.1	25.6	0.	2.8	6.8	27.5
27 0013	MM	0.	0.	0.	0.	0.	0.	0.	0.	0.	0.	0.

* FOR WORK ZONE X ONLY, MINORITY MALE E IS BASED ON POPULATION OF MINORITY MALES TO TOTAL MALES.

03/17/78 EXTERNAL PERCENT FEMALES AND PERCENT MINORITY MALES BY WORK ZONE AND LOCATION

		REPRESENTATION IN EXTERNAL NON-DEGREED COUNTERPARTS TO BE WEIGHTED BY THE INTERNAL PROFILE FOR DETERMINING THE EXTERNAL LABOR MARKET FOR WORK ZONES I AND II.					EXTERNAL LABOR MARKETS FOR WORK ZONES:					
		ENGR	MKTG	FIN	MFG	REL & OTH	III	V	VII	VIII	IX	X*
MINNEAPOLIS-ST. PAUL, MN	FEM	8.3	5.6	26.5	7.1	7.1	8.3	19,9	1.3	2.2	7.4	31.1
5120	MM	2.1	0.7	0.6	1.5	1.5	2.1	2.1	0.9	1.6	1.9	3.8
JACKSON, MS	FEM	20.0	7.4	26.3	8.6	8.6	20.0	23.8	1.8	2.3	4.2	24.0
3560	MM	3.2	3.1	1.5	6.0	6.0	3,2	29.9	15.4	20.7	19.3	58.1
ST. LOUIS, MO-IL	FEM	11.1	8.7	27.1	8.4	8.4	11.1	20.2	1.9	2.1	7.0	23.7
7040	MM	5,1	2.7	2.1	4.3	4.3	5,1	12.1	5,2	7.4	14.2	21.4
SPRINGFIELD, MO	FEM	7.5	9.4	36.5	7.1	7.1	7.5	18.8	2.0	2.6	7.4	32.
7920	MM	3.3	3.9	0.	0.	0.	3.3	1.6	0.	1.3	0.8	1.9
MANCHESTER, NH	FEM	12.5	14.4	30.5	15.7	15.7	12.5	12,2	2.4	2.6	19.7	38,7
4760	MM	0.	0.	0.	0.	0.	0,	0.	0.	0.8	0.	0.4
NASHUA, NH	FEM	5.0	2.7	28.7	7.8	7.8	5.0	20.7	0,	3.2	3.1	44,6
5350	MM	0.	0.	0.	0.6	0.6	0,	0.	0.	0.	1.8	1.7
STRAFFORD, NH	FEM	10.4	0.	19.4	8.1	8.1	10.4	10,3	0.9	3.5	9.3	44.2
33 0017	MM	0.	0.	0.	0.	0.	0.	0.	0.	0.9	0.	0.6
NEWARK, NJ	FEM	12.7	7.7	15.5	10.7	10.7	12.7	17.8	1.2	1.8	14.0	34.8
5640	MM	8.0	2.6	3.0	9.1	9.1	8.0	14.7	5.6	15,1	19.5	33.9
JERSEY CITY, NJ	FEM	11.3	15.9	21.9	19.5	19.5	11,3	18.4	1.7	2.4	9.6	32.1
3640	MM	2.7	2.2	2.4	7.3	7.3	2.7	10.4	2,8	11,2	11.1	18.5
PATERSON-CLIFTON-PASSAIC	FEM	11.1	8.3	12.6	11.4	11.4	11,1	18.4	1,1	1.6	9.8	32.3
6040	MM	1.3	0.7	1.0	3.2	3,2	1,3	7.0	1.6	4.6	7.8	15.0
TRENTON, NJ	FEM	10.8	12.8	13.3	7.2	7.2	10.8	14.2	3.3	1.2	14.6	32.4
8480	MM	4.9	1.1	1.9	4.5	4.5	4.9	6.4	4,5	8,5	9.3	26.8
ALBUQUERQUE, NM	FEM	8.5	7.2	32.1	9.6	9.6	8.5	24.1	2.1	1.9	3.4	14.1
0200	MM	19.8	12.3	16.8	31.3	31.3	19,8	35,7	40.5	35.7	46.5	60.9
CAYUGA, NY	FEM	23.7	0.	20.6	0.	0.	23.7	28.6	4.8	3.3	13.4	39.5
36 0011	MM	0,	0.	4.0	0.	0.	0.	0.	0.	0.7	0.	1.6
BINGHAMTON, NY-PA	FEM	9.9	10.7	23.1	9.1	9.1	9.9	15,9	2.2	2.4	13.8	33.6
0960	MM	0.4	0.	0.4	0.6	0.6	0.4	0.8	0,	0.7	0.4	0.5
ROCHESTER, NY	FEM	8.8	5.5	22.2	6.1	6.1	8.8	17.9	0.9	2.4	11.2	33.9
6840	MM	2.0	0,8	0.7	1.5	1.5	2,0	3.6	1.7	3.7	4.1	11.9
WASHINGTON, NY	FEM	15.1	0.	19.7	42.1	42.1	15.1	7,1	1.4	3.5	28.7	38.9
36 0115	MM	0.	0,	0.	0.	0.	0,	0,	0.	0.	0.	0.1
SUFFOLK, NY	FEM	5.6	3.3	12.0	7.2	7.2	5.6	15.6	1.6	1.8	9.3	28.7
36 0103	MM	5.0	2,9	2.1	1.8	1.8	5.0	9.0	2.4	5.4	7.4	12.8
NEW YORK, NY-NJ	FEM	10.3	9.1	16.8	15.2	15.2	10.3	17,0	1.6	1.9	6.9	26.4
5600	MM	10,0	3.2	4.2	12.8	12.8	10,0	25.8	10.6	18.7	24.1	32.1
ALBANY-SCHENECTADY-TROY,	FEM	9.6	6.2	22.3	8.1	8.1	9.6	17,9	0.7	2.0	3.6	18.8
0160	MM	1.2	0.5	0.4	0.4	0.4	1.2	1.2	0.7	1.5	3.0	5.2
SYRACUSE, NY	FEM	9.9	5.5	25.6	9.3	9.3	9.9	15.7	1.3	2.3	7,2	29.6
8160	MM	0.7	0.	0.2	0.4	0,4	0.7	1.4	0.9	2.3	5.6	5.0
BUFFALO, NY	FEM	10.4	9.8	24.4	4.4	4.4	10,4	17.0	1.1	1.3	6.2	21.1
1280	MM	1.5	0.6	1.0	2.3	2.3	1,5	3.4	1.4	3.8	6.4	12.9
UTICA-ROME, NY	FEM	3.9	11,7	24.8	4.7	4.7	3.9	15.3	1.4	2.9	4.4	28.9
8680	MM	1.0	0.	1.1	0.6	0.6	1.0	1.7	0.2	1.0	2.7	2.5
GREENSBORO—WINSTON-SALE	FEM	14.6	6.2	28.0	11.6	11.6	14.6	22.3	2.5	1.5	8.2	34.1
3120	MM	7.2	1.9	1.8	4.1	4.1	7,2	14.9	4.4	6.8	7.1	30.9

* FOR WORK ZONE X ONLY, MINORITY MALE E IS BASED ON POPULATION OF MINORITY MALES TO TOTAL MALES.

03/17/78 EXTERNAL PERCENT FEMALES AND PERCENT MINORITY MALES BY WORK ZONE AND LOCATION

		REPRESENTATION IN EXTERNAL NON-DEGREED COUNTERPARTS TO BE WEIGHTED BY THE INTERNAL PROFILE FOR DETERMINING THE EXTERNAL LABOR MARKET FOR WORK ZONES I AND II.					EXTERNAL LABOR MARKETS FOR WORK ZONES:					
		ENGR	MKTG	FIN	MFG	REL & OTH	III	V	VII	VIII	IX	X*
CHARLOTTE-GASTONIA, NC	FEM	17.3	6.4	24.5	12.5	12.5	17.3	19.9	2.2	1.9	7.6	31.
1520	MM	4.8	1.2	1.6	5.7	5.7	4.8	24.2	7.5	11.6	18.0	41.5
RALEIGH-DURHAM, NC	FEM	16.3	0.7	26.9	6.8	6.8	16.3	20.7	0.5	3.7	16.6	31.5
6640	MM	1.8	0.	1.8	4.9	4.9	1.8	26.3	9.4	12.5	14.4	40.9
WAYNE, NC	FEM	7.3	0.	33.3	5.0	5.0	7.3	12.1	3.6	0.6	12.8	41.9
37 0191	MM	0.	13.3	0.	0.	0.	0.	15.6	3.3	17.0	35.4	39.7
HENDERSON, NC	FEM	29.8	0.	12.9	50.0	50.0	29.8	10.5	0.	2.1	0.	40.0
37 0089	MM	0.	32.0	0.	0.	0.	0.	2.4	0.	3.8	12.8	3.7
CATAWBA, NC	FEM	12.9	4.3	30.6	0.	0.	12.9	13.6	1.8	0.8	0.	43.0
37 0035	MM	1.8	0.	0.	0.	0.	1.8	7.5	4.6	3.1	5.4	11.4
ORANGE, NC	FEM	29.5	0.	25.6	0.	0.	29.5	13.9	3.1	0.9	18.2	34.2
37 0135	MM	0.	0.	0.	0.	0.	0.	23.3	5.5	16.7	0.	30.4
ROWAN, NC	FEM	42.0	0.	30.9	0.	0.	42.0	20.8	2.8	1.9	0.	41.3
37 0159	MM	0.	0.	0.	0.	0.	0.	11.3	1.6	8.4	3.9	17.4
WILMINGTON, NC	FEM	9.9	15.4	26.9	10.7	10.7	9.9	20.4	3.7	3.3	8.8	23.7
9200	MM	0.	0.	1.1	4.6	4.6	0.	14.9	8.1	8.7	9.3	41.1
ASTABULA, OH	FEM	10.0	0.	47.1	0.	0.	10.0	10.7	0.7	1.5	7.1	34.3
39 0007	MM	5.1	0.	0.	9.8	9.8	5.1	2.5	2.5	1.8	1.3	4.0
YOUNGSTOWN-WARREN, OH	FEM	6.6	6.6	21.6	2.1	2.1	6.6	14.8	1.3	2.8	3.2	23.1
9320	MM	1.3	0.6	2.1	1.8	1.8	1.3	5.1	1.7	3.4	7.6	15.2
CLEVELAND, OH	FEM	10.9	6.8	20.9	5.7	5.7	10.9	20.0	1.5	2.2	8.7	23.
1680	MM	4.4	2.0	2.5	5.1	5.1	4.4	10.2	4.7	9.9	10.6	25.0
HURON, OH	FEM	0.	0.	34.3	0.	0.	0.	16.9	0.	2.4	10.1	44.2
39 0077	MM	0.	0.	0.	0.	0.	0.	1.9	0.	0.	8.2	4.5
CINCINNATI, OH-KY-IN	FEM	10.4	7.6	32.3	8.3	8.3	10.4	17.4	1.5	1.7	6.5	24.2
1640	MM	5.1	1.3	1.8	2.8	2.8	5.1	10.2	3.7	5.4	5.8	16.0
CRAWFORD, OH	FEM	38.2	0.	22.4	0.	0.	38.2	10.4	11.0	0.5	5.2	38.6
39 0033	MM	0.	0.	0.	0.	0.	0.	0.	0.	0.	1.7	0.8
COLUMBUS, OH	FEM	13.5	8.5	26.2	8.1	8.1	13.5	22.8	4.2	2.5	7.6	28.3
1840	MM	4.4	1.1	2.8	2.7	2.7	4.4	9.2	4.0	6.2	9.5	17.6
COSHOCTON, OH	FEM	0.	0.	28.8	0.	0.	0.	12.0	3.1	1.5	22.8	25.5
39 0031	MM	0.	0.	0.	0.	0.	0.	2.4	1.8	1.0	0.	1.5
TUSCARAWUS, OH	FEM	2.1	12.8	22.2	0.	0.	2.1	17.2	0.	2.2	1.5	27.5
39 0157	MM	0.	0.	4.3	0.	0.	0.	0.	2.3	0.	0.	0.9
HOCKING, OH	FEM	7.1	0.	46.2	0.	0.	7.1	16.0	0.	7.7	19.4	34.1
39 0073	MM	0.	0.	0.	0.	0.	0.	0.	0.	0.	0.	0.8
LICKING, OH	FEM	9.1	8.2	31.4	3.3	3.3	9.1	25.4	2.5	5.6	10.4	24.2
39 0089	MM	2.8	0.	0.	4.1	4.1	2.8	1.7	0.	0.8	0.7	1.7
MASKINGUM, OH	FEM	12.7	12.5	32.1	0.	0.	12.7	24.4	1.1	5.8	12.2	38.4
39 0119	MM	0.	0.	0.	0.	0.	0.	3.5	0.5	1.6	0.	7.3
ADAMS, OH	FEM	0.	0.	0.	0.	0.	0.	18.2	0.	5.8	33.9	14.[illegible]
39 0001	MM	0.	0.	0.	0.	0.	0.	0.	0.	0.	0.	0.
AKRON, OH	FEM	9.1	7.7	19.2	3.0	3.0	9.1	16.7	0.8	1.6	5.0	17.2
0080	MM	2.6	1.4	1.1	2.9	2.9	2.6	3.9	3.0	2.8	9.3	12.5
SENECA, OH	FEM	0.	6.2	17.6	0.	0.	0.	8.6	0.	2.3	38.4	31.9
39 0147	MM	3.6	0.	0.	0.	0.	3.6	0.	0.	4.6	2.2	4.5

*FOR WORK ZONE X ONLY, MINORITY MALE % IS BASED ON POPULATION OF MINORITY MALES TO TOTAL MALES.

03/17/78 EXTERNAL PERCENT FEMALES AND PERCENT MINORITY MALES BY WORK ZONE AND LOCATION

		REPRESENTATION IN EXTERNAL NON-DEGREED COUNTERPARTS TO BE WEIGHTED BY THE INTERNAL PROFILE FOR DETERMINING THE EXTERNAL LABOR MARKET FOR WORK ZONES I AND II.					EXTERNAL LABOR MARKETS FOR WORK ZONES:					
		ENGR	MKTG	FIN	MFG	REL & OTH	III	V	VII	VIII	IX	X*
ALLENTOWN-BETHLEHEM-EAST 0240	FEM	5.6	6.5	14.4	11.6	11.6	5.6	15.1	0.4	0.7	6.3	31.6
	MM	0.1	0.6	0.3	0.6	0.6	0.1	0.7	0.8	0.8	2.2	2.8
PITTSBURGH, PA 6280	FEM	5.2	6.6	16.3	3.7	3.7	5.2	12.6	0.7	1.0	2.5	14.0
	MM	2.2	1.2	1.0	1.6	1.6	2.2	3.8	1.8	2.4	3.6	8.6
PHILADELPHIA, PA-NJ 6160	FEM	9.6	6.9	19.8	9.8	9.8	9.6	18.5	1.2	1.7	6.4	28.1
	MM	5.1	1.1	2.1	4.9	4.9	5.1	12.9	5.7	10.1	13.2	26.5
MONROE, PA 42 0089	FEM	18.2	0.	9.5	21.2	21.2	18.2	33.7	0.	3.3	6.3	27.2
	MM	3.2	0.	4.8	0.	0.	3.2	0.	0.	0.	3.7	1.5
ERIE, PA 2360	FEM	9.7	6.0	16.8	6.2	6.2	9.7	14.1	1.2	3.4	6.3	27.5
	MM	0.	0.	0.	0.7	0.7	0.	0.9	0.2	1.9	3.0	5.0
MERCER, PA 42 0085	FEM	3.8	0.	28.4	5.5	5.5	3.8	10.6	0.6	2.3	3.1	15.2
	MM	1.5	0.	1.0	0.	0.	1.5	2.4	0.8	2.6	3.3	4.9
FALL RIVER, MA-RI 2480	FEM	8.7	10.1	23.4	22.6	22.6	8.7	18.5	1.0	1.7	1.1	33.0
	MM	1.2	0.	0.	0.5	0.5	1.2	0.	0.9	0.3	0.4	0.5
PROVIDENCE-WARWICK-PAWTU 6480	FEM	11.3	9.7	21.9	19.2	19.2	11.3	23.0	1.4	2.9	13.7	44.[illegible]
	MM	2.1	0.2	1.0	1.6	1.6	2.1	1.3	1.1	2.0	2.5	3.8
CHARLESTON-NORTH CHARLES 1440	FEM	5.0	9.5	36.0	10.7	10.7	5.0	21.3	2.5	1.7	5.0	18.0
	MM	4.1	6.9	2.8	3.8	3.8	4.1	24.1	14.7	13.0	20.2	55.8
COLUMBIA, SC 1760	FEM	15.2	3.0	29.9	12.7	12.7	15.2	25.1	2.1	1.8	7.7	28.4
	MM	4.9	2.7	1.1	6.0	6.0	4.9	22.7	13.7	16.2	24.2	44.7
FLORENCE, SC 45 0041	FEM	30.8	0.	38.8	0.	0.	30.8	21.5	0.	3.0	2.1	41.1
	MM	2.4	0.	4.3	23.1	23.1	2.4	16.7	7.9	16.5	29.0	36.9
GREENVILLE-SPARTANBURG, 3160	FEM	23.0	10.1	28.3	10.2	10.2	23.0	16.3	3.0	2.1	14.8	34.9
	MM	2.0	0.7	2.5	1.6	1.6	2.0	14.9	4.3	5.2	7.3	26.7
MAURY, TN 47 0119	FEM	13.3	50.0	48.2	36.4	36.4	13.3	20.3	2.3	3.3	4.4	32.3
	MM	0.	0.	0.	0.	0.	0.	14.9	2.3	3.8	0.	21.3
NASHVILLE-DAVIDSON, TN 5360	FEM	18.3	5.2	30.8	9.8	9.8	18.3	21.3	0.8	1.9	8.5	26.7
	MM	3.9	1.9	1.3	4.0	4.0	3.9	17.7	3.2	8.1	8.9	24.2
MEMPHIS, TN-AR-MS 4920	FEM	12.0	9.0	23.3	9.6	9.6	12.0	19.0	1.3	3.4	5.6	25.7
	MM	7.7	2.6	2.7	9.4	9.4	7.7	30.4	8.0	18.6	23.5	56.8
HAMBLIN, TN 47 0063	FEM	0.	23.8	7.1	0.	0.	0.	18.1	4.2	2.2	4.1	33.5
	MM	0.	0.	0.	0.	0.	0.	8.2	2.5	0.7	5.5	6.3
MCNAIRY, TN 47 0109	FEM	0.	0.	0.	0.	0.	0.	24.4	0.	0.	32.6	45.5
	MM	0.	0.	0.	0.	0.	0.	0.	0.	2.8	0.	7.4
DALLAS-FORT WORTH, TX 1920	FEM	15.0	4.8	25.2	9.9	9.9	15.0	22.1	4.1	2.4	10.4	32.[illegible]
	MM	6.5	2.4	3.0	5.7	5.7	6.5	19.6	9.3	12.7	15.2	36.4
HOUSTON, TX 3360	FEM	9.7	8.2	20.1	3.8	3.8	9.7	21.2	1.3	1.5	2.7	13.2
	MM	10.2	5.4	4.0	8.6	8.6	10.2	26.6	10.9	21.8	26.6	45.9
TYLER, TX 8640	FEM	13.7	8.0	19.9	10.0	10.0	13.7	23.0	2.3	0.9	15.8	20.8
	MM	7.6	0.	0.	9.8	9.8	7.6	21.4	18.6	17.0	22.9	40.7
SALT LAKE CITY-OGDEN, UT 7160	FEM	6.9	12.4	23.5	10.5	10.5	6.9	27.8	2.1	1.8	3.2	21.7
	MM	2.6	1.0	0.9	2.1	2.1	2.6	3.2	4.2	4.8	6.5	8.6
CHITTENDEN, VT 50 0007	FEM	5.3	3.3	21.9	0.	0.	5.3	20.2	0.	2.5	0.	20.9
	MM	0.9	0.	0.	0.	0.	0.9	0.	0.	0.	0.	0.
RUTLAND, VT 50 0021	FEM	3.5	0.	36.6	0.	0.	3.5	17.4	2.1	1.3	15.6	32.5
	MM	0.	0.	0.	0.	0.	0.	3.9	0.	0.	7.8	1.8

*FOR WORK ZONE X ONLY, MINORITY MALE % IS BASED ON POPULATION OF MINORITY MALES TO TOTAL MALES.

03/17/78 EXTERNAL PERCENT FEMALES AND PERCENT MINORITY MALES BY WORK ZONE AND LOCATION

		REPRESENTATION IN EXTERNAL NON-DEGREED COUNTERPARTS TO BE WEIGHTED BY THE INTERNAL PROFILE FOR DETERMINING THE EXTERNAL LABOR MARKET FOR WORK ZONES I AND II.					EXTERNAL LABOR MARKETS FOR WORK ZONES:					
		ENGR	MKTG	FIN	MFG	REL & OTH	III	V	VII	VIII	IX	X*
CHARLOTTESVILLE, VA 51 0540	FEM	0.	0.	31.6	0.	0.	0.	24.2	3.6	1.7	0.	29.0
	MM	0.	0.	0.	0.	0.	0.	23.4	0.	4.2	26.3	16.9
NEWPORT NEWS-HAMPTON, VA 5680	FEM	9.1	14.1	35.2	6.3	6.3	9.1	20.4	0.7	1.6	1.7	21.8
	MM	4.3	7.5	2.3	5.0	5.0	4.3	24.7	16.0	16.6	18.7	45.0
LYNCHBURG, VA 4640	FEM	15.7	9.6	31.2	14.7	14.7	15.7	17.6	0.	2.7	5.8	32.4
	MM	3.4	0.	2.7	5.0	5.0	3.4	11.4	9.0	11.4	35.3	31.6
NORFOLK-VIRGINIA BEACH-P 5720	FEM	5.9	10.2	36.3	12.3	12.3	5.9	26.6	2.0	2.3	2.5	17.8
	MM	3.4	1.7	1.5	7.8	7.8	3.4	24.4	12.0	13.5	14.7	53.3
RICHMOND, VA 6760	FEM	19.1	4.6	26.2	7.7	7.7	19.1	25.1	0.4	1.2	1.8	28.0
	MM	6.0	1.5	2.1	4.9	4.9	6.0	26.8	2.7	10.1	18.3	42.6
ROANOKE, VA 6800	FEM	7.9	6.4	26.2	17.0	17.0	7.9	25.0	2.4	1.4	6.0	28.7
	MM	1.5	0.	1.9	2.0	2.0	1.5	5.9	4.7	2.8	7.4	17.5
WAYNESBORO, VA 51 0820	FEM	8.4	22.7	25.5	0.	0.	8.4	18.6	4.2	3.4	42.9	39.1
	MM	10.1	0.	0.	0.	0.	10.1	0.	0.	5.9	0.	7.0
WINCHESTER, VA 51 0840	FEM	22.2	22.7	8.6	0.	0.	22.2	35.1	0.	5.2	0.	35.5
	MM	0.	0.	0.	0.	0.	0.	0.	0.	7.1	25.0	9.2
SEATTLE-EVERETT, WA 7600	FEM	14.1	7.4	36.5	7.3	7.3	14.1	24.9	2.9	2.8	3.9	17.1
	MM	2.0	1.8	2.3	1.1	1.1	2.0	3.4	3.8	3.5	6.5	6.0
TACOMA, WA 8200	FEM	8.6	11.4	40.1	11.4	11.4	8.6	26.3	1.2	1.3	2.3	14.5
	MM	1.3	1.4	1.0	1.7	1.7	1.3	6.1	3.3	3.0	5.6	5.6
MILWAUKEE, WI 5080	FEM	9.3	7.9	24.5	5.6	5.6	9.3	20.8	1.0	2.8	8.6	28.4
	MM	1.9	1.3	1.4	2.4	2.4	1.9	3.8	2.0	4.7	13.0	13.9

*FOR WORK ZONE X ONLY, MINORITY MALE E IS BASED ON POPULATION OF MINORITY MALES TO TOTAL MALES.

APPENDIX E

The Degreed External Labor Market data for Work Zone I and Work Zone II are as follows:

	FEMALES	MINORITY MALES
Engineering Degreed	1.6%	3.1%
Other Technical Degreed	16.6	4.0
Non-Technical Degreed	10.9	3.6

APPENDIX H

HOURLY WAGE ADJUSTMENTS REPORT

Period Covered________________

LOCATION	JOB CLASSIFICATIONS ADJUSTED	TOTAL NO. OF EMPLOYEES	TOTAL ANNUAL INCREASED COMPENSATION $
XXXXXXXXX	XXXX	XXX	XXX
TOTAL	XXXX	XXX	$ XXX

APPENDIX J

HOURLY WAGE LUMP SUM PAYMENTS REPORT

Period Covered ____________________

LOCATION	NO. OF PAYMENTS MADE TO EMPLOYEES	DOLLAR VALUE OF PAYMENTS MADE
XXXXXXXXXXXXXXX	XXX	$ XXX
TOTAL	XXX	$ XXX

APPENDIX K

PROMOTION INCENTIVE PAYMENTS REPORT

Period Covered____________________

WORK ZONE	PAYMENTS MADE: TOT.	FEMALE	MIN. MALE	DOLLAR VALUE: TOT.	FEMALE	MIN. MALE
I	XXX	XXX	XXX	$ XXX	$ XXX	$ XXX
II						
III						
IV						
V						
VII						
VIII						
IX						
TOTAL	XXX	XXX	XXX	$ XXX	$ XXX	$ XXX

APPENDIX L

OPEN PROMOTION SYSTEM PERFORMANCE REPORT

PERIOD____________________

WORK ZONE	NUMBER OPENINGS	APPLICATIONS TOTAL	APPLICATIONS FEMALE	APPLICATIONS MALE MIN.	OFFERS TOTAL	OFFERS FEMALE	OFFERS MALE MIN.	ACCEPTANCES TOTAL	ACCEPTANCES FEMALE	ACCEPTANCES MALE MIN.	REFUSALS TOTAL	REFUSALS FEMALE	REFUSALS MALE MIN.
I	XXX	XXX	XXX	XXX	XXXX	XXX	XXX	XXXX	XXX	XXX	XXXX	XXX	XXX
II													
III													
IV													
V													
VI													
VII													
VIII													
IX													
X													

APPENDIX M

HOURLY TRAINING REPORT

Period Covered________

LOCATION *	WORKZONE VII (APPRENTICE) PROGRAMS			WORKZONE VIII PROGRAMS		
XXXXX						
	ENTERING TRAINEES:			ENTERING TRAINEES:		
	TOT.	FEMALE	MIN. MALE	TOT.	FEMALE	MIN. MALE
		#/%	#/%		#/%	#/%
TOTAL	XXX	XXX	XXX	XXX	XXX	XXX

*Company locations will be identified if they are at or below the minimum female representation for entering trainees pursuant to Paragraph VIII of the Agreement.

APPENDIX N

NUMERICAL OBJECTIVES REPORT

Period______________________

	FEMALES	MALE MINORITIES
	Numerical Objectives	Numerical Objectives
ZONE I	xx.x	xx.x
ZONE II	xx.x	xx.x
ZONE III	xx.x	xx.x
ZONE V	xx.x	xx.x
ZONE VII	xx.x	xx.x
ZONE VIII	xx.x	xx.x
ZONE IX	xx.x	xx.x
ZONE X	xx.x	xx.x

APPENDIX O

NUMERICAL OBJECTIVES PERFORMANCE REPORT

Period ______________________

		FEMALES		MALE MINORITIES	
	OPPORTUNITIES	NUMERICAL OBJECTIVES	PERFORMANCE #/%	NUMERICAL OBJECTIVES	PERFORMANCE #/%
ZONE I	xxxx	xx.x	xx.x	xx.x	xx.x
ZONE II	xxxx	xx.x	xx.x	xx.x	xx.x
ZONE III	xxxx	xx.x	xx.x	xx.x	xx.x
ZONE V	xxxx	xx.x	xx.x	xx.x	xx.x
ZONE VII	xxxx	xx.x	xx.x	xx.x	xx.x
ZONE VIII	xxxx	xx.x	xx.x	xx.x	xx.x
ZONE IX	xxxx	xx.x	xx.x	xx.x	xx.x
ZONE X	xxxx	xx.x	xx.x	xx.x	xx.x

APPENDIX D

Guidelines for Affirmative Action Employment Programs

I. INTRODUCTION

A. State Board Resolution on Affirmative Action
B. Purpose of Guidelines
C. Guideline Inclusions
D. Tailoring Programs to Local Needs
E. Evaluation of Affirmative Action Program

II. SUMMARY OF REQUIREMENTS

III. DEFINITIONS

IV. ESSENTIAL ELEMENTS OF AN AFFIRMATIVE ACTION PROGRAM

A. Governing Board's Affirmative Action Employment Policy Statement
B. Delegation of Affirmative Action Responsibilities and Duties
C. Communication of Policy
D. Utilization Analysis
E. Corrective Action
F. Goals and Timetables
G. Affirmative Action Advisory Committee

V. SUGGESTED TECHNIQUES FOR AFFIRMATIVE ACTION PROGRAM IMPLEMENTATION

A. Recruitment
B. Selection
C. Review of Employment Procedures
D. Training
E. Promotion
F. Assessment of Affirmative Action Program

VI. STATE DEPARTMENT OF EDUCATION RESPONSIBILITY

Prepared under the direction of the Bureau of Intergroup Relations, California State Department of Education, Wilson Riles—Superintendent of Public Instruction, Sacramento, 1975.

CALIFORNIA STATE DEPARTMENT OF EDUCATION
721 Capitol Mall
Sacramento, California 95814

GUIDELINES FOR AFFIRMATIVE ACTION EMPLOYMENT PROGRAMS

I. INTRODUCTION

The State Board of Education has added Chapter 4 (commencing with Section 30) to Division I of Part I of Title 5, California Administrative Code, stating its intention to require educational agencies to adopt and implement plans for increasing the numbers of women and minority persons at all levels of responsibility.

The State Board of Education declares

The State Board of Education maintains as its policy to provide equal opportunity in employment for all persons and to prohibit discrimination based on race, sex, color, religion, age, physical handicap, ancestry, or national origin in every aspect of personnel policy and practice in employment, development, advancement, and treatment of employees; and to promote the total realization of equal employment opportunity through a continuing affirmative action program.

A. State Board Resolution on Affirmative Action

The State Board of Education regulation on affirmative action in employment is a reaffirmation of its commitment to equal employment opportunities. It emphasizes the determination of the State Board of Education that those practices employed by educational agencies under its jurisdiction which result in certain groups of job applicants being excluded and/or under-represented in the agency's work force be eliminated and that the results of its employment practices through affirmative action will be increased representation of minority racial and ethnic groups and women.

Each member of an educational agency's governing board and each agency's administrators is legally and morally bound to uphold the laws of the United States of America and the State of California and to carry out their duties in accordance with them. Generally, this responsibility applies to the laws with respect to the elimination of discrimination based upon race, sex, color, ancestry, national origin, and age.

Failure by a public education agency to develop and implement an Affirmative Action Employment Program constitutes a violation of Title V of the California Administrative Code, and could result in legal action being taken against the district.

B. Purpose of the Guidelines

It is the purpose of the following guidelines to assist governing boards of school districts, county offices of education, and other educational agencies to carry out the requirements of the Administrative Code provisions.

C. Guideline Inclusions

The guidelines include recommendations as to the essential elements of a plan and recommended techniques for its implementation. Key terms are defined and concepts are explained.

D. Tailoring Programs to Local Needs

Local situations differ, and methods for achieving equal employment opportunity for underrepresented and underutilized groups should be designed in accordance with local needs. It is necessary to the success of such efforts that governing boards and chief administrators establish clear policies of equal employment supported by careful planning of affirmative action programs. Successful implementation of such programs will depend on effective administration, responsive personnel, and adequate training.

E. Evaluation of Affirmative Action Programs

A continuing effort must be made to:

1. Evaluate the outcomes of each affirmative action program.
2. Provide a basis for revising goals and timetables.
3. Move toward the ultimate goal of equal participation.

The result is the only criterion of success. Responsibility and accountability must be assigned to achieve the program's objectives.

II. SUMMARY OF REQUIREMENTS

California Administrative Code provisions on affirmative action programs require that

EACH PUBLIC EDUCATION AGENCY* adopt and imple-

*State Department of Education, county superintendents of schools, governing boards of school districts except community college districts.

ment a plan which will result in increased numbers of racial and ethnic minority persons in all operating units and an increased number of racial and ethnic minority persons and women at levels of greater responsibility where it is found that such groups are underrepresented or underutilized. These groups should be equitably assigned among all units within the education agency. The plan will include goals and timetables for implementation and will be a public record.

THE STATE DEPARTMENT OF EDUCATION develop and disseminate guidelines to assist public education agencies in developing and implementing affirmative action employment programs, and render assistance to such agencies in carrying out the requirements.

EACH COUNTY SUPERINTENDENT OF SCHOOLS render assistance in developing and implementing affirmative action employment programs to school districts which during the preceding fiscal year had less than the following number of units of average daily attendance:

Elementary districts, less than 901
High school districts, less than 301
Unified school districts, less than 1501

III. DEFINITIONS

Affirmative Action Program	A comprehensive, result-oriented personnel program designed to increase through active recruitment the number of racial and ethnic minorities and to increase the representation of these groups and women at higher levels of responsibility.
Job Classification	One or a group of jobs having similar content, wage rates, and opportunities.
Qualified	*Certificated Classes*—Those persons who possess relevant skills through training, experience, background, and appropriate certification, as required, by specific job classes and assignments. The qualification of possessing bicultural and bilingual skills may be specified if it is deemed to be a bona fide occupational qualification. *Classified Classes*—Those persons possessing minimum qualifications specified within the job descriptions which have been adopted by the Board of Education. The qualification of possessing bicultural and bilingual skills may be specified if it is deemed to be a bona fide occupational qualification.

Qualifiable	*Certificated Classes* 1. Those persons who possess an undergraduate or graduate degree and student teaching, but lack certain educational requirements to receive the full credential. In this instance, the person is issued a partial credential pending fulfillment of the course or courses required for the full credential. 2. Those persons who possess training and credentials but who lack requisite experience *Classified Classes*—Those persons who possess most of the requisite skills necessary to specific job classes and assignments and who can become fully qualified by limited additional training
Minority Groups	For purpose of these guidelines, minority groups shall include the following: Native American, Asian, Black, Filipino, and Spanish Surnamed. The above designations do not denote scientific definitions of anthropological origins. For purposes of these guidelines, an employee may be included in the group with which he or she identifies, appears to belong, or is regarded in the community as belonging.
Under representation	Those employment situations in which there are significantly fewer persons of a particular grouping (minorities, women, men, etc.) serving at a particular job level or holding a particular kind of position than might be expected when compared to the distribution of that grouping in the available work force
Under-utilization	Those employment situations where minority group individuals and women are not placed in positions commensurate with their educational level, training, experience, and competency
Goal	A realistic level of accomplishment which an educational agency establishes for itself and to which the agency commits itself to increase employment opportunities for minorities and women at all levels (established in terms of the number of projected vacancies and the number of applicants who are qualified or qualifiable in the relevant job market)
Timetable	The maximum time span the agency sets as the long-range and short-range periods for reaching the projected goals, which should be within five years

Test Validation	A planned and systematic process of accumulating evidence that experience and education requirements, written and performance tests, and other employment processes and procedures used as a basis for personnel action are job related and do not have an adverse effect on minorities and women
Adverse Effect	Results of a total employment process which causes a significantly higher percent of racial and ethnic minority groups and women in the candidate population to be rejected for employment, placement, or promotion
Spanish Surnamed	That group which includes persons of Mexican, Puerto Rican, Cuban, Latin American and Spanish descent. This designation, used for state and federal reporting purposes, is shown as a specific ethnic category because of the employment discrimination often encountered by Spanish surnamed persons

IV. ESSENTIAL ELEMENTS OF AN AFFIRMATIVE ACTION PROGRAM

A. Governing Board's Affirmative Action Employment Action Program

Each public educational agency should have a written policy statement adopted by its governing board which sets forth the agency's obligation and commitment to equal employment opportunities through affirmative action. The statement must include a plan to eliminate discrimination in employment, promotion, transfer, and assignment on the basis of race, ethnicity and sex, and must apply this concept to all levels of employment procedure.

B. Delegation of Affirmative Action Responsibilities and Duties

1. Governing Board and Superintendent

The governing board and the superintendent have the overall responsibility for ensuring affirmative action and equal employment opportunity in recruitment, assignment, promotion, retention, compensation, and training; and for improving representation of minority racial and ethnic groups and women.

2. Affirmative Action Officer

The educational agency should designate an affirmative action officer to administer the affirmative action program. This officer should operate within the highest administrative level and be responsible to the district superintendent. (See p. 4)

An affirmative action officer is normally responsible for, but is not necessarily limited to, the following functions:

a. Developing and implementing a districtwide affirmative action program which shall contain specific, timely, relevant, and effective goals and timetables.

b. Developing procedures to assist in the identification of problems and recommending solutions to overcome any deficiencies

c. Providing guidance to all administrative and supervisory staff on matters relating to the implementation of the affirmative action program

d. Developing and monitoring procedures to determine progress being made toward achieving the established goals and timetables

e. Developing and executing result-oriented programs and procedures designed to eliminate underutilization in all areas where underutilization exists

f. Establishing procedures for continuing awareness of equal employment opportunities and providing information concerning the various local, state, and federal requirements for affirmative action

g. Disseminating the agency's affirmative action policy both internally and externally, including its dissemination to minority groups and women's organizations

h. Ensuring that hires, promotions, transfers, assignments, and other personnel procedures are carried out in keeping with the affirmative action policy

i. Ensuring that all selection procedures are job-related and do not adversely affect the opportunities of minorities and women

j. Maintaining an active file of information on training institutions as possible recruitment resources for minorities and women

k. Providing continuing staff development programs to ensure continued personal development and growth of each individual

l. Providing the governing board and superintendent with semi-annual reports as to the success or shortcomings of the program, including statistics detailing the racial, ethnic, and sex composition of district employees by job classification

m. Establishing grievance procedures for employee complaints of discrimination and having the authority to recommend corrective action to the superintendent or the governing board

n. Conducting human relations and awareness training for all staff in the district

C. Communication of Policy

1. Internal Dissemination

a. All agency employees should be apprised of the equal employment opportunity program and affirmative action plan and of the importance of the employee's participation and responsibility in ensuring the plan's implementation

b. Meetings should be conducted with agency staff and site administrators to explain the affirmative action policy and recommend methods to facilitate its implementation

c. Copies of the affirmative action resolution should be displayed in the administrative office of each educational agency and each school site.

2. External Dissemination

a. Written notice should be provided to all recruiting sources of the agency's affirmative action policy

b. Community agencies and organizations and educational institutions should be notified of the policy in order to solicit their assistance in recruiting minority and female candidates.

D. Utilization Analysis

1. The first step in developing an affirmative action program is to determine statistically the racial, ethnic, and sex composition of existing staff by every multiposition job title. Every facet of employment should be examined, including certificated and classified job categories, to determine how the policy of affirmative action can be implemented. Such a review should extend beyond the collecting of statistical data and should include the following:

a. An analysis of all certificated and classified categories of employment (faculty, support staff, and administration) to determine present utilization and underutilization of minorities and women in terms of the racial and ethnic composition of the available work force

b. A systematic and continuing review of special skills, qualifications, and abilities of present minority and women employees to determine the possibility of upgrading or lateral movement into other job classifications to achieve equitable distribution of staff (Career ladders must be established to achieve such upgrading.)

c. An analysis of all positions in the work force to determine if minorities and women are currently being utilized or underutilized in each category with reference to rates of pay, responsibilities, and opportunities

2. In determining whether minorities and women are being underrepresented or underutilized in any job category, the agency should consider all of the following factors:

   a. The numbers and percentages of staff in each position category or job title by ethnic and sex classification

   b. The availability of promotable minority and women employees

   c. The general availability of minorities and women having requisite skills to fill vacancies as they occur

   d. The expansion, reduction, and turnover projected in the work force

   e. The existence of agency training programs such as internships and/or institutions capable of training personnel in the requisite skills for promotional purposes

   f. The programs and training activities which the agency is able to undertake as a means of making all positions and all job classes available to minorities and women

   g. The determination of whether minority and women employees are afforded a full opportunity and are encouraged to participate in all agency-sponsored educational training programs and activities

E. Corrective Action

Corrective action should be initiated when any of the following conditions is found to exist:

1. Minorities and women are underutilized in specific positions or job titles.

2. Lateral or vertical movement of minority or female employees occurs at a lesser rate than that of other employees in all job classifications and titles.

3. Termination rate for minorities and women is higher than that of nonminorities and men.

4. Application forms, tests, interviews, and other related pre-employment material are not in compliance with local, state, federal regulations, executive orders, or guidelines.
5. Entrance qualifications are not consistent with the actual functions and duties required of the position.
6. Sex designation is used when not a bona fide occupational requirement for the job is in question.
7. Minorities and women are underrepresented in staff training or other career improvement programs.
8. Seniority provisions contribute to discrimination (deliberate or inadvertent) against women and racial or ethnic minorities.
9. The wage and salary structure regarding the compensation accorded to male and female employees shows disparity.
10. There is evidence of harrassment, coercion, or other adverse acts.

F. Goals and Timetables

Affirmative action programs are designed to eliminate discriminatory employment practices and to achieve a staff that is representative of the multiracial and mutlicultural society in which the student lives.

Goals, timetables, and affirmative action commitments must be designed to correct any identifiable deficiencies in representation from racial and ethnic minority groups and women at all employment levels within the agency. When deficiencies exist, the agency shall establish and set forth specific goals and timetables. Such goals and timetables shall be documented as part of the agency's written affirmative action program and shall be maintained in the agency's central office. The goals and timetables should be established in terms of the agency's analysis of deficiencies and a projection of anticipated vacancies, expansion, and attrition. Thus, in establishing goals and timetables, the agency should consider the results which could be reasonably expected from its efforts to accomplish the overall goal of the affirmative action program. The educational agency's compliance efforts should be judged by the quality of its affirmative action program and its good-faith efforts exerted toward implementation in conformity with state and federal statutes, regulations, and guidelines.[1]

[1]The FEPA, Sec. 1410-1432 Calif. Labor Code; Title VII of CRA as amended by the Equal Employment Act of 1972; CRA, Title VI; Higher Ed. Act of 1972, Title IX; Presidential directive (Executive Order 11246), October 13, 1968.

The following are factors which should be considered in establishing goals and timetables:

1. Selected staff persons, advisory committees, community representatives, site administrators, employee organizations, and support personnel should be involved in the goal-setting process.
2. Goals should be realistic, measurable, and attainable.
3. Goals should be specific for planned results with timetables for completion.
4. Goals are targets that are reasonably attainable by means of applying every good-faith effort to make all aspects of the affirmative action program work. They are not to be confused with rigid quotas which must be met.
5. In setting goals, reference should be made to the State of California Fair Employment Practice Commission guidelines on affirmative action.

G. Affirmative Action Advisory Committee

An affirmative action advisory committee should be established to assist the agency to achieve understanding and support of these employment policies and programs. This committee should assist in developing the affirmative action programs in conformity with state and federal statutes, regulations, and guidelines, monitoring its progress and acting as an advisory body to the affirmative action officer.

1. Membership of the Committee

   The affirmative action advisory committee should be composed of the affirmative action officer; representatives of employee organizations, both certificated and classified; selected high-level agency administrators; and representatives from those community organizations whose memberships are truly representative of racial and ethnic minority groups and women. Where it seems appropriate in the judgment of the district or agency, existing advisory committees may be used.

2. Functions of the Committee

   a. Advise the administration of its evaluation of the work force profile for both certificated and classified personnel.
   b. Advise the administration as to goals for affirmative action and methods to accomplish these goals within clearly defined timetables.

c. Review progress and results of the affirmative action program and recommend measures for its improvement.

d. Maintain liaison among community, minority groups, women's groups, and other interested organizations on affirmative action matters.

e. Participate in affirmative action training programs.

f. Advise the administration as to special training needs related to affirmative action and assist in planning and implementing training programs to meet these needs.

V. SUGGESTED TECHNIQUES FOR AFFIRMATIVE ACTION PROGRAM IMPLEMENTATION

A. Recruitment

It has been found that educational agencies cannot always rely on conventional methods to create a staff reflecting racial/ethnic and sex diversity. The agency should not wait for minority applicants to appear, but rather it should use affirmative action techniques which require aggressive recruiting programs, tapping all available sources to ensure that men and women of all racial and ethnic backgrounds have an opportunity to compete for employment.

The following are some recommended steps to assist an educational agency in recruiting activities:

1. Post position vacancy notices with employment development agencies and other employment agencies and institutions which comply fully with the State of California Fair Employment Practice Act.
2. Develop a list of various news media with large circulation among minority and women readers. Use such media for advertising job vacancies.
3. Use mass media and professional publications to project an image of the agency as being receptive to employing minority workers and women in positions of responsibility.
4. Use all local minority and women organizations and agencies in recruiting efforts.
5. Encourage minority employees to refer qualified friends and relatives for positions being advertised.
6. Work with community colleges and other higher educational institutions to seek and procure minority and female applicants.

7. Set up an affirmative action recruitment file in order to reach female and minority applicants.

B. Selection

1. State clearly job specifications setting forth those skills necessary to job performance and the required training and experience related to those skills. The requirements should be based on a careful analysis of the job.
2. Choose and design selection devices such as interviews and tests so that they are based solely on the job requirements.
3. Establish selection practices which are job-related and in compliance with existing State of California fair employment practices, laws, federal executive orders, and any other relevant state and federal statutes, regulations, and guidelines.
4. Ensure that tests and other selection procedures are fair to all applicants, keeping in mind the special problems faced by some racial and ethnic minority applicants who may feel that tests tend to exclude them.
5. Provide a rejected candidate for employment or promotion a written explanation for his or her rejection when requested.

C. Review of Employment Procedures

In personnel transactions which relate to selection, assignment, promotion, transfer, demotion, discharge, or termination, the decision should be based on all relevant factors. Such factors include qualifications and capabilities, the goals of the affirmative action program, special requirements to meet minority-group student and community needs and aspirations in counseling, bilingual/multicultural education, school-staff mobility, and special needs for school-community relations. Length of service in the agency should not be used as the sole determinant for such decisions.

The following steps may assist in developing effective employment and personnel procedures:

1. Review procedures to eliminate any possible discriminatory practices based on race, ethnicity, color, or sex.
2. Display State Fair Employment Practice Commission posters where applicants and interviewer will see them.
3. Require that all personnel extend a friendly and courteous reception to all job applicants.
4. Assign staff to units in the agency in order to meet the

educational needs of the students. Such assignments will reflect the racial and ethnic composition of the community served.

5. Survey and analyze entry-level classes and emphasize their availability to minority applicants and women.
6. When possible, place members of the minority groups and women in positions which allow for public interaction.
7. Maintain records on the flow of applicants through the selection process to permit a determination as to whether minorities and females are adversely affected by selection procedures.
8. Review sex-tied job titles and eliminate them when appropriate.
9. Ensure that preemployment inquiries, such as employment application forms and interviews, meet standards set by the Federal Equal Employment Opportunity Commission and the State Fair Employment Practice Commission.
10. Include minority members and women on oral examination boards, recruiting teams, and interviewing and selection panels.
11. Apply sick leave policies equally to men and women in accordance with federal and state guidelines on discrimination because of sex.
12. When necessary, assign persons with bilingual skills to provide services to non-English-speaking persons.

D. Training

1. Encourage minority and women employees to participate in training programs including those which lead to certification.
2. Counsel minority and women employees regarding self-improvement and advancement techniques.
3. Recognize and publicize the advancement of minority and women employees in the local news media.
4. Place minority and women workers in the training positions which lead to skilled or management levels.

E. Promotion

1. Ensure that minority individuals and women are aware of opportunities for promotion and are encouraged to take advantage of such opportunities.

2. Review qualifications and experience records of minority and women employees to determine their eligibility for promotion.

F. Assessment of Affirmative Action Program

1. Conduct surveys at least once annually of the agency's racial/ethnic patterns of employment by organizational unit, ethnic makeup, and sex.
2. Devise ways of correcting any inadequacies found in the results of such surveys.

VI. STATE DEPARTMENT OF EDUCATION RESPONSIBILITY

Each educational agency shall have on file in the district or agency its approved affirmative action plan. Such plans in districts and agencies shall be available for review by the State Department of Education to determine their compliance with the State Board's affirmative action regulations and state and federal statutes, regulations, and guidelines.

The State Department of Education shall:

1. Provide information and assistance to educational agencies with respect to developing and implementing affirmative action policies and programs.
2. Conduct training seminars to assist personnel staff of educational agencies in the implementation and improvement of affirmative action programs.
3. Call to the attention of the Superintendent of Public Instruction those educational agencies which have failed to develop and implement affirmative action programs, and recommend appropriate action.
4. Call to the attention of the district superintendent any instance where assignment of staff conflicts with the intent and purpose of the regulations and these guidelines, and suggest corrective action.

D-12 EDUCATION TITLE 5
(Register 74, No. 16—4-20-74)

31. Policy. The State Board of Education maintains as its policy to provide equal opportunity in employment for all persons and to prohibit discrimination based on race, sex, color, religion, age, physical handicap, ancestry, or national origin in every aspect of personnel policy and practice in employment, development, advancement, and treatment of employees; and to promote the total realization of equal employment opportunity through a continuing affirmative action employment program.

32. Statement of Intent. The State Board of Education recognizes that it is not enough to proclaim that public employers do not discriminate in employment but that we must also strive actively to build a community in which opportunity is equalized. In adopting this chapter, it is the intent of the State Board of Education to require educational agencies to adopt and implement plans for increasing the numbers of women and minority persons at all levels of responsibility.

33. Definitions. As used in this Chapter: (a) "Affirmative action employment program" means planned activities designed to seek, hire, and promote women and persons of minority racial and ethnic backgrounds. It is a conscious, deliberate step taken by a hiring authority to assure equal employment opportunity for all staff, both certificated and classified.

Such programs require the employer to make additional efforts to recruit, employ and promote members of groups formerly excluded at the various levels of responsibility who are qualified or may become qualified through appropriate training or experience within a reasonable length of time. Such programs should be designed to remedy the exclusion, whatever its cause.

Affirmative action requires imaginative, energetic and sustained action by an employer to devise recruiting, training and career advancement opportunities which will result in increased representation of women and minorities.

(b) "Goals and timetables" means projected new levels of employment of women and minority racial and ethnic groups to be attained on a specific schedule, given the expected turnover in the work force and the availability of persons who are qualified or may become qualified through appropriate training or experience within a reasonable length of time. Goals are not "quotas" or rigid proportions. They should relate both to the qualitative and quantitative needs of the employer.

(c) "Public education agency" means the State Department of Education, each office of the county superintendent of schools, and the governing board of each school district in California except community college districts.

34. Development and Implementation of Programs.* Each public education agency will develop and implement an affirmative action employment program for all operating units and at all levels of responsibility within its jurisdiction. The affirmative action employment program shall have goals and timetables for its implementation. The plan will be a public record within the meaning of the California Public Records Act (Government Code Sections 6250 through 6260).

35. Responsibility of Department. The Department of Education shall develop and disseminate to public education agencies guidelines to assist such agencies in developing and implementing affirmative action employment programs and shall render assistance to such agencies in carrying out the requirement of this chapter.

36. Responsibility of County Superintendent of Schools. Each county superintendent of schools shall render assistance in developing and implementing affirmative action employment programs to elementary school districts under his jurisdiction which had fewer than 901 units of average daily attendance during the preceding fiscal year, and in high school districts under his jurisdiction which had fewer than 301 units of average daily attendance during the preceding fiscal year, and in unified school districts under his jurisdiction which had fewer than 1,501 units of average daily attendance during the preceding fiscal year.

CONTINUATION SHEET
FOR FILING ADMINISTRATIVE REGULATIONS
WITH THE SECRETARY OF STATE
(Pursuant to Government Code Section 11380.1)

(Re: Affirmative Action Employment Plans)

ORDER ADOPTING, AMENDING, OR REPEALING REGULATIONS OF STATE BOARD OF EDUCATION

After proceedings had in accordance with the provisions of the Administrative Procedure Act (Gov. Code, Title 2, Div. 3, Part 1, Chapter 4.5) and pursuant to the authority vested by and to implement interpret, or make specific Section 152 of the Education Code; Titles VI and VII of the Civil Rights Act of 1964; Title 45 of the Code of Federal Regulations, Sections 70.1–70.16; Presidential Executive Order 11246 as amended by Executive Order 11375; and the California Fair Em-

*Later amended to require that the plans be developed no later than January 1, 1976.

ployment Practices Act, the State Board of Education hereby adopts and amends its regulations in Title 5 of the California Administrative Code as follows:

(1) Amends Section 34 to read:

34. Development and Implementation of Programs. Each public education agency will develop and implement an affirmative action employment program for all operating units and at all levels of responsibility within its jurisdiction. The affirmative action employment program shall have goals and timetables for its implementation. The plan will be developed no later than January 1, 1976, and will be a public record within the meaning of the California Public Records Act (Government Code Sections 6250 through 6260).

This order shall take effect on the thirtieth day after filing with the Secretary of State as provided in Section 11422 of the Government Code.

The State Board of Education has determined that these regulations are exempt from the provisions of Revenue and Taxation Code Section 2231 because:

(1) They are directed toward school districts.

(2) Duties, obligations, or responsibilities imposed on local governmental entities by these regulations are such that related costs are incurred as a part of their normal operating procedures.

APPENDIX E

Senate Bill No. 179

CHAPTER 1090

An act to add Article 4 (commencing with Section 44100) to Chapter 1 of Part 25 of the Education Code, relating to school employees.

[Approved by Governor September 27, 1977. Filed with Secretary of State September 27, 1977.]

LEGISLATIVE COUNSEL'S DIGEST

SB 179, Greene. Schools: employees; affirmative action.

Existing state and federal law prohibits discrimination in employment. Also, the State Board of Education has adopted regulations requiring each public education agency to develop and implement an affirmative action employment program for both certificated and classified school employees no later than January 1, 1976.

This bill would require each local public education agency, as defined, and the Department of Education to establish and execute an affirmative action employment program, as defined, for school employees. The manner of adoption of such programs and attributes thereof are provided for.

This bill would require the State Board of Education to adopt rules and regulations pertaining to affirmative action employment programs for school employees.

This bill would provide that, notwithstanding Section 2231 of the Revenue and Taxation Code, there shall be no reimbursement pursuant to that section nor shall there be any appropriation made by this bill for a specified reason.

The people of the State of California do enact as follows:

Section 1. Article 4 (commencing with Section 44100) is added to Chapter 1 of Part 25 of the Education Code, to read:

Article 4. Affirmative Action Employment

44100. The Legislature finds and declares that:

(a) Generally, California school districts employ a disproportionately low number of racial and ethnic minority classified and certificated employees and a disproportionately low number of women and members of racial and ethnic minorities in administrative positions.

(b) It is educationally sound for the minority student attending a racially impacted school to have available to him the positive image provided by minority classified and certificated employees. It is likewise educationally sound for the child from the majority group to have positive experiences with minority people which can be provided, in part, by having minority classified and certificated employees at schools where the enrollment is largely made up of majority group students. It is also educationally important for students to observe that women as well as men can assume responsible and diverse roles in society.

(c) Past employment practices created artificial barriers and past efforts to promote additional action in the recruitment, employment, and promotion of women and minorities have not resulted in a substantial increase in employment opportunities for such persons.

(d) Lessons concerning democratic principles and the richness which racial diversity brings to our national heritage can be best taught by the presence of staffs of mixed races and ethnic groups working toward a common goal.

It is the intent of the Legislature to establish and maintain a policy of equal opportunity in employment for all persons and to prohibit discrimination based on race, sex, color, religion, age, handicap, ancestry, or national origin in every aspect of personnel policy and practice in employment, development, advancement, and treatment of persons employed in the public school system, and to promote the total realization of equal employment opportunity through a continuing affirmative action employment program.

The Legislature recognizes that it is not enough to proclaim that public employers do not discriminate in employment but that effort must also be made to build a community in which opportunity is equalized. It is the intent of the Legislature to require educational agencies to adopt and implement plans for increasing the numbers of women and minority persons at all levels of responsibility.

44101. For the purposes of this article:

(a) "Affirmative action employment program" means planned activities designed to seek, hire, and promote persons who are underrepresented in the work force compared to their number in the population, including handicapped persons, women, and persons of minority racial and ethnic backgrounds. It is a conscious, deliberate step taken by a hiring authority to assure equal employment opportunity for all staff, both certificated and classified. Such programs require the employer to make additional efforts to recruit, employ, and promote members of groups formerly excluded at the various levels of responsibility who are qualified or may become qualified through appropriate training or experience within a reasonable length of time. Such programs should be designed to remedy the exclusion, whatever its cause. Affirmative action requires imaginative, energetic, and sustained action by each employer to devise recruiting, training, and career advancement opportunities which will result in an equitable representation of women and minorities in relation to all employees of such employer.

(b) "Goals and timetables" means projected new levels of employment of women and minority racial and ethnic groups to be attained on an annual schedule, given the expected turnover in the work force and the availability of persons who are qualified or may become qualified through appropriate training or experience within a reasonable length of time. Goals are not quotas or rigid proportions. They should relate both to the qualitative and quantitative needs of the employer.

(c) "Public education agency" means the Department of Education, each office of the county superintendent of schools, and the governing board of each school district in California.

44102. Each local public education agency shall submit, not later than January 1, 1979, to the Department of Education an affirmation of compliance with the provisions of this article. The affirmative action employment program shall have goals and timetables for its implementation. The plan shall be a public record within the meaning of the California Public Records Act.

44103. Each county superintendent of schools shall render assistance in developing and implementing affirmative action employment programs to elementary school districts under his jurisdiction which had fewer than 901 units of average daily attendance during the preceding fiscal year, and to high school districts under his jurisdiction which had fewer than 301 units of average daily attendance during the preceding fiscal year, and to unified school districts under his jurisdiction which had fewer than 1,501 units of average daily attendance during the preceding fiscal year.

44104. The Department of Education, out of funds appropriated for such purposes, (1) shall provide assistance to local educational agencies in adopting and maintaining high-quality affirmative action programs; (2) report to the Legislature, by July 1, 1979, regarding the number of districts which have adopted and are maintaining affirmative action programs, including the effectiveness of such programs in meeting the intent of this article; and (3) develop and disseminate to public education agencies guidelines to assist such agencies in developing and implementing affirmative action employment programs.

44105. The State Board of Education shall adopt all necessary rules and regulations to carry out the intent of this article.

Section 2. This act is substantially a codification of regulations adopted by the State Board of Education which require local educational agencies to have developed an affirmative action employment program by January 1, 1976. Since the affirmative action programs mandated by this act are presently required of school districts, it is the intent of the Legislature not to reimburse local educational agencies for program expenditures required prior to the enactment of this act.

Therefore, notwithstanding Sections 2231 and 2234 of the Revenue and Taxation Code, or any provision to the contrary contained in Senate Bill 90 of the 1977 Regular Session, there shall be no reimbursement pursuant to this section nor shall there be any appropriation made by this act because there are no new duties, obligations, or responsibilities imposed on local educational agencies by this act.

Index